An Introduction to the

NEW TESTAMENT

An Introduction to the

NEW TESTAMENT

Charles B. Puskas

HENDRICKSON
PUBLISHERS
PEABODY, MASSACHUSETTS 01961-3473

To Susan, Rita, and Bart
with love

Table of Contents

List of Illustrations, Charts, and Maps

ILLUSTRATIONS

CHARTS

MAPS

Abbreviations and Select Bibliography

Abbreviations of biblical books, ancient texts, periodicals, and reference works are derived from the *The Society of Biblical Literature Member's Handbook* (1980), "Instructions for Contributors," 83–97.

Aharoni and Avi-Yonah, *Bible Atlas*   Y. Aharoni and M. Avi-Yonah, *The Macmillan Bible Atlas*. New York: Macmillan, 1977.

AB   The Anchor Bible. Garden City, N.Y.: Doubleday, 1964–.

Aland, *Synopsis*   *Synopsis of the Four Gospels: Greek-English Edition*. 3rd ed. New York; London: United Bible Societies, 1979.

ANF   *The Ante-Nicene Fathers: Translations of the Writings of the Fathers down to AD 325*. 10 vols. Edited by A. Roberts et al. Buffalo, N.Y., 1884–86; repr. Grand Rapids: Eerdmans, 1951.

Aune, *Prophecy*   D. Aune, *Prophecy in Early Christianity and the Ancient Mediterranean World*. Grand Rapids: Eerdmans, 1983.

Austin, *Hellenistic World*   M. M. Austin, *The Hellenistic World from Alexander to the Roman Conquest, A Selection of Ancient Sources in Trans*. Cambridge: Cambridge University Press, 1981.

Barnstone, *Other Bible*   W. Barnstone, ed. *The Other Bible*. San Francisco: Harper & Row, 1984.

Barrett, *NTB*   C. K. Barrett, ed. *The New Testament Background: Selected Documents*. Harper Torchbooks. New York: Harper & Row, 1961.

BAGD   W. Bauer, *A Greek-English Lexicon of the New Testament and Other Early Christian Literature*. Translated and adapted by W. F. Arndt and F. W. Gingrich. 2nd ed. revised and augmented by F. W. Gingrich and F. W. Danker. Chicago: University of Chicago Press, 1979.

Bauer, *Orthodoxy*   W. Bauer, *Orthodoxy and Heresy in Earliest Christianity*. Translated and edited by R. Kraft et al. from 1934 Ger. ed. Philadelphia: Fortress, 1971.

BC   *The Beginnings of Christianity Part I. The Acts of the Apostles*. 5 vols. Edited by F. J. Foakes-Jackson. London: Macmillan and Co., 1920–33; reprint ed. Grand Rapids: Baker, 1979.

Betz, *Galatians*   H. D. Betz, *Galatians: A Commentary on Paul's Letter to the Churches in Galatia* Hermeneia. Philadelphia: Fortress, 1979.

Biblical Criticism   *Biblical Criticism: Historical, Literary, and Textual*. Edited by D. Guthrie and R. Harrison. Grand Rapids: Zondervan, 1978.

BTB   *Biblical Theology Bulletin*. Jamaica, N.Y.

Bilezikian, *Liberated Gospel*   G. G. Bilezikian, *The Liberated Gospel: A Comparison of the Gospel of Mark and Greek Tragedy*. Grand Rapids: Baker, 1977.

Bornkamm, *Jesus*   G. Bornkamm, *Jesus of Nazareth*. Translated by I. McLuskey et al. New York: Harper & Row, 1960.

Brown, *Beloved Disciple*   R. E. Brown, *The Community of the Beloved Disciple*. New York: Paulist, 1979.

Brown, *Epistles*   R. E. Brown, *The Epistles of John*. AB 30. Garden City, N.Y.: Doubleday, 1982.

Brown, *John*   R. E. Brown, *The Gospel According to John I–XII; XIII–XXI*. 2 vols. AB 29–29A. Garden City, N.Y.: Doubleday, 1966, 1970.

Brown and Meier, *Antioch*   R. E. Brown, J. P. Meier, *Antioch and Rome, New Testament Cradles of Catholic Christianity*. New York: Paulist, 1983.

Bruce, *Book of Acts*   F. F. Bruce, *The Book of Acts*. NIC. Grand Rapids: Eerdmans, 1952.

Bruce, *English Bible*   F. F. Bruce, *The English Bible: A History of Translations from the Earliest English Versions to the New English Bible*. Revised ed. New York; Oxford: Oxford University Press, 1970.

BJRL   *Bulletin of the John Rylands University Library of Manchester*. Manchester, UK.

Bullinger, *Figures of Speech*   E. W. Bullinger, *Figures of Speech Used in the Bible Explained and Illustrated*. London, 1898; repr. Grand Rapids: Baker, 1968.

Bultmann, *Synoptic Tradition*   R. Bultmann, *The History of the Synoptic Tradition*. Translated by J. Marsh New York: Harper & Row, 1963.

Bultmann, *Theology*   R. Bultmann, *Theology of the New Testament*. 2 vols. Translated by K. Grobel. New York: Charles Scribner's Sons, 1951, 1955.

Cadbury, *Making*   H. J. Cadbury, *The Making of Luke–Acts*. London: Macmillan, 1927, reprint ed. London: SPCK, 1968.

Caird, *Language and Imagery*   G. B. Caird, *The Language and Imagery of the Bible*. Philadelphia: Westminster, 1980.

CAH   S. A. Cook, F. E. Adcock, et al., eds. *The Cambridge Ancient History*. Vols. 7–12. Cambridge: University Press, 1928–39.

CHB   *The Cambridge History of the Bible, vol 1: From the Beginnings to Jerome*. Edited by P. R. Ackroyd and C. F. Evans. Cambridge: University Press, 1970.

Cartlidge and Dungan, *Documents*   D. R. Cartlidge and D. L. Dungan, *Documents for the Study of the Gospels*. Philadelphia: Fortress, 1980.

Charlesworth, *OTP*   J. H. Charlesworth, *The Old Testament Pseudepigrapha*. 2 vols. Garden City, N.Y.: Doubleday, 1983, 1985.

Current Issues   *Current Issues in Biblical and Patristic Interpretation*. Edited by G. Hawthorne. Grand Rapids: Eerdmans, 1975.

Deissmann, *LAE*   A. Deissmann, *Light From the Ancient East*. Translated by L. Strachan from 1923 ed. Grand Rapids: Baker, 1978.

Dibelius and Conzelmann, *Pastoral Epistles*   M. Dibelius and H. Conzelmann, *The Pastoral Epistles*. Translated by P. Buttolph and A. Yarbro. Hermeneia. Philadelphia: Fortress, 1972.

Donfried, *Romans Debate*   K. P. Donfried, ed. *The Romans Debate*. Minneapolis: Augsburg, 1977.

Doty, *Letters*   W. G. Doty, *Letters in Primitive Christianity*. Philadelphia: Fortress, 1973.

Dupont-Sommer, *Essene Writings*   A. Dupont-Sommer, *The Essene Writings from Qumran*. Translated by G. Vermes from the 1961 ed. Gloucester, Mass.: Peter Smith, 1973.

Encyclopedia Judaica   *Encyclopedia Judaica*. Edited by C. Roth et al. 16 vols. Jerusalem: Keter; New York: Macmillan, 1971-72.

Eusebius, *Eccl Hist*   Eusebius Pamphilus, *Ecclesiastical History*. Written ca. AD 305-324. Trans. C. F. Cruse, 1850. Grand Rapids: Baker, 1955 repr.

ExBC   *The Expositor's Bible Commentary*. Edited by F. Gaebelein et al. 12 vols. Grand Rapids: Zondervan, 1979.

Farmer and Farkasfalvy, *NT Canon*   W. R. Farmer and D. M. Farkasfalvy, *The Formation of the New Testament Canon, An Ecumenical Approach*. New York: Paulist, 1983.

Farmer, *Synoptic Problem*   W. R. Farmer, *The Synoptic Problem: A Critical Analysis*. Revised ed. Dillsboro, N.C.: Western North Carolina Press, 1976.

Fitzmyer, *Luke*   J. A. Fitzmyer, *The Gospel According to Luke I-X; X-XXIV*. 2 vols. AB 28-28A. Garden City, N.Y.: Doubleday, 1981, 1985.

Francis and Meeks, *Conflict at Colossae*   F. O. Francis and W. A. Meeks, eds. *Conflict at Colossae*. Revised ed. SBS 4. Missoula, Mont.: Scholars Press, 1975.

Georgi, *Opponents*   D. Georgi, *The Opponents of Paul in 2 Corinthians*. Philadelphia: Fortress, 1985.

Godwin, *Mystery Religions*   J. Godwin, *Mystery Religions in the Ancient World*. San Francisco: Harper & Row, 1981.

Greenlee, *INT*   J. H. Greenlee, *Introduction to New Testament Textual Criticism*. Grand Rapids: Eerdmans, 1964.

Gunther, *Opponents*   J. Gunther, *St. Paul's Opponents and Their Background: A Study of Apocalyptic and Jewish Sectarian Teachings*. Leiden: Brill, 1973.

Guthrie, *NTIntro*   D. Guthrie, *New Testament Introduction*. 3rd. ed. Downers Grove, Ill.: InterVarsity Press, 1970.

Haenchen, *Acts*   E. Haenchen, *The Acts of the Apostles, A Commentary*. Translated by B. Noble et al. Philadelphia: Westminster, 1971.

Hanson, *Dawn of Apocalyptic*   P. D. Hanson, *The Dawn of the Apocalyptic*. Philadelphia: Fortress, 1975.

HBD   *Harper's Bible Dictionary*. Edited by P. J. Achtemeier. San Francisco: Harper & Row, 1985.

HNTC   Harper's New Testament Commentaries. New York: Harper & Row, 1957-.

Harrington, *IntNT*   D. J. Harrington, *Interpreting the New Testament, A Practical Guide*. NT Message 1. Wilmington, Del.: Michael Glazier, 1979.

Hayes and Holladay, *Biblical Exegesis*   J. H. Hayes and C. R. Holladay, *Biblical Exegesis, A Beginner's Handbook*. Atlanta: John Knox, 1982.

Hengel, *Jesus and Paul*   M. Hengel, *Between Jesus and Paul*. Translated by J. Bowden. Philadelphia: Fortress, 1983.

Hengel, *Judaism and Hellenism*   M. Hengel, *Judaism and Hellenism*. 2 vols. Translated by J. Bowden. Philadelphia: Fortress, 1974.

Hennecke, *NTA*   E. Hennecke, *New Testament Apocrypha*. 2 vols. Edited by W. Schneemelcher. Translated by R. McL. Wilson et al. Philadelphia: Westminster, 1963, 1965.

HibJ   *Hibbert Journal*.

Hoehner, *Chronological*   H. W. Hoehner, *Chronological Aspects of the Life of Christ*. Grand Rapids: Zondervan, 1977.

IB   *The Interpreter's Bible*. Edited by G. A. Buttrick, et al. 12 vols. Nashville: Abingdon, 1952-57.

ICC   The International Critical Commentary. Edinburgh: T. & T. Clark, 1895-1951; new series, 1975-.

IDB   *The Interpreter's Dictionary of the Bible.* 4 vols. Edited by G. A. Buttrick. New York/Nashville: Abingdon, 1962.

IDBSupp   *The Interpreter's Dictionary of the Bible Supplementary Volume.* Edited by K. Crim. Nashville: Abingdon, 1976.

IOC   *The Interpreter's One-Volume Commentary on the Bible: Introduction and Commentary for Each Book of the Bible Including the Apocrypha.* Edited by C. M. Laymon. Nashville: Abingdon, 1971.

JBC   *The Jerome Biblical Commentary.* Edited by R. E. Brown, J. A. Fitzmyer, and R. E. Murphy. Englewood Cliffs, N.J.: Prentice-Hall, 1968.

Jewett, *Chronology*   R. Jewett, *A Chronology of Paul's Life.* Philadelphia: Fortress, 1979.

Jonas, *Gnostic*   H. Jonas, *The Gnostic Religion.* 2nd ed. Boston: Beacon Press, 1963.

Josephus, *Ant.; War*   Josephus, *Antiquities; The Jewish War.*

Käsemann, *Essays*   E. Käsemann, *Essays on New Testament Themes.* Translated by W. Montague. London: SCM, 1964; Philadelphia: Fortress, 1982.

Kümmel, *Introduction*   W. G. Kümmel, *Introduction to the New Testament.* Revised Eng. ed. Translated by H. C. Kee from 17th Ger. ed. New York/Nashville: Abingdon Press, 1975.

Kümmel, *NT:HIP*   W. G. Kümmel, *The New Testament: The History of the Investigation of its Problems.* Translated by S. MacLean Gilmour and H. C. Kee. Nashville: Abingdon, 1972.

Koester, *Introduction*   H. Koester, *Introduction to the New Testament.* 2 vols. Philadelphia: Fortress Press, 1982.

LCL   *The Loeb Classical Library.* Founded by J. Loeb. 450 vols. Edited by G. P. Goold et al. Cambridge, Mass.: Harvard University Press; London: William Heinemann.

Longenecker, *Biblical Exegesis*   R. N. Longenecker, *Biblical Exegesis in the Apostolic Period.* Grand Rapids: Eerdmans, 1975.

Marshall, *NTI*   I. H. Marshall, ed. *New Testament Interpretation. Essays on Principles and Methods.* Grand Rapids: Eerdmans, 1977.

Martin, *NT Foundations*   R. P. Martin, *New Testament Foundations: A Guide for Christian Students.* 2 vols. Grand Rapids: Eerdmans, 1975, 1978.

Marxsen, *Introduction*   W. Marxsen, *Introduction to the New Testament.* Translated by G. Buswell. Philadelphia: Fortress, 1968.

Meeks, *Writings*   W. A. Meeks, ed. *The Writings of St. Paul.* A Norton Critical Edition. New York: Norton, 1972.

Metzger, *Textual Commentary*   B. M. Metzger, *A Textual Commentary on the Greek New Testament* A Companion Volume to the UBS Greek NT 3rd Edition. New York and London: United Bible Societies, 1971.

Metzger, *TNT*   B. Metzger, *The Text of the New Testament.* 2nd ed. New York and Oxford: Oxford University Press, 1968.

Moulton, *Grammar*   J. H. Moulton, F. W. Howard, N. Turner, *A Grammar of New Testament Greek.* 4 vols. Edinburgh: T. & T. Clark, 1908–76.

Murphy-O'Connor, *Paul's Corinth*   J. Murphy-O'Connor, *St. Paul's Corinth, Texts and Archaeology.* Wilmington, Del.: Michael Glazier, 1983.

NCBC   New Century Bible Commentary. London: Marshall, Morgan and Scott; Grand Rapids: Eerdmans, 1966–.

New Dimensions   *New Dimensions in New Testament Study.* Edited by R. N. Longenecker and M. C. Tenney. Grand Rapids: Zondervan, 1974.

NIC   New International Commentary. Grand Rapids: Eerdmans, 1952–.

NIDNTT   *The New International Dictionary of New Testament Theology.* Edited by C. Brown. 3 vols. Grand Rapids: Zondervan, 1975, 1976, 1978.

NIGTC   New International Greek Testament Commentary. Grand Rapids: Eerdmans, 1978–.

O'Toole, *Unity*   R. F. O'Toole, *The Unity of Luke's Theology: An Analysis of Luke-Acts.* Good News Studies 9. Wilmington, Del.: Michael Glazier, 1984.

Oxford Class Dict   *The Oxford Classical Dictionary.* Edited by N. G. L. Hammond and H. H. Scullard. Oxford: University Press, 1970.

Perrin, *Jesus*   N. Perrin, *Jesus and the Language of the Kingdom: Symbol and Metaphor in New Testament Interpretation.* Philadelphia: Fortress Press, 1976.

Perrin and Duling, *NTIntro*   N. Perrin and D. Duling, *The New Testament: An Introduction.* 2nd ed. New York: Harcourt, Brace, Jovanovich, 1982.

Perrin, *Rediscovering*   N. Perrin, *Rediscovering the Teaching of Jesus.* New York: Harper & Row, 1976.

PerRelSt   Perspectives in Religious Studies. Macon, Ga.

PrC   Proclamation Commentaries, The NT Witnesses for Preaching. Edited by G. Krodel. Philadelphia: Fortress, 1976–.

Reumann, *Jesus*   J. Reumann, *Jesus in the Church's Gospels.* Philadelphia: Fortress, 1968.

Robinson, *Nag Hammadi*   J. M. Robinson, gen. ed. *The Nag Hammadi Library in English.* Translated by members of the Coptic Gnostic Library Project of the Institute for Antiquity and Christianity. San Francisco: Harper & Row, 1977.

Robinson and Koester, *Trajectories*   J. M. Robinson and H. Koester, *Trajectories Through Early Christianity.* Philadelphia: Fortress, 1971.

Roetzel, *Letters*   C. J. Roetzel, *The Letters of Paul, Conversations in Context.* 2nd ed. Atlanta: John Knox, 1982.

Rohde, *Rediscovering*   J. Rohde, *Rediscovering the Teaching of the Evangelists.* Translated by D. Barton. Philadelphia: Westminster, 1968.

Rudolph, *Gnosis*   K. Rudolph, *Gnosis, The Nature and History of Gnosticism.* Translated by R. McL. Wilson et al. San Francisco: Harper & Row, 1983.

Safrai and Stern, *Jewish People*   S. Safrai and M. Stern et al., eds. *The Jewish People in the First Century* Compendia Rerum Iudaicarum ad Novum Testamentum. Section One. 2 vols. Assen, Neth.: Van Gorcum; Philadelphia: Fortress, 1974, 1976.

Sampley, *Eph, Col*   J. Sampley, J. Burgess, G. Krodel, R. Fuller, *Ephesians, Colossians, 2 Thessalonians, The Pastoral Epistles.* PrC. Philadelphia: Fortress, 1978.

Schmithals, *Apocalyptic*   W. Schmithals, *The Apocalyptic Movement, Introduction and Interpretation.* Translated by J. Steely. Nashville: Abingdon, 1975.

Schmithals, *Gnosticism in Corinth*   W. Schmithals, *Gnosticism in Corinth, An Investigation of the Letters to the Corinthians.* Translated by J. Steely. Nashville: Abingdon, 1971.

Schürer and Vermes, *History*   E. Schürer, *The History of the Jewish People In the Age of Jesus Christ (175 B.C.–A.D. 135).* Revised and edited by G. Vermes, F. Millar, et al. 3 vols. Edinburgh: T. & T. Clark, 1973, 1979, 1986.

Semeia   Semeia: An Experimental Journal for Biblical Criticism. Edited by R. Funk, et al. Missoula, Mont.; Chico, Calif.; Atlanta, Ga.: Scholars Press, 1974–.

Sherwin-White, *Roman Society*   A. N. Sherwin-White, *Roman Society and Roman Law in the New Testament.* Oxford, 1963; Grand Rapids: Baker, 1978.

Shuler, *Genre for Gospels*   P. L. Shuler, *A Genre for the Gospels, The Biographical Character of Matthew.* Philadelphia: Fortress, 1982.

Soulen, *Handbook*   R. N. Soulen, *Handbook of Biblical Criticism*. 2nd ed. Atlanta: John Knox, 1981.

Stowers, *Diatribe*   S. K. Stowers, *The Diatribe and Paul's Letter to the Romans*. Chico, Calif.: Scholars Press, 1981.

SLA   *Studies in Luke–Acts*. Edited by L. E. Keck and J. L. Martyn. Nashville: Abingdon, 1966.

Talbert, *Literary Patterns*   C. H. Talbert, *Literary Patterns, Theological Themes and the Genre of Luke–Acts*. SBLMS 20. Missoula, Mont.: Scholars Press, 1974.

Talbert, *Gospel?*   C. H. Talbert, *What Is A Gospel? The Genre of the Canonical Gospels*. Philadelphia: Fortress, 1977.

Theissen, *Sociology*   G. Theissen, *Sociology of Early Palestinian Christianity*. Translated by J. Bowden. Philadelphia: Fortress, 1978.

TDNT   *Theological Dictionary of the New Testament*. 10 vols. Edited by G. Kittel and G. Friedrich. Translated by G. W. Bromiley. Grand Rapids: Eerdmans, 1964–76.

Throckmorton, *Gospel Parallels*   B. H. Throckmorton, *Gospel Parallels: A Synopsis of the First Three Gospels*. 4th rev ed. New York; Nashville: Thomas Nelson Sons, 1979.

Vermes, *Jesus the Jew*   G. Vermes, *Jesus the Jew, A Historian's Reading of the Gospels*. London: Collins, 1973; Philadelphia: Fortress, 1981.

Vermes, *Scrolls*   G. Vermes, *The Dead Sea Scrolls in English*. Revised ed. Baltimore, Md.: Penguin, 1968.

WBC   Word Biblical Commentary. Edited by D. A. Hubbard et al. Waco, Tex.: Word, 1982–.

ZPE   *The Zondervan Pictorial Encyclopedia*. 5 vols. Edited by M. C. Tenney. Grand Rapids: Zondervan, 1975.

Introduction

THE INFLUENCE OF THE NEW TESTAMENT

Probably no group of religious writings has influenced the Western world more than the New Testament. It inspired such literary classics as Augustine's *City of God* and Bunyan's *Pilgrim's Progress*. New Testament stories are rehearsed in the cultural celebrations of both Christmas and Easter; and the Protestant work ethic derived from the New Testament. In the academic areas of ethics and philosophy, this provocative collection confronts the modern person with the ageless questions of ultimate concern: Who am I? Why am I here? Is there life after death? The New Testament challenges each generation to formulate anew a response to these enduring questions. Finally, in the discipline of ancient history, the New Testament serves as a significant historical source for understanding first-century Judaism, the early Roman Empire, and the roots of Christianity.

THE DIFFICULTIES IN READING THE NEW TESTAMENT

Even though it has been an influential document throughout human culture, the New Testament is a difficult book to read. This ancient collection not only assumes social structures and customs different from our own, but many of its teachings reflect diverse perspectives on similar topics (AD 30–140). Note, for example, the shocking saying in Luke 14:26 about hating one's family in order to become a disciple and the authoritarian teaching about submission in the household in 1 Peter 3:1–6. Both passages presuppose social structures unlike our own, and both reflect distinct perspectives on faith and family issues.

DISTINCT FEATURES OF THIS BOOK

The focus of this volume is on the development of early Christianity in its historical context. A presentation of the Greco-Roman world and Jewish environment of early Christianity is essential to bridging the historical and cultural gap that separates us from the New Testament. An outline tracing early Christianity from Jesus to emerging orthodoxy is vital for understanding the different New Testament teachings in their respective historical contexts.

Since the New Testament is our basic source for this historical inquiry, chapters on the New Testament language, text, methods of interpretation, literary genres, and an appendix on canon and English translations are included. These sections seek to answer fundamental questions, such as, In what type of language was the New Testament written? How reliable is our New Testament text? How do we interpret the New Testament? Why are there only twenty-seven books in the New Testament? What type of translation should I read?

Although separate discussions for every book are not included, my own conclusions regarding questions of authorship and dating are evident in the historical presentation of Jesus and early Christianity. Some treatment of these issues is found in the footnotes, with alternate views noted. Illustrations and charts should greatly assist the reader in comprehending the material. Primary and secondary sources are also provided for further study. A select bibliography at the beginning and indexes at the end should also prove helpful. Studying the New Testament can be a fascinating enterprise, but it takes time, it takes tools, and it takes a determination to encounter this collection on its own terms.

Part I
Backgrounds to the New Testament

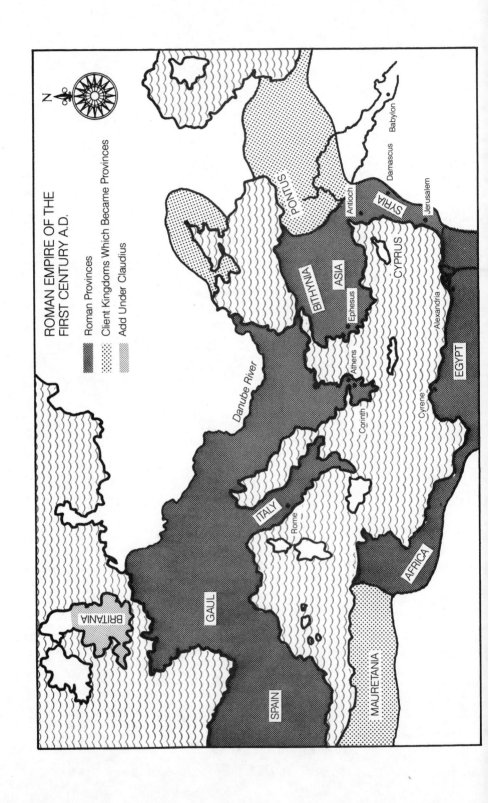

ROMAN EMPIRE OF THE
FIRST CENTURY A.D.

Roman Provinces

Client Kingdoms Which Became Provinces

Add Under Claudius

1

The Greco-Roman Context of the New Testament

Understanding the historical context is crucial for the serious study of any written document. For example, no earnest interpreter of the United States Constitution can ignore the importance of eighteenth-century mercantilism and the prevalent teaching of social contract and popular sovereignty. So it is also with the study of the NT. If we are to interpret accurately these early Christian writings, the significant provincial policies of first-century Rome and the influential thought of both Judaism and Hellenism cannot be ignored. No document is immune to the influences of its historical setting.

A PERVASIVE HELLENISM

The NT was not written in Aramaic, the native language of Jesus and his disciples, or in Latin, the language of Rome, but in a common Greek dialect of the first century. Why was it written in Greek? This linguistic phenomenon is chiefly due to the efforts of one extraordinary man: Alexander of Macedon (356–323 BC).

Hellenization under Alexander the Great

Alexander's background is impressive and his achievements are astonishing.[1] As the son of an ambitious Macedonian ruler (Philip II), Alexander studied ethics, geography, and Homer's *Iliad* under the famous Greek philosopher, Aristotle; he also received intensive military training from experienced warriors. When he succeeded his father in 336 BC, young Alexander sought to consolidate his father's power and launch a

---

1. Primary sources for Alexander and his accomplishments are the works of Diodorus of Sicily (1st cent. BC), Quintus of Curtius (1st cent. AD), Plutarch of Chaeronea (early 2nd cent. AD) and Arrian of Nicodemia (2nd cent. AD). Pertinent selections from the above are found in Austin, *Hellenistic World* 8–46. For a helpful survey, see W. W. Tarn, *Alexander the Great* (Boston: Beacon Press, 1956).

fantastic campaign eastward. Within ten short years, Alexander and his great army of 30,000 infantry and 4,500 cavalry would conquer Asia Minor (modern Turkey), Syria, Palestine, Egypt, Babylonia (modern Iraq), Persia (Iran) and northwestern India.[2]

As Alexander marched eastward, he brought his Greek culture with him. Although "Hellenization," or the spread of Greek culture away from its homeland, began centuries earlier with Greek traders and colonists, the process was greatly accelerated by the campaigns of Alexander. As a student of Greek learning, he envisioned a union of the East and West through Greek culture and took definite steps to fulfill it. First, he married Persian women and encouraged his soldiers to do the same (Arrian, *Anabasis* 7.4.4). Second, he and his successors built a network of Greek cities throughout the empire, sixteen of which were called "Alexandria." These became centers of Greek culture. Many other Hellenistic aspirations and achievements of Alexander are highlighted, with some exaggeration, in Plutarch, *The Fortunes and Virtues of Alexander the Great* I.328C–329D.

The type of Greek language disseminated by Alexander and his men was not the classical Attic of Aristotle (although it was dominant), but *koinē* or "common" Greek. This type was a vernacular Greek, a more vigorous and simplified form of Attic (Athens) with elements of Ionic (Ephesus). It may have evolved in the following manner. Alexander probably emphasized the Attic dialect in which he was schooled. It was later modified by his troops whose native dialects were diverse, and it underwent further changes when adopted by the Eastern "barbarians" (non-Greeks). This simplified and adaptable Greek dialect soon supplanted Aramaic, the language of the Persian Empire. It became the international tongue of the Mediterranean world, just as Latin did in medieval Europe and English has done in our contemporary world. The use of Hellenistic Greek as a common language would last almost a millennium (322 BC–AD 529).

Hellenization After Alexander the Great

Although the cultural effects of his conquests would endure, the political unity of the empire would not survive after Alexander. In 323 BC, burdened with administration and suffering from a fever, he died at the age of thirty-two with no legal heir. His generals struggled for control of his empire and soon dismantled it into small, petty kingdoms. Ptolemy took

2. The above military statistics from Diodorus, *Library of History* 17.7.3–4, are probably not an exaggeration. The geographical extent of Alexander's conquest are most evident (ironically) in the accounts narrating the division of his kingdom, e.g., fragment of Greek history attributed to Arrian, 156F (in Austin, *Hellenistic World* 41–43).

Alexander the Great. From a first-century Roman mosaic depicting the battle of Issus, Pompeii. *Naples National Museum.* Used with permission.

Egypt and southern Syria; Antigonus claimed most of northern Syria and western Babylonia; Lysimachus held Thrace and western Asia Minor; and Cassander ruled Macedonia and Greece. The territory of Antigonus was taken by Seleucus I after the battle of Ipsus (301 BC), and the kingdom of Lysimachus was also absorbed into the realm of Seleucus. For centuries the dynasties established by Seleucus and Ptolemy fought against each other for more territory. For example, Palestine, which served as a buffer zone between the two kingdoms, was first under Ptolemaic control and then under Seleucid rule after 198 BC.[3]

3. Primary sources for this complicated period after Alexander are found in Austin, *Hellenistic World* 39–92. A helpful survey is found in W. W. Tarn and G. T. Griffith, *Hellenistic Civilisation* (London: Arnold Press, 1952) 5–46.

The Hellenization process begun by Alexander, however, continued under the Seleucids and Ptolemies. Cities like Alexandria of Egypt, Antioch of Syria, and Seleucia on the Tigris River (near modern Baghdad), were model Hellenistic cities. Most of them had great walls which enclosed private homes, a central marketplace (Gk. *agora*) with temples and government buildings, a gymnasium, a theater, and a bathhouse. Alexandria of Egypt was a trade center with a great library and museum. Seleucia on the Tigris was a wealthy banking city, and Antioch of Syria later became the capital of the Seleucid Empire.[4]

Although the luxuries of these Hellenistic cities were enjoyed by the king and his Greek associates, privileges were extended to influential non-Greeks who assimilated Greek language and customs. Upper-class non-Greeks formed their own associations, and the people were allowed to observe either Greek laws or their own statutes unless they conflicted with those of the king.[5] This arrangement also applied to Palestine, where numerous Hellenistic cities existed in Phoenicia (e.g., Ptolemais-Acco, Jamnia, Ascalon, Gaza) and the regions near Galilee (e.g., Sepphoris, Pella, Gadara, Scythapolis).[6] Areas least affected by Hellenism were certain rural areas, although some of the Greek vernacular and Hellenistic customs were probably adopted.

The conquests of Alexander set in motion cultural trends that could not be reversed despite the splintering of his empire among his generals and the continued rivalry among their own descendants. After centuries of political conflict each small kingdom fell in turn to Rome in the first century BC. By that time, however, a distinctive culture had emerged: a curious blend of Greek and oriental.

A STABLE ROMAN EMPIRE

The United States and the Soviet Union are two modern examples of "world powers"; their interests and concerns greatly affect the rest of the world. The history of civilization is replete with such examples of world powers, and the time of the NT is no exception. The early Christian documents were written at a time when Rome controlled the Mediterranean world.

4. An early (20 BC) description of the above three cities is found in Strabo, *Geography* 16.1.5 (Seleucis); 16.2.4–10 (Antioch); 17.1.6–10 (Alexandria); 16.2.5 (all three). For further discussion, see Koester, *Introduction* 1:67–73; Tarn and Griffith, *Hellenistic* 150–52, 183–86.

5. M. Hadas, *Hellenistic Culture Fusion and Diffusion* (New York: Columbia University Press, 1959) 30–44; Koester, *Introduction* 1:56–58.

6. For the pervasive influence of Hellenism on the Jews of Palestine in late antiquity, see Hengel, *Judaism and Hellenism* 1:58–88.

When Rome became a world empire it also became the heir to Hellenism.[7] By the sixth century BC, Rome had evolved from a monarchy into a republic ruled by two consuls in cooperation with a senate and two assemblies. Because of their fear of invaders and additional reasons (e.g., economic interests, political mission), the Romans sought to neutralize their frontiers. By the third century they had gained control of Italy (275 BC) and had finally defeated Carthage (207 BC), which secured domination of the western Mediterranean world. In the second and first centuries BC, when Rome expanded its borders eastward, it inherited much of the Hellenistic world founded by Alexander. Macedonia and Achaia became Roman provinces in 148 BC, Asia in 133 BC, Syria in 64 BC, and Egypt in 30 BC. By the first century BC the eastern Mediterranean kingdoms linked together by Greek culture were absorbed into the one political entity of Rome.

Augustus Caesar

After a half century of bitter power struggles involving Julius Caesar, Pompey, Mark Antony, and Octavian, Rome became an imperial government under Octavian, Caesar's grandnephew. In 27 BC, when Octavian emerged as undisputed victor of the power struggle, the Senate responded by granting him numerous titles and offices: he was *Princeps* or "first citizen," proconsul, tribune, and he assumed the title "Augustus" or "revered one." Although he pledged to restore the republic, in practice Augustus was head of state, governor of the important provinces, and had veto power over the Senate. Augustus also assigned to his imperial household the daily business of managing the government, which also lessened the influence of the Senate. Because the Roman republic was inefficient in handling its vast dominion, the transition to a strong central authority was a considerable improvement.[8]

In a testament prepared by himself, called the *res gestae*, or "achievements," Augustus could boast of: (1) securing peace by extending and neutralizing the frontiers; (2) encouraging religion by building temples and shrines; (3) strengthening morality by enforcing laws governing personal behavior; and (4) beautifying the city of Rome with magnificent

---

7. Primary sources for the history of Rome are: Dio Cassius, *Roman History* (2nd cent. AD), the works of Livy (1st cent. AD), C. Tacitus, *Histories* and *Annals* (1st cent. AD), and Suetonius, *Lives of the Caesars* (early 2nd cent. AD). Excellent summaries of Roman history are found in M. Grant, *The World of Rome* (Cleveland: World Publishing Co., 1960); M. Hadas, *Imperial Rome*, rev. ed. (Alexandria, Va.: Time-Life Books, 1979) 35–44, 57–68; Koester, *Introduction* 1:281–322.

8. Hadas, *Imperial Rome* 44, 57–59.

Caesar Augustus.
Statue of Caesar Au-
gustus located on the
island of Capri in the
Bay of Naples, Italy.
Photo by Ralph Harris.

buildings.[9] Most of these achievements would serve as standard policy goals in the imperial administrations that would follow.

The reorganization of the provinces by Augustus is noteworthy. The Senate retained control of the pacified provinces without a standing army (e.g., Macedonia, Achaia, Crete, Cyprus). Both Sergius Paulus, procon-

9. The *Res Gestae Divi Augusti* inscription (AD 13) was discovered in the temple of Rome and Augustus at Ancyra in Galatia (*Monumentum Ancyranum*). Other writings extolling the accomplishments of Augustus are: Suetonius, *Augustus* and Horace, *Secular Ode* 51f., selections of which are found in Barrett, *NTB* 1–8. See also: Hadas, *Imperial Rome* 58–59.

sul (Gk. *anthypatos*) of Cyprus (Acts 13:4,7), and Gallio, proconsul of Achaia (Acts 18:12–17), were governors of senatorial provinces appointed for one-year terms. Those provinces, requiring legions of troops because they were newly acquired or frontier territories, were under the direct control of the emperor, who appointed a "legate" as governor (e.g., Syria, Pamphylia, Galatia). In some districts the emperor ruled through a "prefect" or (after AD 41) a "procurator" (e.g., Egypt, Judea). The Gospel of Luke identifies both the legate of Syria (Quirinius, 2:2) and prefect of Judea (Pontius Pilate, 3:1), although both offices are given the general title of "imperial governor" (Gk. *hēgēmon*). All provinces were ruled by Romans, but certain responsibilities were delegated to local magistrates, especially in the senatorial provinces.

The governors of the provinces had both financial and legal responsibilities. They supervised the collection of taxes and administered justice. Any lawsuit in the provinces could be transferred to the imperial court. This appeal to Caesar was important, for example, in cases of extortion against officials or for alleged crimes against the Roman people and their emperor (e.g., treason, conspiracy). Roman law was equitable for loyal taxpaying provincials but harsh for those convicted of extortion or treason.[10]

Augustus also created new offices for the construction and repair of public buildings, roads, and aqueducts. The great network of roads built by Augustus and his successors was an impressive accomplishment. Roads extended throughout the empire, making even the remote frontiers accessible. Durable and well-constructed, some of these roads are still in use today. Military posts, postal stations, and inns were set up at regular intervals, and maps were provided indicating distances and major points of interest. This engineering feat greatly enhanced travel, trade, and communication in a manner unparalleled in ancient history. It also was a significant factor in the mission and expansion of Christianity.

The Julio-Claudian Emperors

Most of the emperors after Augustus (27 BC–AD 14) either continued or expanded his provincial policies.[11] The four who followed him are known as the Julio-Claudian emperors because they were descendants of the Julians and Claudians, two families of ancient Roman nobility.

10. For more information on the Roman provincial system, see A. H. M. Jones, *Studies in Roman Government and Law* (Oxford: Blackwell, 1960); A. N. Sherwin-White, *Roman Foreign Policy in the East* (Norman, Okla.: University of Oklahoma Press, 1983); idem, *Roman Society*; G. H. Stevenson, *Roman Provincial Administration* (Oxford: Blackwell, 1939).

11. Primary sources for the Roman emperors are: Suetonius, *The Twelve Caesars*; Tacitus, *Annals* and *Histories of Rome*; Dio Cassius, *Roman History*. Selections of

Tiberius (AD 14–37) was the stepson of Augustus. He assumed the office with an experienced military and administrative background. Although he tried to emulate the accomplishments of Augustus, domestic problems and his fear of conspiracy (e.g., by his lieutenant Sejanus) made his reign an unfavorable time for the Senate and provincial governors like Pontius Pilate.

Gaius Caligula (AD 37–41) was the greatnephew of Tiberius, and his rule was at first popular (e.g., he pardoned political prisoners, reduced taxes); but his demand to be addressed as a god (the embodiment of Jupiter) offended the Romans and outraged the Jews (Philo, *Embassy to Gaius*). He also drained the treasury with his reckless expenditures and was killed by his own guards.

Claudius (AD 41–54) was the uncle of Caligula and proved to be a sensible and competent ruler, despite his problems with a physical paralysis. He expanded the offices of the imperial household into an efficient government bureaucracy and also extended Roman citizenship to many prominent provincials. He is mentioned as expelling the Jews from Rome for rioting (because of Christian preaching?) according to Acts 18:2 and Suetonius, *Claudius* 25. He was unfortunately poisoned by his second wife, Agrippina, who had previously forced him to adopt her son, T. Claudius Nero, as legal heir to the throne.

Nero (AD 54–68), stepson of Claudius, had a successful early reign under capable advisors (Seneca, G. Burrus), but it began to deteriorate when he took full control. He had members of his own family murdered, emptied the treasury with his extravagant spending, and resorted to violence in replenishing it. He was accused of setting fire to Rome (64) but fixed the blame on the Christians. According to tradition, Peter and Paul were executed then. After failing to lead a military campaign in the east, Nero, forced by his pretorian guards to flee the city of Rome, committed suicide.

After the Julio-Claudian emperors, a year of civil war saw the reign of three short-lived emperors from the military ranks: Galbo, Otho, and Vitellius.

The Flavian Dynasty

The Flavian dynasty, unlike the Julio-Claudians, descended from an "equestrian" family, the middle class of military commanders and merchants.

T. Flavius Vespasian (AD 69–79) was an experienced general who was completing the campaign to end the Judean revolt of 66–70 when his supporters proclaimed him emperor. Leaving the siege against Jerusalem to his son, Titus, he seized Egypt, thereby controlling Rome's grain supply, and then proceeded to the city with his army to receive from the Senate their official confirmation of his imperial authority. His wise rule brought a new era of peace. He weakened the political control of the army by returning power to the emperor and Senate. The bankrupt treasury was replenished and appointments in the imperial household attracted equestrians and senators. He strengthened the frontiers through

---

these and other sources are found in M. P. Charlesworth, *Documents Illustrating the Reigns of Claudius and Nero* (London: Cambridge University Press, 1939), and E. M. Smallwood, *Documents Illustrating the Principates of Nerva, Trajan and Hadrian* (London: Cambridge University Press, 1966).

The Roman Political System

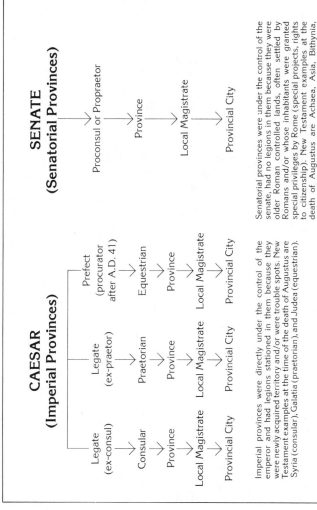

CAESAR
(Imperial Provinces)

Legate (ex-consul) → Consular → Province → Local Magistrate → Provincial City

Legate (ex-praetor) → Praetorian → Province → Local Magistrate → Provincial City

Prefect (procurator after A.D. 41) → Equestrian → Province → Local Magistrate → Provincial City

Imperial provinces were directly under the control of the emperor and had legions stationed in them because they were newly acquired territory and/or were trouble spots. New Testament examples at the time of the death of Augustus are Syria (consular), Galatia (praetorian), and Judea (equestrian).

SENATE
(Senatorial Provinces)

Proconsul or Propraetor → Province → Local Magistrate → Provincial City

Senatorial provinces were under the control of the senate, had no legions in them because they were older Roman controlled lands, often settled by Romans and/or whose inhabitants were granted special privileges by Rome (special projects, rights to citizenship). New Testament examples are Achaea, Asia, Bithynia, Crete, Cyprus, Macedonia.

Taken from CHRONOLOGICAL AND BACKGROUND CHARTS OF THE NEW TESTAMENT, by H. Wayne House.
Copyright ©1981 by The Zondervan Corporation. Used by permission.

The Roman Military System

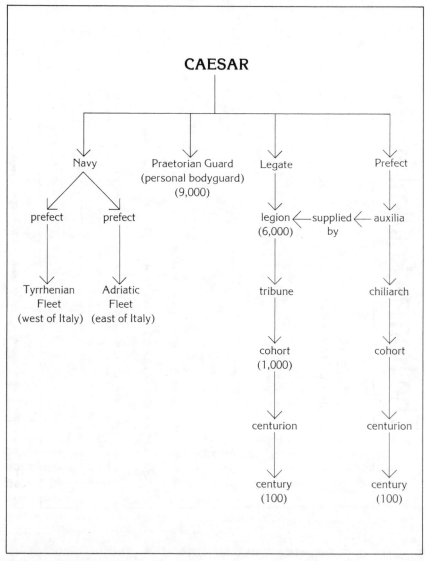

a system of new roads and forts, and the granting of Roman citizenship was made more available to provincials.

Titus (AD 79–81) had replaced his father, Vespasian, as general, overseeing the destruction of Jerusalem in 70 before becoming emperor. His short reign, mainly concerned with relief work to victims of catastrophe (e.g., volcanic destruction of Pompeii and Herculaneum, fire at Rome, plagues), was a popular one.

Domitian (AD 81–96), brother of Titus, was a cruel and vengeful emperor who had his opponents murdered and heavily taxed his subjects. He sought to revive the emperor religion and demanded worship as a god. This policy probably caused the persecution of many Jews and Christians. Many of the anti-Roman motifs in the book of Revelation may reflect his reign (Rev 13; 17). Domitian was killed by members of his imperial household.

The Emperors of the "Golden Age"

The "five good emperors" that followed Domitian saw the "golden age" of the empire. Each emperor made provisions for his own successor and special attention was given to the welfare of provincial cities during this time of peace and prosperity. All except Nerva were provincials.

Nerva (AD 97–98) was a respectable old Roman lawyer who sought to rebuild the state treasury, distribute land to the poor, and encourage building construction. He took definite steps in the choosing and training of a successor.

Trajan (AD 98–117), from an equestrian Roman family of Spain, was Nerva's appointed successor. Trajan was an ambitious ruler who waged war against the Parthians (115–117) and suppressed a Jewish revolt to expand the eastern frontiers. Under his reign the empire reached its peak geographically. To prevent abuse and extravagance, he appointed curators to supervise the local affairs of provincial cities. During this time of prosperity Trajan also encouraged public and private philanthropy. His famous correspondence with Pliny the Younger, governor of Bithynia, provides insights regarding Rome's dealings with Christians.

Hadrian (AD 117–138), also from Spain, was Trajan's adopted son and successor. Although he did not continue Trajan's policies of conquest, he sought to neutralize the frontiers through negotiation (with the Parthians) and fortification (e.g., Hadrian's wall in Britain). Hadrian was a cosmopolitan emperor who traveled extensively throughout the empire, promoting Greek culture and numerous building projects. He granted citizenship to a growing number of new towns and cities which applied for it and standardized Roman legal procedure throughout the empire. In reaction to Hadrian's attempts to rebuild Jerusalem into a Roman city with a temple dedicated to Jupiter, the Jews revolted under Simon Bar Kochba (132–135). The insurrection was suppressed after much effort, and it resulted in the expulsion of all Jews from Palestine.

Antoninus Pius (AD 138–161), from a Roman family of southern Gaul, was Hadrian's appointed successor. He quietly furthered the centralization of the government (e.g., had imperial cabinet of advisors) but maintained good relations with the Senate. Despite border clashes in the northern and eastern frontiers, he enjoyed a reign of peace and prosperity as expressed in the oration, *To Rome* by Aelius Aristides (tutor of Marcus Aurelius). Aristides, a provincial from Asia Minor, pictured the empire as a commonwealth of peaceful and prosperous city-states under Rome's beneficent leadership and protection.

Marcus Aurelius (AD 161–180), adopted son of Antonius, came from a consular family of Spain. At an early age he gained the favor of Hadrian, who supervised his fine education. When he assumed the imperial throne, Aurelius was an accomplished soldier, administrator, and philosopher. He composed his *Meditations*, breathing high Stoic principles, between military campaigns. Despite wars on the Rhine, Danube, and Euphrates rivers, there was a remarkable sense of unity in the empire. Grants of Roman citizenship were freely given, and qualified provincial citizens also served in the Senate.

Despite the sporadic periods of tyranny in the reigns of Caligula, Nero, and Domitian, the emperors of Rome continued and even refined the fair provincial policies of Augustus. They maintained political order and economic stability in an otherwise turbulent Mediterranean world. By the "golden age," emperors were taking an active role in the safety and welfare of provincial cities. Early Christianity would benefit from such imperial policies. Full-scale persecution of Christians for refusing to pay homage to the emperor would not begin until the reigns of Decius and Valerian (250–260). These efforts ended with the reign of Constantine (324–337), who declared Christianity a legal religion of Rome.

AN AGE OF ANXIETY AND ASPIRATION[12]

Rapid change in any society can both inspire new hopes and arouse new fears. From the years following World War II to the present, our Western society has experienced great scientific and technological advances which have given it a sense of both achievement and anxiety. Our rocket systems are so advanced that we can make shuttle trips to the moon or send guided missiles to destroy any locality in the world. Genetic engineering capable of creating new life forms in a laboratory may help solve some current problems or produce many unforeseen ones. Our great advances in computer technology can enhance the productivity of some people or limit the employment opportunities of others. This paradox of aspiration and anxiety through rapid change was also characteristic of the

---

12. The title, "Age of Anxiety And Aspiration," is derived in part from: E. R. Dodds, *The Greeks and the Irrational* (Berkeley: University of California Press, 1951) 44, 78, 97; idem, *Pagan and Christian in an Age of Anxiety* (London: Cambridge University Press, 1965) 3–4, 133; and H. C. Kee and F. W. Young, *Understanding the NT* (Englewood Cliffs, N.J.: Prentice-Hall, 1957) 7–8. Although the second book by Dodds mainly concerns the 2nd–4th cents. AD, much of it has relevance for our period of discussion. The English word, "anxiety," is derived from the Latin, *anxietas*, which denoted "worry, trouble" and "fear" in Latin literature; and "aspiration" also has a Latin derivative, *aspiratio*, "exhalation," which also conveyed the figurative meaning of "hope" or "aspiration."

NT world. With the cultural revolution caused by Hellenism and improved travel, goods and ideas were either exchanged or exploited; old traditions were either transformed or forgotten; and people left their native lands either as hopeful travelers or despairing slaves. Rapid change in any age generates new aspirations and anxieties.

The Anxieties of the Age

Before looking at the new aspirations, we will survey some of the anxieties and the circumstances that produced them. Improved travel, improved trade, and pervasive Hellenism certainly produced favorable changes in the Greco-Roman world. But such changes also brought with them numerous problems or sources of anxiety. Improved travel not only enhanced communication and trade, but also increased the spread of diseases, causing illness, death, or the fear of disease.[13.] Improved trade not only stimulated the accumulation of wealth for some, but caused the exploitation and displacement of people from their homelands to serve as slaves for a new prosperous merchant class.[14] Such a situation would produce in these oppressed peoples, feelings of despair and vulnerability and would result in the loss of ethnic identity. Pervasive Hellenism in the East resulted in the emergence of oriental thought in Greek dress. Such a transformation brought new life to both oriental religions and Greek philosophy, but it also carried with it a pessimism of the old traditions and an obsession with fate that would lead to moods of hopelessness and helplessness.[15]

13. The movement of goods and people was easy and cheap in the empire, see for examples, the travels of apostle Paul, Aquila, and Priscilla in Acts and the accounts of traveling merchants, cited in M. P. Charlesworth, *Roman Empire* (London: Oxford University Press, 1967) 86–87. The spread of disease was also unprecedented, for example, during the reigns of both Titus and Marcus Aurelius, terrible plagues swept across the empire. Note also the diverse list of diseases in *Asclepius: Testimonies*, ed., E. J. and L. Edelstein (Baltimore: Johns Hopkins Press, 1945).

14. The correspondence of Zeno, steward of a large estate in Fayum, Egypt, addressed to Apollonius, the finance minister under Ptolemy II (282–246 BC), and the king's extensive "Revenue Laws" indicate the vast amounts of trade in which money-making Egypt was engaged (Austin, *Hellenistic World* 395–411). On prosperous Roman trading, see Charlesworth, *Roman Empire* 81–91. The importance of slaves in labor and commerce cannot be underestimated. In the 1st cent. BC, one third of Rome's population were slaves. Most were acquired through military conquest, e.g., the Jewish historian, Josephus, stated that Rome took 97,000 prisoners from Palestine during the Jewish revolt of AD 66–70, *War* 6.420. See T. Wiedermann, *Greek and Roman Slavery* (Baltimore: Johns Hopkins, 1981).

15. See the concern for deliverance from fate in Apuleius, *Golden Ass* 11.6,15; Corpus Hermetica 12.9, in R. Bultmann, *Primitive Christianity* (Cleveland: World Publishing, 1956) 154. For the view of the revival of Eastern religions in Greek language and thought-forms, see Jonas, *Gnostic* 3–27.

The Temple of Athena Parthenos (maiden) built on the highest part of the Acropolis of Athens, 438 BC. The outer colonades have been rebuilt in modern times. *Photo by Ralph Harris.*

Belief in fatalism dominated Hellenistic thought. Since the classical period, the Greeks believed that each person received his "appointed portion" in life (Gk. *moira* in Homer). But in Hellenism, human life was predetermined by higher powers (e.g., Stoicism, apocalypticism) which were often identified as fate (Gk. *heimarmenē* or *anankē*; Lat. *fatum*). Fate, sometimes personified, would determine the outcome of nations, individuals, and events, with little or no human control.[16]

The preoccupation with fate was greatly influenced by astrology. The belief that the stars were deities which determined the destiny of humans, probably began in Mesopotamia (700 BC) and spread throughout the Mediterranean world after Alexander.[17] Astrology affected every aspect of society: religion, war, politics, trade, and personal matters. The old Greek gods were identified with the planets: Zeus = Jupiter, Aphrodite = Venus, Ares = Mars, Kronos = Saturn, Hermes = Mercury. Symbols of the Zodiac figure prominently in a sculpture of Zeus from Italy and a relief of Cybele the Asian Mother-goddess (Transjordan area),

16. Examples of fatalism in Stoicism are Zeno, *Fragments* 175–76 and Chrysippus, *Fragment* 625 (both in Barrett, *NTB* 61–64); Seneca, *On Providence* 5.7–9 and *To Marcia* 18.5–6; see also: Pliny, *Natural History* 2.22 and the histories of Suetonius and Tacitus. The following are examples of the apocalyptic view that the events preceding the end are predetermined: Dan 9:24; 1 Enoch 92.2; 4 Ezra 4:36–37; 6:1–6; 2 Bar 25; see also Jewish Wisdom: Eccl 3:2–8; Sir 23:20; 39:25,30.

17. See examples of Hellenistic astrology: Papyri Tebtunis 276 (late 2nd cent. AD) and Chrysippus, *Fragment* 625 (both in Barrett, *NTB* 35–36, 61–62); Philo, *Migration of Abraham* 179 (early 1st cent. AD); 4Q186 and 4QMess (Qumran Scrolls). Note statues and reliefs of Greek gods and zodiac in Godwin, *Mystery Religions* plates 2 (Jupiter in zodiac), 8 (zodiac and intermediate deities), 142 (Orphic deity and zodiac); see also: plates 75 (Asian goddess Cybele and zodiac) 50 (Jewish zodiac, 6th cent. AD).

Public ceremony of Isis cult with priest officiating; wall painting from Pompeii, first century AD. *Naples National Museum.* Used with permission.

both dated in the early second century AD. Horoscopes were so prevalent in the early Roman Empire that Augustus sought to standardize them by publishing his own.

The Aspirations of the Age

Appearing as either symptoms of or responses to the above anxieties and obsessions were the aspirations of this age. They were numerous and diverse, but primarily religious and philosophical. Many of these spiritual pilgrimages or quests for meaning are a resurgence of Eastern thought transformed by Hellenism. They represent a new synthesis of oriental religion in Greek dress. For example, the ancient Egyptian cult of Isis (representing the earth) and Osiris (personification of the Nile river) are Hellenized into Isis, the "Mother of all things," and Sarapis, who is portrayed in the likeness of Zeus.[18]

Most of these Hellenistic religions and philosophies offered people security, identity, and a sense of community in the midst of growing fears. They also provided ways of dealing with the problem of fate.

Astrology, Magic, and Divination

Specific attempts at circumventing one's fate were the practices of astrology, magic, and divination. Although astrology led to the preoccupation with fate, it also sought to deal with the problem. If the order of

18. See plates of oriental deities in Hellenistic dress with universalistic titles, in Godwin, *Mystery Religions* plates ii (Mithra), ix (Isis), 63–71 (Mithra), 85–89 (Isis and Sarapis).

the stars determines one's destiny, then a *knowledge* of one's fate could be known by a study of the stars. This explains the wide use of personal horoscopes in such diverse places as the imperial household and Jewish Qumran. It also accounts for the depiction of Hellenistic deities in the zodiac, implying their control of the stellar movements. Closely associated with astrology was the practice of magic. It was an attempt to gain mastery over both the good and evil powers that determine one's fate. The "Great Magical Papyri" from Egypt (3rd cent. AD) contain various prescriptions and rituals to deal with the good and bad spirits (demons) that affect one's destiny.[19] Prophetic oracles were also consulted at places like the shrine of Apollo at Delphi, Greece, and divination was practiced to discern the future.[20]

The Mystery Religions

The so-called mystery religions sought to deal with the problem of fate and the fears of the age with promises of immortality and personal communion with a deity.[21] Although they were given the name, "mystery religions," because of their stress on secret initiations, many also included public processionals and celebrations. Most of these mystery cults included both the recital and reenactment of a myth celebrating the death and resurrection of a deity. This myth corresponded to the annual vegetation cycle when life is renewed each spring and dies each fall. The "mysteries" also promised their initiates immortality, personal communion with a deity, and membership in a close-knit organization of fellow adherents. Although all of the mystery cults were influenced by Hellenism and cir-

---

19. Both Jewish and pagan magical texts are found in these Egyptian papyri, now preserved in the National Library of Paris. The texts are reproduced, translated, and discussed in Deissmann, *LAE* 254–64.

20. Originally prophetic women, called sibyls, resided at places like the temple of Delphi and gave ecstatic predictions. Later, prophecies ascribed to these sibyls were published in books, called the Sibylline Oracles. See translations and critical discussion of the vast corpus of the Sibylline Oracles (2nd cent. BC–7th cent. AD) by J. J. Collins, in J. H. Charlesworth, *OTP* 1:317–472. Underscoring their popularity in the Roman world, the emperors also consulted oracles and participated in divination (e.g., Suetonius, *Julius Caesar* 81; *Vespasian* 5; Tacitus, *Histories* 5.13).

21. Primary sources for the mystery religions are from a variety of Greek and Latin authors and inscriptions. Selections are found in J. Ferguson, *Greek and Roman Religion A Source Book* (Park Ridge, N.J.: Noyes Press, 1980) and F. C. Grant, *Ancient Roman Religion* (Indianapolis, Ind.: Bobbs-Merrill Co., 1957). Informative illustrations of ancient artifacts and excavated sites are also found in J. Ferguson, *The Religions of the Roman Empire* (Ithaca, N.Y.: Cornell Univ. Press, 1970); Godwin, *Mystery Religions* (1981) and *The New Larousse Encyclopedia of Mythology*, new ed. (London/New York: Hamlyn Publishing, 1968).

culated throughout the Mediterranean world, we have conveniently grouped them according to their places of origin:

Greece. The cult of Demeter (goddess of soil and farming) and Kore (her daughter) originated at Eleusis (near Athens) in the 15th cent. BC. The myth concerns the kidnap of Kore to Hades, her search by Demeter, and Kore's release as Persephone. These events were memorialized in great festivals. The departure of Kore/Persephone was celebrated in October and her return in February. In September a great procession en route from Athens to Eleusis was held in honor of Demeter. Rites of purification and initiation were also performed.

The cult of Dionysius began in Thrace (modern Bulgaria) but came to Boeotia, Greece at an early date. Originally, Dionysius was the god of wine (Roman name: Bacchus), and later the god of vegetation, life, and pleasure. In the myth, Dionysius was born from a union between Zeus and a human mother (Semele) and was raised by the nymphs of Nysa. As an adult he discovered the art of making wine and shared this gift with mortals throughout his many travels. Cultic festivals were held in December (new wine offering) and late February (last vintage of wine). Animal sacrifices were also offered. In early March a great festival took place with dramatic representations. In addition, orgiastic revelries occurred (e.g., on the slopes of Mt. Cithaeron).

The Orphic cult identified Dionysius with the Cretan god Zagreus, son of Zeus and Demeter (or Kore), who was slain and dismembered by jealous Titans, his heart was rescued by Athena and from it Zeus created Dionysius, the Orphic god of life and death. Later Orphics eliminated the orgiastic features of the early Dionysian cult and produced sacred writings of hymns and cosmological myths.

Egypt. The Isis-Sarapis cult (300 BC) utilized ancient myths about the deities Isis, Osiris, and Horus, as early as 3000 BC. In Plutarch's version, Osiris (the personification of the Nile river) was slain and dismembered by the evil god Typhon (associated with desert and sea water). Isis, a goddess representing earth and the forces that cause the Nile flood, recovered the scattered pieces of Osiris and revived him. As his waters began to flow once more over the land, the union of these two divine principles gave birth to Horus, the personification of Egypt. In the Hellenistic period Osiris took the name Sarapis and was often portrayed as Zeus-Jupiter. Isis also appeared as Juno or Venus and was regarded as a divine queen, the mother of all, savior, and ruler of fate. Temples of Isis and Sarapis were found throughout the Mediterranean world. For example, hellenized sanctuaries of Isis (called "Iseia") have been found in Pompeii, Rome, and on the Aegean island of Delos. Temples of Sarapis ("Sarapeia") have been excavated at Alexandria, Ostia near Rome, Pergamum, Ephesus, and Miletus. Many of them had assembly halls to contain a large number of people. These temples indicate a structured organization under the leadership of priests. Membership was obtained through a rite of initiation, and participation in sacred meals also occurred. Elaborate public processions were also part of the Isis-Sarapis cult. As a Hellenistic mystery religion it flourished from 300 BC to AD 400.

Persia. The origin of Mithraism goes back to the Mitra of the Indo-Aryans with some modifications. The god Mithras appears to be lower than the Persian Supreme Deity of Light (Ahura Mazda) but higher than the visible sun. He was also a mediator between light and the power of darkness (Ahriman). In the cult legend, Mithras was born from a rock on December 25 as witnessed by shepherds with gifts. While hunting, Mithras encounters a bull, overcomes it, and carries it into a cave where he kills the bull with a short sword. From its blood and semen grows new life, but a snake tries to drink the blood and a scorpion poisons the semen. The sun, the moon, the planets, and the winds witness the sacrifice; Mithras meets with the sun (i.e., Helios/Sol), both eat the meat and drink the bull's blood and make a covenant; Sol kneels before Mithras, receives the accolade, and they shake hands. The initiation into the mystery comprised seven steps of endurance, which probably corresponded to the seven planets. The initiate is called "reborn," and through an oath he becomes a soldier of Mithras. Military discipline and subordination are part of the cult's hierarchical structure. The Mithraeia at Ostia and Rome are cave-like structures with carvings of Mithras slaying the bull surrounded by benches for worshipers. It was a cult restricted to males but had fraternal relations with the Cybele cult. Mithraism flourished in the Roman Empire from the 1st to the 4th cents. AD.

Asia Minor. Although the Cybele cult had early connections with Syria, it expanded to Asia Minor by the second millennium BC where it flourished for centuries. The goddess Cybele was viewed as the Great Mother of life and a mighty and fierce fertility god. Attis was a Phrygian shepherd or son of a mountain deity, beloved by the Great Mother. Although the Hellenistic legends of the couple are diverse, they concern Cybele's vengeance at the infidelity of Attis and his tragic death by castration. Some legends included a death and restoration to life of Attis by Cybele. Her cult was accompanied by orgiastic rites leading to a climax at which devotees would castrate themselves in ecstatic frenzy. Although the cult came to Rome in the early 3rd cent. BC, its worship was in secret because it was too barbaric for the Romans. In Greece the castration rite disappeared. A well known rite of the cult was the taurobolium, in which initiates were washed in the blood of a slaughtered bull.[22] The cult attracted many female devotees.

Because they were close-knit associations attempting to overcome fate and promising immortality and intimate communion with a deity, the so-called mystery religions spread throughout the Roman world. Hellenization and syncretism ("mixing of religions") contributed to their wide influence. Although a direct dependency of early Christianity on the mystery cults is difficult to establish, both had parallel patterns of development because they shared the same cultural environment. In many cities of the empire, the Romans probably viewed early Christians as devotees of a new mystery cult (e.g., Tacitus, Suetonius, Pliny the Younger).

Gnosticism

Another spiritual phenomenon that competed with the mystery cults was Gnosticism, a widespread religious and philosophical movement of

---

22. A vivid account of the taurobolium is found in a Christian work from the 2nd cent., Prudentius, *Peristephanon* 10.1011–50. For discussion of relevant source material and the inclusion of informative archaeological photographs and illustrations, see M. J. Vermaseren, *Cybele and Attis: The Myth and the Cult* (London: Thames & Hudson, 1977).

the first three centuries AD.[23] This diverse movement, like the mystery cults, is the product of Hellenistic syncretism, the mingling of Greek and oriental traditions and ideas (i.e., Greek, Jewish, Iranian, Christian influences). Although there was no uniform gnostic system, certain myths and motifs were dominant.

A first major concept was *gnōsis* (Gk. "knowledge"). It was a secret revealed knowledge to initiates which had both liberating and redeeming effects. The content of this *gnōsis* consisted of basic insights into the divine nature of humanity and the cosmos. The possession of it freed the individual from ignorance and bondage in the world.

A second characteristic was a central myth which consisted of the following: the presence of a divine "spark" in humans, which proceeded from the divine realm and had fallen into our world. The earth is also the tragic result of a downward movement from the divine realm. The recovery of this divine "spark" in the world by its own divine counterpart is necessary for liberation and redemption to take place.

A third concept presupposed in gnostic systems is radical dualism ("two opposite realms") interwoven with a monistic conception ("supreme unknown God"). The spiritual realm of the unknowable God which incorporates a "fullness" (*plērōma*) of subordinate angels and heavenly beings is in "direct opposition" to our own physical world which is characterized by chaos, darkness, ignorance, and death. The structure of this scheme consists of the following elements. At the center is the earth, surrounded by air and eight heavenly spheres. The eight spheres consist of the seven planets and the fixed stars that close them off. They were believed to be inhabited by demons, spirits, or "rulers" (Gk. *archons*). Above them lies the realm of the "unknown God" and the Pleroma ("fullness") with its graduated worlds (aeons). These gnostic cosmologies or "schemes of the world" varied particularly in the number of heavenly beings and spheres and the different names ascribed to them. For example, the so-called Valentinian system consisted of pairs of aeons ("dyads"), called "Nous-Truth, Logos-Life, Man-Church." The so-called Basilidian system gave prominence to the "archons," called "Ogdoad and Hebdomad." Yet, the basic scheme mentioned above is presupposed in both.

---

23. Primary sources for Gnosticism are found in Robinson, *Nag Hammadi;* W. Foerster, *Gnosis: A Selection of Gnostic Texts,* 2 vols. (London: Oxford University Press, 1972, 1974); R. M. Grant, *Gnosticism* (New York, 1961); Hennecke, *NTA,* 2 vols.; selections of Mandean, Manichean and other gnostic texts are found in W. Barnstone, ed., *The Other Bible* (San Francisco: Harper & Row, 1984). For a comprehensive survey and critical discussion of sources, see Rudolph, *Gnosis.* For a brief survey, see *Nag Hammadi, Gnosticism, and Early Christianity,* ed. C. W. Hedrick and R. Hodgson (Peabody, Mass.: Hendrickson, 1986) 1–11.

Fourth, connected with these cosmologies was a myth of the creation of the world ("cosmogony") offered as an explanation for the present dilemma of humanity, remote from God. Most are influenced by the Genesis creation story and consist of a downward fall of a heavenly being (e.g., Sophia), who through a series of complicated or tragic circumstances brings about the creation of the world (often called the "Abortion"). Like diamonds in mud, a divine spark is hidden within human inhabitants of this dark and ignorant world. Salvation for humans and the cosmos is accomplished when people receive gnosis about their divine origins through a Gnostic Redeemer and when the divine soul takes its heavenly journey through the hostile spheres to be reunited in the divine realm. This final phase of restoration also constitutes the gnostic teaching of last things.

Our understanding of gnostic cult and community is derived from gnostic writings, patristic reports (often exaggerated), and later manifestations found among the Manicheans (6th–10th cents.) and Mandeans (4th–20th cents.). Gnostic practices are as diverse as the sources, ranging from ascetic and monastic to libertine and licentious activities. Our primary sources confirm the ascetic and monastic features, whereas evidence for libertine activities is deduced from secondary reports of the church fathers. The Manicheans were an ascetic communal organization with a common meal and a so-called mass for the dead. The practices of the Mandeans were similar but are distinguished primarily by their baptismal ceremonies in flowing ("living") water.

The origins of Gnosticism are difficult to ascertain, since our earliest sources are second and third century AD. Evidence from church fathers, like Justin Martyr and Irenaeus make it clear that there were Christian Gnostics in conflict with early catholic Christians at that time. Some concluded from the patristic data that Gnosticism began as a Christian heresy. However, the discovery of the Nag Hammadi texts in southern Egypt, 1945, has challenged this view. The Nag Hammadi collection seems to indicate the existence of fully developed non-Christian and Jewish gnostic systems that may have preceded Christianity. This is a significant point since some scholars believe that the concept of a Gnostic Redeemer may have influenced the way some early Christians portrayed Jesus (e.g., Phil 2; Jn 1), although there is no consensus on this view. Later Mandean, Manichean, and Hermetic texts (2nd to 6th cents. AD) show the prevalence of Gnosticism in the East and possibly contain early traditions contemporary with the NT.

Gods and Divinized Heroes

The Greco-Roman world, as we have seen, had many gods and goddesses. Some were mythical deities who dwelt in the heavens or on some mythical mountain, and others were associated with the cycles of the seasons. Some of these immortal gods, like the Gnostic Redeemer figure, descended from heaven to earth or were sent to fulfill some important mission on behalf of humanity.

There were also human figures of both history and legend who were so endowed with divinity that they performed miraculous deeds.[24] Some were believed to be the offspring of gods and humans. What is most characteristic of them is their wisdom and special powers. Usually they were considered to be great benefactors of humanity. In this category were divinized rulers, military leaders, politicians, philosophers, physicians, and healers. The idea of emperor worship, for example, was an adaptation of Eastern beliefs about the divinity of the king or pharaoh. But Western conquerors fostered such ideas on their marches eastward, for example, in the eastern provinces the Roman emperor was often believed to be divine. At home, Greeks and Romans tolerated such views for political unity, but were disillusioned with them. It was customary, however, to pay homage to emperors as gods after they died.

Especially widespread was the notion of a hero or philosopher who was revered for his ability to perform miracles or impart great wisdom. These great abilities were believed to be a manifestation of deity, and some of these heroes, such as the legendary Hercules, were granted immortality after death. Another example was the itinerant Pythagorean philosopher, Apollonius of Tyana (Asia Minor), who had a miraculous birth, gathered followers, taught, healed, and appeared to his followers after death. He lived in the first Christian century, and shortly after AD 217 a *Life of Apollonius*, which resembles a Synoptic Gospel, was written by Philostratus.

Hellenistic Philosophies

Like the mystery religions and Gnosticism, Hellenistic philosophies also promised deliverance from the fears and uncertainties of life.[25] Unlike most religious cults, these philosophical schools offered a comprehen-

24. A selection of primary sources and comments on gods and divinized heroes is found in Cartlidge and Dungan, *Documents*; F. C. Grant, *Ancient Roman Religion* (Indianapolis: Bobbs-Merrill, 1957) 169–243; M. Hadas and M. Smith, *Heroes and Gods* (New York: Harper & Row, 1965); J. Campbell, *The Hero with a Thousand Faces*, 2nd ed. (Princeton: Princeton University, 1968) 49–254, 315–64. See also the survey in Talbert, *Gospel?*.

25. For the pragmatic focus in Greco-Roman philosophies, see E. Bevan, "Hellenistic Popular Philosophy," in J. B. Bury et al., *The Hellenistic Age* (London: Cambridge University Press, 1925) 79–107. For primary sources and comments, see Barrett, *NTB* 54–79; G. H. Clark, *Selections from Hellenistic Philosophy* (New York: Appleton-Century-Crofts, 1940); J. Ferguson, *Greek and Roman Religion* 90–117; F. Grant, *Ancient Roman Religion* 59–156.

sive picture of the origin and structure of the universe. Such teachings were not formulated in the interests of pure science but were intended to explain a person's place and destiny in the universe and how that person might best conduct his or her life. By the Hellenistic period, the golden age of Greek philosophy was past. In a pragmatic age disillusioned with the past ideals of human reason, the Hellenistic philosophies were popular quasi-religious movements of wandering preacher-philosophers and healers.

The influential ideas of Plato (d. 347 BC) were continued in what is labeled Middle Platonism (68 BC–AD 205).[26] These Platonists followed the three characteristic aspects of Plato's dualism. (1) A distinction was made between two levels of reality: the imperfect, temporal, changing, material world of particulars over against the perfect, eternal, unchanging, spiritual world of Forms. (2) True knowledge of the Forms can only be attained by reason, not sense experience. (3) The immortal soul is imprisoned by the mortal body (also Pythagorean). Plato's theological speculations were also developed by his disciples and the later Platonists. Plato's conception of the Good as the highest of Forms was identified as a supreme Deity (Middle Platonism). His Demiurge (Divine Craftsman in *Timaeus*) was equated with Aristotle's Unmoved Mover (Albinus of Smyrna), and his mention of intermediaries (*daimones*) between heaven and earth was delineated into good and evil demons (Xenocrates of Chalcedon).

Platonism influenced Alexandrian Jews like Philo, the gnostic movement, and early Christianity. A few examples will be given. Philo stated that an invisible plan of Ideas was conceived by God before he created the world (*Creation* 4). He also used biblical stories, like Abraham's migration to Canaan, to illustrate the soul's migration from physical bondage. Gnosticism regarded the soul ("inner spirit") as needing liberation from the body, made extensive use of intermediate beings, and went beyond Platonic dualism in viewing the earthly world and divine realm as irreconcilable opposites. The NT book of Hebrews may have been influenced by Platonic (or Philonic) dualism in its constant analogies between shadow and reality, earthly and heavenly, and transitory and enduring. Early catholic Christians, like Justin Martyr, and Alexandrian Christians, like Clement and Origen, were especially indebted to Middle Platonism.

26. A selection of sources for Plato and Middle Platonism are: Plato, *The Republic, Symposium, Timaeus, Parmenides*; Diogenes Laertius, *Lives*, Bk 3; Albinus of Smyrna (AD 150); Plutarch, *Platonic Essays* (AD 120). Helpful secondary sources are: J. Dillon, *The Middle Platonists, 80 BC to AD 220* (Ithaca, N.Y.: Cornell University Press, 1977); P. Merlan, *From Platonism to Neoplatonism*, 2nd ed. (Hague: Nijhoff, 1960); P. Shorey, *Platonism, Ancient and Modern* (Berkeley: University of California Press, 1938).

The founder of Epicureanism was Epicurus of Samos (342–270 BC). His basic teachings were rarely altered by his followers.[27] Although maligned by contemporaries for his professed hedonism, he advocated a rational pursuit of pleasures that would free one from pain and despair. In order to lead such a pleasant life, Epicurus believed that one must be released from groundless fears that would cause mental anguish. For this reason, Epicurus based his ethics on a materialist view of the universe. Whereas Aristotle valued the perception of our senses, Epicurus regarded them as the *only* true source of knowledge (empiricism). Epicurus also adopted the atomistic view of reality from Democritus (405 BC). This atomistic theory gave a natural explanation of the origins of the universe without reference to the gods: everything originated from the determined movements of atoms (*atomoi*) in a vacuum (*kenos*). This view, Epicurus believed, could deliver one from the fear of the gods, the dread of death, and the terrors of superstition. It would liberate the individual from the fear of the gods since they did not create the world, are made of a different element, and are unconcerned with human affairs. It would release one from the dread of death, because when the atoms and void that constitute a person come apart, there is nothing more to experience. (Both the body and soul, or vital spirit, are mortal.) It would finally set free the person from the terror of Destiny, because everything that occurs is either the result of atoms colliding in a vacuum (chance) or our own human choices (modifying Democritus with the inclusion of human volition).

Stoicism was probably the most popular Hellenistic philosophy.[28] Its name was derived from the *Stoa Poikile*, or "painted porch," a public hall in Athens where its founder, Zeno (336–263 BC), taught. Because of its diverse development, Stoicism has been divided into three periods: Early Stoa (300–185 BC), Middle Stoa (185–46 BC), and Later Stoa (46 BC–AD 180).

In the early period, Zeno and his students sought to develop a complete philosophical system of physics, ethics, and logic. In physics, he followed the teachings of Heraclitus (500 BC), who saw the world ordered by divine reason or "Logos," which he identified with the primal element of fire, from which everything came and to which all would return.

---

27. Sources for Epicureanism are: Leucippus and Democritus in Diogenes Laertius, *Lives* 9.30–49; life and teachings of Epicurus in D. Laertius, *Lives* 10; Lucretius, *On the Nature of the Universe* (50 BC). For secondary information, see R. D. Hicks, *Stoic and Epicurean* (New York: Russell and Russell, 1962).

28. The lives and teachings of Heraclitus, Zeno, and his students is found in D. Laertius, *Lives* 7; 9.1–17. The works of Epictetus and Seneca are found in the LCL. Collections of Stoic writings are found in Arnim, *Stoicorum Veterum Fragmenta*, 4 vols. (1921–24); G. H. Clark, *Selections from Hellenistic Philosophy* (New York, 1940) 50–105; Barrett, *NTB* 61–71. For discussion, see Hicks, *Stoic and Epicurean*; J. M. Rist, *Stoic Philosophy* (Cambridge: University Press, 1969).

Zeno and his student Cleanthes identified the Logos with Zeus, the supreme (but impersonal) governor of the universe. Zeno's disciple, Chrysippus, believed that the world would perpetually undergo a process of destruction by fire and restoration to life (i.e., a universal and recurring conflagration). In ethics, conformity with the natural laws of divine reason was viewed as imperative by Zeno and his followers. One conforms to divine reason by pursuing the good (virtue) and avoiding evil (vice). Since all adversities are determined occurrences, they should be endured with self-control and composure. Destiny is overcome by not being emotionally swayed by the circumstances of life. In logic Zeno was influenced by his teachers: Diodorus for his dialectics and Antisthenes (4th cent. BC) for his linguistic analyses. Logical discussion mainly concerned the nature and manner of perceiving and understanding reality.

The Middle Stoa was characterized by further revisions and accommodations to contemporary philosophical and religious views. Panaetius (185–109 BC) rejected the doctrine of universal conflagration and advocated the (Peripatetic) belief in the eternal quality of the world. Posidonius (135–46 BC) believed that a "seminal reason" of the divine Logos dwelt within all humans and that obedience to this "seed of the Logos" would bring one in harmony with the universe.

The later period was almost exclusively devoted to ethical teachings. Seneca (AD 60), Nero's advisor, wrote essays on practical moral topics. The ethical *Discourses* and *Manual* ascribed to the Roman slave, Epictetus (130), utilize the so-called diatribe form of argumentation: i.e., objections by fictional opponents, rhetorical questions, use of hyperbole, and anecdote. This form of debate was also used by the apostle Paul and the book of James. The *Meditations* of Marcus Aurelius (AD 121–180) includes Epictetus and Plato as its sources.

Much of Stoicism was derived from Cynicism. Zeno, the founder of Stoicism, was a student of Crates, a disciple of Diogenes (400–325 BC), whose detached and independent lifestyle gave him the label "dog" (Gk. *kyōn*), from which the sect derived its name. Diogenes based his teaching on the Socratic ideals of Antisthenes (445–360 BC), who advocated the independent pursuit of virtue. Crates developed, in a moderate direction, the teachings of Diogenes, who stressed self-sufficiency and individualism with little interest in theoretical or speculative knowledge.[29] During this period, literary disciples, like Bion and Teles, developed the diatribe form of argumentation and the listing of vices and virtues. Both

---

29. For primary data on Antisthenes, Diogenes and his followers, see D. Laertius, *Lives* Bk 6. See also the following Cynic writings, mostly from the third and second cent., BC: A. Malherbe (ed.), *The Cynic Epistles* (Missoula, Mont.: Scholars Press, 1977); idem, "Cynics" in *IDBSupp*, 21–23; Kee, *NT Context* 230–31.

of these literary forms are found in the NT. By the first century AD, much of Cynicism was absorbed into Stoicism, although the former persisted in its characteristic scorn of conventional morality and religion.

In the Hellenistic world, the teachings and practices of philosophical leaders were often preserved and continued in schools of disciples. By the sixth century BC, the followers of Pythagoras gathered around him in Italy, forming a close brotherhood. Many other schools were also established in Athens, for example, Plato's Academy and Zeno's public hall Stoa. This school tradition was also prevalent among the Jewish Essenes and Pharisees, having roots in the prophetic guilds of the ancient Near East (e.g., 1 Sam 10:5-11; 19:20-24; Isa 8:16; Jer 36:4). It also seems apparent that early Christianity developed schools or communities along similar lines (e.g., Johannine community, Origen).[30]

Hellenistic Judaism

In competition with the religious and philosophical aspirations of the Greco-Roman world was Hellenistic Judaism, especially the "Diaspora" Jews who lived outside of Palestine.[31] Despite its distinctive adherence to the "law of Moses," Judaism was a Hellenistic religion. By the third century BC, most Jews of the Diaspora and Palestine had learned to speak Greek. Shortly afterward, a Greek translation of the Hebrew Bible, the Septuagint, was begun in Alexandria.[32] It was later used by early Christians. Jewish philosophers, like Philo of Alexandria (AD 20-50), interpreted the Jewish Scriptures figuratively or allegorically to underscore biblical agreement with Hellenistic philosophy.[33] It was Philo who sought to present the religion of the Jews as a type of mystery cult (*On Cherubim* 48-50), although he was not favorably disposed to the pagan mysteries (*On Special Laws* 1.319-21). Jews such as Josephus wrote histories of their people to show that their cultural heritage was as good as that of the Greeks (e.g., *Against Apion* 2.164-71). Archaeological excavations have shown that synagogues, serving as gathering places for worship and in-

30. For the best example of philosophical schools and the succession of tradition, see Diogenes Laertius, *Lives of Eminent Philosophers*. See also the surveys in R. A. Culpepper, *The Johannine School: An Examination of the Johannine-School Hypothesis Based on the Investigation of the Nature of Ancient Schools*, SBLDS (Missoula, Mont.: Scholars Press, 1975); Talbert, *Literary Patterns* 89-110, 125-34.

31. See the mention of Diaspora in Josephus, *Ant.* 14.110-18 and Philo, *Against Flaccus* 73-77. See also J. Barlett, *Jews in the Hellenistic World* (Cambridge: University Press, 1985); Schürer and Vermes, *History* 3:1-176. For further discussion, see ch 2, Jewish Background of NT.

32. *Letter of Aristeas* 1-12, 28-51, 301-11 (2nd cent. BC); Philo, *On the Life of Moses* 2.26-42 (1st cent. AD).

33. Examples of Philo's allegorical exegesis can be found in his: *On the Migration of Abraham* 89-93; *On the Posterity and Exile of Cain* 1-11.

struction, were located throughout the Mediterranean world.

The Jews maintained a belief in only one God (monotheism) who created the world and controls its future. For those who live according to the will of God as expressed in the Jewish law (Torah) there is everlasting life; for the disobedient there is everlasting judgment (e.g., Dan 12:2–3; 1 Enoch; 1QS 4.6–14; Mishnah, *Aboth*). These beliefs were appealing responses to the fears and problems connected with fatalism in Hellenism. As a result, Judaism attracted converts and admirers (e.g., Acts 2:5–13; 13:43,50; 17:4,17). Some Jews were probably engaged in missionary activity (Mt 23:15; Numbers Rabbah 8.3; *b. Yebamoth* 47 a,b). Converts became sons of Abraham the father of all nations, and adopted partners in a covenant relationship with the God of Israel. Judaism's greatest influence was upon early Christianity which began as an apocalyptic (end-time oriented) Jewish sect.[34]

SUMMARY

A common language in a world of many dialects, improved travel and political stability under a world power, combined with fears and aspirations of an age in rapid transition—these are major characteristics of the NT Greco-Roman world. It was an age when vernacular Greek was spoken by diverse peoples of the East and West. It was a time when Greek culture penetrated every major city of the Mediterranean world. It was a Roman age when political peace and economic stability were long-awaited realities in a war-torn and politically fragmented world. Roman resourcefulness and efficiency improved travel and trade in an unprecedented manner. Despite the irrational actions of a few despots, most Roman emperors and provincial rulers were fair and tolerant to those willing to live peaceably under their rule. This period was a time of rapid change through improved communication and increased mobility.

The sudden and pervasive changes mentioned above also generated new fears and aspirations. New fears were caused by the spread of disease, the shift of wealth, the dislocation of peoples, and the breakdown of old traditions. These fears expressed themselves in a variety of ways: anxieties about the future, loss of social or ethnic identity, and especially—obsession with fate or destiny. In this age of anxiety, there were also a variety of human aspirations that were either symptoms of or responses to the fears and uncertainties. These aspirations appear to be either re-

---

34. See our section on Jewish Apocalypticism in ch 2, Jewish Background of the NT.

ligious or philosophical. The popular religious responses to this anxiety attempted to provide security and community through personal experiences with the gods. The popular philosophical responses sought to provide security and tranquility through a comprehensive picture of the universe and a specific ethical orientation to life.

It is into such an environment of cultural exchange, increased mobility, political stability, along with new hopes and fears, that Christianity was born and developed. Nevertheless, just as Freudian psychologists remind us that the behavioral development of a child cannot be determined solely by his or her environment but must include the genetic relationship to the parents, so also we must include the parent religion that gave birth to Christianity: Judaism. Although we have briefly surveyed the phenomenon of Hellenistic Judaism, it is now necessary to examine more closely the development of Judaism and its beliefs, especially in the context of its homeland, Palestine.

2

The Jewish Background of the New Testament

Heredity or environment? Which of these factors most determines the behavioral development of a child? This question has been debated vigorously among psychologists in the twentieth century. No doubt most would conclude today that both hereditary and environmental factors are important, and that both should be considered. This is also the case with the development of early Christianity, if we may employ an analogy between human growth and the historical development of a religious movement. Judaism is the parent religion of Christianity. Jesus and his disciples were Jews, and for some time Christianity was a sect within Judaism. We cannot fully appreciate the beliefs and practices of first-century Judaism without a grasp of the history which shaped them.

THE TRAGIC HISTORY OF JUDAISM

Israel's history of foreign domination is not unlike that of twentieth-century Poland. Despite Poland's great cultural and economic achievements, its history in the twentieth century can be viewed as a tragic history.[1] Throughout this modern period, Poland can be seen as a nation overcome by foreign powers. In World War I, it was the battleground for much of the fighting on the "eastern front" between Germany and Russia. During World War II, it was occupied by Nazi Germany, and after

1. The provocative title of this section is based primarily on the history of Israel as one of domination by foreign oppressors (e.g., Assyrians, Babylonians, Egyptians, Syrian Greeks, Romans). A secondary consideration is Israel's interpretation of its own history as one of disobedience to the works of Yahweh (e.g., see Isa 6:9-10; 8:17; Jer 5:20-31; Third Isa 64:5-7; Ezk 2-3; Dt 32; 1 Kgs 22; Neh 9; Damascus Document of Qumran [CD]). See also the early Christian interpretations of Israel (Acts 7; 28:24-28; Rom 9-11). The titles, "Tragic History" and "Persistent Faith" have also been applied to Judaism in R. A. Spivey and D. M. Smith, *Anatomy of the NT* (New York: Macmillan, 1969) 7, 13.

that period to the present, Poland has been under the foreign dominance of Soviet Russia. Poland's history in the twentieth century appears tragic, because larger nations have used its territory as a battlefield or have struggled to gain control of it. Jewish history is not unlike that of modern Poland.

From the sixth century BC to the second century AD, the history of Israel can be viewed as one of foreign dominance with a brief interlude of independence. This "tragic history" of Israel can be outlined in five series of events: the Babylonian Exile, the problematic resettlement under Persia, Greco-Syrian oppression, a disappointing interlude of independence, and conflicts with Rome.

The Babylonian Exile

The Babylonian Exile (587 BC) marked the end of a great period of Israelite independence under such notable kings as David, Solomon, Hezekiah, and Josiah. Although the northern kingdom had seceded from unified Israel in 922 BC and had fallen to the Assyrians in 722 BC, the southern kingdom of Judah (west of the Dead Sea and including Jerusalem) had a relatively stable government and economy before the fateful years leading to its conquest by the Neobabylonians under Nebuchadnezzar II.[2]

The Babylonian Exile meant for the people of Judah the loss of a king, land, and temple. From 598 to 587 BC there was a rapid succession of three Judean kings who were deported or killed by the Neobabylonians.[3] By 587 BC, a large number of citizens had been deported as slaves to Babylon; the city of Jerusalem lay in ruins; and the magnificent temple built by Solomon had been destroyed. This terrible series of events, as indicated by the sources, produced negative responses of fear, loneliness, anger, despair, and the loss of both cultural and religious identity among the people of Judah.[4]

2. The rise and fall of the Israelite monarchy is narrated in the Hebrew Bible: 1 and 2 Samuel; 1 and 2 Kings; 1 and 2 Chronicles; and also Josephus, *Ant.* Books 7–9. See the following modern studies: J. Bright, *A History of Israel*, 3rd ed. (Philadelphia: Westminster, 1981) 183–339; J. H. Hayes and J. M. Miller, eds., *Israelite and Judean History* (Philadelphia: Westminster, 1977); S. Herrmann, *A History of Israel in OT Times*, trans. J. Bowden (Philadelphia: Fortress, 1975); Y. Kauffmann, *The Religion of Israel* (Chicago: University of Chicago Press, 1960).

3. For biblical accounts of the fall of Judah, see 2 Kgs 24–25; 2 Chr 36; Jer 52; Lamentations. See also Josephus, *Ant.* 10.74–185. For modern studies, see P. R. Ackroyd, *Exile and Restoration* (Philadelphia: Westminster, 1968); Bright, *History of Israel* 343–59; Herrmann, *History of Israel*, 289–97; R. W. Klein, *Israel in Exile* (Philadelphia: Fortress, 1979).

4. See, e.g., Lamentations; Pss 44; 74; 79; 102; 103.

But these fifty years of Babylonian Exile were also a time of reorganization and growth for Judaism.[5] It was a time when many old traditions were written down and collected as sacred literature. The rite of circumcision and the institution of Sabbath-day observance had a special binding force. The Jewish belief in only one God (monotheism) reached its classical definition. The emergence of the synagogue, the meeting place for prayer and study of the law of Moses, also occurred. Finally, in the course of fifty years, many of the Jews who were dispersed throughout the Near East as slaves, soon earned their freedom and entered trade and commerce. The dispersement of the Jews is the beginning of what is called the "Diaspora," or Jews "scattered" throughout the world. During the Greco-Roman period, the Diaspora is almost synonymous with Hellenistic Judaism.[6]

The Resettlement under Persia

Even though the conquest of Babylon by the Persians and the Edict of Cyrus (538 BC) permitted the Jews to return home, there were many problems involved in the resettlement.[7] First, not many exiled Jews wished to return to their homeland. Most of them were descendants of the exiles who were comfortably settled in Babylon and elsewhere. Second, there was much work to be done if Palestine was to be reestablished as a Jewish nation. Jerusalem lay in ruins and there was no temple to unify the Jews in worship. Third, the exiles that arrived in Palestine were not welcomed by the current inhabitants. There was conflict with the scattered Jewish communities that were not deported in 587 BC, who were practicing a form of Judaism less structured than that of the exiles. There also was opposition from the Samaritans, a Jewish-like people who claimed to be the descendants of the northern kingdom, although this area had been resettled by Assyrian colonists after the fall of the north in 722 BC. Finally, there was also armed conflict with Arab tribes of surrounding nations (e.g., Edomites).

Despite many problems, groups of exiles returned to Palestine from 536 to 444 BC. A modest temple was constructed around 515 BC, and the walls of Jerusalem were rebuilt under Nehemiah (437 BC). About this time, Ezra,

5. See the exilic and post–exilic writings of the so-called Deuteronomistic Historian (Dt to 2 Kgs), the Priestly Writer (Lev and related cultic legislation of the Pentateuch), Second and Third Isa (40–66), and Ezk. See also the following studies: Ackroyd, *Exile and Restoration*; Bright, *History of Israel* 347–51; Klein, *Israel in Exile*.

6. Josephus, *Ant.* 10.186–187; 14.110–118; *War* 7.43; Philo, *Against Flaccus* 73–75. See also the discussion in Safrai and Stern, *Jewish People* 1:117–215; J. A. Sanders, "Dispersion," *IDB* 1:854–56.

7. See Ackroyd, *Exile and Restoration* 138–231; Bright, *History of Israel* 360–402.

"a scribe skilled in the law of Moses" (Ezra 7:6) arrived bringing the sacred Torah, which contained laws for the life and faith of the people. By this time, not all Jews were conversant in Hebrew, but instead spoke Aramaic, a related Semitic language. It became the international language of commerce in the western Persian Empire. Aramaic remained the chief native dialect of Palestine during the time of Jesus, although most spoke Hellenistic Greek.

The Greco-Syrian Oppression

The Hellenization of the Near East began with the conquests of Alexander the Great (332–323 BC) and continued under his two generals: Ptolemy and Seleucus.[8] Both divided up Alexander's eastern empire after his death and established dynasties: the Ptolemies of Egypt and the Seleucids of Syria.

For one century the Seleucids sought control of Palestine from the Ptolemies, because it served as an excellent buffer zone between the two kingdoms. When the Seleucids, under Antiochus III, finally controlled Palestine in 198 BC, the Jews welcomed their new overlords and Antiochus granted them special privileges.[9] Under the rule of his son, Antiochus IV Epiphanes, this peaceful coexistence would end.

Because of heavy taxation under the Seleucids and the political infighting of the priestly families of Jerusalem, Palestine was in a turbulent state under Antiochus IV. The situation reached a crisis in 168 BC, when Antiochus plundered the temple treasury of Jerusalem between campaigns against Egypt. Conservative Jewish factions revolted in response. By this time the Egyptian campaign of Antiochus ended in defeat because of Roman intervention. The humiliated Seleucid king then returned to Jerusalem intent on subduing the rebellion.[10] He captured Jerusalem, killed or expelled its Jewish inhabitants, and repopulated the city with Syrian Greeks. As a result, the Jewish temple was devoted to the worship of Zeus, the Jewish religion was outlawed in Judea, and pious Jews were persecuted.[11]

---

8. For further discussion of Alexander and his successors, see the previous chapter: "The Greco-Roman Context of the NT, 'A Pervasive Hellenism.' "

9. See Josephus, Ant. 12.129–153.

10. See 1 Macc 1; 2 Macc 4–5; Josephus, Ant. 12.242–264. See also E. Bickerman, The God of the Maccabees: Studies on the Meaning and Origin of the Maccabean Revolt (Leiden: Brill, 1979); Koester, Introduction 1:210–15; H. Jagersma, A History of Israel from Alexander the Great to Bar Kochba, trans. J. Bowden (Philadelphia: Fortress, 1986) 44–67.

11. Because of his anti-Jewish legislation, the figure of Antiochus IV has been portrayed as the archetypal villain in Jewish apocalyptic and historical writings: e.g., Dan 11:20–39; 1 Macc 1; 4 Macc 4:15–5:38; Josephus, Ant. 12.242–286; T Adam 4:6-7.

The Interval of Jewish Independence

In response to these tragic events, the Maccabean revolt of 167 occurred. Many Jews who defied the laws of Antiochus IV fled to the hills of Judea and joined the guerrilla forces of Judas called *Maccabeus* ("the Hammer").[12] This resistance was actively supported by the *Hasidim* ("pious ones") who advocated traditional Jewish values and discouraged Hellenistic reform. Judas waged an effective guerrilla warfare against the Syrian Greeks. In 164 BC he and his forces captured Jerusalem and reestablished Jewish worship in the temple.[13] Judaism has commemorated this event in the Feast of Dedication or Lights, also called Hanukkah.[14]

The Maccabean revolt restored freedom of worship to Judea, but independence would not take place until the ruling house of Simon was established, also called the Hasmonean dynasty.[15] Through the efforts of Simon and his brother, Jonathan, the Syrian garrison was expelled from Jerusalem (142 BC). Shortly afterward, Simon was heralded by the Jewish people as both ruler and high priest (140 BC).[16] During the reign of his son, John Hyrcanus (134–104 BC), Syrian interference in the Jewish state finally ended.[17]

The dynasty established by Simon had the appearance of Hellenistic royalty.[18] As rulers of the people, Simon and his descendants had full military and political power. Only they were permitted to be clothed in purple and wear a gold buckle. As high priests, they were in charge of the sanctuary and its priests. Although the establishment of the dynasty was a welcomed alternative to foreign rule, certain priests regarded the Hasmonean office of high priest as illegitimate because these rulers were not descendants of Zadok.[19] It was probably at this time that the Essenes,

---

12. Judas appears to have been the founder of the resistance movement in 2 Macc 5:27; 8:1, whereas in 1 Macc 2–3, it seems to be Mattathias of Modein, the father of Judas. The discrepancy may be explained by the fact that 1 Maccabees was composed by a Hasmonean court historian. The Hasmonean dynasty was founded by Simon, who was also a son of Mattathias.

13. Jerusalem's temple was *officially* returned to traditional Jewish worship by Antiochus (probably Antiochus V, 2 Macc 11:22–26). The remaining correspondences in 2 Macc 11:16–38 presuppose a lengthy period negotiation, probably 164–162 BC.

14. See 1 Macc 4:36–59; 2 Macc 10:5–8; Josephus, *Ant.* 12.323–326.

15. Simon was the brother of Judas and son of Mattathias of Modein. Josephus calls Simon's family the "Asmoneans," probably the name of one of Simon's ancestors, *Ant.* 16.187; 20.190; 20.238.

16. 1 Macc 14:41–49.

17. Josephus, *Ant.* 13.254–300.

18. 1 Macc 14:41–49 and Josephus, *Ant.* 13.213–217.

19. In the Chronicler's history, Zadok was a descendant of Aaron (1 Chr 6:50–53) who was appointed high priest by King David (16:39–40; 29:22). Ezekiel under-

a faction of the Hasidim whose leader was a Zadokite priest (the "Teacher of Righteousness"), left Jerusalem to establish their own community near the Dead Sea: Qumran.[20]Another faction of the Hasidim, the Pharisees, would also be persecuted under a later Hasmonean, Alexander Jannaeus (104–78 BC).[21]

Under the reigns of John Hyrcanus and his son, Alexander Jannaeus, most of Palestine became a Jewish state through conquest. Although they were practicing Hellenists, the Hasmoneans compelled the inhabitants of the Greek cities to emigrate or convert to Judaism. Under coercion, Idumean males were circumcised and Samaritans submitted to the religious jurisdiction of Jerusalem.[22] Much of this expansionism was more the result of political ambition than religious zeal, as indicated by the Jewish revolt against the policies of Alexander Jannaeus (94 BC).[23]

After the reigns of Jannaeus and his widow, Alexandra (76–67 BC), the Hasmonean dynasty came to a close with the intrigues and fighting of their two sons. In 65 BC, there was such a struggle for power between Aristobulus II and Hyrcanus II, that the latter requested Rome to intervene, thereby ending Jewish independence.[24]

The Roman Occupation

When the Roman general Pompey ended the dispute between the two Hasmoneans in 64 BC, he sided with Hyrcanus II and one of his supporters, Antipater II, who was ruler of Idumea (south of Judea).[25] Palestine was then controlled by Rome and in the reorganization under Augustus (AD 27), it became part of the imperial province of Syria.[26] In Antioch, a military governor called a legate commanded thousands of Roman troops. Around AD 6, Samaria and Judea were governed directly by the emperor through his prefect (later procurator). Pontius Pilate served as prefect of these regions in AD 26–36. His chief responsibilities were to

---

scores the case that only descendants of Zadok could serve as high priests (Ezk 40:46; 48:11).

20. Some of the writings of this Qumran community, called the "Dead Sea Scrolls," underscore both the preeminence of the Zadokite priesthood (CD 3.18–4.4; 1QS 5.1–3) and the corruption of the Jerusalem (Hasmonean) priests (1QpHab 9.4–5; 12.7–9). References are from Dupont-Sommer, *Essene Writings*.

21. Josephus, *Ant*. 13.372–376. Pharisees were probably among the thousands of Jewish rioters punished by Alexander Jannaeus since they were outspoken critics of Hyrcanus, his father. See *Ant*. 13.288–292.

22. For the conquests of Hyrcanus, see Josephus, *Ant*. 13.230–300.

23. *Ant*. 13.131–186.

24. *Ant*. 14.1–79.

25. Ibid.

26. For more discussion of the Augustan provincial policies, see the previous chapter: "Greco-Roman Context of the NT, 'A Stable Roman Empire.' "

Chronology of Jewish and Christian History

Major Empires	General History	Jewish Events	Select Authors or Writings
Neo-Babylonian (597–538)	586 Destruction of Jerusalem by Neo-Babylonians	Babylonian Exile Jerusalem temple destroyed	Lamentations Job Second Isaiah
Persian (538–336)	538 Cyrus' edict of toleration	Return of exiles to Palestine	Third Isaiah Haggai/Zechariah
	509 Founding of Roman Republic		
	507 Democracy at Athens		Malachi
		445 Nehemiah governs	Ezra/Nehemiah
		428 Ezra's reforms	
	431–404 Peloponnesian Wars		Herodotus/Thucydides Plato
		320–290 Onias I, high priest	
Hellenistic (336–148)	336–323 Conquests of Alexander the Great		Cynics Aristotle
	175–164 Rule of Selucid Antiochus IV Epiphanes	171–161 Menelaus, high priest	Stoics, Epicureans
		167 Maccabean Revolt against Seleucids	Chronicles, Daniel/ Apocalyptic writings Greek Septuagint
		167–163 Independent Jewish state	1 Maccabees
Roman (148–AD 455)	150–146 Destruction of Carthage and Corinth by Rome	Hasmoneans 135–104 John Hyrcanus 103–76 Alexander Jannaeus; Pharisees and Sadducees emerge	Psalms of Solomon Cicero (106–43) Virgil (70–19) Lucretius (60)
	44 Julius Caesar killed	63 Rome acquires Syria and Palestine	
	30–AD 14 Augustus	37–4 Herod the Great	
	14 Tiberius	6–4 Jesus born	
	37 Gaius Caligula	4 BC–39 AD Herod Antipas	Philo (30–42)
	41 Claudius	30–33 Ministry of Jesus	
	54 Nero	62 Paul in Rome	Paul (50–62)
	66–70 1st Jewish Revolt	70 Fall of Jerusalem	Four Gospels (65–95)
	69 Vespasian		
	79 Titus		Josephus (75–95)
	81 Domitian	90 Jamnia	1 Clement (95)
	98 Trajan		Didache (100)
	117 Hadrian	130 Simon bar Kochba	Gosp. of Thomas (100)
	132–135 Second Jewish Revolt		

Section of Roman aqueduct on the outskirts of Caesarea, first century AD. *Photo by C. B. Puskas.*

maintain order and collect taxes. Although the Jews were granted certain privileges by the emperor, these were not always honored by the provincial governors (e.g., Pilate, G. Florus).[27]

The Roman provincial system also used the services of local magistrates. In the case of Palestine, the Idumeans, Antipater and his son Herod, obtained this derived authority. These shrewd politicians were able to shift allegiances to a succession of Romans (e.g., Pompey, Julius Caesar, Antony, Octavian), and as a result Herod became a powerful vassal king of Rome (37–4 BC). Herod was a crafty politician, a magnificent builder, and a ruthless tyrant. He may have won the favor of Augustus as a passionate Hellenizer. Herod surrounded himself with Greek scholars and undertook many building projects: an impressive fortified palace, the magnificent Jerusalem temple, the fortress of Masada (35 miles south of Jerusalem), and numerous Greek cities with theaters, baths, and amphitheaters. The last years of Herod's reign were characterized by suspicion and cruelty. He had many opponents and relatives executed, including his wife (a Hasmonean princess). Because of his acts of cruelty and the fact that he was an Idumean convert to Judaism, Herod was never greatly liked by the Jews. Before Herod died, Jesus of Nazareth was born.[28]

27. All of the prefects and procurators of Palestine are mentioned in Josephus, *Ant.* 18.1–108; 19.360–365; 20.1–53, 148–223; *War* 2.117–183, 204–249, 271–404. Pilate is also mentioned in Philo, *On the Embassy to Gaius* 38. See also G. W. Stevenson, *Roman Provincial Administration*, 2nd ed. (Oxford: Blackwell, 1959).

28. For extensive material on Herod the Great, see Josephus, *Ant.* Books 14–17 and *War* 1.195–673. See also M. Grant, *Herod the Great* (New York: American Heritage, 1971); S. Perowne, *The Life and Times of Herod the Great* (London: Hodder and Stoughton, 1956).

First-Century Emperors, Roman Procurators over Judea, and Rulers in Palestine

EMPERORS	PROCURATORS	KINGS, TETRARCHS, ETHNARCH
AUGUSTUS, 27 B.C.–A.D. 14	Coponius, A.D. 6-10	HEROD the Great, King over all Palestine, 37-4 B.C. (Matt. 2:1-19; Luke 1:5)
		ARCHELAUS, Ethnarch of Judea, Samaria, and Idumea, 4 B.C.–A.D. 6 (Mark 2:22)
TIBERIUS, A.D. 14-37	M. Ambivius, 10-13 Annius Rufus, 13-15	
	Valerius Gratus, 15-26 PONTIUS PILATE, 26-36 (Luke 3:1; 23:1)	HEROD PHILIP, Tetrarch of Iturea, Trachonitus, Gaulanitis, Auranitis, and Batanea, 4 B.C.–A.D. 34 (Luke 3:1)
Caligula, 37-41	Marcellus, 36-38	HEROD ANTIPAS, Tetrarch of Galilee and Perea, 4 B.C.–A.D. 39 (Mark 6:14-29; Luke 3:1; 13:31-35; 23:7-12)
CLAUDIUS, 41-54	Marullus, 38-41	HEROD AGRIPPA I, 37-44; by A.D. 41, King over all Palestine (Acts 12:1-24)
Nero, 54-68 (Emperor at deaths of Paul and Peter)	Cuspius Fadus, 44-46 Tiberius Alexander, 46-48 Ventidius Cumanus, 48-52 M. Antonius FELIX, 52-59 (Acts 23:26-24:27) Porcius FESTUS, 59-61 (Acts 25) Albinus, 61-65 Gessius Florus, 65-70	HEROD AGRIPPA II, 48-70, Tetrarch of Chalcis and northern territory (Acts 25:13-26:32)
Galba, 68 Otho, 69 Vitellius, 69 Vespasian, 69-79 Titus, 79-81 Domitian, 81-96	Vettulenus Cerialis, 70-72 Lucilius Bassus, 72-75 M. Salvienus, 75-86 Flavius Silva Pompeius Longinus, 86	
Nerva, 96-98 Trajan, 98-117		

Names in caps are mentioned by name in the New Testament.

After Herod's death, his kingdom was divided among his three sons. Philip became tetrarch of the largely non-Jewish areas northeast of the Sea of Galilee (4 BC–AD 34). Herod Antipas was named tetrarch of Galilee and Perea across the Jordan River (4 BC–AD 39). Herod Antipas had John the Baptist executed (Mk 6:14–29), and it was before him that Jesus appeared (Lk 23:6–12). Antipas was eventually exiled by the emperor, Caligula (AD 39). Archelaus was given Samaria and Judea. Because his rule was challenged by both his subjects and Antipas, and because there was general unrest brewing in Galilee, Archelaus was dismissed by Rome and banished to Gaul in AD 6. Except for the short reign of Herod Agrippa I over all Palestine (41–44), the entire region was under Roman procurators after AD 44.[29]

According to ancient Jewish sources, life for the Jews under the prefects and procurators was difficult. Pontius Pilate ignored Jewish customs, confiscated temple monies, and killed many Jews and Samaritans.[30] Pilate was eventually sent to Rome to account for his actions and was exiled (AD 36). After the interim reign of King Agrippa I ended (AD 44), the situation under the procurators became worse. At this time there arose Jewish revolutionaries who sought to rekindle the spirit of the Maccabean revolt. Self-styled prophets and messiahs also appeared, as well as a radical group of assassins, the Sicarii.[31] The procurators, Felix (AD 52–60) and Festus (AD 60–62), spent a great deal of time putting down Jewish revolts (both are mentioned in Acts 23–24).

Gessius Florus (AD 64–66) one of the last and worst procurators, fanned the flames of revolt in Palestine.[32] In AD 66, his embezzlement of funds from the temple treasury outraged the people. Florus responded to their outcries by having his troops plunder the city. When mediation attempts failed, a fierce struggle occurred in the area between the Roman fortress of Antonia and the temple court. Shortly afterwards, sacrifices offered for Rome and the emperor ceased and the fortress of Masada, thirty-five miles south, was captured. These events marked the beginning of the

29. For information on the later Herods, see Josephus, *Ant.* Books 17–19; *War* Books 1–2. See also H. Hoehner, *Herod Antipas* (Cambridge: Cambridge University, 1972); A. H. M. Jones, *The Herods of Judea*, 2nd ed. (Oxford: Clarendon, 1967); S. Perowne, *The Later Herods* (New York: Abingdon, 1959).

30. *Ant.* 18.55–59; 18.85–89; *War* 2.175–177; Philo, *To Gaius* 38.

31. For example, see Judas the Galilean who inspired the Zealot sect (*Ant.* 17.271–272; 18.1–10; *War* 2.117–118), Theudas the false prophet (*Ant.* 20.97–99), the Egyptian prophet (*Ant.* 20.167–172) and other false prophets (*War* 6.285–287). For datum on the Sicarii and Zealots, see *War* 7.252–274; 7.407–419. See also D. M. Rhoads, *Israel in Revolution 6–74 C.E.* (Philadelphia: Fortress, 1976).

32. Josephus, *War* 2.77–341.

The Arch of Titus on the Via Sacra of Rome was erected (ca. AD 94) to commemorate Titus' capture of Jerusalem in AD 70. On it, Jewish captives are shown marching in procession and carrying spoils from the temple. *Photo by Ralph Harris.*

Jewish resistance party called the Zealots.[33]

After some successful attacks by the rebels, Nero dispatched his able general, Vespasian, to quell the revolt that was spreading throughout Palestine. With the aid of his son, Titus, who commanded the forces of Egypt, Vespasian made a successful assault upon Galilee with a massive army.[34] Jerusalem at this time was caught in a bitter civil war between moderate and radical Jewish rebels. The experienced Vespasian subdued the surrounding areas and waited for the Jews to exhaust themselves in Jerusalem. But before Vespasian could end the revolt in Jerusalem, his actions were delayed by the death of Nero and the rapid succession of emperors from 68 to 69. In 69, Vespasian left his command post to his son Titus and went to Rome to become its ninth emperor.[35]

In the spring of 70, Titus began his siege of Jerusalem.[36] Although the Jewish factions finally united in combat, the military entrenchment around the city made it impossible for the rebels to receive supplies. Hunger and

33. *War* 2.405–456. Although many resistance groups existed before AD 66, a case can be made for the emergence of a specific "Zealot" party only after AD 66. See Josephus, *War* 2.441–448; 2.564; 4.158–161; 7.268–270; Rhoads, *Israel in Revolution* 52–58, 97–110; M. Borg, "The Currency of the Term 'Zealot' " *JTS* 22 (1971) 504–12.

34. *War* 3.1–4.120

35. *War* 4.486–502, 545–555; 4.588–663; Suetonius, *Vespasian* 4–6.

36. *War* 5.1–20, 39–46.

thirst took their toll and the city was gradually taken. The great temple was lost to fire in the midst of the battle.[37] Many men, women, and children died because the Jews refused to surrender. When the battle was over, the city and temple were in ruins and Titus returned to Rome with hundreds of prisoners to exhibit for the victory parade through the city, commemorated (shortly afterwards) by the arch of Titus, still standing in the Roman Forum today.[38]

Despite a decisive victory, the Romans needed to subdue several fortresses, particularly the fortress of Masada.[39] Built by Herod the Great on a mesa along the Dead Sea, the fortress was almost impregnable. The rebels occupying Masada were under the command of Eleazar son of Yair. Flavius Silva, the Roman commander, was forced to build a tremendous landbridge in order to transport a large battering ram to penetrate the wall. When Eleazer realized that their cause was lost, he addressed his garrison, and requested that they kill their families and themselves rather than surrender. When the Romans finally breached the wall, there was no battle left to be fought.

The destruction of Jerusalem and the second temple was a terrible blow to Judaism. What survived was a reorganized religion under the Pharisees who gathered at the coastal town of Jamnia (Hebrew "Jabneh").[40] This religion without a temple and priests became known as Rabbinic Judaism.[41] Influential Jewish communities continued to develop outside of Palestine (e.g., Egypt, Babylon). Palestinian Judaism lingered until the Judean uprising lead by Simon bar Kochba ("Son of the Star") in 132–135.[42] The revolt was in reaction to Emperor Hadrian's attempt to rebuild

37. Ibid., 6.1–8, 15–53.

38. The Arch of Titus was completed after his death (AD 94). The following references recount his triumph over the Jews. War 7.116–162; Suetonius, Titus 4–5.

39. War 7.252–406; Y. Yadin, Masada: Herod's Fortress and The Zealot's Last Stand (London, 1966; Jerusalem: Steimatzky, Ltd., 1984).

40. The Hebrew name, "Jabneh" is mentioned in 2 Chr. 26:6; the Greek name, "Jamnia," in 1 Macc 4:15; 5:58; 2 Macc 12:8–9; Josephus, War 2.335. The Jewish Mishnah (ca. AD 220) mentions the transfer of the court ("Beth-Din") or college ("Yeshiva") of seventy-two elders from Jerusalem to Jabneh in the following tractates: Rosh Ha-Shana 4.1–2; Zebahim 1.3; Ketuboth 4.6. Jabneh was the center of Judaism from AD 70 to the early second century. J. P. Lewis, "What Do We Mean By Jabneh?" JBR 32 (1964) 125–32.

41. Third-century rabbinic sources containing earlier traditions are: the Mishnah, legal interpretations of the Torah; the early Midrashim, commentaries on the Hebrew Bible; the Tosefta, additions to the Mishnah. See also J. Neusner, Early Rabbinic Judaism (Leiden: Brill, 1975) and Method and Meaning in Ancient Judaism (Missoula, Mont: Scholars Press, 1979).

42. Spartian Hadrian 4; Dio Cassius, Roman History 69.12–15; Eusebius, Eccl Hist 4.6.1–4; 8.4. See recently discovered letter from Simon Bar Kochba in Y. Yadin, Bar Kochba (New York: Random House, 1971).

Jerusalem into a Greco-Roman city with a temple for Jupiter. Hadrian ended the revolt and carried out his plans, forbidding Jews to enter the city. From that time on, until the establishment of a Jewish state in 1948, Judaism was primarily a religion of the Diaspora.[43]

THE PERSISTENT FAITH OF JUDAISM

Although Judaism's history was characterized by foreign dominance, its traditions and beliefs persisted for centuries. This is true of many nations and peoples who struggle under foreign dominance. Let us return to our example of twentieth-century Poland. Here is a nation that in the past century has been under the domination of Germany and now Soviet Russia, yet the basic beliefs and convictions of the Polish people have persisted. Although under the dominance of Soviet Russia, Poland remains one of the most Roman Catholic nations in the world and its people have fought hard for their liberties and rights. This is also the case with Judaism. Despite the domination of foreign powers, Judaism has persisted in its religious beliefs and practices.

Unlike the diverse religions of their foreign conquerors, the Jews retained their belief in only one God, offered sacrifices at only one temple, observed feasts that repeated their history as a people, sought to follow laws of God written in sacred books, worshipped God and studied the laws in meeting houses called synagogues, and maintained confidence in their destiny as the people of God. Even though foreign thought forms (e.g., Babylonian, Persian, and Greek) influenced Jewish beliefs and practices, their appropriation into a complete system of monotheism, law, and religious history, made Judaism a distinct religious phenomenon. We will now look more closely at these Jewish beliefs and practices.

The One God

Allegiance to only one God, or practical monotheism, came to its fullest expression in Judaism during the exile, when the sovereignty of other gods was rejected.[44] However, stress on the oneness of God and the need for exclusive obedience to him occurred before the Exile, when Israel's classic expression of faith was framed: "Hear, O Israel, the Lord our God, the Lord is one" (Dt 6:4; cf. 4:35,39). After the Exile, God's name, Yahweh, became too sacred to be pronounced and was substituted with

43. See the popular history which underscores this point: A. Ebban, *My People. The Story of the Jews*, new ed. (New York: Random House, 1984).
44. Second Isa 43:10–11; 44:8; 45:5–6,21–22; 46:8–9. See also: B. W. Anderson, "God, OT View of," *IDB* 2:427-28.

Adonai ("Lord").[45] The Jews also viewed their God in distinction from
the world as its creator, yet active in the world as provider and savior.
During the Greco-Roman period, the Jews were often accused of athe-
ism by the Gentiles (non-Jews) because they refused to recognize the sovereignty of any other deity except their own.[46]

Connected with the Jewish belief in only one God, was the idea of a
covenant that bound the people with their God. Many of the covenant
formulations found in the Jewish Scriptures were based on secular trea-
ties of the ancient Near East that were instituted by kings on behalf of
their vassal subjects.[47] These covenants or binding agreements with God
usually included: (1) a list of gracious acts that God had performed on
Israel's behalf, such as delivering it from bondage in Egypt (Ex 19:4-6)
and (2) stipulations that Israel was expected to carry out in response to
God's acts of favor (20:1; 23:19). The circumcision of every male child was
also required as a sign of the covenant (Gen 17:10-14). This covenant with
God gave the people both a special status as God's elect and a sacred
responsibility to carry out God's statutes and laws.

The Sacrificial System

Although attempts were made to construct rival temples,[48] the temple
of Jerusalem[49] remained the exclusive place of sacrificial worship for almost all Jews. The first temple was built by Solomon 1000 years before
the Christian era, and was destroyed by the Neobabylonians in 587 BC.
A modest temple was built by the returning exiles in 515 BC and rebuilt
on a much grander scale in the Herodian period. This temple was begun
under Herod the Great (20 BC) but was not completed until AD 60, ten
years before its destruction.[50] The guardians of the temple and its wor-

45. Mishnah *Sanhedrin* 7.5; *Yoma* 6.2; *Soteh* 7.6; and Mt 5:34-35; 23:21-22.

46. For Roman suspicions of Judaism, see Seneca *Epistulae Morales* 95.57; Tacitus, *Histories* 5.2-13. For Jewish opposition to emperor worship, see Josephus, *Ant.*
18.257-268; Philo, *On the Embassy to Gaius* (concerning the deification of emperors Caligula and Augustus).

47. For modern discussion with primary sources, see D. J. McCarthy, *Treaty
and Covenant*, new ed. (Rome: Biblical Institute Press, 1978) and *OT Covenant*
(Atlanta: John Knox, 1972); G. E. Mendenhall, "Covenant Forms in Israelite Tradition," in *BAReader* 3 (Garden City, N.Y.: Anchor Books, 1970) 25-53.

48. W. F. Stinespring, "Temple, Jerusalem," *IDB* 4:534-60; M. Ben-Dov, "Temple
of Herod," *IDBSupp* 870-72; M. Haran, "Priests and Priesthood," *Encyclopedia Judaica* 13:1069-88.

49. When the Jerusalem temple was captured by Antiochus IV, the high priest,
Onias IV, built a similar but inferior temple in Heliopolis, Egypt, see Josephus,
Ant. 13.62-68.

50. The earliest descriptions of the Herodian temple and priesthood are: Josephus, *Ant.* 15.380-425; high priests 20.224-251; *War* 5.184-247; Mishnah *Middoth*
("Measurements" of the temple) 1-5.

Jerusalem viewed from the east, near the Mt. of Olives.
The Dome of the Rock (center) was built in AD 691 on
the Herodian Temple area. The current walls, rebuilt in
the 16th century, follow roughly the contours of Herod's
construction. *Photo by C. B. Puskas.*

ship were the priests. When temple worship was restored in 515 BC, they
regained much of the influence they had lost during the Exile, especially
the high priest, who had both civil and religious authority. Under the
Seleucid Greeks, the high priesthood became a political position sought
after by competing priestly families (e.g., Jedaiah, Bilgah). During the brief
interlude of independence, the Hasmoneans (not of Zadokite descent)
assumed the prerogatives of high priest and king. As a result, the pro-
Zadokite Essenes withdrew from Jerusalem and the pro-Hasmonean Sadducees (mostly of the house of Boethus) rose to power. In the Herodian
period, high priests were appointed from priestly families of the Diaspora
(e.g., Phiabi of Babylon, Boethus of Egypt). They presided over both the
temple worship and the Great Sanhedrin, the high court of Judaism.[51]
The power of the priesthood ended with the destruction of the Jerusalem
in AD 70.

51. For an excellent survey, see H. Mantel, "Sanhedrin," *IDBSupp* 784–86.

Scale model of the Herodian Temple of Jerusalem recon- structed by Y. Aha- roni and displayed at the Holyland Hotel of Jerusalem.
Photo by Ralph Harris.

The major religious functions of the priests were to maintain purity through the sacrificial system at the temple.[52] In ancient Israel a whole system of sacrifices had arisen to set sinful people right with the one holy God. This system was administered by the priests and sacrifices were offered on an altar at least twice daily.

Even the architectural design of the Herodian temple reflects the vari- ous degrees of holiness.[53] Only the outermost part of the temple was ac- cessible to Gentiles. Moving toward the central buildings (for Jews) came the Court of Women, the Court of Israel (men), the Court of Priests where daily sacrifices took place, the Holy Place where the priests regularly burned incense, and the Holy of Holies into which the high priest entered only once a year on the day of Atonement.

Even though the temple was a holy center where the priest interceded for the people, it was also the center of commercial activity. It housed the national treasury collected from an annual temple tax into which every Jew was expected to pay. The priests were also responsible for the col- lection and allocation of these funds.

The Feasts

Closely related to the temple worship were the religious festivals and holy days of the Jews.[54] The Jewish civil year began around September/

---

52. Lev 1–10; 16; 21–23; 27; Ezk 44–46. See also L. H. Schiffman, "Priests," *HBD* 821–23.

53. Josephus, *Ant.* 15.380–425; *War* 5.184–247; Mishnah *Middoth* 1–5.

54. Early sources outside the Bible are: Josephus, *Ant.* 3.237–257; 11.109–113; 12.323–326; *War* 2.42–44; 6.423–427; Mishnah: *Moed* ("Set Feasts"), second major division. For a listing of some Mishnaic texts with comments, see Barrett, *NTB* 153–62.

October whereas the religious year was about March/April. Regulations for the feasts are prescribed in the books of the law (Exodus, Leviticus), with the exception of Hanukkah and Purim, which were instituted later. Pilgrims from outside Jerusalem and Palestine thronged to the holy city for the three main festivals: Passover-Unleavened Bread, Pentecost, and Booths. The biblical significance of the feasts was retained in the Herodian period.

Feast	Purpose	Date
Passover and Unleavened Bread	Commemorates the Exodus from Egypt and marks the beginning of the wheat harvest (Ex 12–13; Num 9; Dt 16; 2 Chr 30; 35).	Nisan 15 (March/April) 7 days
Pentecost or Weeks	Commemorates the giving of the Law on Mt. Sinai (Lev 23:15–16) and marks the end of wheat harvest (Ex 23:14–17; 34:18–24; Dt 16:10)	Sivan 6 (May/June) 50 days after Passover
Trumpets or Rosh Hashanah	Inaugurates both the civil year and the end of the grape and olive harvest (Lev 23:23–25; Num 29).	Tishri 1 (Sept./Oct.)
Day of Atonement or Yom Kippur	Day of national repentance, fasting and atonement (not called a feast) (Lev 16; 23:26–32).	Tishri 10 (Sept./Oct.)
Booths or Succoth	Commemorates the living in tents leaving Egypt for Canaan—a joyous festival when people would live in temporary huts made of branches (Ex 23:14–17; Lev 23:34–36).	Tishri 15–22 (Sept./Oct.)
Lights or Dedication, Hannukah	Commemorates the rededication of the temple by Judas Maccabeus, with brilliant lights in temple area and Jewish homes (1 Macc 4:42–58).	Kislev 25 (Nov./Dec.) 8 days
Purim or Lots	Commemorates the deliverance of Israel during Persian period, with public reading of book of Esther in synagogue (2 Macc 15:36).	Adar 14–15 (Feb./March)

The Law

After the Exile, Judaism began to stress obedience to God's will in its collection of sacred writings.[55] By this time the Deuteronomic History (Dt

---

55. H. Mantel, "The Development of the Oral Law During the Second Temple Period," in M. Avi-Yonah and Z. Baras, eds. *World History of the Jewish People 8: Society and Religion in the Second Temple Period* (Jerusalem: Massada, 1977) 41–64,

This stone pavement was first constructed by Herod the Great as part of the temple courtyard in Jerusalem. The buildings and arches are Muslim. *Photo by C. B. Puskas.*

through 2 Kgs) had been added to Genesis, Exodus, Leviticus and Numbers to serve as Israel's primary history. Several prophetic books were also added: Isaiah 1–39; Jeremiah, Ezekiel, and some "minor prophets" (e.g., Amos, Hos, Mic). Supplements to Isaiah (40–66) and additional minor prophets were added shortly afterward. This collection of the Law (Gen–Dt) and Prophets (Jos–2 Kgs, Isa–Ezk, and 12 minor prophets) was closed by the second century BC (prologue, Sirach) but a third undefined group of "other books" remained open. This third general category included such writings as the Psalms, Proverbs, Esther, and Daniel. This third group was probably not closed until years after the destruction of Jerusalem, perhaps AD 90–100 at Jabneh (Jamnia). The broader collections of Scripture in the Dead Sea Scrolls at Qumran and the Greek translation of the Jewish Scripture, called the Septuagint (LXX) from Alexandria (both before

---

325–37; "Torah Scholarship," 314–80 and "Life and Law," 464–87 in Schürer and Vermes, *History* 2; H. L. Strack, *Introduction to the Talmud and Midrash* (Philadelphia: Jewish Publication Society, 1931).

the NT), support the thesis of a later closed Jewish Scripture.[56]

Obedience to the Torah ("instruction"), particularly the legal material of the "Law" collection (Ex–Dt) was of primary importance in Judaism. To know the law was to know the will of God. To study and do the law is the greatest blessing. By the Hasmonean period, there were different attitudes to the Torah. The Pharisees were concerned with interpreting and applying the law in a manner applicable to contemporary problems. They held that God had given Moses two laws, a written one (Law, Prophets, and other Writings) and an oral one to interpret the written.[57] The Sadducees rejected the concept of oral law and did not regard the prophetic or "other books" as binding in authority. The Essenes, like the Pharisees, devoted themselves to the study of the Law, Prophets, and Writings, but focused on ascetic practices and prophetic predictions in their communities outside of Jerusalem.[58] After AD 70, the position of the Pharisees was assumed by Rabbinic Judaism. The practice of the Pharisees and their descendants—to expand the written word by oral tradition in order to apply it to new conditions—is documented in the Mishnah and Talmud. It consisted of restatement and revision through discussion and debate. By the first century there were already differing "schools of interpretation" within the Pharisees (e.g., Hillel and Shammai). Debate and discussion was necessary to make a hedge for the Torah, i.e., to keep it from being transgressed. To preserve the Sabbath commandment (Ex 20:11) one should not work. But what is work? Oral tradition, transcribed into the Mishnah by AD 220, would set out to define precisely what activities constitute "work." So important was the Torah to the Jews that all aspects of life and thought were to be inspired and guided by it.[59]

56. D. N. Freedman, "Canon of the OT," 130–36 and J. A. Sanders, "Torah," 909–11 in *IDBSupp*; A. C. Sundberg, " 'The OT': A Christian Canon," *CBQ* 30 (1968) 143–55; S. Z. Leiman, *The Canonization of the Hebrew Scriptures. The Talmudic and Mishnaic Evidence* (Hamden, Conn.: Archon Books, 1976).

57. On Pharisees and oral law, see Josephus, *Ant.* 13.297. For an example of oral traditions codified in writing, see Mishnah *Aboth* ("Fathers"), selections of maxims in praise of the law handed down in the names of 60 teachers of the law who lived between 300 BC and AD 200.

58. Josephus, *Ant.* 18.18–22; *War* 2.119–161; the Dead Sea Scrolls of the Qumran community (an Essene sect).

59. Some English translations of major rabbinic works are H. Danby, *The Mishnah* (London: Oxford University Press, 1933); I. Epstein, ed., *The Babylonian Talmud*, 35 vols. (London: Soncino Press, 1935–52); H. Freedman and M. Simon, *Midrash Rabbah*, 10 vols. (London: Soncino Press, 1951). The Mishnah and Talmud, contain "halakah" (exposition of law) and "haggadah" (stories and maxims). The Midrash is primarily haggadah.

The Synagogue

The synagogue ("gathering place")[60] played an important part in the growth and persistence of Judaism. In the Roman period, synagogues were in most regions of the empire.[61] Although the Talmud mentions their origins during the exile,[62] the earliest archaeological evidence is from the Christian era.[63] The synagogue was a meeting place for prayer and an educational center for the study of the law. No sacrifices were offered there. The synagogue services probably consisted of a recitation of the Shema (Dt 6:4), Scripture readings, expositions, blessings, and prayers.[64] The popular Jewish sect of the Pharisees, who excelled in the study of the law, were closely associated with the synagogue.

The Final Destiny

Judaism was not only concerned with remembering the past and living faithfully in the present, but also with understanding its future destiny.[65] In reaction to the tragic events of Jewish history (e.g., the Babylonian Exile, Syrian oppression and the disappointing Hasmonean rule), two alternative lines of thought developed regarding the future. First, Judaism could repeat the lofty nationalistic hopes of the ancient prophets (e.g., Isa 11; Mic 4), and leave to God the time and circumstances under which these glorious promises would be fulfilled. Second, it could assess the national tragedies as the work of a demonic power opposed to God and shift the sphere of God's final triumph from a future time in plain history to the cosmic realms of heaven and earth at the *end* of time.

---

60. "The Synagogue," in Safrai and Stern, *Jewish People* 2:908–44; "Synagogue," in Schürer and Vermes, *History* 2:423–63.

61. Allusions to these synagogues can be found in the four Gospels, Acts, Josephus, Philo, and rabbinic sources.

62. Palestinian Talmud, *Megillah* 3.73d; Babylonian Talmud, *Megillah* 29d alluding to Ezk 11:16, a "sanctuary" (*mikdash*) for the Diaspora.

63. See archaeological illustrations with comments of synagogues in Palestine, Babylon, Egypt, Asia, Greece and Italy: I. Sonne, "Synagogue," *IDB* 4:480–84 and E. Meyers, "Synagogue, Architecture," *IDBSupp* 842–44.

64. For the two versions of the "Eighteen Benedictions" (*Shemoneh 'Esreh*) used in early synagogue worship, see Schürer and Vermes, *History* 2:455–63; and other prayers with some Christian interpolations: D. R. Darnell and D. A. Fiensy, "Hellenistic Synagogal Prayers (Second to Third Century AD)," Charlesworth, *OTP* 2:671–97.

65. For primary sources, see Charlesworth, *OTP* vol. 1; Vermes, *Scrolls*; H. S. Ryle and M. R. James, *Psalmoi Solomontos: Psalms of the Pharisees* (Cambridge, 1891). For important studies, see P. D. Hanson, "Jewish Apocalyptic Against Its Near Eastern Environment," *Revue Biblique* 78 (1971) 31–58; idem, *Dawn of Apocalyptic*; K. Koch, *The Rediscovery of the Apocalyptic* (London: SCM Press, 1972).

Rabbinic Writings

WRITINGS	DIVISIONS	DATES	CONTRIBUTORS	CONTENTS	COMMENTS
MIDRASH*	Halakah†	100 B.C.-A.D. 300	Tannaim■	Legal sections commenting only on Torah	Halakah is the legal part of the Gemara, usually derived from OT.
MIDRASH*	Haggadah‡	100 B.C.-A.D. 300	Tannaim	Narratives and sermons on entire Old Testament	Haggadah embraces nonlegal interests (such as history, folklore, parables, and scientific knowledge such as medicine and astronomy) infrequently encountered in the Mishnah.
TOSEFTA°		A.D. 100-300	Tannaim	Teachings not found in the Mishnah	
PALESTINIAN TALMUD	Gemara•	A.D. 200	Amoraim**	Commentary on the Mishnah	
BABYLONIAN TALMUD	Mishnah††	A.D. 200	Tannaim	Legal portions commenting only on the Mishnah	The Mishnah was divided into six sections: Seeds, concerning ritual laws dealing with cultivation of the soil; Festivals, concerning rules and regulations on the Sabbath and holy days; Women, on marriage, divorce, and other family issues; Damages, mainly regarding compensation on damages; Holy Things, rules and laws on sacrifices, and other issues pertaining to the ancient Temple and its ritual; Purifications, pertaining to the subject of cleanness and purity.
BABYLONIAN TALMUD	Gemara	A.D. 500	Amoraim	Commentary on the Mishnah	

° Midrash refers to the exposition of the Law in running commentary.
† Halakah literally means "going" or "walking" and was extended to the statements by which one is guided.
‡ Haggadah is a type of Jewish interpretation intended for edification.
■ The Tannaim are "repeaters" or teachers of the Oral Law before the completion of the Mishnah. They date from Ezra—through Hillel, Akiba, and Meir—to Judah Hanasi.
° Tosefta means "supplement."
• Gemara literally means the "completion" of the Talmud.
** The Amoraim were sages who labored in Judaism after the completion of the Mishnah.
†† Mishnah means "repetition"; the Oral Law had to be repeated verbally with great accuracy from generation to generation.

Taken from CHRONOLOGICAL AND BACKGROUND CHARTS OF THE NEW TESTAMENT, by H. Wayne House. Copyright ©1981 by The Zondervan Corporation. Used by permission.

Remains of a Capernaum synagogue with Corinthian caps and Doric-style columns, third or fourth century AD. It may have been built on the earlier site of the synagogue mentioned in Mark 1:21–23; Luke 4:31–33.
Photo by C. B. Puskas.

Nationalistic Hopes

By the first century BC, most Jews assumed the first alternative of repeating the nationalistic hopes of the earlier prophets. Documentation for this outlook is found in the Psalms of Solomon.[66] The unknown author was a Jew who longed for the establishment of a Davidic ruler as God's viceregent over Israel (17:4–5,32) and saw the Hasmonean Sadducees as the opponents of the devout (8:12,22; 17:5–8,22,45). His teaching of divine providence (5:3–4) and final retribution (2:34–5; 15:12–13) reflects a Pharisaic or Essene viewpoint. But the book is probably Pharisaic instead of Essene, because it lacks those end-time features which are characteristic of Essene prophecies.[67]

Like the Essenes, Pharisees, and Zealots, most Jews hoped for a coming messiah ("anointed one") who would be of the dynasty of King David.[68] In contrast to the early Christians, this Jewish hope concerned a political ruler who would defeat the foreign oppressors and establish Israel as a great political kingdom. Unlike the revolutionary Zealots (who attracted many Pharisees and Essenes in AD 66), this would not come

66. The following text has been used: R. B. Wright, "Psalms of Solomon," Charlesworth, *OTP* 2:639–70.

67. The Pss Sol contain no predictions about the "trials of the faithful" before the Messiah's coming nor any cryptic clues as to when the event will occur. God will establish the rule of the Davidic Messiah at a time determined by him (17:21). For more information, see Kee, *NT Context* 85–87; Ryle and James, *Psalmoi Solomontos*.

68. Jer 23:4–5; 33:14–22; Zec 6:12–13; 9:9–10; Pss Sol 17; Philo, *On Rewards and Punishments* 16.95–97 (conquering Messiah); Josephus, *War* 6.288–315 (6.312, on messianic oracles); Qumran scrolls on Davidic Messiah, 1QSa 2.11–27; 4QPatrBless 1–8; 4QFlor 1.11–13; early Christian accounts of Jewish messianism, Mk 8:11–12; 12:35–37; 15:43; Lk 23:2–3; Jn 1:41,49; 6:15; Mishnah *Berakoth* 1.5 and *Sotah* 9.15 (approaching age of the messiah); Midrash Rabbah on Psalms 60.9–10, where Rabbi Akiba hails Simon Bar Kosiba as messiah in AD 132–135.

about through violent resistance to Rome but through the hand of God. In distinction from the Essenes and other esoteric groups of end-time orientation, this nationalistic hope would take place in the real politics of plain history, sometime in the future. Like the Sadducees, who did not entertain such hopes, the Pharisees were involved in Jewish politics.[69] However, the Pharisees did not espouse these future hopes out of patriotic interests alone. The teachings of a resurrection of the dead and a final judgment of both good and evil (Dan 12:2) were adhered to by the Pharisees (as well as Essenes, Zealots, and Christians) although the Sadducees rejected them (Mk 12:18; Acts 23:8).

Apocalyptic Eschatology

The Essenes, certain early Christians, and other related messianic or prophetic groups, assumed the second alternative of "apocalyptic eschatology" or "mysterious unveilings about the end of the age."[70] They taught that God had revealed to them the secret schedule of his plan by which the evil powers would be overcome and God's eternal rule established. They did not expect the restoration of all Israel or the world, but rather the vindication of a small faithful remnant, usually identical with the sect that propagated the teaching. The type of literature produced by these groups was highly symbolic and esoteric in style. It was filled with veiled references to historical events structured in a certain time frame that lead to a final conflict followed by a new age of salvation. All was predetermined by God and only those within the group could decipher the revelations ("apocalypses") and discern the movement of the divine purpose. Ultimate deliverance would come from God through a messianic figure: a Davidic king, a prophet like Moses, an ideal priest, a leader of eschatological (end-time) war, or a heavenly Son of Man. Unlike the Pharisaic hope of national deliverance, these disclosures of the end time were no longer translated in terms of plain history, real politics, and human instrumentality. They were portrayed as cosmic battles between heaven and earth, angels and demons, with ultimate salvation coming from God alone. Examples of apocalyptic literature are Daniel, 1 Enoch, 2 Baruch, Testament of Moses, 4 Ezra, Mark 13, Revelation, and many of the Dead Sea Scrolls from Qumran. Most of the books listed above are written in the name of famous individuals, like Daniel, Moses, and Enoch. Although

---

69. For example, the Pharisees opposed the policies of John Hyrcanus (*Ant.* 13.288–298), and a Pharisee named Zadok helped Judas the Galilean organize a resistance group against the Romans (*Ant.* 18.1–10).

70. For a convenient collection of the literature, see Charlesworth, *OTP.* For studies, see Schmithals, *Apocalyptic;* Special Issue on Apocalyptic Literature, *CBQ* 39 (3, 1977) 307–409; P. D. Hanson, "Apocalypse, Genre" and "Apocalypticism," *IDBSupp* 27–34.

the real authors are unknown, this procedure (called "pseudonymity") was a feature of apocalyptic books designed to lend the writing a certain authority.

The origins of apocalyptic eschatology are complex and diverse. They show influences of Hebrew prophecy and wisdom literature, as well as Persian dualism (angels vs. demons) and Babylonian astrology (predetermined events). It is also a product of hope and despair. It resulted from the unswerving hope in the power of God and the ultimate plan he has established for his people. It was also a product of despair in the course of Judaism's tragic history of foreign dominance which smashed hopes of establishing a successful independent Jewish nation.

THE COMPETING PARTIES WITHIN JUDAISM

The type of Judaism that persisted through a tragic history was one of competing parties. Although there was basic agreement on such points as monotheism, Torah, Sabbath, and the Feasts, there was much diversity regarding how to interpret and implement them. Since we have already discussed Hellenistic Judaism of the Diaspora, we will limit our discussion to the four major parties of Palestinian Judaism: the Sadducees, Pharisees, Essenes, and Zealots.[71]

The Sadducees

The Sadducees,[72] whose name was probably derived from Zadok, a high priest of Solomon's time (1 Kgs 2:35, 950 BC), first made their appearance during the reign of the Hasmonean John Hyrcanus I (130 BC). They were the party of priestly urban aristocrats who were favorably disposed to Hellenistic culture but conservative in politics and religion. In

71. See the following studies: M. Simon, *Jewish Sects at the Time of Jesus*, trans. J. H. Farley (Philadelphia: Fortress, 1967); Schürer and Vermes, *History* 2:381–414, 562–90, 598–606; Avi-Yonah and Baras, *World History* 8:99–152, 263–302; G. W. E. Nickelsburg and M. E. Stone, *Faith and Piety in Early Judaism* (Philadelphia: Fortress, 1983) 24–40.

72. For primary sources, see Josephus *Ant.* 13.171–173 (their denial of fate); 13.293–298 (adhere only to written law, not oral traditions of the fathers; 13.297); 18.16–17 (deny immortality of the soul); *War* 2.162–166 (only concerned with human free will and deny final rewards and punishments; 2.164–165); Mk 12:18; Acts 23:8 (they deny there is a resurrection from the dead); Mishnah *Berakoth* 9.5 (classified with "heretics" for denying a world to come?); *Parah* 3.3,7 (scrupulous in temple sacrifices); *Yadaim* 4.6–8 (disagreements with Pharisees on legal issues); *Menahoth* 10.3; Babylonian Talmud *Pesahim* 57a (identified with the house of Boethus, from Alexandria, 23 BC, *Ant.* 15.320); J. Goldin, *The Fathers According to Rabbi Nathan* (New Haven: Yale University Press, 1955) 5 (supposed split of Boethusian and Sadducean parties over doctrine of final reward).

the area of politics, they were generally supportive of the ruling establishment. For example, they supported the policies of the Hasmoneans and later sought to secure the favor of the Herods and Romans. As priests, they officiated the sacrificial offerings at the temple, and it was from their ranks that the high priest was appointed. It was also their members who dominated the Jewish high court of the Sanhedrin. In both politics and religion they came in conflict with the popular Pharisee party, whose members were generally more antagonistic to Roman rule and tended to associate themselves with the synagogue and its particular emphases. In their understanding of Torah, the Sadducees and Pharisees were the most dissimilar. Moreover, the Pharisees adhered to a written Torah consisting of the Law and the Prophets, as well as an oral Torah of tradition, but the Sadducees only regarded the five books of Moses as binding. Whereas the Pharisees sought to apply the Torah to all aspects of life through the assistance of oral tradition, the Sadducees sought to limit the scope of the Torah by a more literal interpretation without employing oral tradition as an authoritative guide. Whereas the Pharisees held to the belief of angels and a resurrection of the dead as derived from the authority of the written prophets and oral tradition, the Sadducees rejected these beliefs because they were later formulations not derived from the authoritative books of Moses. After the destruction of the temple in AD 70, the priestly group of the Sadducees lost its power and eventually disappeared.

The Pharisees

The Pharisees[73] were probably the most influential and significant Jewish group of the Greco-Roman times. Their name is probably derived from the Hebrew *perushim*, meaning "the separated ones." Although it may have been a pejorative nickname, "Persian" (Aramaic *Parsh'ah*), because they shared certain Persian beliefs (e.g., resurrection, angels vs. demons). Their intense devotion to the law makes them the spiritual descendants of the Hasidim ("pious ones") who joined the Maccabean revolt to op-

---

73. For primary sources, see Josephus, *Ant.* 13.288–298; 13.408–415; 17.32–45 (their politics, popularity and adherence to the traditions of the fathers); 13.171–173 (fate is balanced with human freedom); 18.11 (their lifestyle of moderation, belief in immortality of the soul, final rewards and punishments); *War* 1.110–112 (their piety, precise interpretation of the law, and political influence); *Life* 189–194 (their accurate knowledge of Jewish law); Mt 23 (a Christian critique of their religious zeal and legalism). Much of the teaching of the Mishnah and Talmud which can be traced back to the so-called Tannaitic period (200 BC–AD 200) is from Pharisaic schools. See J. Neusner, *The Rabbinic Traditions About the Pharisees Before 70*, 3 vols. (Leiden: Brill, 1971); W. D. Davies, *Introduction to the Pharisees* (Philadelphia: Fortress, 1967); L. Finkelstein, *The Pharisees*, 2 vols., 3rd ed. (Philadelphia: Jewish Publication Society, 1963). H. F. Weiss, "Pharisaios," *TDNT* 9:1–48.

pose religious persecution under the Syrian Greeks (1 Macc 2:42). Like the Sadducees, the Pharisees first appear under the Hasmonean reign of John Hyrcanus I. Unlike the Sadducees, most Pharisees were not priests, but lay scholars who were responsible for the development and preservation of the oral legal tradition. Therefore they were connected with the synagogue, known for pious living (prayer, fasting, almsgiving, tithing) and precise interpretations of the law, especially in the areas of food purity, crops, sabbaths, festivals, and family affairs. In contrast to the Sadducees, the Pharisees accepted the larger notion of Scripture (Law and Prophets) as well as "new doctrines" about angels, demons, and the resurrection of the dead. The Pharisees also divided into various schools of interpretation, for example, the schools of Hillel and Shammai in the first century AD. It was the Pharisees who survived the war with Rome and reorganized Judaism along Pharisaic lines at the coastal town of Jabneh (Jamnia).

The Essenes

The Essenes[74] were an ascetic group who maintained a strict adherence to the law. Those who resided at Qumran near the Dead Sea were a strict monastic community with a profound eschatological perspective of themselves and the world. Their name may have been derived from the Aramaic *Hasayyah* or "pious ones," reflecting their close associations with the Hasidim of the Maccabean Revolt. They first appear when the Hasmonean, Jonathan, assumed the high priesthood (161–143 BC). Both Philo and Josephus mentioned that thousands of Essenes lived in towns and villages of Judea. The discovery of the Dead Sea Scrolls at Khirbet Qumran in 1947, revealed a monastic end-time-oriented wilderness community which was probably a major Essene center. The location confirmed

74. Primary sources: Josephus, *Ant.* 13.171–173 (fate governs everything); 15.373–379 (foreknowledge of the future and knowledge of divine revelations ascribed to Menahem the Essene); 17.345–348 (the interpretation of dreams ascribed to Simon the Essene); 18.18–22 (their belief in immortality and resurrection, strict ascetic and communal lifestyle, do not worship in the Jerusalem temple); *War* 2.119–136 (ascetic practices, abstain from marriage, communal living in towns of Judea, their study of ancient writings); Philo, *Every Good Man is Free* 12.75–91 (they do not offer sacrifices, live in villages, ethical concerns, synagogues, sharing of goods and monies); Pliny, *Natural History* 5.15.73 (their community near the Dead Sea, celibacy, recruitment of members). The Dead Sea Scrolls and community discovered at Khirbet Qumran (1947) are from an Essene group. For English texts, see Dupont- Sommer, *Essene Writings*, Vermes, *Scrolls*, and T. H. Gaster, *The Dead Sea Scriptures*, rev. ed. (Garden City, N.Y.: Anchor, 1976). See also F. M. Cross, *The Ancient Library of Qumran and Modern Biblical Study*, rev. ed. (Grand Rapids: Baker, 1980); G. Vermes, *The Dead Sea Scrolls, Qumran in Perspective*, rev. ed. (Philadelphia: Fortress, 1981).

Caves near Qumran where the Dead Sea Scrolls were discovered. *Photo by R. Hodge.*

the reports of the Roman scholar, Pliny the Elder (AD 70). The founder of the Qumran community was a Zadokite priest, called the Teacher of Righteousness, who opposed the (non-Zadokite) Hasmonean priesthood and left Jerusalem with a sizable group of followers. Probably in fulfillment of the prophetic utterance, "in the wilderness prepare the way of the Lord" (Isa 40:3), the group founded a center in the wilderness of Judea near the Dead Sea. There a community of scribes ("experts in the law of Moses") under the direction of the Zadokite priest awaited the end of the age, interpreting future prophecies as if they spoke to its situation in an exclusive manner. Members worked, copied religious texts, composed religious books, worshipped according to the community's calendar and customs, baptized, shared in a common meal, and sought to live undefiled ascetic lives.[75] The "Dead Sea Scrolls" produced by this community are also important for understanding apocalyptic and messianic groups like early Christianity.

The Zealots

The Zealots[76] were a Jewish resistance group that sought to revive the spirit of the Maccabeans in their revolt against Rome (AD 67-70). Their

75. Although some Essenes in outlying towns ("camps") married and reared children (CD 7.6-8; 12.1, 2, 19; Josephus *War* 2.160-161) and the bones of a few women and children were found on the periphery of the Qumran graveyard (where only adult male skeletons have been uncovered), the Qumran sect was primarily a male celibate community. See 1QS 1.6; 11.21; Josephus, *War* 2.120-121; Philo; Pliny; Vermes, *Dead Sea Scrolls* (1981) 96-97, 126, 181-82; Cross, *Ancient Library* 97-99.

76. Most of our information is from Josephus, see *War* 2.647-651 (their conflicts with the high priest; 2.651); 4.158-161 (they profess to be zealous for a good

Western wall of Jerusalem with large stones from the Herodian temple, commonly called the "Wailing Wall." *Photo by C. B. Puskas.*

name is probably derived from Phineas, who was "zealous for God" (Num 25:13), or from statements like a "zealot for the laws" (2 Macc 4:2). Like the Pharisees, they envisioned Israel's national deliverance under a messiah. Unlike (most of) the Pharisees, the Zealots sought to bring this about through armed resistance.

Even though the Zealot movement probably began in Jerusalem shortly after the revolt against procurator Florus (AD 66), it was influenced by many rebels and resistance movements that preceded it. An important ancestor of two Zealot leaders, Menahem and Eleazar ben Yair, was Judas the Galilean.[77] In AD 6 Judas rebelled against the Roman legate of Syria because of a provincial census. The Sicarii (Lat. "daggers, assassins")[78] were identified with the Zealots at Masada (AD 72). They may

cause; 4.160–161); 4.300–304 (Zealot raids on Jerusalem); 4.556–576 (fighting against other Jewish factions); 5.1–10 (their seizure of the temple); 5.98–105 (more fighting in the temple); 5.248–257 (uniting with other factions to fight the Romans); 7.252–274 (their violent activities summarized). See also Rhoads, *Israel in Revolution* 94–181; M. Stern, "Zealots," *Encyclopedia Judaica*; M. Hengel, *Was Jesus A Revolutionist?* (Philadelphia: Fortress, 1971).

77. *Ant.* 18.4–10, (author of the fourth sect of the Jews); 20.97–104 (concerning the rebel Theudas and the sons of the Judas the Galilean; 20.98, 102); *War* 2.117–118 (the revolt against Roman taxation; 2.118); Acts 5:36–37 (Theudas and Judas); Acts 21:38 (the Egyptian and Assassins). See also W. R. Farmer, *Maccabees, Zealots and Josephus* (New York: Columbia University Press, 1956).

78. *War* 2.254–265 (the rise of the Sicarii, rebels, and false prophets under the Roman procurator Felix); 2.425–429 (Sicarii known for attacking opponents with concealed daggers; 2.425); 4.398–409 (their occupation of Masada and the banditry throughout Judea); 4.514–520 (their raids against the temple); 7.252–406 (their

have had some connection with the brigands and assassins that arose at the time of the procurator Felix (AD 52–60). This earlier group was also called the Sicarii by Josephus because they mingled in the crowds and assassinated their opponents with concealed knives.

The Zealot movement of AD 66–70 was one of several rival factions whose rebel leaders each sought control of Jerusalem. John of Gischala, who lead a rebellion in Galilee, fled to Jerusalem in AD 67 to form another revolutionary faction. His group probably joined with the Zealots near the end of the war. Simon bar Giora was an Idumean guerrilla leader who fought the Zealots for control of the temple. He later joined forces with John of Gischala and the Zealots to feebly oppose the mighty Roman army under Titus. Many of the Zealots and Sicarii under Eleazar Ben Yair fled to the Herodian fortress of Masada, where they all committed suicide rather than surrender to the Romans in AD 72. In reaction to the Hellenizing policies of Emperor Hadrian, the spirit of the Zealot resistance revived in the revolt under Simon Bar Kosiba (AD 132–35). This rebel leader was also called Simon Bar Kochba by the famous Rabbi Akiba. "Bar Kochba" means "Son of the Star," a messianic title from Num 24:17. The messianic and apocalyptic overtones of this revolt were also characteristic of many rebel movements in first-century Palestine.[79]

Rebels and brigands, such as the Zealots and Sicarii, were part of life in the restless province of Palestine. Mention is made of rebels in the NT (Mk 15:7; Acts 5:36–37; 21:38). Even one of Jesus' disciples was thought to have been a Zealot ("Simon the Zealot," Lk 6:15; Acts 1:13).

SUMMARY

A tragic history of foreign dominance could not stifle the persistent faith of Judaism in the first Christian era. Through such tragedies as the Babylonian Exile, the struggles in resettlement of Palestine, Syrian oppression, a disappointing interval of independence, and revolts against Rome, Judaism revived, readjusted, and reorganized as a monotheistic faith devoted to the law, the Sabbath, circumcision, and the feasts. This unifying faith of Judaism also persisted in a diversity of expressions, as we have seen in the parties of the Sadducees, Pharisees, Essenes, and Zealots. Despite this diversity of the first century AD, we begin to see after AD 90 a con-

---

stand against the Romans at Masada); 7.407–425 (some fled to Egypt); 7.437–442 (some fled to Cyrene).

79. See Midrash Rabbah on Psalms 60:9–10, where Rabbi Akiba hails Simon Bar Kosiba as Messiah, and Eusebius, *Eccl Hist* 4.6.1–4; 8.4. See also note 42 of this chapter.

solidation of beliefs and practices brought about by the surviving Pharisaic party, a trajectory that leads to the complex legal systems of Rabbinic Judaism. This trend from diversity to conformity, as we will note, also took place in early Christianity about the same time.

This was the situation into which Christianity emerged: in a Greco-Roman environment of pervasive Hellenism, under a stable Roman government, in an age of anxiety and aspiration, conceived and mothered by Judaism, its parent religion. Both the environmental and hereditary factors must be considered in our attempt to understand the growth and development of early Christianity and its written legacy, the NT.

3

The Language of the New Testament

In what language was the NT originally written? Almost all of the NT authors were Jews, but not a single book was written in Hebrew or Aramaic (a related Semitic language).[1] All of the NT books were written when Rome ruled the Mediterranean world, but none were written in Latin. Therefore, we must turn to the one language prevalent during that period: ancient Greek. We have over 5000 manuscript copies of the NT written in Greek from the mid-second to the twelfth centuries. The earliest versions of the NT were in Syriac, Coptic, and Latin (as early as the second and third centuries); all presuppose a Greek original.

Unfortunately, the question of the NT language is not sufficiently answered with the statement that it was written in ancient Greek. This general statement prompts us to ask a more specific question: in what *dialect* of ancient Greek was the NT written? Or, stating it another way: was the NT written in the Old Ionic of Homer, the Attic of Plato, or the literary Koine of Philo? We will attempt to answer this complex question, first, by reviewing briefly the history of the development of the Greek language up to the present and, then, by briefly examining the characteristics of NT Greek.

THE HISTORY OF THE GREEK LANGUAGE

Greek has been a spoken language for more than 3000 years. Like all

---

1. The Aramaic of first-century Palestine was a Semitic dialect closely related to Hebrew with a long historical development (12th cent. BC to 7th cent. AD). It was the native language of Palestinian Judaism that was used by Jesus and primitive Jewish Christianity. Although some scholars have argued that the Gospels were originally *composed* in Aramaic (e.g., C. C. Torrey, *The Four Gospels* [New York, 1933]), a consensus of scholars today rejects this thesis. Aramaic influence on NT Greek is probable, however, see e.g., J. Fitzmyer, *A Wandering Aramean: Collected Aramaic Essays* (Missoula, Mont.: Scholars Press, 1979).

spoken languages, it has experienced constant changes, generally from more complex to simpler linguistic forms.[2] The periods of Greek can be divided approximately into the following four categories:[3]

Classical Period, from Homer to Aristotle (1000–322 BC)

Hellenistic period, from Alexander the Great to the Roman emperor Justinian I (322 BC–AD 529)

Byzantine period, from Justinian I to the fall of Constantinople (529–1453)

Modern period, from 1453 to present.

The Classical Period (1000–322 BC)

The classical period was characterized by a variety of different dialects, resulting from differences in culture and geographical location. Some of the dialects of this early period were:

Old Ionic. This dialect of Achaea was in use from the 10th to the 8th cent. BC. The epic writings of Homer employ this type of Greek.

Ionic. Used throughout the classical period, it was the Greek of Herodotus the historian and Hippocrates the physician. Ionic was the dialect of the southwest Asia Minor coast.

Attic. This sophisticated Greek of Athens was dominant in the classical period and greatly influenced the Hellenistic dialect. The Attic language was the linguistic medium of the philosophers Plato and Aristotle. It was the dialect of historians, like Thucydides and Xenophon. Attic was a smooth and harmonious dialect (like Ionic) in comparison with later NT Greek. It was also characterized by complex linguistic forms.

The grammar of Attic Greek was sophisticated and precise. It made ample use of the subjunctive and optative moods in verbs, the dual number in nouns and adjectives, and a bewildering maze of particles.[4] One example of preciseness in Attic Greek is that it could state in three words what would taken ten in the English language: "I have been called up for service throughout the wars" (Thucydides). Such precision with an economy of expression was done by adding prefixes, suffixes, and infixes to the three words. This compound formation of words is called synthesis.[5] In the next period with wider use among people of different cultures there would be a trend away from synthesis to analysis, e.g., some inserted a series of helping words rather than building on the same stem.

Attic Greek had an enduring influence for two reasons: (1) it was the

---

2. For further information, see E. C. Colwell, "Greek Language," *IDB* 2:479–82.

3. The four categories are from: B. Metzger, "Language of the New Testament," *IB* 7:44–46.

4. White, "Greek Language," *ZPE* 2:827.

5. Colwell "Greek," *IDB* 2:480.

dialect of Athens, the city which had dominance over the other Greek communities after the Persian war. It also took part in the colonization of the Aegean Sea region. (2) The last great representative of the classical Attic dialect was Aristotle, the teacher of Alexander the Great. Although Aristotle's death marks the end of the classical period, the influence of Attic Greek continued.

The Hellenistic period (322 BC–AD 529)

Alexander's conquest of the eastern Mediterranean world began the Hellenistic period. Two developments took place after the establishment of Alexander's empire: (1) The Greek language and culture penetrated into the orient (for example: Palestine, Egypt, and Persia); and (2) a new form of Greek emerged, Hellenistic or Koine (common) Greek.

This new Koine Greek was the result of internal and external factors. The following examples might have been some of them. First, within Alexander's army were men from all parts of Greece. Their close associations during the campaigns played a significant role in the emergence of a new type of Greek (which had already begun through increasing contact between Greek city-states). Those elements of speech which were most widely current and readily adapted from various dialects tended to survive, whereas the less functional were dropped. Since Attic was the predominant language also spoken by Alexander, there was a tendency to conform to Attic standards. Second, wherever the army of Alexander went, this language was disseminated and took root in oriental soil with all the adaptations and modifications that generally accompany such assimilation. It must be noted, however, that the use of native dialects continued alongside the newly acquired Greek. For example in Palestine most of the people spoke their native Aramaic as well as the Koine Greek.

In a relatively short period of time Koine Greek became the common means of communication in the Hellenistic age. After Alexander's death the Greek language spread extensively throughout the Mediterranean world so that by the first century AD, Koine Greek was spoken from Spain to northwestern India and was the chief language of Rome.

Characteristics of Koine involve the simplification of forms and the use of emphatic and vigorous expressions. Simplified forms involved the limited use of the optative verb mood, dual number, and particle. Emphatic and vivid expressions were conveyed by compound verbs, use of the present instead of future tense, use of the active instead of middle voice, and the greater use of direct discourse.

Varieties of Koine included: literary Koine, Attic, and vernacular Koine. Literary Koine comes closest to being a natural development of the Attic.

It became the most suitable vehicle for formal literature. This was the Koine of Polybius the historian, Strabo the geographer, Epictetus the philosopher, and the Jewish writers, Josephus and Philo.

The Atticist dialect was developed by a few literary men to imitate the Attic of the classical age. It was an artificial literary language in reaction to Koine Greek and only lasted a short period. Some of the participants in this short-lived Attic revival were: Dionysius and Dio Chrysostom.

Vernacular or nonliterary Koine was the most influential of the period. It was the language of the street, home, marketplace, and farm. In comparison with Attic Greek, it was crude, often ungrammatical. A wealth of information concerning this vernacular Greek was found in the Egyptian papyri, pottery fragments, and inscriptions dating from the third century BC to the fourth century AD discovered in the late nineteenth and early twentieth centuries.[6]

Before the discoveries of the Egyptian papyri and their evaluation by such men as Grenfell, Hunt, Deissmann, and Moulton, scholars were divided in their understanding of the NT language into at least two camps of interpretation. First, there was the camp that regarded it as a distinct Hebraic or biblical Greek because of its use of the Greek OT and its lack of extrabiblical parallels (at that time). Critics accused this camp of advocating a "Holy Ghost Greek" for the NT. The second camp evaluated the language according to the high standards of classical Attic. They generally regarded the NT Greek as decidedly inferior to its classical ancestor and concluded that it was a vulgar imitation by writers who used Greek as foreigners.

With the discovery of the Egyptian papyri our understanding of the NT language changed radically. No longer was the language of the NT viewed as a special biblical Greek or a vulgar imitation of Attic, but as the colloquial language of the people of that day. The NT was no longer to be seen as a unique work of art but as a record of life (Deissmann). Special NT words now had parallels in the everyday language of the people. Even the literary forms of Paul's letters have close parallels in the private and business correspondence of the Hellenistic people.

The Byzantine Period (AD 529–1453)

This period continues the process of simplification typical of the Hellenistic period. The Byzantine period begins with the influential reign of

6. For information on the discoveries of the Egyptian papyri and inscriptions see Deissmann, *LAE* 1–61. See also A. S. Hunt and C. C. Edgar, *Select Papyri*, 2 vols. LCL (1932); B. P. Grenfell and A. S. Hunt, *New Classical Fragments and Other Greek and Latin Papyri* (London: Oxford, 1897); J. H. Moulton and G. Milligan, *The Vocabulary of the Greek Testament* (London, 1930; repr. Grand Rapids: Eerdmans, 1980) vii–xx.

Emperor Justinianus from Constantinople (e.g., Justinian Code of 529). It was a low ebb in learning and much of the distinctiveness of the Greek was lost through changes in syntax and borrowings from other languages. The takeover of the Turks in 1453 ends the Byzantine period.

The Modern Period (AD 1453–Present)

This period also continues the process of simplification typical of the Hellenistic period. And although the modern Greek contains a variety of changes and foreign influences, it differs more from the classical language of Homer than the Koine dialect of Polybius.[7]

THE GREEK LANGUAGE OF THE NT

Although they fit very comfortably into the common vernacular of the day, the literary styles of the NT authors vary. Certain books approach the literary Koine, whereas most fall within the broader vernacular style. Hebrews and Luke–Acts are nearest to literary Koine. Both exhibit a breadth of culture and a rich vocabulary (e.g., Heb 1:1–3; Lk 1:1–4). The Gospels of Mark and John and the book of Revelation are typical of the popular colloquial Koine. They evidence a limited vocabulary and even a disregard for the ordinary rules of Greek syntax (e.g., Revelation). Mark, John, and Revelation also retain many Semitic and Aramaic idioms. The letters of Paul fit somewhere between these two tendencies. Although he is steeped in both the Greek OT and the colloquial language, Paul speaks with the Koine of an educated man (e.g., Epictetus).

Semitisms

Because most of the NT books were either written by Jews, reflect a Palestinian setting, or utilize Palestinian sources, there is evidence of Semitic influence. The Semitisms of the NT originate from a number of sources: (1) borrowings from the language of Greek OT (the LXX); (2) the occurrence of Aramaic terms and constructions; and (3) possible Hebrew constructions. Most Semitisms are borrowings from the language of the Greek OT, which is "translation Greek" in the Koine tradition. A number of Aramaic terms are retained in the Gospels, especially Mark (e.g., *Gethsemane, abba, eloi, eloi lama sabachtani, Golgotha, rabbi*), and some alleged Aramaic constructions occur. Although many Jews of Jesus' day knew Hebrew, its influence on the NT is difficult to discern. Much of the Hebraic style in NT Greek was derived from the LXX rather than from the

7. A. T. Robertson, *A Grammar of the Greek NT*, 4th ed. (Nashville: Broadman, 1934) 45.

Hebrew Bible. Nevertheless, it has been argued by some that such expressions as "with joy you will rejoice" (you will rejoice greatly, Jn 3:27) or "before the face of his way" (Acts 13:24) are Hebrew constructions.[8] However, it is difficult to refute the claim that these "Hebrew constructions" were conveyed through Greek translations of the OT.

Latinisms

Latinisms are sparsely represented in the NT. They are chiefly military and commercial terminology, e.g., centurion, legion, speculator, denarius, colony. The occurrence of Latinism in the NT is probably due to the presence of the Roman military throughout the Mediterranean world. These isolated terms probably filtered into the popular colloquial Koine.[9]

Christian Vocabulary

The possibility of a specific Christian element in the NT language must be approached with some reservation. Upon the discovery of the Egyptian papyri, many special "biblical terms"[10] (Thayer) were actually found to be part of the everyday language of the people (A. Deissmann, W. Bauer). Thayer originally argued for over 700 "biblical terms" in the NT. Deissmann in his research brought this special list down to 50 and W. Bauer reduced this number even more.[11] Of course the Christian communities used popular vocabulary and gave it a different nuance in the context of their worship and proclamation. But reservations should be made concerning the possibility of the *creation* of new Christian terms and phrases.

---

8. Also paratactic constructions connecting a series of independent clauses by conjunctions "and . . . and . . . and" are considered to be (Semitic) Hebraic constructions.

9. There are also a number of NT phrases that seem awkward in Greek but resemble familiar Latin idioms, e.g., Mk 15:15,19; 14:65; Lk 12:58; Acts 17:9; 19:38. See C. F. D. Moule, *An Idiom Book of NT Greek*, 2nd ed. (Cambridge: University Press, 1971) 192.

10. See, for example, the long list of "Biblical or NT" Greek words in J. Thayer, *A Greek–English Lexicon of the NT*, 1889 ed. (Wheaton, Ill.: Evangel, 1974) Appendix III, 693–710.

11. See how the list of "Christian terminology" is considerably shortened in *BAGD* xix–xxviii.

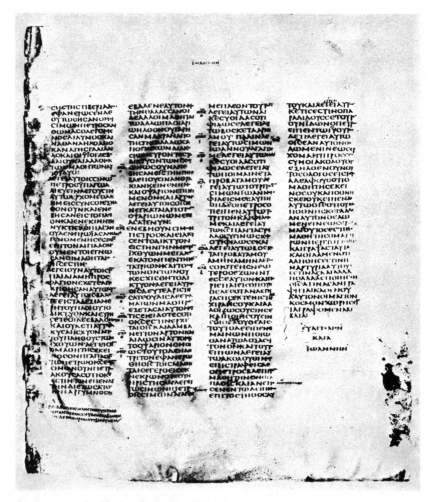

Codex Sinaiticus (ℵ, 4th cent.), showing last folio of
John's Gospel (Jn 21:1–25); approximate size 14″ by 13″.
British Museum. Used with permission.

4

The Text of the New Testament

The Manuscripts of the NT Text

Certain questions are essential for interpretation. One question to be addressed before asking what a text originally meant is: "Did the text originally state that?" For example, if we want to understand what the author of 1 John originally meant by the phrase, "the Spirit, the water, and the blood" (5:7–8), we had better be certain that the author of 1 John composed it.[1] How reliable are the Greek manuscripts on which our modern translations are based?

All extant (existing and known) Greek manuscripts of the NT are of codex (book) form, and those before the ninth century were written in uncial capital letters.[2] The codex, or leaf-form book, came into extensive use by the second century. Codices were folded sheets (quires) bound by waxed tablets and fastened together by a thong hinge. It was much easier to use than the older scroll book form, which was a roll of sheets fastened together up to 35 feet in length and wound around a stick. Some of the early writings of the NT may have been composed on a scroll book form but we do not possess any of the originals. Greek manuscripts before the ninth century were written in the literary uncial (or "majuscule") style. Uncials (Latin "inch high") were capital letters written separately with little or no punctuation and spacing between words. It was the style used for

1. The KJV in 1 Jn 5:7 has a long theological interpretation of these three (Spirit, water, blood) as symbols of the Trinity; this is derived from late manuscripts. The RSV, NEB, JB, NAB, NIV and almost all other modern translations omit this statement.

2. Material in this section has been derived from: K. Aland and B. Aland, *The Text of the NT*, trans. E. Rhodes (Leiden: Brill; Grand Rapids: Eerdmans, 1987); G. D. Fee, "Textual Criticism of the NT," *Biblical Criticism*; J. Finegan, *Encountering NT Manuscripts* (Grand Rapids: Eerdmans, 1974); Greenlee, *INT* 18–58; idem, "Text and Manuscripts of the New Testament" in *ZPE* 5:697–707; Metzger, *TNT* 3–92.

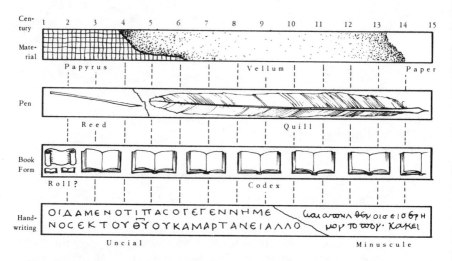

Paleographic chart of Greek NT manuscripts. *J. H. Green-lee, Introduction to New Testament Criticism © 1964.* Used with permission.

literary writing. There existed at the same time a cursive (running) handwriting that was used for personal or nonliterary purposes (e.g., personal letters of the nonbiblical Egyptian papyri). Some of Paul's letters, for example, may have been written originally in a cursive handwriting, but we do not possess the originals.

There are over 5000 extant Greek manuscripts of the NT. This is a quantity greater than any other ancient body of literature. These Greek manuscripts fall under five major categories: papyri (88), parchments (270), uncials and minuscules (2800), ancient versions, and patristic citations. We will briefly examine all five.

Papyri

The eighty-eight or more extant papyri manuscripts of the Greek NT date from the early second to the eighth centuries. Most were discovered in the sands of Egypt in the late nineteenth century. These manuscripts are sheets of papyri made from the spongy center of the stalk from the papyrus plant grown mostly in the Nile delta region. The sheets usually ranged in size from 6 x 9 to 12 x 15 inches. All extant papyri texts are in the codex book form. Although most are fragmentary, together they include a considerable part of the NT. Most of the papyri represent an early Alexandrian (Egyptian) text type. In spite of their early date, the reliability of the papyri is reduced by the fact that many of them were

Chester Beatty Papyrus II (p[46], 3rd. cent.) showing the
text of Romans 15:29–33; 16:25–27; actual size 6″ by 9″.
Chester Beatty Museum. Used with permission.

copied by nonprofessional scribes.[3]

Two of the most important collections of NT papyrus manuscripts were acquired in 1930–31 by Chester Beatty of London and M. M. Bodmer of Geneva in 1955–56. The oldest known fragment of the Greek NT is p^{52} of the John Rylands Library in Manchester. It contains a few lines of John 18 and is dated around AD 125.

The Beatty Collection is found mostly in Dublin, although some fragments are located at the University of Michigan and in Vienna. All of the papyri of the Beatty collection date in the early third century. They include almost one-seventh of the Gospels and Acts (p^{45}), a large portion of Paul's letters plus Hebrews (p^{46}), and about one third of the book of Revelation (p^{47}).

The Bodmer Collection is located in Geneva, Switzerland. The papyri range in date form the second (p^{66}, p^{75}) and third (p^{72}) to the seventh (p^{74}) centuries. They include a large portion of John's Gospel (p^{66}, p^{75}), most of Luke (p^{75}), Jude, 1 and 2 Peter (p^{72}), Acts, James, and 1, 2, and 3 John (p^{74}). The manuscript p^{72} also includes a number of apocryphal writings (e.g., the Nativity of Mary, the apocryphal correspondence of Paul to the Corinthians).

Parchment Uncials

The parchment uncials presently number about 270, varying in size from a few verses to the complete NT, and ranging in date from the fourth to the tenth centuries. These manuscripts are durable sheets made from animal skins which were soaked, scraped, dried, and rubbed down to a smooth writing surface (also called "vellum"). This form of writing material replaced papyri by the fourth century. All parchment uncials were written in the codex book form. By the parchment uncial period, Christianity had become a legitimate religion of the Roman Empire and consequently most uncial manuscripts were copied by professional scribes.

The Codices Sinaiticus, Alexandrinus, Vaticanus, and Bezae are four of the more significant or representative parchment uncials. Codex Sinaiticus, (ℵ) from the fourth century, contains all of the New and most of the Old Testaments. It is located in the British Museum of London. It is one of the most important manuscripts of the NT and its discovery by Constantine von Tischendorf around 1840 is a fascinating story. Codex Sinaiticus belongs in general to the Alexandrian (Egyptian) text type with which most of the early papyri are identified.

Codex Alexandrinus (A), a fifth-century manuscript lacks almost all of Matthew, most of 2 Corinthians, and part of John. It is displayed in the

---

3. Greenlee, *ZPE* 5:702. For further discussion on the preparation and use of papyri, see Pliny, *Natural History* 13.68–83; Barrett, *NTB* 23–25; Finegan, *Encountering* 19–22; *CHB* 1:30–32, 48–66.

British Museum of London. It contains a mixed text type: the Gospels are of the later Byzantine type and the rest of the NT resembles the Alexandrian type.

Codex Vaticanus (B), written in the mid-fourth century, is located in the Vatican library of Rome. It ranks with Sinaiticus as one of the two most important Greek manuscripts of the NT. It lacks part of the OT, and in the NT, part of Hebrews and all of Titus, Timothy, Philemon, and Revelation are missing. Like Sinaiticus it is considered a good representative of the Alexandrian text type. Some believe that Vaticanus and Sinaiticus were two of the fifty copies of the Bible which Emperor Constantine ordered (331), but this is difficult to prove.[4]

Codex Bezae (D) is a sixth-century manuscript of the Gospels and Acts, now located in the Cambridge University library. The text of Codex D, also known as Cantabrigiensis, has both Greek and Latin facing each other on opposite pages (diglot). It is the chief representative of the "Western text" known for its extensive paraphrases and additions, especially in Acts. Other minor Greek manuscripts are designated by letters of the Greek alphabet (Δ, Π) and numerals preceded by zero (048, 0242).

Minuscules

The third major manuscript category is that of the minuscules. These manuscripts outnumber the uncials ten to one and range in date from the ninth to the fourteenth centuries. The minuscule ("small letter") handwriting style was a ninth-century refinement of the early nonliterary cursive style which completely displaced the use of uncials in formal literature. Like the early cursive ("running") style the minuscule letters were connected (including words!) which made writing (if not interpreting) much easier than the uncial style.

The minuscule manuscripts are designated by numerals (33, 2127) and vary from one or two pages to the complete NT. Only two examples will be given: Manuscripts 1 and 13. Manuscript 1 is a twelfth-century manuscript containing all of the NT except Revelation. It is located in Basel, Switzerland. It was one of the manuscripts used by Erasmus in the preparation of the first published edition of the Greek NT. Manuscript 1 is closely related to a group of minuscules (118, 131, 209, and 1582) called "family 1."

Manuscript 13 is a thirteenth-century codex of the Gospels located in Paris. It is closely related to a group of minuscules (e.g., 69, 124, 346, 828)

---

4. Metzger, TNT 47. K. Aland concurs in a general manner, feeling that the Age of Constantine produced the right conditions for church scriptoria to be established at such centers of learning as Alexandria and Antioch; Aland, TNT 64–67, 70–71.

known as "family 13," which is textually related to "family 1." In the family 13 group the woman taken in adultery follows Lk 21:36 instead of Jn 7:52.

The lectionaries are also classed with the minuscules. They are selections from the Gospels and "apostolic writings" used for reading in church services. There are over 2000 of these minuscule manuscripts dating from the fifth to the eighth centuries. They are identified by the following symbols: l^{60}, l^{680}.

Ancient Versions

In addition to the Greek manuscripts there were also early versions of the NT in other languages. The important Latin versions of the West date from the late second to the fourth centuries (Jerome's Vulgate, ca. 384). The Syriac translations of the East date from the mid-second (Tatian's *Diatessaron*) to the seventh centuries (the Peshitta revisions). The Coptic versions of Egypt date from the early third (Sahidic) to the fourth centuries (Bohairic). Through textual criticism, a version can sometimes indicate what type of Greek manuscript was used as well as its approximate date and geographical origin. The versions therefore make a significant contribution to the study of the Greek NT manuscripts. Designations for versions are: e.g., it^a, it^s (Latin), syr^s, syr^p (Syriac), cop^{sa} (Coptic).

Patristic Citations

A final source for recovering the original Greek text is in the quotations and allusions of the catholic (and non-catholic) Christian writers of the first eight centuries (also called church fathers or patristic writers). Most of their works are in Greek and Latin with a lesser amount in Syriac and other languages.

Although the NT quotations are extensive, a number of problems arise in attempting to recover the Greek text utilized by them. First, the Christian writers often cited the NT from memory and it is therefore difficult to determine the actual wording of their Greek text. Second, a patristic writer may have used several different copies of the NT. Finally, most available texts of the patristic writings are also late and sometimes corrupt copies.[5] Yet when the difficult task of reconstructing the NT text of the patristic writers is done, it is of great value, since it provides a datable and geographically identifiable witness to the NT available to an early Christian writer. Designations for church fathers are generally the first few letters of their names: e.g., Ir (Irenaeus), Tert (Tertullian).

---

5. Fee, "Textual Criticism" 133. See the following difficulties in establishing the NT text of the church fathers in: Aland, *TNT* 166–80.

THE TRANSMISSION OF THE NT TEXT

The history of the transmission of the NT text will be surveyed from two major periods.[6] First, the period of the handwritten text (before 1516). Second, the period of the printed text (1516 to present).

The Handwritten Text

The period of the handwritten text (before 1516) was characterized by three developments: a divergence of manuscripts, a convergence of texts, and the dominance of the Byzantine texts.

The Divergence of Manuscripts

The period of the divergence of manuscripts begins with the writing of the first NT books (ca. 50) and declines with the request for fifty copies of the Bible by Emperor Constantine (ca. 331). During this period of divergence many errors in the copying of the NT took place. At this time, NT books were generally copied by Christians who were not professionally trained scribes. These early copyists introduced thousands of changes in the text. The majority of their errors were unintentional and are easily discernible as slips of the eye, ear, or mind. Hundreds of changes, however, were intentional. Early scribes often "smoothed out" the Greek of the NT author by changing word order or tenses of verbs and by adding conjunctions. They also tended to clarify ambiguous passages by adding nouns or pronouns, by substituting common synonyms for uncommon words, and even by rewriting difficult phrases. There was also a tendency to harmonize one passage with another, especially in the Synoptic Gospels.[7]

This period also saw the rise of local texts. Copies of NT books were carried to various localities by Christians, each manuscript containing its own characteristic textual variants. Over a period of time, the manuscripts circulating in a given locality would tend to resemble each other more nearly than manuscripts of any other locality.[8] Current evidence suggests that different local texts may have been present in the regions around Rome, Alexandria, Caesarea (or Jerusalem), and Constantinople.

From the surrounding areas dominated by the centers of local texts (e.g., Rome, Caesarea, Alexandria) early translations of the Greek manuscripts also emerged. Examples from three versions will be given. Translations of certain NT books into Latin (N. Africa) and Syria (east) began in the

---

6. Material for this section has been adapted from: Aland, *TNT* 48–71; Fee, "Textual Criticism," 138–48; Greenlee, *INT* 59–95; idem,"Text and Manuscripts" *ZPE*, 5:707–13; Metzger, *TNT* 95–146.

7. Fee, "Textual Criticism" 139; Aland, *TNT* 285–86.

8. Greenlee, *INT* 61; Aland, *TNT* 53–56.

mid-second century. By the third century, Coptic translations of the NT began in Egypt. This development contributed to the divergence of NT manuscripts.

The Convergence of Texts

The most important contribution to the convergence of NT Greek manuscripts was the commission by Constantine to produce fifty new copies of the Bible for churches of Constantinople (AD 331).[9] Although other earlier causes were at work, like the toleration of Christianity and its sacred writings (AD 313), Constantine's imperial edict marked a period of standardization. This imperial commission gave opportunity for official comparison of various manuscripts and indicated the need for uniting divergent local texts in a single text tradition.[10] Professional scribes could now be employed for copying the manuscripts, which helped reduce variations in the text. Therefore, at Constantinople, the center of the Greek-speaking church, a convergence of Greek NT manuscripts took place that influenced most of the church. The process of converging NT manuscripts and displacing older text types continued from the fourth to the eighth centuries.

The Dominance of Byzantine Texts

Factors such as the prevalence of Latin in the West and the weakening of Christian influence in Egypt[11] eliminated the competition of other local text types and contributed to the *dominance* of the Constantinople text tradition, or "Byzantine text," from the eighth to the fifteenth centuries. More than nine-tenths of the existing manuscripts of the NT are from the eighth and later centuries. Very few of these manuscripts differ from the Byzantine text. Although copying manuscripts by hand increased variations, the text after eighth century was basically Byzantine. The printed Greek NT was also essentially a Byzantine type until the late nineteenth century.[12]

The Printed Text

The next historical phase of the transmission of the NT text was the period of the printed text (1516 to present). This period was characterized by at least four developments: (1) the establishment of the "received text"; (2) the accumulation of textual evidence; (3) the struggle for the critical text; and (4) the period of the critical text.

---

9. The city of Byzantium had its name changed to Constantinople by Emperor Constantine around AD 330.
10. Greenlee, *INT* 62; Aland, *TNT* 70-71.
11. Fee, "Textual Criticism" 140.
12. Greenlee, *INT* 62.

The Period of the "Received Text"

Johannes Gutenberg's invention of the printing press (ca. 1450) marked a new period in the history of the NT text. Although the first Greek NT to be printed was the Polyglot Bible edited by Cardinal Ximenes (1514), the first text put on the market was edited by the Dutch humanist Erasmus in 1516.

Unfortunately, these first editions, which served as the basis for all subsequent editions until the nineteenth century, were derived from late medieval manuscripts of inferior quality. In fact, Erasmus' only manuscript of Revelation was so badly mutilated that he supplied the missing portions with the Latin Vulgate translated into Greek (the last six verses). These readings have never been found in any Greek manuscripts.

Three subsequent editions are of special importance in the history of the text.[13] First, the third edition of Robert Stephanus, which was dependent on the text of Erasmus, served as the basis for the King James Version (1611). The fourth edition of Stephanus (1551) was also the first to be numbered into chapters and verses as they are today. Second, Theodore Beza, Calvin's successor in Geneva, published nine editions from 1565 to 1604 which gave the text of Erasmus a stamp of approval. Two of his editions were also used in the King James Version. Third, a Greek text very similar to those of Erasmus, Stephanus, and Beza was edited by the Elzevir brothers in 1633. It became the standard Greek text of Europe. The term "received text" (textus receptus) is from the preface of their 1633 edition: "You therefore have the text which is now received by all, in which we give nothing changed or corrupted." This boast held good for over two hundred years.

The Period of New Textual Evidence

The period from 1633 to 1831 is characterized by the accumulation of new evidence from Greek manuscripts, versions, and patristic writers. During this period, the dominance of the "received text" was not broken, but evidence was collected which eventually led to a better Greek text.

At least three scholars made significant contributions in this period: Bengel, Wettstein, and Griesbach. In 1734 J. A. Bengel published a Greek text in which he first suggested the classification of manuscripts into text types, and devised a system for evaluating textual variants. J. J. Wettstein's edition of the Greek text (1751–52) presupposed certain principles of textual criticism and used a system for designating manuscripts by symbols. J. J. Griesbach, in his editions from 1774 to 1807, modified Bengel's classification of text groups to three, defined the basic principles of textual criticism, and showed great skill in evaluating textual variants. Although the

13. Fee, "Textual Criticism" 141; Aland, *TNT* 3–11.

above works followed the "received text," valuable new evidence was relegated to the critical notes.

The Period of the Struggle for the Critical Text

The period from 1831 to 1881 saw the overthrow of the "received text" and the struggle for a new critical edition. The first important break with the "received text" came with the Greek text published by Karl Lachmann (1831).[14] His was the first attempt to reconstruct a text from scientific principles instead of reproducing the medieval text.

The impressive work of Constantine von Tischendorf brought to light many unknown manuscripts (e.g., Codex Sinaiticus). He also published critical editions of the Greek text. The last edition (1872) gave a critical apparatus noting all the known variants of the uncials, minuscules, versions, and patristic readings.

The Period of the Critical Text

In 1881 two Cambridge scholars, B. F. Westcott and F. J. A. Hort, combined their efforts to produce a monumental critical edition of the Greek NT. It was based on the earlier research of Griesbach, Lachmann, and Tischendorf, and it established a foundation for further study. The Westcott-Hort text was the basis for the English Revised (1881) and American Standard (1901) Versions of the NT.

In the introduction to the critical edition, F. J. A. Hort laid to rest the "received text" with three basic arguments against the Byzantine text type.[15] First, manuscripts of the Syrian (Byzantine) text type contain readings that *combine* elements found in the earlier text types. Second, the readings peculiar to the Syrian text type are *never* found in Christian writings before the fourth century. Third, when readings peculiar to this text-type are compared with rival readings, the Syrian claim to originality disappears.

After careful examination of the early text types and their variants, Westcott and Hort concluded that the Egyptian text ($\aleph$, B, which they called "Neutral") preserved the original text with minimal change. Their critical Greek text was therefore based on this "neutral" text type, except in cases where internal evidence was clearly against it.

Subsequent research after Westcott and Hort (1881) has seen further refinements in the reconstruction of the critical text. In 1913, H. von Soden published a massive work that included a critical text, an extensive apparatus (critical notes) and lengthy descriptions of manuscripts. Although

14. Fee, 143; Aland, 11.
15. B. F. Westcott and F. J. A. Hort, *The NT in Original Greek* (Cambridge: University Press, 1881) 93–119; summary of three points from Metzger, *TNT* 135.

Theories Concerning the History of the Text

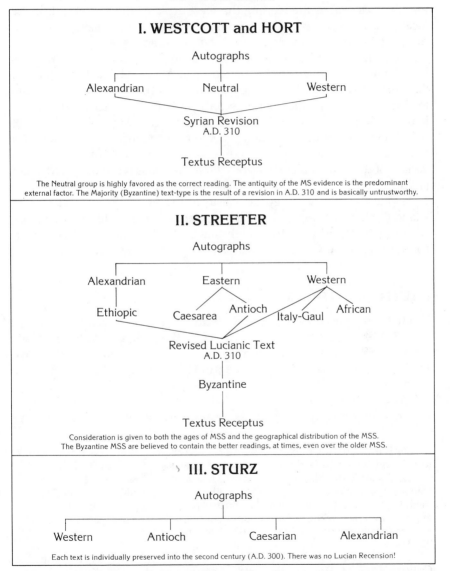

I. WESTCOTT and HORT

Autographs

Alexandrian   Neutral   Western

Syrian Revision
A.D. 310

Textus Receptus

The Neutral group is highly favored as the correct reading. The antiquity of the MS evidence is the predominant external factor. The Majority (Byzantine) text-type is the result of a revision in A.D. 310 and is basically untrustworthy.

II. STREETER

Autographs

Alexandrian   Eastern   Western

Ethiopic   Caesarea   Antioch   Italy-Gaul   African

Revised Lucianic Text
A.D. 310

Byzantine

Textus Receptus

Consideration is given to both the ages of MSS and the geographical distribution of the MSS. The Byzantine MSS are believed to contain the better readings, at times, even over the older MSS.

III. STURZ

Autographs

Western   Antioch   Caesarian   Alexandrian

Each text is individually preserved into the second century (A.D. 300). There was no Lucian Recension!

his textual theories became controversial, von Soden's text is a treasure of information.[16]

Since 1898, pocket editions of Greek NT began under the editorship of Eberhard Nestle. Recently, a completely revised twenty-sixth edition appeared in 1979 under the supervision of K. Aland. In this edition, dual consideration is given to the geographical location of the text (e.g., Alexandria) as well as the reading that best explains the others (called the local-genealogical method).[17] This latter genealogical consideration is a modification of the Westcott-Hort local text theory.

In 1966 the United Bible Societies (New York; London; Stuttgart) published a new handbook edition edited by K. Aland, M. Black, B. Metzger, A. Wikgren, and later C. Martini. This text has been prepared especially for Bible translators and therefore only variants that make a difference in translation are included. The third edition of this text (1975, 1983), except for disagreements on punctuation, is almost identical in wording with the Nestle-Aland, twenty-sixth edition. A commentary on each textual variant of the United Bible Societies' Greek text was written by B. Metzger (1973).

Despite the advances beyond Westcott and Hort, the texts of Nestle-Aland (26th ed.) or the United Bible Societies (3rd ed.) differ much more with the "received text" than with that of Westcott and Hort. The contribution of these Cambridge scholars appears to be enduring.

TEXTUAL CRITICISM OF THE NT

What principles are employed in deciding between variant readings of a text? What criteria are used for detecting the earliest possible reading? These questions are the concern of the science of textual criticism. We will now give a basic survey of the principles employed in this method of inquiry.[18]

One criterion above others affects the scholar's choice at every point of variation: *the variation that best explains the origin of all the others is most*

16. Fee, "Textual Criticism" 147; Aland detects too many deficiencies in the text of von Soden to find much commendable in it, Aland, *TNT* 22–23.

17. E. Nestle, K. Aland, et al., *Novum Testamentum Graece*, 26th ed. (Stuttgart: Deutsche Bibelstiftung, 1979) 43. This method is also called by some the "eclectic method" because it presupposes a reconstruction of the earliest and best text variant by variant according to critical judgment without favoring any particular text type as preserving the original. See Fee, "Textual Criticism" 150; Aland, *TNT* 20–22, 31–36.

18. For a more complete discussion, see Aland, *TNT* 275–311; Fee, "Textual Criticism" 148–53; Finegan, *Encountering* 54–75; Greenlee, *INT* 96–134; Metzger, *TNT* 149–246. Several key points from Fee's article have been utilized in this section.

likely to be the original. In order to "best explain the origin of the others," there are two factors that scholars must consider: external evidence (the manuscripts themselves) and internal evidence (the authors or the scribes).

Concerning external evidence, one must first weigh the manuscript evidence supporting each variant. The age, quality, and geographical distribution of the witnesses and their text supporting each variant are important considerations for isolating the best readings and their documents.

Internal evidence is of two types: (1) *transcriptional probability*, which deals with what kind of error or change the scribe probably made; and (2) *intrinsic probability* or what the author was most likely to have written. The detection of scribal errors (1) is based on inductive reasoning. For example, it is usually true that the *more difficult reading* is probably the original one, because it was the tendency of scribes to make the text easier to read. Also, the shorter reading is often the original one, because scribes tended to add to the text (although the scribes sometimes made omissions). Finally, a textual variant differing from quoted or parallel material is almost always original, since the scribes tended to harmonize.[19] Detecting what the author most likely would have written (2) is the most subjective aspect of textual criticism. It has to deal with the style, vocabulary, and ideas of the author as they are found elsewhere and in the immediate context. (This aspect of internal evidence is given special weight by G. D. Kilpatrick.)

Not all the criteria mentioned above are equally applicable in every case, sometimes they even oppose one another. In such stalemates the text critic is usually forced back to the external evidence (the manuscripts themselves) as final arbiter. It is significant that for most scholars over 90% of all the variations of the NT text are resolved, since the variant that best explains the origin of the others is also supported by the earliest and best witnesses.[20]

19. Fee, "Textual Criticism" 149; Metzger, *TNT* 197–98.
20. Fee, "Textual Criticism" 150.

Part II
Methods for Interpreting the New Testament

5

The Historical Methods of Criticism

Why does a "popular" collection of writings require such careful interpretation to be understood properly? This or a similar question might be raised by the reader after noting the technical title of this chapter. But this predicament of interpreting popular writings is not restricted to the NT. It also applies to the United States Constitution. To use a simple analogy: both the NT collection and the U.S. Constitution were written for the benefit of "common people," and both require careful interpretation to be understood properly.

The reasons for the predicament in interpretation are analogous for the two documents. First, both are a diverse collection of documents. The NT contains twenty-seven books. The Constitution contains seven Articles and twenty-six Amendments. Second, both are products of a lengthy historical process. The NT includes over a century of tradition and composition (AD 30–140). The Constitution and its Amendments represent almost two centuries of tradition (1789 to present). Third, both contain technical language belonging to specific communities: the religious communities that produced the NT, and the legislative bodies that produced the Constitution.

The above reasons also substantiate two key points: (1) both the NT and the U.S. Constitution are difficult documents to read, and (2) a proper understanding of them necessitates the assistance of specialists. Despite the above difficulties and necessities, there are some positive aspects of the analogy: both sets of writings were compiled for the benefit of nonspecialists who are encouraged to be familiar with their contents. Therefore, these documents of the common people which require such careful interpretation were also intended to be understood by common people.

TWO PRESUPPOSITIONS

The NT methods that we are concerned with presuppose two kinds of historical distance: (a) that which exists between the modern reader and the ancient texts, and (b) that which exists between the time of writing and the events narrated.

Modern Reader and Ancient Texts

The first type of distance concerns the great span of about 2000 years that exists between us and the NT. On the one hand, there is our situation: we live in a modern industrial age of computer technology and space exploration. On the other hand, there is the NT period: it was a feudalistic agricultural age of primitive machinery and slow travel. Clearly, these are two different worlds, separated historically by almost two millennia. The methods that we are about to discuss presuppose this historical distance. It is a basic premise of all objective historical study. It is also a necessary prerequisite for interpreting ancient texts. Once the historical gap is recognized, steps can be taken to establish a common ground of understanding between the modern reader and ancient documents. For example, in order to become acquainted with a foreign culture, one must also be able to understand the differences between one's own and that foreign culture. This understanding of historical and cultural differences is presupposed in the historical methods of literary criticism. With this historical premise in view, we approach the NT in a manner different from that of reading the daily newspaper.

The Writings and the Events

Another type of distance which these literary methods presuppose is that between the time of writing (AD 65–150) and the time of the events narrated (e.g., life of Jesus and the apostles, AD 30–62). This is especially the case between the time when the four Gospels were written (AD 65–95) and the date of the ministry of Jesus (AD 30–33).[1]

Why would historical distance imply a change in viewpoint from the time of Jesus to the time of the Evangelists? Did not the ancient person have a greater propensity to preserve and transmit old traditions than we do today? Were not some of the words and deeds of Jesus committed to writing during his lifetime? The historical gap of thirty-five to sixty-five years includes many social, cultural, and political changes. For example, the destruction of both the city of Jerusalem and its temple by the Romans in AD 70 is only one event that produced diverse changes in Palestinian Judaism, Diaspora Judaism, and early Christianity. In reply to the second question, people of the ancient world did devote themselves to preserving and transmitting old traditions, but subtle and some-

1. See chart on facing page.

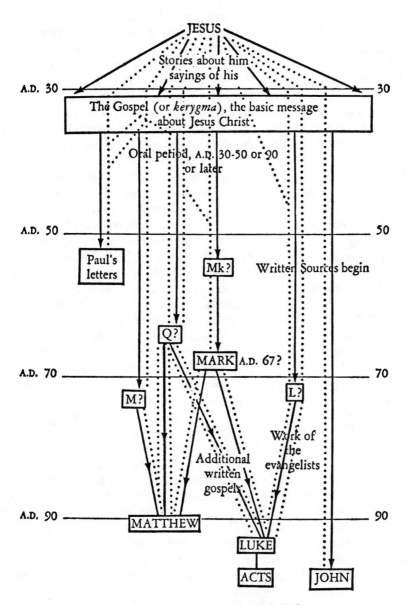

THE GROWTH OF THE GOSPELS

Growth of the Gospels. *J. H. Reumann,* Jesus in the
Church's Gospels. © *1968 by Fortress Press.* Used with
permission.

times substantial changes took place in the process. Some changes took place to assist in memorization (e.g., mnemonics). The transmitters of the traditions would also adapt the materials for their respective audiences or revise them when combined with other traditions. As a result, different versions of the same tradition appeared.

Several reasons can be given in response to the third question: were there not early written documents about Jesus that would minimize any different perspectives between Jesus and the Evangelists? First, we have no evidence that material about Jesus was committed to writing during his lifetime. It is clear from the Gospels that Jesus did not lecture in a classroom with students taking class notes. He taught where the common people of the Jews worked and gathered (e.g., marketplace, synagogue).

Although many of Jesus' disciples were probably literate, it is uncertain if any were skilled in writing documents for use in their communities (cf. Acts 4:13). Most of Jesus' disciples worked in manual trades, like fishing. Second, immediately after Jesus' death, his followers did not devote themselves to writing his "memoirs," but rather to preaching the gospel. Evangelization was undertaken with a special sense of urgency, because they believed that Jesus would soon return as a conquering Messiah and divine judge. Third, the writing down of oral traditions about Jesus became a great necessity only after the death of most of the eyewitnesses. Second and third generation Christians, who were probably confronted by diverse teachings, concerned about their heritage, and convinced that the return of Jesus would be delayed, were the ones who devoted themselves to the task of writing for posterity. These later compilers and writers had conceptions and perceptions that differed from their predecessors. Ancient documents that evidence a similar distance between the historical person and its author include: the *Dialogues* of Plato, which eulogize the life and teachings of Socrates, and the laudatory accounts of Apollonius of Tyana by Philostratus, a later disciple. Both documents are attempts by students to maximize the positive and minimize the negative features of their teachers. Socrates and Apollonius would have told their own stories differently. The above are some reasons why the writings of the Gospel tradition were relatively late and why they would reflect the special concerns of later generations.

The problem of historical distance between (a) us and the ancient text and (b) the time of writing and the events narrated is a working presupposition of the historical methods of literary criticism. In a similar manner the science of textual criticism presupposed the historical distance between our Greek copies of the NT (e.g., 2nd to 4th cent.) and the autographs (1st cent.). Awareness of these historical gaps should underscore the importance of carefully considering the differences between the two time periods, before drawing conclusions about the common features.

COMMON OBJECTIVES AND CONCLUSIONS

The historical methods of literary criticism trace and define the long process involved in the collection and composition of the NT writings. It is their common objective to investigate the three periods of: oral transmission, the transcription of oral traditions, and their incorporation into complete narrative books. Although these methods concentrate on the four Gospels and Acts, they also apply to the study of the remaining NT books. These historical methods seek to reveal the historical dynamics at work in the production of ancient texts.

The historical methods of criticism enable us to view the NT books as intricate works with ingenious literary patterns and highly developed interpretations.[2] This perception of the NT is a modern discovery of the past two centuries. Before this period of modern research, the Gospels were often viewed as a simple collection thrown together and told in a very straightforward manner. The story of Jesus, for example, was viewed as a verbatim report of the busy itinerary of Jesus narrated in a precise chronological order. The specific problems with this view will be discussed under form and redaction criticism.

Modern research, however, draws certain historical conclusions about the NT books.[3] First, they are not merely a collection of factual reports, but reflect various sociological and religious concerns, different contexts, and different literary purposes. Second, the religious topics discussed in the text are not precise images of reality, but are reflections of the faith and life of early communities and their authors. Third, all historical reconstructions of modern research are subject to refinement and revision. Because every age has its biases, limited knowledge, and perspectives, one should avoid all cultural chauvinism. Uncritical loyalty to either our own modern age or the ancient culture of the NT hinders the interpretive process.

THREE METHODS OF CRITICISM

The three methods of criticism to be examined in this chapter are: source, form, and redaction criticism. *Source criticism* seeks to detect the primary documents used in a book. In the nineteenth century it became a well-defined method. *Form criticism* determines the original setting and function of the traditional forms used in a book. It was applied to the

2. Old and new perceptions of the NT are from D. Via in foreword to E. McKnight, *What Is Form Criticism?* (Philadelphia: Fortress, 1969) v.

3. Three points on modern biblical research are derived from Hayes and Holladay, *Biblical Exegesis* 116–17.

Bible in the first decades of our century. *Redaction criticism* underscores the final writer's editing of traditional materials for his own readers. Shortly after World War II, it was employed in NT research. Prior to their use in interpreting Scripture, these critical tools were employed in the study of classical Greek and early Western literature. Although they are technical approaches to the ancient texts, they can be understood and employed by the nonspecialists.

Before approaching a text with the historical methods it is important to be familiar with the literary and historical context of the passage to be studied. First, consult and use modern English translations that are based on the most reliable Greek manuscripts (e.g., RSV, NAB, NEB, NIV, NJB). Second, read the passage carefully. Be alert to the literary relationship of your passage to its immediate context (e.g., paragraph, chapter, section) and the book in which it occurs. Familiarity with the general outline of the book is helpful. Third, get acquainted with the names, places, and concepts in the passage. This can be done by consulting a current Bible encyclopedia, such as: *IDB, IDBSupp, HDB,* or *ZPE.* Fourth, outline the passage to discover and highlight the major points (i.e., grammatical analysis). Fifth, check your research by consulting a Bible commentary on the NT passage, for example: HNTC, AB, Hermeneia, NCBC, NIC, WBC.[4] This process of understanding the text need not be followed in the exact order listed above, nor does it have to be a long, time-consuming project since you will learn more as you utilize the historical methods of literary criticism.

Source Criticism

The method of source criticism seeks to determine the following in a written document: (1) the presence and meaning of sources, and (2) the author's use of these sources.[5]

The Importance of Detecting Sources
Knowing sources is especially important if one encounters startling in-

---

4. See our *Abbreviations and Select Bibliography* for further information on the above works. For specific books on tools for NT study, see J. A. Fitzmyer, *An Introductory Bibliography for the Study of Scripture,* rev. ed. (Rome: Biblical Institute Press, 1981); R. P. Martin, *NT Books for Pastor and Teacher* (Philadelphia: Westminster, 1984); D. M. Scholer, *A Basic Bibliographic Guide for NT Exegesis,* 2nd ed. (Grand Rapids: Eerdmans, 1973). On the practice of NT interpretation (Gk. *exegesis*), see G. D. Fee, *NT Exegesis, A Handbook for Students and Pastors* (Philadelphia: Westminster, 1983); W. G. Kümmel, *Exegetical Method: A Student's Handbook,* rev. ed. (New York: Seabury, 1981); Hayes and Holladay, *Biblical Exegesis.*
5. For introductions to source criticism, see Harrington, *IntNT* 56–57; D. Wenham, "Source Criticism," Marshall, *NTI* 139–52.

formation or conflicting accounts. Consider the following scenario. You are driving home from school and suddenly hear on the radio that the Soviet Union has invaded Iran! Certainly you would want to know the source of information for such startling news—especially if you are of a draftable age! When you arrive home to view the evening news on television, you hear that the Soviet Union has not invaded Iran. A Marxist revolution had successfully taken place within that nation! Certainly you would be interested in knowing the sources behind these two conflicting reports. You would either want to learn more about the event, or weigh carefully the credibility of the sources used (e.g., foreign correspondents, Pentagon officials). Startling information and conflicting reports are at least two reasons why it is important to have access to primary sources.

The above scenario is similar to the situation often faced in NT studies. For example, in the narrative of Mt 8:28–34, there are *two* demoniacs from *Gadarenes* but in Mk 5:1–20 there is only *one* demoniac from *Gerasenes* mentioned. Do the two accounts presuppose two different sources or two variations of the same source? The issues raised by these two passages are part of the concern of source criticism.

The Basic Assumptions

Source criticism assumes that the NT authors used written as well as oral traditions in the production of their works.[6] In the Gospels, the gap of thirty-five to sixty-five years from the time of the events to the time of their written narration lends good support to this assumption. Because of this presupposition, source criticism excludes from its approach two extreme positions. First, is the view that the events narrated in the NT are complete literary fabrications of the author. Many of them correspond too closely to what we know from archaeology and other ancient literature to support this view. Second is the view that the NT writers were merely "stenographers for God" who wrote at his dictation. Such an extreme confessional position would require a much greater degree of uniformity in content, style, and purpose than exists in the NT. Source criticism presupposes that the NT was the product of a human process of collecting

6. For background on the history of source-critical research, note the following scholars with dates of major works reflecting this concern: OT source criticism (mainly the Pentateuch) had a long history originating in the late 17th cent. with R. Simon and later developed by, e.g., A. Kuenen (1860), K. H. Graf (1860) and J. Wellhausen (1870). Scholars of early European history also employed the method, e.g., B. G. Niebuhr (1811), L. von Ranke (1824). NT source criticism focused on the Synoptic Gospels, beginning with, e.g., J. J. Griesbach (1776), J. G. Eichhorn (1795), K. Lachmann (1835) and developed further by, e.g., H. J. Holtzmann (1863), B. H. Streeter (1924), W. R. Farmer (1964). For more discussion, see Kümmel, *NT:HIP* 74–88, 144–61, 325–41.

oral and written traditions and committing them to writing. This assumption does not conflict with any view that is historically informed.

The NT writers made use of written traditions. This is evident, first of all, by the explicit use of passages from the Jewish Scriptures, especially the Septuagint (LXX). There are approximately 1600 citations in the NT of over 1200 different passages from the Jewish Scriptures, as well as several thousand allusions. The author of Luke–Acts also mentions written accounts of Jesus, which he probably utilized in his own work (Lk 1:1–4). Unfortunately he does not tell us when he is relying on these written Jesus traditions.

How to Detect Sources

How does one detect the presence of sources in the NT writings? Sometimes explicit reference is made of a source before it is cited. This is especially the case with citations of the Jewish Scriptures. They are often preceded by such formulas as: "it is written" (Rom 1:17) or "as Isaiah predicted" (Rom 9:29). There are over 200 instances of OT citations introduced by these formulas.[7] Another example of the explicit use of a written document is stated by the Apostle Paul in his first letter to the Corinthian church: "now concerning the matters about which you wrote" (1 Cor 7:1). A final example is to introduce a source with a stereotyped phrase designating it as traditional material: "for I delivered to you . . . what I also received" (1 Cor 15:3). It is unclear in this last instance whether the author is using an oral or a written source.

When the use of sources is not mentioned, the task becomes more difficult, but source criticism has provided us with internal criteria for detecting them. They include: (a) the displacement or discontinuity of thought and literary style; and (b) the use of unusual vocabulary that is uncharacteristic of the rest of the book. Other criteria will be introduced in our comparisons of Matthew, Mark, and Luke.

An example can be given: 2 Cor 6:1–7:4. If one carefully reads the entire passage, the contents of 6:14–7:1 seem to interrupt the thought pattern. The topic of 6:1–13 (an appeal for openness) abruptly changes at v 14 and does not resume until 7:2. The vocabulary and style of 6:14–7:1 are also different from the rest of 2 Corinthians, specifically, and Paul's other letters, generally. The contents of this displaced passage are similar to teaching found in the Dead Sea Scrolls of Qumran, and some even speculate that it was an Essene document revised by Christians. As we

---

7. H. M. Shires, *Finding the Old Testament in the New* (Philadelphia: Westminster 1974) 15. See especially indexes of quotations, allusions, and parallels in K. Aland et al., *The Greek New Testament*, corrected 3rd. ed. (New York/Stuttgart: United Bible Societies, 1983) 897–911.

have seen, displacement of thought and the presence of unusual vocabulary are two important internal criteria for detecting sources, especially when the writer of a work does not identify them. Other significant examples will be given to better understand the methodology of source criticism.

A Case Study in Mark
Let us apply these principles of source criticism to a passage in the Gospel of Mark (the second Gospel) 1:1-3:

> The beginning of the gospel of Jesus Christ, the Son of God. As it is written in Isaiah the prophet, "Behold, I send my messenger before your face, who shall prepare your way; the voice of one crying in the wilderness: Prepare the way of the Lord, make his paths straight."

The source used by Mark in this passage is clearly introduced by the stereotypical formula: "as it is written in Isaiah the prophet." Most modern translations also indent the quotation. However, a difficulty arises in attempting to identify precisely what source or sources are used. The passage cited in Mark is from Isa 40:3, probably in a Greek translation of the Hebrew Bible:[8]

> The voice of one crying in the wilderness: Prepare the way of the Lord, make *our God's* path straight.

With only one modification (italicized) Mark makes use of the passage of Isa 40:3 in a Greek translation similar to the one from which I have translated, i.e., the Septuagint. But the Isaiah 40 passage only accounts for the second part of the quotation. No where in Isaiah 40 or in the entire book of Isaiah (1–66) is there found the first part of Mark's quote attributed to Isaiah! It is, however, found in Mal 3:1, and follows closely a Hebrew text similar to the one from which our OT is translated:[9]

> Behold, I send my messenger before *my face* to prepare the way.

Some of the wording in Mark's quote may have been influenced by a Greek translation of Ex 23:30 since part of it agrees verbatim with Mark: "behold, I send my messenger before your face."[10] But the quote in Mk 1:2, ascribed to Isaiah, is clearly referring to the passage of Mal 3:1.

8. Our translation of the LXX is based on: A. Rahlfs, ed., *Septuaginta*, 9th ed. (Stuttgart, 1905) 2:619.
9. Our translation of the Hebrew Bible is based on K. Elliger and W. Rudolph, eds., *Biblia Hebraica Stuttgartensia* (Stuttgart: Deutsche Bibelstiftung, 1967-77) 1084.
10. Translation based on Rahlfs, ed., *Septuaginta*, 9th ed.

Matt. 3:1–3	Mark 1:1–3	Luke 3:1–6
	[1] The beginning of the gospel of Jesus Christ, the Son of God.	
[1] In those days		[1] In the fifteenth year of the reign of Tiberius Caesar, Pontius Pilate being governor of Judea, and Herod being tetrarch of Galilee, and his brother Philip tetrarch of the region of Ituraea and Trachonitis and Lysanias tetrarch of Abilene, [2] in the high-priesthood of Annas and Caiaphas, the word of God came to
came John the Baptist, preaching in the wilderness of Judea		John the son of Zechariah in the wilderness;[3] and he went into all the region about the Jordan, preaching a baptism of repentance for the forgiveness
[2] "Repent, for the kingdom of heaven is at hand." [3] For this is he who was spoken of by the prophet Isaiah when he said,	[2] As it is written in Isaiah the prophet, "Behold, I send my messenger before thy face, who shall prepare thy way;	of sins. [4] As it is written in the book of the words of Isaiah the prophet,
"The voice of one crying in the wilderness: Prepare the way of the Lord, make his paths straight."	[3]"The voice of one crying in the wilderness: Prepare the way of the Lord, make his paths straight—"	"The voice of one crying in the wilderness Prepare the way of the Lord, make his paths straight." [5] Every valley shall be filled, and every mountain and hill shall be brought low, and the crooked shall be made straight, and the rough ways shall be made smooth; [6] and all flesh shall see the salvation of God."

The Synoptic Problem

Now compare Mark with the Gospels of Matthew and Luke.[11] All three are called the "Synoptic" Gospels because they share a "common vision"

11. The following work has been used in our comparison: Throckmorton, *Gospel Parallels*; Aland, *Synopsis*; see also R. J. Swanson, *The Horizontal Line Synopsis of the Gospels* (Dillsboro, N.C.: Western North Carolina Press, 1975).

of the life of Jesus. Note that all three accounts deal with John the Baptist, and both Matthew and Luke cite the passage from Isa 40 found in Mark: "The voice of one crying in the wilderness." But what happened to that problematic Malachi passage found in Mk 1:2? It is omitted in the accounts of both Matthew and Luke. These two Gospels use the Malachi passage in another context, perhaps influenced by another source (Mt 11:10; Lk 7:27 = Q). It almost appears that Matthew and Luke are improving on Mark at this point.

We should also note how Matthew and Luke employ the Isaiah 40 quote differently from Mark, by observing what precedes and follows in all three Gospel accounts. First, neither Matthew nor Luke employ Mark's superscription, "The beginning of the gospel." The basic reason for this omission is because Matthew and Luke begin their gospels ("good news announcements") not with the account of John (cf. Mk), but with the birth and infancy narratives. Second, Luke begins his account of John with a chronological notation (Lk 3:1-2) endeavoring to link his narrative with secular history, a distinctive concern of Luke. Third, both Matthew and Luke felt it necessary to first acquaint their readers with the message of John's preaching before the Isaiah quote, whereas Mark includes this after it (Mk 1:4). Fourth, although Luke retains Mark's phrasing of John's message, "preaching a baptism of repentance for the forgiveness of sins," Matthew changed this to: "Repent, for the kingdom of heaven is at hand," which is a special emphasis in his Gospel (e.g., Mt 3:11; 4:17). Fifth, only Luke expands upon the Isaiah quote, citing 40:3-5 (LXX with two words and a phrase omitted from 40:4-5). This was done especially to highlight the statement, "all flesh shall see God's salvation," which is another distinctive emphasis of the author of Luke–Acts (e.g., Lk 2:30; Acts 28:28). The above five points show how differently the Isaiah 40 passage in Mark is employed by Matthew and Luke.

It also appears from our comparison that Matthew and Luke are dependent on Mark. There are several reasons to support this observation, and problems are raised by resisting it. First, we saw that both Matthew and Luke, possibly influenced by a common source, omit the problematic Malachi passage that Mark had ascribed to Isaiah (Mk 1:2). Second, Matthew and Luke either arranged in different order or revised material they seem to have gotten from Mark (e.g., the content of John's preaching). Third, there is an example of one Gospel apparently expanding upon the quotation originally cited in Mark: Luke's expansion of the Isaiah 40 quote in Mark. The theory of the primacy of Mark appears to provide the best explanation of the evidence as we have shown by the three observations listed above.

There are more problems raised by resisting the conclusion of Markan primacy.[12] First, why would anyone want to abbreviate or conflate Matthew and Luke to produce a Gospel like Mark? Second, why would Mark have omitted so much material from Matthew and Luke? For example, why would Mark have ignored the infancy stories and post-resurrection appearances? Third, what kind of author and religious teacher would Mark have been if he really had copies of Matthew and Luke but omitted so much from them? Should he not be compared to the reductionist Marcion or the reactionary Tatian? (For discussion of Marcion and Tatian, see Appendix A.) The above problems are raised to support the view that Mark was the first Gospel and that Matthew and Luke used Mark independently. This hypothesis, for a majority of scholars, best explains the phenomena of similarities and differences between Matthew, Mark, and Luke (i.e., the Synoptic Problem).

There is also a second problem encountered in the Synoptic Gospels. This concerns the close similarities between Matthew and Luke that are not found in Mark. Let us look again at our Synoptic comparison. After following Mark's account of John the Baptist and his ministry, both Matthew and Luke add an account that it is not found in Mark:

Matt. 3:7–10	Luke 3:7–9
[7] But when he saw many of the Pharisees and Sadducees coming for baptism, he said to them, "You brood of vipers! Who warned you to flee from the wrath to come? [8] Bear fruit that befits repentance, [9] and do not presume to say to yourselves, 'We have Abraham as our father'; for I tell you, God is able from these stones to raise up children to Abraham. [10] Even now the axe is laid to the root of the trees; every tree therefore that does not bear good fruit is cut down and thrown into the fire."	[7] He said therefore to the multitudes that came out to be baptized by him, "You brood of vipers! Who warned you to flee from the wrath to come? [8] Bear fruits that befit repentance, and do not begin to say to yourselves, 'We have Abraham as our father'; for I tell you, God is able from these stones to raise up children to Abraham. [9] Even now the axe is laid to the root of the trees; every tree therefore that does not bear good fruit is cut down and thrown into the fire."

12. The three points concerning Markan priority are from Harrington, *IntNT* 61–62. For further arguments, see J. A. Fitzmyer, "The Priority of Mark and the 'Q' Source in Luke," *Jesus and Man's Hope* [=*JMH*], 2 vols., ed. D. Miller (Pittsburgh: Pickwick, 1970) 1:131–70; Kümmel, *Introduction* 35–63; B. H. Streeter, *The Four Gospels* (London: Macmillan, 1924); G. M. Styler, "The Priority of Mark," *The Birth of the NT*, ed. C. F. D. Moule (New York: Harper & Row, 1962) 223–32. Note, however, the following works which dispute Markan priority and favor Markan dependency on both Matthew and Luke (i.e., Griesbach hypothesis): D. L. Dungan, "Mark—The Abridgement of Matthew and Luke," *JMH* 1:51–97; Farmer, *Synoptic Problem*; idem, "Modern Developments of Griesbach's Hypothesis," *NTS* 23 (1976–77) 275–95; T. R. Longstaff, *Evidence of Conflation in Mark?* (Missoula, Mont.: Scholars Press, 1977).

Synoptic Parallels

	MATTHEW	MARK	LUKE	JOHN
Preaching of John the Baptist	3:1-2	1:1-8	3:1-20	1:19-28
Baptism of Jesus	3:13-17	1:9-11	3:21-22	
Temptation	4:1-11	1:12-13	4:1-13	
Beginning of Galilee ministry	4:12-17	1:14-15	4:14-15	
Rejection at Nazareth	13:53-58	6:1-6	4:16-30	
Healing of Peter's mother-in-law and others	8:14-17	1:29-34	4:38-41	
Cleansing of a leper	8:1-4	1:40-45	5:12-16	
Healing of the paralytic	9:1-8	2:1-12	5:17-26	
Calling of Levi	9:9-13	2:13-17	5:27-32	
Fasting	9:14-17	2:18-22	5:33-39	
Grain plucking on the Sabbath	12:1-8	2:23-28	6:1-5	
Healing of withered hand	12:9-14	3:1-6	6:6-11	
Choosing of the Twelve	10:1-4	3:13-19	6:12-16	
Parable of the sower	13:1-23	4:1-20	8:4-15	
Jesus' true family	12:46-50	3:31-35	8:19-21	
Calming of a storm	8:23-27	4:35-41	8:22-25	
Healing of demon-possessed man	8:28-34	5:1-20	8:26-39	
Jairus's daughter and woman with hemorrhage	9:18-26	5:21-43	8:40-56	
The Twelve sent out	10:5-15	6:7-13	9:1-6	
John the Baptist beheaded	14:1-12	6:14-29	9:7-9	
Five thousand fed	14:13-21	6:30-44	9:10-17	6:1-14
Peter's confession	16:13-19	8:27-29	9:18-20	
Jesus' foretelling of death and resurrection	16:20-28	8:30-9:1	9:21-27	
Transfiguration	17:1-8	9:2-8	9:28-36	
Casting out of unclean spirit	17:14-18	9:14-27	9:37-43	
Second Prediction of death and resurrection	17:22-23	9:30-32	9:43-45	
"Who is greatest?"	18:1-5	9:33-37	9:46-48	
Jesus and Beelzebub	12:22-30	3:20-27	11:14-23	
Demand for a sign	12:38-42	8:11-12	11:29-32	
Parable of the mustard seed	13:31-32	4:30-32	13:18-19	
Blessing of little children	19:13-15	10:13-16	18:15-17	
Rich young ruler	19:16-30	10:17-31	18:18-30	
Third Prediction of death and resurrection	20:17-19	10:32-34	18:31-34	
Healing of blind Bartimaeus (and another)	20:29-34	10:46-52	18:35-42	
THE FINAL WEEK				
Triumphal entry into Jerusalem	21:1-11	11:1-11	19:28-40	12:12-19
"By what authority . . .?"	21:23-27	11:27-33	20:1-8	
Vineyard and tenants	21:33-46	12:1-12	20:9-19	
"Render to Caesar"	22:15-22	12:13-17	20:20-26	
The resurrection	22:23-33	12:18-27	20:27-40	
David's son	22:41-46	12:35-37	20:41-44	
Sermon on the last days	24:1-36	13:1-32	21:5-33	
Passover plot	26:1-5, 14-16	14:1-2, 10-11	22:1-6	
Preparing of Passover	26:17-20	14:12-17	22:7-14	
Foretelling of betrayal	26:21-25	14:18-21	22:21-23	13:21-30
The Lord's Supper	26:26-30	14:22-26	22:14-20	
Prediction of Peter's denial	26:31-35	14:27-31	22:31-34	13:36-38
Gethsemane	26:36-46	14:32-42	22:39-46	
Arrest of Jesus	26:47-56	14:43-50	22:47-53	18:3-12
Sanhedrin (Peter's denial)	26:57-75	14:53-72	22:54-71	18:13-27
Jesus before Pilate	27:1, 2, 11-14	15:1-5	23:1-5	18:28-38
Sentencing of Jesus	27:15-26	15:6-15	23:17-25	18:39-19:16
Crucifixion, Death, Burial	27:32-61	15:21-47	23:26-56	19:27-42
Resurrection	28:1-8	16:1-8	24:1-12	20:1-10

Despite the differences in the opening sentence between Mt 3:7 and Lk 3:7, the rest of the two passages are verbatim in the Greek, with the exception of one word and one case ending (cf. Gk., *doxēte* and *arxēsthe, axion* and *axious,* Luke also adds *kai*). These two passages show such close verbal similarities that it is probable that a common written source is used here. This parallel is only one of many (e.g., Mt 6:24/Lk 16:13; Mt 23:37–39/Lk 13:34–35). Often this common non-Markan material is arranged in different places by Matthew and Luke, indicating that both utilized this source independently. This common written source, not found in Mark, is often called "Q" from the German *Quelle,* meaning "source." It is also called the Synoptic Sayings Source, because it contains mostly sayings of Jesus, rather than stories about him.[13]

The theory that Matthew and Luke used both Mark and Q as sources is called the Two Document Hypothesis. In addition to these two written documents, two oral (or written) sources have been postulated to explain the presence of distinctive Matthean and Lukan material. "M" refers to that material only found in Matthew, such as: the Coming of the Magi, the Slaughter of Children by Herod, and the Flight and Return of Jesus and his Family from Egypt. "L" refers to that material only found in Luke, such as: the Birth of John the Baptist, Mary's Magnificat, the Visit of the Shepherds, and the Presentation of the Infant Jesus in the Temple. Unlike Mark and Q, it is difficult to determine if M and L are: (a) oral or written sources, or (b) the literary creations of the authors. The documentary hypothesis we have outlined above has been followed by a majority of biblical scholars since the beginning of this century.

One problem raised by the Two Document Hypothesis concerns the minor agreements of Matthew and Luke against Mark.[14] If they used Mark independently, they really should not agree in their modifications of it. Four responses to this problem can be given. First, on certain topics, Q and Mark may have overlapped and here Matthew and Luke may have relied on Q instead of Mark. Second, Matthew and Luke may have had access to a slightly different edition of Mark from what we have. Third,

13. See B. W. Bacon, "The Nature and Design of Q, The Second Synoptic Source," *HibJ* 22 (1923/24) 674–88; R. A. Edwards, *A Concordance to Q* (Missoula, Mont.: Scholars Press, 1975) and *A Theology of Q* (Philadelphia: Fortress, 1976); J. M. Robinson and H. Koester, *Trajectories Through Early Christianity* (Philadelphia: Fortress, 1971) 71–113, 158–204; V. Taylor, "The Order of Q," *JTS* 4 (1953) 27–31; N. Turner, "Q in Recent Thought," *ExpT* 80 (1969) 324–28; J. S. Kloppenborg, *Q Parallels. Synopsis, Critical Notes, & Concordance* (Sonoma, Calif.: Polebridge, 1988).

14. F. Neirynck, *Minor Agreements of Matthew and Luke Against Mark with a Cumulative List* (Gembloux: Duculot, 1974); R. T. Simpson, "The Major Agreements of Matthew and Luke against Mark," *NTS* 12 (1965–66) 273–84. Problems and responses from Harrington, *IntNT* 63.

those who copied the early Greek manuscripts may have harmonized the Matthean and Lukan texts. Fourth, just as two competent teachers independently reading a student's paper will naturally introduce many of the same corrections, so Matthew and Luke may have independently yet harmoniously corrected Mark's rough Greek style. The Two Document explanation of the Synoptic Problem is only a hypothesis, although it is a plausible explanation of the facts and explains more evidence than any alternate theories.

Source Criticism: Conclusions
Source criticism attempts to do three things: (1) detect the presence of a source, (2) determine the contents of the source, and (3) understand how the source was used. Source criticism seeks to deal seriously with the NT as a historical document. Its importance is obvious to anyone who is confronted with startling or conflicting information. When the reader of the NT encounters a problem passage or two conflicting accounts of one event, the quest for sources can often help clarify or explain the problem. Although most of our examples for source criticism have been taken from the Synoptic Gospels, this method is used throughout the NT. The relationship of 2 Peter and Jude, for example, has raised several source-critical questions not unlike those of the Synoptic Problem. The usefulness of source criticism is augmented by the historical methods of form and redaction criticism.

Form Criticism

Form criticism concentrates on the traditional units that originated in an oral or preliterary setting. It attempts to get behind the written sources to the oral period before the literary forms were put into writing. Before discussing form criticism, the nature and significance of literary forms will be examined.

Literary forms are various modes of communication available to the writer for his readers.[15] There are numerous assortments of literary forms in every culture, ancient and modern. Note the diverse examples of literary forms in our culture: a personal letter, an obituary notice in the newspaper, a school drama script, and the love poem on a greeting card. All of the above examples are modes of communication used by writers for various audiences. As we see, literary forms are an important and pervasive phenomenon in human culture.

15. The NT literary forms will be classified under the following categories: (1) Sayings (i.e., direct discourse, e.g., proverbs, parables) and (2) Stories (i.e., indirect discourse, e.g., miracle accounts, legends). See Bultmann, *Synoptic Tradition* vii–viii, 11.

Basic Features of Literary Forms

There are at least five basic characteristics of literary forms in culture which are underscored in form criticism. First, all literary forms have fixed patterns. In our culture, for example, even a personal letter will usually contain: (a) an indication of place and date, (b) the name of the recipient (e.g., Dear Aunt Sue), (c) an apology for not writing sooner, and (d) a statement of the writer's health and expression of hope that the recipient is in good health. Giving another example, newspaper obituary notices generally contain the following pattern: (a) name of the deceased, (b) brief description of life and career, (c) mention of surviving relatives, (d) age, (e) date of death, and (f) proposed funeral arrangements. Every culture has fixed patterns for its literary forms of communication.

Second, literary forms change in history. For example, a personal letter written in Egypt around the second century BC has features different from those of our own time and culture:

Greeting: Isias to her brother Hephaestion, greeting.

Thanksgiving: If you are well and other things are going right, it would accord with the prayer which I make continually to the gods. I myself and the child and all the household are in good health and think of you always.

Body: When I received your letter from Horus, in which you announce that you are in detention in the Sarapeum at Memphis . . . when all the others who had been secluded there have come, I am ill-pleased. . . . please return to the city, if nothing more pressing holds you back. . . .

Closing: Goodbye. Year 2, Epeiph 30. (Addressed) To Hephaestion.

Although the basic pattern of a greeting, body, and closing are similar to our modern letter form, its basic arrangement and formal contents are different. The above features are typical of most personal letters written in the ancient Hellenistic world.[16]

Historians of literature, by studying the external and formal features (as well as language and style) can arrive at a relatively accurate date and location for the above literary forms, even when such information is not given. Sensitivity to the changes of a literary form in the history of a culture is an important concern in form criticism.

A third characteristic of literary forms is that each form has a unique linguistic intent associated with it. For example, personal letters are intended to renew acquaintances, obituary notices serve as memorial notices for the deceased and family, dramatic plays entertain, and love poems endear one individual to another.

---

16. For an additional example of an obituary's form see G. Lohfink, *The Bible, Now I Get It! A Form-Criticism Handbook* (New York: Doubleday, 1979) 19.

Although there may be exceptions to the above generalizations, every literary form has a specific intent. This linguistic intent or purpose is also fully understood by the specific audience addressed. The intent of a literary form is usually so familiar to the audience or readers that it signals certain expectations in them. We are so familiar with our literary forms, that we have some idea of their contents even before reading them! For example, we approach a love poem differently than we would an obituary notice, a dramatic play with different expectations than a special documentary report. Each literary form has a specific intent that is fully understood by the audience addressed and triggers certain expectations in them.

A fourth characteristic of literary forms is that they are connected with certain social and institutional settings. The setting of a personal letter, for example, would be a private relationship between two friends (in most cases). The setting presupposed in an obituary notice is that of grief shared by friends and relatives of the deceased. The setting of a dramatic play, in our culture, would be on a stage in a public theatre. The setting generally presupposed in a love poem is a private relationship between two people in love. Literary forms are either the products of certain settings or only comprehensible in certain contexts.

A fifth and final characteristic is that the setting for certain literary forms changes over a period of years. An illustration of this will be taken from the broad category (or genre) of drama. The modern setting of a dramatic play is generally on the stage of a public theatre, a secular or popular setting. Originally, drama did not have such a setting. Both tragedy and comedy originated in the religious festivals of Greek cities of the classical and Hellenistic periods. Despite their diverse themes and plots, dramatic plays were performed in honor of the Greek god Dionysius, and they generally followed a private religious ceremony of the cult in a nearby temple of the god! Consider the origins of this literary category the next time you watch your favorite television drama. The settings of literary forms change in the history of a culture. This is an important observation in the study of those traditional units of folk literature which presuppose an oral setting (e.g., poems, songs, riddles). When these oral forms are put into writing, the literary context often differs from its original oral setting.[17]

NT Case Studies
Our discussion on the nature and significance of literary forms is a rele-

17. See Lohfink, *Now I Get It!* 45–51, for a similar example taken from a love poem. See also C. S. Lewis, *The Allegory of Love: A Study in Medieval Tradition* (London: Oxford University Press, 1936, 1938).

vant preface to the form-critical study of the NT. This method was first applied to old European folk literature before its use in biblical writings.[18] The popular and social character of both types of literature almost required such a method. Because of the nature of literary forms (as we have seen), form criticism seeks to comprehend the following: (1) the character of each literary form and the fixed patterns in which it is framed, (2) the linguistic intent that the readers were accustomed to expect, and (3) the social and institutional setting that produced the literary form. These three concerns of form criticism will be applied to two traditional forms found in Mark's Gospel: the miracle story of the healing of the leper (1:40–45) and the parable of the mustard seed (4:30–32). Each is a prevalent form in the Synoptic Gospels, each reflects an oral setting and has been the focus of much form-critical research.

Like all literary forms, the account of the healing of the leper in Mk 1:40–45 follows a fixed pattern, characteristic of most miracle stories of that period:

Diagnosis: a leper in need of cleansing, v 40

Therapy: the healing touch of Jesus, v 41

Proof of Restoration: the leper left—cleansed! v 42.

Reading the entire account, one will note that the story centers upon this basic three-point pattern. All details are reduced to essential descriptions. Nothing is known of the leper's name, nor of the specific time or place, nor is anything else mentioned of him after his restoration to health. Why? Assuming that healings took place in the ministry of Jesus, the incident was probably reduced after years of oral circulation to a simple fixed pattern so that the story could be remembered easily and transmitted to others. This was an acceptable way of telling miracle stories in the ancient Mediterranean world (and elsewhere). For example, many similar stories with the same fixed forms were circulated about the healer-

---

18. Two examples of early works that influenced the form criticism of the Bible were L. von Ranke, *Geschichte der romanischen und germanischen Völker* (1824) and E. Nordern, *Agnostos Theos* (1913). The following studies pioneered the approach in biblical studies: H. Gunkel, *Genesis* (1901) and *Ausgewählte Psalmen* (1917); M. Dibelius, *Die Formgeschichte des Evangeliums* (1919); R. Bultmann, *Die Geschichte der synoptischen Tradition* (1921) [*Synoptic Tradition*, trans. from 1958 ed.]. For later research on form criticism, see B. Gerhardsson, *Memory and Manuscript*, trans. E. Sharpe (Lund: Gleerup, 1961); R. H. Lightfoot, *History and Interpretation in the Gospels* (London: Hodder & Stoughton, 1935); H. Riesenfeld, *The Gospel Tradition and Its Beginnings* (London: A. R. Mowbray, 1957); V. Taylor, *The Formation of the Gospel Tradition* (London: Macmillan, 1933). For surveys, see Harrington, *IntNT* 70–84; McKnight, *What Is Form Criticism?*; S. H. Travis, "Form Criticism," Marshall, *NTI* 153–64.

philosophers Pythagoras and Apollonius.[19]

The essential points to which it is reduced make plain the linguistic intent of this form. The healing of the leper story seeks to glorify Jesus as the instrument of God's power. It might also have sought to encourage its hearers by impressing them with Jesus' special ability to relieve a human affliction.

The sociological setting that produced the present framework of the miracle story is more difficult to ascertain. There are *at least* three stages in the history of the transmission of this Gospel tradition (e.g., Jesus-Church-Gospel), and we will concentrate on the stages preceding the Gospel of Mark.[20] According to most form critics, many of the miracle stories of Jesus were widely circulated among urban Gentile communities that were attracted to Jesus as a divine miracle-worker superior to other healer-philosophers. However, the concluding proof of restoration in the story indicates that it probably originated in a Jewish-Christian community of Palestine: "go present yourself to the priest and offer for your cure what Moses prescribed" (Mk 1:44). Although the literary framework of the story is characteristic of many miracle stories in the ancient Mediterranean world, the vocabulary and religious contents reflect the beliefs and perceptions of Jewish Christians of Palestine. This proposed setting also lends some credibility to the view that the story points back to an incident that took place in the ministry of Jesus.[21]

The saying in Mk 4:30–32 is called a parable. It is like our modern form of simile because it is a comparison of an abstract concept with a common situation of everyday life. Unlike the allegory and other similitudes which have many hidden or implicit meanings in the analogy, the parable focuses on one central message. It is a saying or story that seeks to

---

19. Iamblichus, *Life of Pythagoras* 36, 60–61, 134–36; Philostratus, *The Life of Apollonius* 2.4; 3.38; 4.20, 45; see also the healing accounts at the temple of Asclepius in the Epidaurus inscriptions (4th cent. BC). All of the above healing accounts are found in Cartlidge and Dungan, *Documents*, 151–55, 220, 225–26, 229–31. For studies on NT miracles, see R. H. Fuller, *Interpreting the Miracles* (London: SCM, 1963); H. C. Kee, *Miracle in the Early Christian World* (New Haven: Yale University Press, 1983); E. and M.-L. Keller, *Miracles in Dispute A Continuing Debate*, trans. M. Kohl (London: SCM, 1969); G. Thiessen, *The Miracles of the Early Christian Tradition*, trans. F. McDonagh (Philadelphia: Fortress, 1983).

20. If we were to trace the history of the tradition from its inception to its final shape in the Gospel, it would be more appropriate to posit four or more stages, for example: (1) the ministry of Jesus; (2) the earliest followers after Jesus; (3) early Christianity adjusting to its environment; and (4) the writing of the Gospels. See our chart in this section on the growth of the Gospels.

21. See the following studies which argue that the Gospel tradition was derived from Jesus himself: Riesenfeld, *Gospel Tradition*; Gerhardsson, *Memory and Manuscript*.

drive home a central point by illustrating it from some familiar situation in life.[22]

Using the parable of the mustard seed in Mark, we note the following fixed pattern: (a) a starting point, usually with the opening phrase, "the kingdom of God is like"; (b) the illustration from life (e.g., a mustard seed); and (x) the central point (e.g., miraculous growth).

Many form critics believe that Jesus taught about the kingdom of God using concise and simple parables like that of the mustard seed. If this parable stems from the ministry of Jesus (as most scholars believe), it was probably intended as a defense of Jesus' ministry against Jewish critics. Many Jews of Jesus' day did not see the end-time glories of God's kingdom that they anticipated in Jesus' ministry. Telling a parable like the mustard seed would be an appropriate response of Jesus to that situation.

The following interpretation is a possible rendering of the original intent of Jesus' parable of the mustard seed. Although it is small and insignificant when it is planted, the mustard seed miraculously grows into a large bushy shrub providing shelter for the birds. So it is also with the kingdom of God in Jesus' ministry. Although it appears small and insignificant, when God's reign is truly recognized in the ministry of Jesus, it will become something great, providing shelter for people. This emphasis on the small beginnings of God's kingdom with the promise that it would develop into something great would be an appropriate response of Jesus to the charges of his critics.[23]

Form Criticism: Conclusions

Although much form-critical research has been done in the Synoptic Gospels, attention has also been directed to other areas, for examples: early Christian hymns (e.g., Phil 2:6–11; Col 1:15–20; 1 Pet 3:18–22; 1 Tim 3:16) and household rules (e.g., Col 3:18–4:1; Eph 5:21–6:9; Titus 2:1–10). Most of the hymns emphasize the divine mission of Christ and presuppose original oral settings in the life and worship of early communities. The household rules are drawn from the traditional ethics of the Hellenistic world. Other traditional forms analyzed in the NT Epistles are: creeds, confessions, baptismal formulas, catechetical teachings, diatribes

---

22. For studies on parables, see J. D. Crossan, *In Parables* (New York: Harper & Row, 1973); C. H. Dodd, *The Parables of the Kingdom*, rev. ed. (New York: Charles Scribner's Sons, 1961); A. M. Hunter, *Interpreting the Parables* (Philadelphia: Westminster, 1960); J. Jeremias, *The Parables of Jesus*, 2nd rev. ed., trans. S. H. Hooke (New York: Charles Scribner's Sons, 1972); Perrin, *Jesus*; M. Tolbert, *Perspectives on the Parables: An Approach to Multiple Interpretation* (Philadelphia: Fortress, 1979).

23. For more discussion on the teachings of Jesus, see 179, "The Message of Jesus."

(or philosophical dialogues), and pareneses (i.e., moral exhortations).[24]

The special concerns of form criticism are significant for the study of early Christianity. First, it seeks to get behind the sources discovered by source criticism to learn something about the earliest communities and Jesus. Second, it takes seriously the fixed literary forms of the NT and seeks to understand their practical function within the communities that produced them. Third, it takes seriously the preliterary period of oral transmission as a time of growth and adaptation for the literary forms within the communities who used them. Finally, form criticism regards many of these literary forms with their long preliterary history as "windows" from which the existence of early Christian communities can be viewed and studied.

Redaction Criticism

"Redaction" is the process of putting information into a suitable literary form; the act of revising or editing. Using an example from our modern day, redaction is the work of a newspaper reporter who selectively organizes information from an interview and brings it together into a final written report. It is also the task of anyone today who revises a written proposal from a committee meeting by correcting it or adding important information that was overlooked. Redaction is concerned with the selection, omission, addition, correction, or abridgement of information to produce a final written document.

Basic Concerns

In the NT, redaction criticism is concerned with the activity of the final writer of a book: (1) how the writer employed (revised, edited) sources; (2) his or her particular emphases and distinctive viewpoint; and (3) the author's own life-setting and the needs of the specific audience being addressed.[25]

24. Special attention will be given to the NT epistolary forms below. For surveys of the various early Christian forms, see Doty, *Letters* 55–63; G. W. H. Lampe, "The Evidence in the NT for Early Creeds, Catechisms and Liturgy," *ExpT* 71 (1959–60), 359–63; C. J. Roetzel, *Letters* 41–49. For specific form-critical studies, see D. L. Balch, *Let Wives Be Submissive: The Domestic Code in 1 Peter* (Chico, Calif.: Scholars Press, 1981); R. P. Martin, *Carmen Christi, Philippians 2:5–11*, rev. ed. (Grand Rapids: Eerdmans, 1983); V. H. Neufeld, *The Earliest Christian Confessions* (Leiden: Brill, 1963); J. T. Sanders, *NT Christological Hymns* (Cambridge: University Press, 1971); Stowers, *Diatribe*.

25. For redaction-critical studies, see G. Bornkamm et al., *Tradition and Interpretation in Matthew*, trans. P. Scott (Philadelphia: Westminster, 1963); Harrington, *IntNT* 96–107 (survey); W. Marxsen, *Mark the Evangelist*, trans. J. Boyce (Nashville: Abingdon, 1969); N. Perrin, *What Is Redaction Criticism?* (Philadelphia:

Mark 1:1–3

¹The beginning of the gospel of Jesus Christ, the Son of God.

² As it is written in Isaiah the prophet
"Behold, I send my messenger
    before thy face,
    who shall prepare thy way;
³ the voice of one crying in
    the wilderness:
Prepare the way of the Lord,
    make his paths straight—"

⁴ John the baptizer appeared in the wilderness, preaching a baptism of repentance for the forgiveness of sins.

Luke 3:1–6

¹ In the fifteenth year of the reign of Tiberius Caesar, Pontius Pilate being governor of Judea, and Herod being tetrarch of Galilee, and his brother Philip tetrarch of the region of Ituraea and Trachonitis and Lysanias tetrarch of Abilene, ² in the high-priesthood of Annas and Caiaphas, the word of God came to John the son of Zechariah in the wilderness; ³ and he went into all the region about the Jordan, preaching a baptism of repentance for the forgiveness of sins. ⁴ As it is written in the book of the words of Isaiah the prophet,

The voice of one crying in
    the wilderness:
Prepare the way of the Lord,
    make his paths straight.
⁵ Every valley shall be filled,
    and every mountain and hill
        shall be brought low,
    and the crooked shall be
        made straight,
    and the rough ways shall
        be made smooth;
⁶ and all flesh shall see
    the salvation of God."

Redaction criticism both draws upon the literary and historical concerns of source and form criticism and also goes beyond them by focusing on a different aspect of the text. It presupposes source criticism by investigating the author's use of sources, but goes beyond this method by con-

Fortress, 1969); Rohde, *Rediscovering*; R. H. Stein, "What is Redaktions-geschichte?" *JBL* 83 (1969) 45–56.

centrating on the work of the *final author*. It serves as a complement to form criticism because it concerns the final stage of the history of tradition. It, however, distinguishes itself from form criticism on at least three points: (a) redaction criticism focuses on the final text, not the preliterary history of tradition; (b) it works towards a synthesis of the smaller literary units which form criticism seeks to analyze; and (c) it only deals with the final author's life-setting and not the various oral and written settings of the traditions.

A Case Study from Luke

Let us again look at our comparison of the Synoptic Gospels, concentrating on Luke 3:1-6 and its use of Mark. We see from the comparison chart that our analysis will presuppose from form criticism that Mark is a source for Luke. Even though redaction criticism can be undertaken with documents whose sources are not clearly delineated (e.g., Mark's Gospel and the Acts of the Apostles), the evidence of defined sources makes the analysis less complicated. Mark is a complete work in itself, but in the history of the Synoptic tradition it, along with Q, functions as a precursor to the completed stages of the Synoptic tradition in which the Gospels of Matthew and Luke are classified.

As we concentrate on Luke's use of Mark, we would like to point out five redactional techniques employed by Luke: addition, omission, expansion, rearrangement, and inclusion. Some overlap may occur.

Let us look at *addition*. It is clear from the chapter headings that Luke does not begin his Gospel at the same place that Mark does. Luke adds to his source two chapters of material not found elsewhere: a prologue with birth and infancy narratives (Lk 1:1-2:52) and a historical preface (Lk 3:1-2a). Luke's prologue (1:1-4) not only introduces his Gospel, but also his second volume, Acts of the Apostles (cf. Acts 1:1). The birth narratives also include accounts of John the Baptist (Lk 1:5-25, 57-80), who is also the subject of our comparison chart (Lk 3:1-6; Mk 1). This background of John is not found in Mark. Luke's additions (1:1-3:2a) provide much that is lacking in his Markan source and give Luke's Gospel ancient biographical or historical characteristics. The historical notations, found in 2:1-3 and 3:1-2, may signify Luke's special concern to place the stories of John and Jesus in the context of Roman secular history, since these notations are found elsewhere (e.g., Acts 11:28; 18:2,12).

The second technique concerns a Lukan *omission*. Looking at our comparison chart, we note that Luke omits the Malachi passage found in his source (Mk 1:2/Mal 3:1). Luke's omission was probably influenced by Q, since the Malachi passage appears elsewhere in a tradition common to both Luke and Matthew (Lk 7:27 and Mt 11:10 = Q).

Lukan *expansion* of his source is the third redactional technique. In Lk 3:5-6, the author expands his source by quoting more extensively the Isaiah 40 passage found in his Markan source. Luke continues to follow a Greek text similar to Mark. In his expanded citation of Isa 40:3-5, Luke omits a word ("all") and a phrase ("the glory of the Lord") and appears to underscore the statement: "all flesh shall see the salvation of God." This statement in the Greek resembles both Lk 2:30 (God's salvation anticipated) and Acts 28:28 (God's salvation extended to all people). This theme of worldwide salvation (for Jews and Gentiles) is an important concern for the author of Luke–Acts (e.g., Lk 2:32; 24:27; Acts 13:47; 26:23). On the basis of historical clues and such Lukan emphases as worldwide salvation, tension with Judaism, and appeals for Roman tolerance, one can draw some tentative conclusions about the situation of Luke and his readers. They appear to be part of a growing Gentile-Christian community that is experiencing a loss of identity or purpose as a result of Jewish and pagan antagonism (ca. AD 80–90).

The fourth device used by Luke in this passage is the *rearrangement* of his source. Luke makes it clear to his readers "about whom this prophet speaks" by relocating his source about John's preaching (Mk 1:4) before the Isaiah passage is cited (Lk 3:3). Luke also prefaces this Markan preaching summary with an introduction that appears to identify John as a prophet: "the word of God came to John" (3:2). John is identified as a prophet elsewhere (e.g., Lk 7:26-27; 20:4-6). By rearranging his source Luke provides a "topical sentence" to introduce and preview the discussion on John that follows.

Luke uses a fifth redaction technique in this passage: *inclusion*. Luke not only begins his discussion of John with a description of John's preaching (3:3) but concludes with it as well (v 18). Substantial blocks of material on John's preaching are also included from Q, Luke's second source (Lk 3:7-9/Mt 3:7-10), and from Luke's own special material (Lk 3:10-14). All of this extra material probably serves as Luke's interpretation of the Markan source. According to Luke, John is the prophet who preaches "repentance for the forgiveness of sins" in anticipation of God's worldwide salvation. John is both subordinate to Jesus the Messiah (3:15-16) and is united with Jesus in his preaching and prophetic role (cf. 3:2b-20 with 4:16-30).

It has been evident from our study that much of the information on Luke's redactional activity was collected by approaching the text from two perspectives. First, by looking *in* the text for redactional changes, and then, by looking *through* the text into the entire literary work to verify whether the themes of the text are typical emphases and concerns of the author. From this last perspective we sought to reconstruct the author's life-setting.

Contents of Hypothetical Q

I. THE PREPARATION
A. John's preaching of repentance (Luke 3:7-9; Matt. 3:7-10)
B. The temptation of Jesus (Luke 4:1-13; Matt. 4:1-11)

II. SAYINGS
A. Beatitudes (Luke 6:20-23; Matt. 5:3, 4, 6, 11, 12)
B. Love to one's enemies (Luke 6:27-36; Matt. 5:39-42, 44-48; 7:12)
C. Judging (Luke 6:37-42; Matt. 7:1-5; 10:24; 15:14)
D. Hearers and doers of the Word (Luke 6:47-49; Matt. 7:24-27)

III. NARRATIVE
A. The centurion's servant (Luke 7:1-10; Matt. 7:28a; 8:5-10, 13)
B. The Baptist's question (Luke 7:18-20; Matt. 11:2, 3)
C. Christ's answer (Luke 7:22-35; Matt. 11:4-19)

IV. DISCIPLESHIP
A. On the cost of discipleship (Luke 9:57-60; Matt. 8:19-22)
B. The mission charge (Luke 10:2-16; Matt. 9:37, 38; 10:9-15; 11:21-23)
C. Christ's thanksgiving to the Father (Luke 10:21-24; Matt. 11:25-27; 13:16, 17)

V. VARIOUS SAYINGS
A. The pattern prayer (Luke 11:2-4; Matt. 6:9-13)
B. An answer to prayer (Luke 11:9-13; Matt. 7:7-11)
C. The Beelzebub discussion and its sequel (Luke 11:14-23; Matt. 12:22-30)
D. Sign of the prophet Jonah (Luke 11:29-32; Matt. 12:38-42)
E. About light (Luke 11:33-36; Matt. 5:15; 6:22, 23)

VI. DISCOURSE AGAINST THE PHARISEES
(Luke 11:37-12:1; Matt. 23)

VII. SAYINGS
A. About fearless confession (Luke 12:2-12; Matt. 10:19, 26-33; 12:32)
B. On cares about earthly things (Luke 12:22-34; Matt. 6:19-21, 25-33)
C. On faithfulness (Luke 12:39-46; Matt. 24:43-51)
D. On signs for this age (Luke 12:51-56; Matt. 10:34-36; 16:2, 3)
E. On agreeing with one's adversaries (Luke 12:57-59; Matt. 5:25, 26)

VIII. PARABLES OF THE MUSTARD SEED AND LEAVEN
(Luke 13:18-21; Matt. 13:31-33)

IX. OTHER SAYINGS
A. Condemnation of Israel (Luke 13:23-30; Matt. 7:13, 14, 22, 23; 8:11, 12)
B. Lament over Jerusalem (Luke 13:34, 35; Matt. 23:37-39)
C. Cost of discipleship (Luke 14:26-35; Matt. 10:37, 38; 5:13)
D. On serving two masters (Luke 16:13; Matt. 6:24)
E. On law and divorce (Luke 16:16-18; Matt. 11:12, 13; 5:18, 32)
F. On offenses, forgiveness, and faith (Luke 17:1-6; Matt. 18:6, 7, 15, 20-22)
G. The day of the Son of Man (Luke 17:23-27, 33-37; Matt. 24:17, 18, 26-28, 37-41)

Scholars vary as to the contents of Q.

Adapted from Ralph Martin, New Testament Foundations: A Guide for Christian Students, vol. 1 (Grand Rapids: Eerdmans, 1975), by permission.

Redaction Criticism: Conclusions

As we have mentioned, redaction criticism can be applied to other books of the NT. It is can be applied to books that have no clearly delineated sources, such as Mark's Gospel and the Acts of the Apostles. Here (without the close comparison of a specific written source) concentration must be placed on the unique vocabulary, style, structure, and key themes of each author. Redaction-critical study of the NT letters and homilies has also been done, especially where the use of traditional material can be detected (e.g., hymns, confessions, household rules).[26]

The method of redaction criticism concentrates on the time of the final authors, their setting and audience, their special concerns and intentions. It is not concerned with the preliterary oral traditions, but with the literary text in its *final form*. This focus of redaction criticism has also prepared the way for more recent methods of literary criticism pioneered by scholars of European literature: genre, style, and poetic analysis. All of these methods are concerned with the language, diction, structure, and imagery of the literary work in its final form. These new methods are often helpful for understanding the intrinsic qualities of the NT writings, regardless of the historical-critical problems.[27]

26. Redaction-critical research of the so-called NT epistles is evident, for example, in the following commentaries of the Hermeneia series (Philadelphia: Fortress, 1971–): Conzelmann, *1 Corinthians*; Betz, *Galatians*; Lohse, *Colossians and Philemon*; Dibelius and Conzelmann, *Pastoral Epistles*; Dibelius and Greeven, *James*.

27. Examples of the new literary-critical approaches to NT study are W. A. Beardslee, *The Literary Criticism of the New Testament* (Philadelphia: Fortress, 1970); Crossan, *In Parables*; R. W. Funk, *Jesus as Precursor* (Missoula, Mont.: Scholars Press; Philadelphia: Fortress, 1975); E. V. McKnight, *The Bible and the Reader: An Introduction to Literary Criticism* (Philadelphia: Fortress, 1985); D. Patte, *What Is Structural Exegesis?* (Philadelphia: Fortress, 1976); N. R. Petersen, *Literary Criticism for New Testament Critics* (Philadelphia: Fortress, 1978); D. O. Via, *Kerygma and Comedy in the New Testament* (Philadelphia: Fortress, 1975); and volumes 2, 4, 6, 10, 14, 20, 23, 26, 29, 30–32 in *Semeia*.

6

The Genres of the Gospels and Acts

The question of the genre of the four Gospels and Acts is a difficult one. Most scholars avoid generic categories for these five books and merely label them as unique Christian literature. In order to simplify discussion we will first examine Acts and the Synoptic Gospels, then treat the Gospel of John in a separate section.

Genre is commonly understood as the broad category of artistic, musical, or literary composition characterized by a particular style, form, purpose, or content. In modern literature, for example, there are the genres of exposition, fiction, drama, and poetry. These categories are often self-evident to the modern reader because he or she is accustomed to their style, form, and content. The classification of ancient writings is more difficult because the modern reader is not familiar with them. Nevertheless, the discipline of genre criticism is important for interpreting and understanding.[1] It greatly assists our understanding of an ancient classic when we know what to expect from it and can discover what the work sought to accomplish.

One of the reasons why there is so much disagreement about the nature of the Gospels is because there is general confusion about the type of literature that one is reading. For example, some lay people read the prophecies of Mark 13 like weather predictions in today's newspaper. They also tend to read the ministry of Jesus in the Gospels like the daily itinerary of Pope John Paul II. The general reader certainly does not treat modern literature in the same naive manner as the Gospels. For instance, most people correctly read Martin Gilbert's *Winston Churchill* as biography

---

1. E. D. Hirsch, *Validity in Interpretation* (New Haven: Yale University Press, 1967) 78, 86. See also T. Todorov, *The Fantastic: A Structural Approach to the Literary Genre* (Cleveland: Case Western Reserve, 1973); M. Gerhart, "Generic Studies: Their Renewed Importance in Religious and Literary Interpretation," *JAAR* 45 (3, 1977) 309–25; J. P. Strelka, ed., *Theories of Literary Genre* (University Park, Pa.: Pennsylvania State University Press, 1978).

and John Irving's *The World According to Garp* as fiction. Despite our current fascination with historical novels, such as *Space* by James Michener, modern readers are cautious not to read too much fact into fiction. Why, therefore, is there so much confusion about interpreting the Gospels?

Reading the Gospels as ancient literature raises another problem. The Gospels are not only classic writings but are also part of a canon of religious literature. This fact tends to encumber the Gospels with various kinds of traditional interpretations. This point might explain some of the confusion about interpreting the Gospels. But whatever our attitude towards these sacred books, our common goal is accurate interpretation (i.e., *exegesis*). The achievement of this objective requires some adherence to the basic methodologies discussed in ch 5. Genre criticism also assists in this goal by complementing, correcting, or clarifying internal analysis through external classification.

We will begin our discussion of genre by looking at the Gospels of Mark, Matthew, and Luke–Acts. From our study of source and redaction criticism, we have seen that Mark was probably the earliest gospel and Luke–Acts was a two-volume work written by one author. Furthermore, Matthew, Mark, and Luke are called the Synoptic Gospels because they share a similar vision of the life of Christ.

Under what categories do we classify Matthew, Mark, and Luke–Acts? To illustrate the practical importance of this question, let us imagine ourselves in different roles at a different place and time. We are a group of librarians at the magnificent library of Alexandria in the third century AD. We have just received copies of Mark, Matthew, and Luke–Acts for the library. The head librarian orders us to categorize and shelve them with appropriate identifying tags. We must go through these documents and classify them according to the existing generic categories,[2] and not according to some religious predisposition (i.e., canon). Under what genres do we classify these books? Three prevalent categories of the Hellenistic world might be suggested: history, biography, and tragic drama.[3]

2. The Christian category of "gospel" is not helpful in this context. The term "gospel" (*euangelion*), for Hellenistic non-Christians, probably had the meaning of a joyful announcement connected with the eventful appearance or activity of a great ruler. The titles "Gospel of Matthew, Gospel of Mark, Gospel of Luke, and Gospel of John" were applied to the first four books of our NT by Christians of the second and third centuries as convenient identifying labels; they do not represent a precise category of genre nor are they infallible indicators of authorship. Each of the Gospels and Acts should also be examined separately, since the source dependence of the Synoptic Gospels does not automatically mean genre dependence, see Shuler, *Genre for the Gospels* 30–31.

3. Before discussion it is necessary to clarify our approach with several preliminary remarks. First, other so-called genres could also be considered (e.g., historical romance), but most of them are variations of the three major ones that

THE HISTORICAL GENRE: A COMPARISON WITH LUKE–ACTS

Why would any of the Gospels or Acts be compared to ancient history? They are not secular or comprehensive in scope like the Greek and Roman histories. Even when compared to the more religious Israelite-Jewish histories, they are still not as inclusive. In contrast to most ancient histories, the Gospels and Acts do not focus on politics and war or generals and kings. In comparison with the great Greek histories of Herodotus, Thucydides, and Polybius, their style and composition is less cultivated. Finally, when Eusebius of Caesarea wrote *Ecclesiastical History* in the early fourth century AD, he considered it to be the first of its kind (1.1).

Despite the above contrasts, Luke–Acts lends itself to some comparison with ancient history. There are at least seven points of analogy: (1) prefaces stating the author's method and purpose; (2) chronological notations; (3) attention to factual details; (4) political bias; (5) assumptions about fate or providence; (6) speeches that express the author's understanding of the events; and (7) selective arrangement of events in a linear succession.[4] Before discussing the points of comparison we will first identify some ancient histories, then mention the similarities and differences of Greco-Roman and Israelite-Jewish histories.

Jewish and Greco-Roman Histories

Examples of Israelite histories are the Deuteronomistic History (i.e., the final edition of Dt through 2 Kgs in the Hebrew Bible) and the Chronicler's

---

we shall discuss. To illustrate the dominance in antiquity of the genres of history, biography, and tragic drama, see, e.g., the mosaic (ca. AD 100) found at Hadrumetum in Africa (now in the Bardo museum) where Virgil is flanked by the muses of both history and tragedy as he composes the Aeneid. Virgil describes his own work as an account of the deeds and hardships of Aeneas as he traveled from Troy to found Rome (1.1-7; an epic biography?). Another example is from Lucian, *How to Write History* 7 (2nd cent. AD), where Lucian makes sharp distinctions between history and laudatory biography (or *encomium*). Second, it is not our purpose in this chapter to develop a technical criterion of "genre" and apply it consistently to each Gospel as in Talbert, *Gospel?* 2-5. This approach places too much confidence on the accuracy of the criterion and assumes too much uniformity of style, structure, and intent in all four Gospels. Our purpose is to introduce the reader to a sampling of diverse genre categories that a reading of the Gospels might have evoked from the ancient reader. Consistent with our purpose, we consulted the authors of antiquity (e.g., Aristotle, Lucian) for definitions of the genres and the criteria for understanding their forms and functions. Third, our approach assumes that the first four books of our NT are not necessarily of the same literary genre merely because they contain common traditions and were labeled "Gospels" by later Christians. It also recognizes the difficulty of categorizing the Gospels according to genre because each book seems to combine several literary types.

history (1 and 2 Chron, Ezra, Neh). Examples of Jewish histories are 1 and 2 Maccabees, and Josephus' *Antiquities* and *War of the Jews*. Examples of Greek histories are Herodotus' *The Histories,* Thucydides' *The Peloponne-sian Wars,* and Polybius' *The Histories.* Examples of Roman histories are the works of Livy and Tacitus.

Although the Israelite-Jewish histories are not as secular and anthropo-centric as most Greco-Roman histories, they have similarities. Both types deal with the similar topics of politics and wars of nations, as well as the words and activities of rulers and generals. It was probably for this rea-son that Eusebius in the fourth century labeled his history of Christian-ity, *Ecclesiastical History,* although he is selective in his mention of political events and the activities of rulers. Both Jewish and Greco-Roman histor-ies attempt to be comprehensive in their recording of events and people in a linear progression of time (i.e., the origin and development of a people).[5] It also must be pointed out that the pervasive influence of Hel-lenism made Jewish and Greco-Roman histories increasingly similar (cf. the works of Josephus and Tacitus).

Fate, providence, moralism, and value judgments can be found in both Israelite-Jewish and Greco-Roman histories with differences only in em-phasis and interpretation. For example, the works of Herodotus, Poly-

---

4. The above points are derived from comparisons of Luke–Acts with several ancient histories (e.g., Thucydides, Josephus, Polybius) and the following sources: Lucian, *How To Write History,* 7, 23–27, 40, 51–53, 58–60; Polybius, *The Histories,* 10.21.8; "Historiography, Greek and Latin," *The Oxford Classical Dictionary,* 2nd ed., ed. N. G. L. Hammond and H. H. Scullard (London: Oxford University Press, 1970) 521–23; H. Attridge, *The Interpretation of Biblical History in the Antiquities of Judaica of Flavius Josephus* (Missoula, Mont.: Scholars Press, 1976); H. J. Cadbury, "The Greek and Jewish Traditions of Writing History," *BC* 2:7–29; M. Dibelius, *Studies in Acts of the Apostles,* trans. M. Ling (London: SCM, 1956) 125, 133–38; A. W. Gomme, *A Historical Commentary on Thucydides* (London: Oxford Univer-sity Press, 1956) 1:1–2, 25–30; M. Grant, *The Ancient Historians* (New York: Charles Scribner's Sons, 1970); A. Momigliano, *Essays in Ancient and Modern Historiography* (Middletown, Conn.: Wesleyan University Press, 1977). Most of the Greek and Latin histories cited in this section are derived from the LCL.

5. It has been held that the basic difference between Israelite-Jewish and Greco-Roman histories consisted in their respective concepts of time. The former was considered linear, the latter cyclical. See T. Boman, *Hebrew Thought Compared with Greek,* trans. J. L. Moreau from 1954 ed. (London: SCM, 1960). But recent re-search has raised doubts about this distinction. Whereas cyclical concepts of time have roots in the religious experiences of both Jews and Greeks (e.g., religious calendars), both tended to view the writing of history as the selecting and gradu-ating of events in a linear continuum. See Momigliano, "Time in Ancient His-toriography," in *Essays in Ancient and Modern Historiography,* 184–89. For further critiques of the old view, see J. Barr, *Biblical Words for Time,* 2nd. ed. (London: SCM, 1969).

bius, and Tacitus include instances where Fate seems to rule in the affairs of people; in Israelite-Jewish histories, however, Fate is explicitly ascribed to the providence of God and occurs more frequently in their accounts.[6] Value judgments and moralism also occur more often in Israelite-Jewish histories, probably because they are more religious in nature than most Greco-Roman histories.

The basic differences between Israelite-Jewish and Greco-Roman histories would be in the areas of religious or philosophical bias, reliability of evidence, and motives for writing history. Concerning bias, Israelite-Jewish histories give prominence to the role of the prophet who interprets the *religious significance* of the events. In Greco-Roman histories we find no such collaboration of the historian with the philosopher, their counterpart to the "prophet."[7] Regarding the attention to the reliability of evidence, Greco-Roman histories generally placed a higher priority on it as a criterion for writing history. Most Israelite-Jewish histories incorporated religious traditions and myths without questioning their reliability (e.g., spectacular or bizarre miracles). Differences also included the motives for writing history. For Greeks it was to cherish the examples of the ancestors and to rescue what was in danger of being unknown. For Israelite history, it was a religious duty to remember the past (Ex 32:13; Dt 7:18). The *motives* for writing Jewish history, however, are not profoundly different from the Greeks and Romans.

It is with the above the similarities and differences between Greco-Roman and Israelite-Jewish historiography in view, that we compare Luke–Acts with "ancient history." Let us now look at the seven points of comparison.

Points of Comparison with Luke–Acts

Similar Prefaces
The first point of correspondence between Luke–Acts and ancient history is found in the prefaces: Lk 1:1–4 and Acts 1:1–2. Because papyri scrolls were limited in length, an ancient author had to divide his work into separate volumes. He would prefix to the first a preface for the whole and add secondary prefaces to the beginning of each later one.[8] This is apparently the case with the Lukan prefaces. Both are addressed to Theophilus, probably a Roman patron to whom the work is dedicated.

6. For discussion of fate and providence with primary sources, see C. H. Talbert, "Prophecy and Fulfillment in Luke–Acts," *Luke–Acts. New Perspectives from the Society of Biblical Literature*, ed. C. H. Talbert (New York: Crossroad, 1984) 91–103; idem, *Reading Luke: A Literary and Theological Commentary on the Third Gospel* (New York: Crossroad, 1982) 234–40.

7. Momigliano, "Time," 194–95.

8. Cadbury, "Commentary on the Preface of Luke," *BC* 2:491.

There are parallels to this practice in the work of the historians Josephus (*Against Apion* 1.1 and 2.1) and Polybius (*Histories* 1.1 and 3.1). Like the preface in ancient histories (e.g., Polybius), Luke alludes to the work of his predecessors (Lk 1:1). The Lukan preface also reflects the historical concern to utilize eyewitness material (Lk 1:2; Polybius, Tacitus). "Events accomplished among us" (Lk 1:1) echoes the focus of ancient historiography on the facts of the near past (e.g., Herodotus, Thucydides, Polybius). Luke's concerns to "follow all things closely" and "write an orderly account" (1:3) are in keeping with the practices of ancient historians to work carefully through reports and memoranda and arrange them in an orderly manner.[9] We know that Luke made use of at least two documents in his composition, Mark and Q (the alleged source common to Mt and Lk). Like the ancient histories, Luke's general purpose is to "preserve the memory of the past" for posterity (Herodotus 1.1).

Similar Chronological Notations

A second point of comparison is chronological notation. These synchronisms are found in Luke–Acts at numerous points. They link the birth of Jesus with the reign of Emperor Augustus and the census of Quirinius, legate of Syria (Lk 2:1). They also connect the ministry of John the Baptist with the rules of Emperor Tiberius, Pontius Pilate, prefect of Judea, and the Herodian ethnarchs (3.1). Further references are made to: the famine under Emperor Claudius (Acts 11:28); the death of Herod Agrippa I (11:20–23); the expelling of Jews from Rome under Claudius (18:2); Paul's appearances before Gallio, proconsul of Achaia (18:12–17); the procurators Felix and Festus (24–25); and the ethnarch Agrippa II (25:13–14). Such chronological notes are characteristic of ancient histories (Thucydides 2.2; Polybius, *Histories* 1.3; Josephus, *Ant.* 18.106). They are also Luke's attempt to link his account of Jesus and early Christianity with the secular Roman world.

Similar Attention to Detail

Related to synchronisms is the third point: attention to factual details. This concern for specific names, dates, places, titles, and technical terms is especially evident in the histories of Herodotus, Thucydides, Polybius, and Josephus. However, Luke's concern for factual details is no guarantee of their accuracy. Discrepancies do occur, as in all ancient writing, for example: the linking of Jesus' birth (4 BC) with the census of Quirinius (AD 6) in Lk 2:1, the conflicts with Josephus on the dating of Theudas the rebel (Acts 5:36; *Ant.* 20.97–98) and disagreements with Paul's letters on the apostle's visits to Jerusalem (Acts 9; 11; 15 with Gal 1–2).

9. Lucian, *How to Write History* 43–44.

Despite the above discrepancies in its narrative, Luke–Acts includes many accurate details. The author's knowledge of the Aegean Sea region is extensive (Acts 15:36–19:20) and numerous localities are correctly identified. Luke's account of Paul's basic itinerary finds many points of agreement with Paul's letters. The narrative of Paul's sea voyage to Rome is one of the most instructive accounts of ancient seamanship (Acts 27:1–28:15). The book of Acts alone contains more than one hundred personal names: Jewish, Christian, and pagan. The identities of many of the personages are corroborated by Paul's letters and ancient history (e.g., Paul's co-workers, Gallio, Claudius, Felix, Festus).

Details of time and place, as well as concern for technical terms, also figure prominently. Note for example, the time and place notations on Paul's itinerary: three sabbaths in the synagogue of Thessalonica (17:2), eighteen months in Corinth (18:11), three months in the synagogue of Ephesus (19:8), and three months in Achaia (20:3). Luke also has an impressive grasp of the technical terms of Roman administration. He correctly distinguishes between imperial provinces governed by legates and senatorial provinces ruled by proconsuls (e.g., Acts 13:7; 16:20,22; 18:12). He is familiar with other titles of local provincial magistrates: "politarchs" (17:6), "city clerk" (19:31). Furthermore, he is informed about appropriate military titles (10:1; 21:31; 27:1).

Similar Bias

The fourth point of comparison is that of political bias. Since ancient history deals with politics and war, and all historians are partial to certain viewpoints, political bias often surfaces in their work. Herodotus and Thucydides were pro-Athenian, Polybius, Tacitus, and Josephus were pro-Roman. This is also the case with Luke–Acts, which portrays imperial Rome in a favorable light. Numerous examples can be given. In Luke's Gospel, both the Roman prefect Pilate and a Roman centurion, on separate occasions, declare Jesus innocent (23:4,14,22,47). In Acts, prominent Roman officials are converted to Christianity (Acts 10–11; 13:7–12; 28:7–10), Paul himself is a Roman citizen and enjoys all the privileges connected with that honor (16:37–39; 22:24–29), and in Rome Paul is permitted to live under house arrest and receive visitors (28:16,30–31). Luke's motive for this pro-Roman bias is probably similar to that of the Jewish historian Josephus: to achieve a favorable standing with Rome for him-

10. For example, Herodotus discussed how oracles come true, *Histories* 7.14f.; Suetonius recounts prophecies that Vespasian would become emperor of Rome, *Vespasian* 5; See also Tacitus, *Histories* 5.13, Virgil, *Ecologues* 4 (predictions of a coming ruler) and Sibylline Oracles. See other pagan prophecies in Talbert, *Reading Luke* 234–40.

self and his people. Luke sought to win Rome's favor towards Christianity, whereas Josephus had the same objective on behalf of Judaism.

Similar Views on Providence

The fifth basis of comparison concerns assumptions about fate or providence. Even though Luke's notion of divine necessity in human affairs (e.g., Lk 17:25; 22:22; 24:26; Acts 4:28; 10:42; 13:48; 17:31) has similar functions to the Greco-Roman concept of fate in history, the best context for understanding this theme is in Israelite-Jewish history. In Luke–Acts, divine necessity is closely related to fulfillment of the Jewish Scriptures (Lk 24:26–27,44–47; Acts 4:24–29; 10:42–43; 13:46–48). Although it also appears in pagan literature,[10] proof-from-prophecy in Luke–Acts is biblical. Much of Luke's thought on divine election is also informed by biblical texts (Lk 9:35; 23:35; cf. Isa 42:1; Lk 2:31–32; Acts 1:8; 13:47; cf. Isa 49:6).

In Israelite-Jewish history, the themes of divine necessity and election occur in the context of God's activity on behalf of his people, called "salvation history." Two examples of this divine activity are God's delivering Israel from Egypt and bringing it into the land of Canaan. In Luke–Acts, salvation history is identified with the appearance of Jesus as savior of the world (Lk 1:30–33; 2:10–14,27–32; Acts 3:13–15; 4:10–12) and the extension of salvation to the nations (Lk 24:46–48; Acts 1:8; 9:15; 13:47).[11]

Similar Use of Speeches

The sixth point of comparison is the use of speeches that express the author's interpretation of the events. It was common practice in ancient times to adorn historical works with speeches of the actors that expressed the historian's perspective on the events narrated. Thucydides in his introduction to the *Peloponnesian Wars* (1.22.1) states his method of employing speeches. Although its was difficult for him to follow precise wordings, Thucydides would try to keep to the general sense of the word to make the speakers say, in his opinion, what was called for by each situation. Instances can be cited, however, where Thucydides falls short of his methodological objective. Let us look at some examples. The famous funeral oration of Pericles makes little reference to the minor occasion in which it is placed (2.34–46); detailed forensic speeches make little reference to the event that prompted the debate (3.36–50); and the favorite themes of Thucydides are repeated on the mouths of different speakers

11. The following works treat the themes of divine necessity, election, and proof-from-prophecy under Luke's salvation-history scheme: H. Conzelmann, *The Theology of St. Luke*, trans. G. Buswell (New York: Harper & Row, 1961) 149–69; N. A. Dahl, "The Story of Abraham in Luke–Acts," in *SLA* 139–58; O'Toole, *Unity* 17–32.

addressing different audiences (1.120–24; 140–44). Even though some of the above examples may capture the memory of the occasion, the speeches as ancient history reflect the author's purpose and contain teaching to instruct the reader.[12]

Approximately one-fifth of the book of Acts, like the history of Thucydides, is speech material. In Acts, there are speeches that proclaim the passion, resurrection, and exaltation of Jesus (e.g., Acts 2:14–39; 3:11–26; 4:18–22; 13:16–41) and those that defend Paul and the Christian mission to the Gentiles (22:3–21; 26:1–23; 28:16–28). As in ancient history, the speeches of Acts enhance the significance of the events, advance the action of the narrative, and allow the author to address his audience through his characters. Although some speeches may capture the essence of the original event, they primarily reflect the author's interpretation and perspective. Many speeches do not even apply to the specific setting in which they are found, but go beyond the historical situation to address the readers of the book.[13]

Similar Arrangement in Linear Progression

Both Greco-Roman and Israelite-Jewish histories basically follow a linear progression of time, although both were acquainted with cyclical patterns. For example, the Greek Herodotus begins his *Histories* with the rise of the Persian Empire from its beginnings to the sixth century BC (1.1–5.27). He then progresses to the Greek and the Persian wars of the sixth and fifth centuries BC (5.28–9.1). The Jewish historian, Josephus, in his *Antiquities*, follows the progression of biblical history in his first eleven books: Creation, to the Exodus (12th cent. BC), to the Exile and Restoration (6th

12. Cadbury, "The Speeches in Acts," *BC* 5:405 (402–27). For other studies on the Lukan speeches, see M. Dibelius, *Studies in Acts of the Apostles* 138–91; E. Schweizer, "Concerning the Speeches in Acts," *SLA* 208–16. Two examples from the Roman period revealing the authors' creative use of speeches will also be given. The speech of Caesar to his soldiers in Dio Cassius, *Roman History* 38.36–46, is very different from the brief address reported by Caesar himself in *Gallic Wars* 1.40. Josephus, reporting on the same event in different books, puts two different speeches in the mouth of Herod in *War* 1.373–379 and *Ant.* 15.53.

13. The author of Luke–Acts appears to make creative use of his speeches as in ancient history. First, the speeches and narratives are dominated by the style and thought of Luke. Second, the author's favorite scriptural quotes occur in the mouths of different speakers on different occasions, for example: Ps 16 in both Acts 2:27 (Peter) and 13:35 (Paul); Dt 18 in both 3:22 (Peter) and 7:37 (Stephen); Ex 20 in both 4:24 (the disciples) and 14:15 (Paul). Third, a similar logic of interpreting biblical quotes is presupposed in all of the above speeches: (a) Scripture says this; (b) this must apply to the speaker's time or another era; (c) it does not apply to the speaker's time; (d) therefore since it was fulfilled in Jesus, it may be applied to him. All the Christian speakers of Acts interpret Scripture in the same manner. Cadbury, "Speeches," *BC* 5:408.

and 5th cents. BC). In the remaining nine books, Josephus continues from the death of Alexander the Great (4th cent. BC) to the Maccabean and Hasmonean periods (2nd and 1st cents. BC), ending with the outset of the Jewish revolt (AD 66). The *War of the Jews* by Josephus begins with a survey of events from Antiochus IV Epiphanes (168 BC) to the death of Herod the Great (4 BC). He continues from the death of Herod up to the time Vespasian was sent to the subdue the Jewish revolt (AD 66) and then focuses on the Jewish revolt in the remaining five books (AD 66–73).

Luke–Acts covers not the centuries outlined by Herodotus and Josephus, but less than sixty years from the birth of Jesus to the imprisonment of Paul at Rome (4 BC–AD 62). The reason for this brevity is that Luke, like ancient historians, is selective. He reports only what is "important, essential, personal or useful."[14] Luke–Acts moves in a geographical and chronological progression from Jesus to the Jerusalem church and Paul. The book of Acts begins with the emergence of Christianity in Jerusalem (1:15–8:3 [AD 33?]). It continues with the spread of Christianity into Samaria and the coastal regions of Palestine (8:4–11:18 [AD 34–36?]). Acts then focuses on the development of Christianity in Antioch, Asia Minor (11:19–15:35 [AD 37–48]), and the Aegean Sea region (15:36–19:20 [AD 48–55]). It concludes with the progression of Christianity from Jerusalem to Rome in the story of Paul's journeys, imprisonment, and appeal to Caesar (19:21–28:31 [AD 57–62]).[15]

THE BIOGRAPHICAL GENRE: A COMPARISON WITH MATTHEW

Let us turn to the second ancient genre to be examined: biography.[16] Why would any of the Gospels and Acts be comparable to biography?

---

14. Lucian, *How to Write History* 53.
15. Cf. Cadbury, "Greek and Jewish Traditions of Writing History," *BC* 2:22–29, for other comparisons, see 7–21.
16. Most of the primary sources of ancient biography cited in this section are from the LCL. See also A. N. Athanassakis, *The Life of Pachomius* (Missoula, Mont.: Scholars Press, 1975); D. Aune, "The Problem of the Genre of the Gospels: A Critique of C. H. Talbert's What is a Gospel?" *Gospel Perspectives*, vol. 2, ed. R. T. France and D. Wenham (Sheffield: JSOT Press, 1981); idem, "Greco-Roman Biography," *Greco-Roman Literature and the NT*, ed. D. Aune (Atlanta: Scholars Press, 1988), 107–26; D. L. Barr and J. L. Wentling, "Conventions of Classical Biography and the Genre of Luke–Acts: A Preliminary Study," *Luke–Acts* 63–88; Cartlidge and Dungan, *Documents*; P. Cox, *Biography in Late Antiquity* (Berkeley: University of California Press, 1983); R. H. Gundry, "Recent Investigations into the Literary Genre 'Gospel,' " *New Dimensions* 97–114; M. Hadas and M. Smith, *Heroes and Gods, Spiritual Biographies in Antiquity* (New York: Harper & Row, 1965); Shuler, *A Genre for the Gospels*; Talbert, *Literary Patterns*; "Prophecies of Future Greatness:

They have little to say about Jesus' human personality, his appearance and character, his origin, education, and development. The Gospels and Acts are not as cultivated in techniques of composition as great literature of this type. They are also rich in traditions of divine activity and reflect a communal setting of worship, which are not typical of ancient biographies.[17]

Despite the above difficulties, the Gospels (especially Matthew) and most ancient biographies share a common *bios* or life pattern. The pattern manifests itself in at least three areas: (1) similar *topoi* or topics relevant to the praise of an individual, (2) analogous literary techniques of creative arrangement, amplification, and comparison, and (3) a common intent to praise and honor a great individual.[18] It will now be shown that the above elements are found in both the Gospel of Matthew and ancient biography.

Before discussing the basic features of ancient biography, we will first address some of the difficulties raised. Next, we will define what type of biography with which we are comparing Matthew's Gospel. Then, we will give examples of the genre.

The Basic Objections Addressed

Let us now respond to the three difficulties raised. First, concerning the comment about no mention of Jesus' human personality, appearance, character, origin, education, and development, it will be shown that books which follow the three aspects of a *bios* pattern need not include all of the above characteristics to be a biography. Second, concerning the literary quality of the Gospels, although they were not written in the Attic Greek of Polybius and Xenophon, they are more than loosely joined collections of folk traditions produced by sectarian communities. Redaction and literary criticisms have established that the final forms of the Gospels and Acts are the designed literary products of creative authors. The

---

The Contribution of Greco-Roman Biographies to an Understanding of Luke 1:– 4:15," *The Divine Helmsman*, ed. J. Crenshaw and S. Sandmel (New York: Ktav, 1980), 129–41; idem, *Gospel?*; C. W. Votaw, *The Gospels and Contemporary Biographies in the Greco-Roman World*, 1915 ed. (Philadelphia: Fortress, 1970); A. Wardman, *Plutarch's Lives* (Berkeley and Los Angeles: University of California Press, 1974).

17. Bultmann, *Synoptic Tradition* 371–74.

18. These three characteristics apply to a certain type of ancient biography, *encomium*, which was well known in late antiquity. The three points are derived from both the remarks of Greek and Latin rhetoricians and a comparison of ancient biographies, as outlined in Shuler, *Genre for the Gospels* 85–87, 92–106. These characteristics would not include biographies which seek to discredit a teacher (e.g., Lucian, *Alexander the False Prophet*) or those which combine genres (e.g., *Life of Aesop*, a romantic type of biography).

Gospels and Acts are not polished Attic Greek but reflect definite techniques of composition and style. Third, it can be shown that numerous ancient biographies: (a) contain myths of immortals and divine men (e.g., Alexander the Great, Augustus, Pythagoras, Apollonius of Tyana); and (b) are linked to communities founded by, or connected with, the hero of the narratives (e.g., emperor cults of Alexander and Augustus, religious communities of Pythagoras, shrines and temples of Apollonius).[19]

Characteristics of Laudatory Biography

The type of ancient biography with which we are concerned is called *encomium* or laudatory biography. This was a distinct type of literature in the ancient Mediterranean world whose primary concern was to show individual greatness and merit.[20]

The three characteristics of *encomium* (i.e., *topoi*, literary techniques, and common intent) are derived from Greek and Roman experts on rhetoric: Aristotle (4th cent. BC), Cicero (1st cent. BC), Quintilian (1st cent. AD), Theon of Egypt (2nd cent. AD), and Hermogenes of Tarsus (2nd cent. AD). Because of the far reaching influence of many of the above rhetoricians, the techniques of writing *encomia* would have been known in most areas of the first-century Mediterranean world.[21]

Similar Topoi

The first identifiable characteristic of ancient biography is *topoi* (i.e., "topics, common-places, or elements"). This feature of *encomium* consists of topics of birth, ancestry, character, deeds, virtues, and type of death. The use of such *topoi* was determined by the design of the author. Detailed explanations of them are given by Quintilian and Theon of Smyrna.

Matthew's Gospel contains the following *topoi* in the accounts of Jesus' birth and infancy: (a) his illustrious lineage through his earthly father (1:1–17); (b) his upright earthly father (1:19); (c) the time and place of his birth (2:1); (d) his escape from death as an infant (2:13–15); and (e) his hometown (2:23). These *topoi* are accented by dreams, stellar illumination, and the adoration of the child. Many of these elements appear in ancient biog-

---

19. Talbert, *Gospel?* 25–113;
20. On formal *encomia* and the characteristics of the laudatory biography genre cf. Isocrates, *Helen, Busiris, Evagoras*; Tacitus, *Agricola*; Lucian, *Demonax*; Philostratus, *Life of Apollonius*; Shuler, *Genre for the Gospels* 57. For further discussion on the criteria for determining genre, see Barr and Wentling, "Classical Biography," *Luke–Acts* 63–88.
21. See e.g., H. I. Marrou, *A History of Education in Antiquity*, trans. G. Lamb from 1948 ed. (Madison, Wis.: University of Wisconsin Press, 1982) 198–99.

raphies (e.g., Isocrates, *Evagoras*, Philo, *Life of Moses*, Tacitus, *Agricola*).[22]

In Matthew 3–4, Jesus' baptism and temptation can be viewed as substitutes for stories about the virtues of his childhood and youth. In ch 3, Jesus is empowered by God's Spirit and his identity is revealed as God's Son. After his messianic identity is disclosed, it is tried and proven in the next scene (4:3,6). Matthew 4 presents Jesus as a strong messianic figure who can withstand temptation and provide spiritual leadership. In several laudatory biographies, heroes were praised because their vocational choices were not altered by other tempting possibilities. For example, Agricola resisted fame, Moses his royal inheritance in Egypt, and Demonax, wealth.

Other *topoi* of significance are connected with Jesus' death and resurrection. By focusing on these aspects that underscore Jesus' innocence, uprightness, and messianic identity, Matthew transforms a scandalous form of death into a victorious glorification. For example, the predictions of Jesus' impending death (16:21; 18:22–23; 20:17–19; 26:2) underscore its significance. By emphasizing the following two points, Matthew also affirms Jesus' innocence: (1) his death was the result of a treacherous scheme by his opponents (26:3–5; 27:1); and (2) the betrayer Judas realized he was wrong and feebly tried to rectify it (27:3–10).

As in the narrative of Jesus' birth, supernatural events surround his death, affirming his innocence and messianic identity. Through his wife's dream (27:19), Pilate is warned to have nothing to do with the upright Jesus. Pilate, Jesus' judge, then becomes convinced of his innocence (27:24–26). The divine necessity of Jesus' death is indicated by darkness over the land at his death (27:45) and the tearing of the temple curtain (27:51). There is also mention of an earthquake with a resurrection and appearance of the dead (27:51–53). A second earthquake also appears on the first day of the week before the women visit Jesus' tomb (28:1). Even his humiliating death is presented in such a way as to elicit faith and praise from the reader. In response to the events connected with Jesus' death the centurion and his men exclaim in unison: "Certainly this was the Son of God" (27:54).

Finally, Matthew gives special evidence of the resurrection. In Mt 27:62–66, Pilate sets up guards to prevent the theft of Jesus' body and squelch all rumors of a resurrection. Shortly afterward (28:4) it is the soldiers themselves who witness the magnificent angel rolling the stone away from the tomb, and their response is one of fear. Still later (28:11–15) the soldiers are bribed and told to falsify their testimony by stating that the disciples stole the body. Consequently, Matthew's readers can have confidence in

22. The above analysis of Matthew as ancient encomium is derived from Shuler, *Genre for the Gospels* 98–106.

the resurrection of Jesus through this carefully worked out defense.

Analogous Techniques

The second characteristic of ancient biography is found in the literary techniques of creative arrangement, amplification, and comparison. By creative *arrangement* we mean the subordination of geography and chronology to the author's design. For example, in *Agricola* by Tacitus, the author's apologetic is veiled in a conquest of Britain without a real concern for geographical accuracy.

In Matthew's Gospel, there is no attempt to trace a chronology of Jesus' life. Matthew uses the *bios* form as an outline on which to organize the traditions that commend Jesus. Traditions which eulogize the hero are historicized, like the Sermon on the Mount and the speeches of both Calgarus and Agricola in *Agricola* 29–36. Matthew further validates his presentation with numerous Scripture quotations, each prefaced by a fixed formula (e.g., 1:22; 2:15,17,23). In a similar manner, Plutarch incorporates quotations from ancient poets to support the praiseworthiness of its subjects (e.g., Philopoemen 11:2–3 and Aristides 3.4 in *Lives*).

Matthew also tends to arrange materials thematically. For example, the Sermon on the Mount (5–7) concerns righteousness; miracle stories are combined in one unit (8–9), the mission charge (10) focuses on discipleship; the section on parables (13) concerns the kingdom and its growth; rules of church discipline are collected in ch 18; teachings against the Pharisees are in ch 23; and discourses on the return of the Lord and final judgment are collected in chs 24–25. Traditions are also organized in both Philo (*Life of Moses*) and Xenophon (*Agesilaus*) to convey special themes of the authors.

Amplification is the technique used by laudatory biographers to accent the positive attributes and minimize the negative qualities of their heroes. It is a basic feature of *encomium*. Polybius described it as a "somewhat exaggerated account of . . . achievements" (*Histories* 10.21.8). Cicero described it as eulogizing actions in a way that enhances merit to the point of exaggeration (*Letters* 5.12.3). *Encomium* seeks to magnify the merits of a great person, and not to dissect or criticize that individual (cf. also Josephus, *Life*; Plutarch, *Lives*; Cornelius Nepos, *Lives of Great Men* [Pelopidas 16.1.1]).

The literary convention of amplification is used often by Matthew. The progressive disclosure of Jesus' identity as the Son of God (1–4) and the extraordinary *topoi* surrounding his death (27–28) are two examples of amplification. Both sections are heightened by the use of dreams, supernatural phenomena, and the testimony of eyewitnesses. Amplification is also evidenced in the particular segments of Jesus' life chosen by Matthew for presentation. Following most ancient biographies, Matthew concentrates on certain segments of the adult years. Matthew includes Jesus' birth and the beginning of his ministry, but only as preliminary accounts. The ministry itself focuses on a small segment of Jesus' life in comparison with the accounts of his final week. From these concentrated traditions, one can discern the identity and character of Jesus, his message proclaimed, his actions performed, the nature of the opposition as a rationale for his death, and the purposes of God throughout the entire process.

The literary technique of *comparison* was prevalent in laudatory biography. In Isocrates, *Helen* 16, the technique is used to elevate Helen to a rank above the great Hercules. Much of Helen's praiseworthiness is also derived from the character of her suitors, like the noble Theseus (38). In Isocrates, *Evagoras*, Cyrus and Conon are compared to Evagoras but neither excels him in greatness (33). In Philo, *Life of Moses* 2.19–20, the law of Moses is regarded as superior to that of other nations. It was Ptolemy Philadelphus, whose qualities are unequaled, that recognized the value of Moses' law and commissioned its translation into Greek (2.29–37).[23]

Use of comparison is evident in Matthew's Gospel. Impressive personages, like John the Baptist, Jesus' opponents, and Roman officials are shown by comparison to neither excel nor equal Jesus in greatness or authority. In Mt 3, John appears as an impressive figure: preaching, baptizing, and attracting disciples. His preaching is identical with that of Jesus (3:2; 4:17). The groups that John denounces become the opponents of Jesus (Pharisees and Sadducees, 3:7). These parallels, for Matthew, are not to argue that John and Jesus are equals or that Jesus was a disciple of John. In Mt 3:14, John's hesitation to baptize Jesus and his own willingness to be baptized by Jesus point to the *superiority* of Jesus over John. John's identification with Elijah (3:3; 11:14) also indicates Jesus' supremacy: John is the one preparing the way for another greater than he. Following the baptism, both the heavenly voice and the descent of the dove confirm this conclusion. The implication of this comparison is that, since John can be considered great, how much greater is Jesus.[24]

Matthew's depiction of Jesus and his opponents also reveals comparison. Although direct conflict begins at Matthew 12, readers are alerted earlier to impending conflict. After the Sermon on the Mount it is stated that Jesus taught with authority not as the scribes (7:28–29). In response to an indicting question (9:11) Jesus gives only a general answer (9:12–

23. In the *Letter of Aristeas*, Ptolemy Philadelphus (285–247 BC) is purported to be the backer of the Jewish translation of the Hebrew Bible into Greek (LXX) in Alexandria, Egypt.

24. This type of comparison was frequently used in rabbinic interpretation. In the hermeneutical rules of Hillel (1st cent.) it was called, *qal waḥomer* or "inference from minor and major."

13), and to charges by the Pharisees (9:34) he gives a reply later in the narrative (12:24-32). When Jesus commissions his disciples he warns them that they will encounter the same opposition that he is about to face (10:16-25). These clues alert the reader to expect greater conflicts in the narrative between Jesus and his opponents.

In Matthew 12-22 the conflict stories are more direct and intense. The Pharisees criticize Jesus for allowing his disciples to pluck grain on the Sabbath and even condemn him for healing on that sacred day (Mt 12:1-15a). The clever responses of Jesus to the accusations of his opponents (vv 3-13) indicates his superiority over them. Therefore, since they are incapable of defeating him in debate, they must destroy him (v 14). The conflict stories again become concentrated at Mt 21:23 and climax in 22:45f. Now Jesus appears as the aggressor. After a series of confrontations, the Pharisees refuse to answer a question Jesus initiates and Matthew states that "no one dared . . . to ask him any more questions" (22:46). The reader therefore concludes that Jesus is superior to his opponents. Even though Jesus answered all his opponents charges and questions, they were at a loss to answer his challenge, and so their only course of action was to seek his death.

In ancient biography, similar comparisons of the hero with his inferior opponents occur. The jealousy encountered by Moses prior to his first flight from Egypt (Philo, *Life of Moses* 1.46) and the envy successfully avoided by the humble actions of Agricola, which accounted for his longevity (Tacitus, *Agricola* 44), are two examples.

Common Intent to Praise

The third element common to the *encomium* is the intent to praise and honor a great individual. Cornelius Nepos, in his life of *Pelopidas*, was concerned about building a case for greatness (16.1.1). Xenophon in *Agesilaus* endeavored to write an "appreciation of Agesilaus" that would be "worthy of his virtue and glory" (1.1). Philo, in his *Life of Moses*, sought to present "the story of this greatest and most perfect of men" (6.1-2,4). This chief aim of the laudatory biographers determined the content and arrangement of the materials with which they worked.

In a manner characteristic of *encomium*, Matthew sought to focus on the following: (1) Jesus' prominent identity, (2) the significance of his words and deeds, and (3) the kind of response his readers should emulate towards him. This threefold purpose has parallels in Philo, *Life of Moses*, Lucian, *Demonax*, and Philostratus, *Life of Apollonius*. Matthew's distinctive focus might be in the type of response he wished to inspire in his readers: e.g., faith, praise, and obedience.

In the narrative, Matthew progressively unfolds the identity of Jesus as the "Son of God." The importance of this identification is evident from the key positions it occupies in the text (e.g., 4:3,6; 14:33; 16:16; 26:63; 27:40,54). The authentication of this identity by numerous scriptural prophecies confirms for the reader the messianic identity of Jesus. The question asked of Peter, "whom do you say I am" (16:15), with its appropriate answer, "you are the Christ . . . " (v 16), is also asked of the reader.

The second laudatory focus of Matthew is the recognition of Jesus' messianic activity. The summary of Jesus' messianic activity in Mt 4:23-25 serves as a programmatic statement which introduces both the Sermon on the Mount (5-7) and section on miracles (8-9). The proper response to this messianic activity is both heeding and doing what Jesus proclaims (7:24).

To inspire emulation of the messiah's activity, chs 1-9 constitute a paradigm of discipleship. There is no direct conflict during this period in Jesus' ministry. For Matthew this time of Jesus seems to be identical with the time of the reader, who is being taught and trained before being sent out (ch 10).[25] After announcing Jesus' messianic identity, Matthew presents his teaching on the Sermon on the Mount (cf. Lucian, *Demonax*). Matthew concludes chs 1-9 with important instruction for his readers on true discipleship (8:18-22; 9:10-13, 35-38). Only after such instruction is the disciple ready for commissioning (10). In a similar manner as Mt 1-9, chs 12-28 can be understood as providing a model for facing trials, since the teaching to the disciples in Mt 10 includes warnings of future opposition (vv 16-25).[26]

The Biographical Genre: Conclusions

Much of what we have concluded about Matthew and laudatory biog-

---

25. The Gospel of Matthew seems to presuppose a three-epoch scheme: (a) time of Israel (Jewish Scriptures); (b) time of Jesus; and (c) time of the church (rules for church, mission to Gentiles, all ministry after the resurrection) with some overlap in the last two epochs (the presence of the exalted Christ with his church, Mt 28:20). See J. D. Kingsbury, *Matthew*, PrC (Philadelphia: Fortress, 1977) 27-28; J. Meier, "Salvation-History in Matthew: In Search of a Starting Point," *CBQ* 37 (1975) 203-15.

26. In the *Lives of Eminent Philosophers*, the life of Plato (3.1-45) is recounted, followed by a listing of his disciples (3.46-47) and a summary of his doctrine (3.47-109). The same pattern is followed for other founders of philosophical schools (e.g., Pythagoras, Epicurus). In the Christian *Life of Pachomius*, the early part of the biography deals with the career of Pachomius, the founder of this particular monastic community. In section 117, he appoints Orsisius to succeed him. In sections 118-29 the life and teaching of Orsisius is recounted as one who emulates the life of Pachomius. Then Orsisius appoints Theodore as successor (130). For more discussion on these points, see the following works by Talbert: *Gospel?* 95-6; *Literary Patterns* 125-34; and *Acts*, Knox Preaching Guides (Atlanta: John Knox, 1984) 1-3.

raphy is also applicable to the other Gospels and Acts. One can hardly deny to Mark, Luke, and John, the basic *bios* pattern that we find in Matthew. Mark's Gospel, for example, is a major source for Matthew's outline of Jesus' ministry. Also, both Luke and Matthew contain redactional additions that are of a biographical nature (e.g., birth, infancy, ancestry) and employ many of the same *topoi* and literary techniques that seek to glorify Jesus.

THE DRAMATIC GENRE: A COMPARISON WITH MARK

Let us look at the last ancient genre to examine: tragic drama.[27] Why would any of the Gospels be regarded as drama? The Gospels were designed for sectarian reading, not stage presentation. They were written in colloquial prose and not in poetic verse as most dramas were. Although large sections of the Gospels consist of dialogue, it is more conversational and less poetic than most dramatic dialogue.

Reasons for a Comparison with Mark

Despite the above differences, there are a number of significant reasons for comparing the Gospels, especially Mark, with tragic drama. First, both were religious in origin and dealt with religious questions. Second, drama was so prevalent and influential in the Roman era that the Gospel writers must have been acquainted with it. Third, by that time period, drama had become diverse enough in form and function to include a work like Mark's Gospel, written by a religious teacher for a sectarian audience. Fourth, the Gospel of Mark tends to follow many of the basic components of Greek tragedy outlined in the influential Aristotle's *Poetics*.

A Well-known Genre
By the Roman period, drama was prevalent throughout the Mediterranean world. Theaters, where comedies and tragedies were performed by a chorus and actors before a live audience, have been discovered in Italy, Greece, France, Asia Minor, Egypt, Syria, Palestine, and Phoenicia.

---

27. For English translations and critical discussions of Greek and Roman drama, see W. J. Oates and E. O'Neill, eds., *The Complete Greek Drama* 2 vols. (New York: Random House, 1938) and G. E. Duckworth, ed., *The Complete Roman Drama*, 2 vols. (New York: Random House, 1942). For the Greek and Latin texts, see the LCL. For comparisons of Mark and Greek Tragedy, see Bilezikian, *Liberated Gospel*; E. W. Burch, "Tragic Action in the Second Gospel," *JR* 11 (1931) 346–58; A. Stock, *Call to Discipleship. A Literary Study of Mark's Gospel* (Wilmington, Del.: Michael Glazier, 1982); J. H. Stone, "The Gospel of Mark and *Oedipus the King*: Two Tragic Visions," *Soundings* 67 (Nashville, 1/84) 55–69.

Unlike its modern descendant, ancient drama was connected with religion. Drama was also studied in the classroom.[28] Wherever Hellenism
took root, there existed educational institutions to transmit the Greek literary heritage. Therefore, the Gospel writers were probably familiar with
ancient drama, as well as other classical literature.

A Diverse Genre

The form and function of ancient drama also became diverse during
the Roman period. There were literary or "closet plays" written for small
select groups instead of the public theater. Most of these "closet dramas"
were not written by dramatic poets but by philosophers and historiographers who generally used them as a medium for propagating their teachings. Some of these closet plays reflected contemporary historical events.
Some examples are: the nine dramas attributed to the Stoic philosopher,
Seneca; the play of *Daniel and Susanna* by the Jewish historiographer, Nicolaus of Damascus; the Latin drama, *Octavia*, reflecting the turbulent reign
of Emperor Nero. Therefore Mark's Gospel could not be excluded from
the category of drama, simply because it was not written by a dramatic
poet for public stage presentation.

A Misunderstood Genre

The Gospels, especially Mark, share more basic components with Greek
tragedy than with comedy. Although some of his actions and his associations with the "riffraff" might recall ancient comedy,[29] Jesus' purpose
and fate in Mark qualify him as a tragic hero. This Gospel also follows
many of the components of tragedy outlined in Aristotle's *Poetics*.

Whatever the relationship of the Gospels to Greek tragedy, it is an over-
simplification to associate ancient tragedy only with disaster and misfortune. The religious soul of tragedy has been described as the affirmation
of moral order, the assertion of transcendence, the mimesis of sacrifice,
and faith in the overruling of justice. The tragic element does not neces-
sitate the destruction of the whole world. In fact, "the stormy heavens
may break to shed the light of salvation."[30]

Points of Comparison with Mark

Now we will see to what extent Mark follows the characteristics of Greek
tragedy as outlined in Aristotle's *Poetics*. Although the views of this influential philosopher of the fourth century BC are not infallible, they are

28. Marrou, *History of Education in Antiquity* 161–65, 277–78, 403–4.
29. D. O. Via, *Kerygma and Comedy* 100.
30. Bilezikian, *Liberated Gospel* 26–27.

a helpful guide to the basic features of Greek tragedy as understood in antiquity. Aristotle's *Poetics* reveals a keen perception of Greek tragedy, and it is possible that his widely acclaimed views on the subject influenced the subsequent writing of tragedy.

Aristotle held that tragedy was basically an imitation of human beings in action rather than the disposition of the characters (*Poetics* 6.2).[31] Therefore, for him, the most important component of tragedy was its plot, which supplies the action in the play (6.12–18).

According to Aristotle, the plot in a tragedy includes a complication and denouement (18.1). The complication, or "tying of the knot," includes the incidents from the beginning of the story to the point just before the change in the hero's situation. The denouement or "untying of the knot," consists of everything from the beginning of the change to the end (18.1–3).

In Aristotle's plot-structure scheme, the transition between complication and denouement is called the crisis or turning point. It brings about the change in the course of action. To summarize what has taken place before the beginning of the play there is a "prologue" or opening scene. An "epilogue" also closes the play and is generally brief. Complication-denouement plot structure, prologue, and epilogue are evident in most Greek and Roman plays.

Like most Greek plays, Mark's Gospel begins with a prologue (1:1–13). This convention of providing an introduction and background for the contemporary audience is found in most tragedies (e.g., Hippolytus, Ajax). The entrance of the protagonist, Jesus, is announced by John the Baptist who soon leaves the scene (1:2–9). The statements of the messianic identity of Jesus (1:1,11), the prophetic expectation (1:2–3), and the conflict with evil (1:13), set the tone and inform the audience of the subject matter.

In the complication (1:14–8:26), Jesus is unable to proclaim his messiahship because his contemporaries are unable to recognize the nature of his vocation. Instead, he discloses it only to those who have "eyes to see and ears to hear." Jesus proclaims God's reign and performs various miracles. But those around him fail to perceive the significance of his words and deeds. Their conceptions of a political messiah or great miracle worker have blinded their understanding.

The dramatic tension created by the complication of the unrecognized messiah is partially relaxed when the disciples begin to recognize the messianic identity of Jesus (8:27–30). This pericope of Peter's confession at Caesarea Philippi serves as the crisis, or turning point, of the narrative. As a result of Peter's confession, the plot moves to its resolution or de-

31. Chapters and verses of Aristotle's *Poetics* follow LCL (Cambridge, Mass.: Harvard University Press). See also F. Lucas, *Tragedy: Serious Drama in Relation to Aristotle's "Poetics,"* rev. ed. (New York: Macmillan, 1958).

nouement (8:31–15:47). The ministry of Jesus now has a central focus: the accomplishment of his messianic task. The denouement unfolds along two lines: (1) Jesus prepares the disciples for his death, and (2) the opponents succeed in putting him to death. Jesus instructs his disciples on the necessity of his suffering and death, but they fail to understand and desert him when he is arrested. After Jesus has effectively challenged the Jewish leaders, they succeed in their scheme to kill him. Even though the death of Jesus was a tragic act, it was also the accomplished goal of his messianic mission. It was a goal to which he, as a tragic hero, nobly submitted.

Mark 16:1–8 serves as an effective closure or epilogue. As in the prologue, the contemporary audience of Mark is addressed in the scene. The audience is informed of the successful outcome of the protagonist by a young man (messenger): "He has risen, he is not here . . . but go tell his disciples . . . that he is going before you to Galilee, there you will see him." (16:6–7). This finale is a dramatic counterpoint to the denouement (the necessity of the Messiah's death). The young man's message is directed to the audience as well as the women at the tomb. The audience also shares with the women the response of fear and awe at this final scene. The brief and sudden closure (16:8) appears to evoke a dramatic suddenness that leaves the audience pondering over the meaning of the story. A stage suddenly left vacant by the character is an acceptable and effective device for ending tragedies.[32]

Following his essential component of plot, Aristotle's second component of tragedy is character or *ethos* (6:9). Although his understanding is not limited to it, much of Aristotle's discussion presupposes one dominant figure or hero, which is typical in most tragedies. According to Aristotle, the tragic hero should be: (a) characterized by moral purpose, (b) true to type (appropriate), (c) realistic, and (d) consistent in character throughout the play (15.1–6). Aristotle also mentioned that the main character or hero should be of high station and good fortune (13.6). He continues with his noteworthy statement: "This is the sort of man who is not preeminently virtuous and just" and yet it is through no evil or villainy of his own that he falls into misfortune, but rather through some "flaw in him" (13.5). Aristotle's mention of "not pre-eminently virtuous and just," coincides with his discussion of appropriate and realistic characterization. Aristotle's reference to the hero's falling into misfortune by some "flaw in him," does not connote moral deficiency, but some error of judgment (Gk. *hamartia*). It may even consist of a moral bent or quality that is turned

32. This dramatic effect is achieved in the endings of Aeschylus's *Choerphoroe, Eumenides* and Seneca's *Troades*. See also Bilezikian, *Liberated Gospel* 135–36; Stock, *Call to Discipleship* 50–53.

into a liability for the hero in unusual circumstances.[33]

In Mark's Gospel, Jesus appears as the tragic hero. His words and deeds are typical of a messianic prophet of first-century Palestine. Exclusive titles, like "Son of God," are used to enhance the nobility of his character. The humanness of his feelings and perceptions gives us a realistic portrayal.

The moral purpose of Jesus is consistently depicted in his unshakable determination to fulfill his work. Jesus' drive to complete his mission, his refusal to escape his fate, and his passive acceptance of violence, however, can also be viewed as heroic moral qualities turned into liability and misfortune by an exceptional set of circumstances (i.e., *hamartia*).

Aristotle's third component of tragedy is the "element of thought" or the message of the play. It should be intelligible and evoke the appropriate response from the listener (19.2–8). The literary techniques of arrangement in Mark's Gospel also imply a concern for the proper transmission of ideas and the responses they should elicit from the reader.

Diction, or the choice of words, expressions, and style figured prominently in Aristotle's discussion (19.7–22.19). He recommended that diction be clear and not commonplace, a style worthy of tragedy but not so ornamental as to be unintelligible (22.1). This advice was important since ancient tragedy was intended for public oral presentation.

The choice of vocabulary and style in Mark's Gospel accords with Aristotle's recommendation that clarity in expression should have priority over nobility in form. "Mark's style and syntax produce an effect of actuation similar to the animated reality of dramatic performances."[34] The following can be cited as examples: descriptive use of the Greek historical present, the impression of immediacy with auxiliary verbs of action, use of direct discourse and imperatives to intensify dramatic situations, vividly described scenes, and realism. The Koine Greek of Mark also has close affinities with the spoken dialect of everyday life. Aristotle himself pointed out the similarities between the typical "iambic meter" of Greek tragedy and conversational dialogue (*Poetics* 4.18–19). Furthermore, it was noted earlier that dramatic poetry contains colloquial expressions and descriptive verbs not unlike those of Mark's Gospel.

Aristotle's fifth and sixth components of spectacle and song, are not directly relevant to Mark's Gospel. Both melody (singing and dance) and

33. For example, in *Hippolytus* by Euripides, it was the determination of young Hippolytus to resist temptation and remain chaste for the goddess Artemis that caused his downfall. Also, in *Oedipus the King* by Sophocles, it is the tragic hero's obsession to know the truth that revealed his own crime. See Bilezikian, *Liberated Gospel* 110; O. Mandel, *Definition of Tragedy* (New York: New York University Press, 1961) 114, Jesus had a certain *hybris*, passion or obsession, typical of prophets and tragic heroes.

34. Bilezikian, *Liberated Gospel* 113.

spectacle (stage presentation) lost much of their prominence in the Roman period. The literary plays by Seneca, which do not emphasize these components, are an example.

The Gospel of Mark also contains many literary techniques of tragedy mentioned by Aristotle. Concerning the plot (*Poetics* 11), Aristotle recommended achieving the ideal tragic effect, (which was, for him, the arousing of pity and fear) by the following three ways: discovery (Mk 8:27–30), reversal of situation (8:31–33) and suffering or *pathos* (14:43–15:32). Concerning other literary devices, there are at least seven parallels: the use of irony or paradox (1:11–13; 16:6), foreshadowings or forewarnings of disaster (3:6; 8:31), forensic debates between protagonists and antagonists (11:27–33; 12:13–27), *hyporcheme* or outbursts of joy (11:7–10), final oracles of judgment on antagonists (13), messengers (1:4–9; 16:5–7), and *deus ex machina* (Lat. "god from the machine"), a divine or human character brought out to resolve quickly some desperate situation in the play (16:5–7).

The Dramatic Genre: Conclusion

The foregoing analysis indicates that Mark corresponds with many of Aristotle's characteristics of Greek tragedy. Furthermore, the prevalence of the genre in the Roman world, and its diversity which included literary or closet plays, contribute to the similarities of Mark's Gospel with the ancient category of tragic drama. Certainly there are other ancient genres with which Mark could be compared. Our purpose in this section was to show that the content of Mark's Gospel is diverse enough to include characteristics from the genre of tragic drama.

THE GOSPEL OF JOHN AND GENRE

John and the Synoptics: A Comparison

Differences

When we read the Gospel of John we seem to enter a different narrative world than that of the Synoptic Gospels. In contrast to the synoptics, John introduces us to a distinctly different Jesus: the preexistent Logos (Word) who is God's only Son, the Lamb of God, messiah, and king of Israel (Jn 1). In the Fourth Gospel, we do not find the straightforward Synoptic parables of Jesus, but rather a few complex allegories. The concise Synoptic aphorisms have become extended discourses in the form of dramatic dialogues or monologues (Jn 4; 9; 10). The miracle stories are limited to seven "signs" that glorify Jesus and teach the meaning of belief. John's emphasis on the Judean ministry of Jesus is evident by the five trips Jesus makes to Jerusalem (2:13; 5:1; 7:10; 10:22,23; 12:12) in contrast to one visit in Mark (Mk 11) and two in Luke (Lk 2:22; 19:45). In Mk 1:14, Jesus' ministry begins as John the Baptist is imprisoned; whereas in Jn 3:24 the two preachers work side by side.

According to the Synoptic Gospels, the temple was cleansed at the close of Jesus' ministry (Mk 11:15–19; Lk 19:45–46; Mt 21:12–13); in John's account it occurs at the beginning (2:13–22). The dialogue on the eating of flesh and drinking of blood (Jn 6) replaces the Last Supper words in the Synoptic tradition (e.g., Mk 14:17–25). John also includes a long farewell discourse of Jesus (chs 13–17) related to the Synoptic prayer at Gethsemane (e.g., Mk 14:32–42). The Synoptic Gospels agree that the crucifixion of Jesus took place on the Passover (Nisan 15), but John has it before the Passover to coincide with the sacrifice of lambs (Jn 1:29,36; 19:30–37). Finally, the length of Jesus' ministry in John is at least three years, whereas in the Synoptic tradition it appears to be only one.

It becomes evident from a comparison of John with the Synoptic Gospels that the structural arrangement and thematic emphases of the former are distinctive. John 1:19–12:50 seems to be built around the theme of signs (2:11; 4:54; 12:37); chs 13–17 are thematic discourses and a prayer, and chs 18:1–20:31 are a passion narrative. In distinction from the Synoptic tradition, we also find in John a high Christology (e.g., preexistent Word), a moral dualism (light/darkness, life/death), an emphasis on faith, the presence of the Paraclete (chs 14–16), and realized eschatology (e.g., 3:17–19; 11:25–26).

The Gospel of John also contains stories and discourses not found in the Synoptic Gospels: the wedding at Cana (2:1–11), the narratives concerning Nicodemus (3:1–21) and the Samaritan woman (4:7–42), the healing at the pool of Bethzatha (5:1–9), the healing of the man born blind (9:1–12), the raising of Lazarus (11:1–44), and Jesus' farewell discourse and prayer (13–17).

Similarities

Despite numerous differences, there are noteworthy similarities. Narratives that John has in common with the Synoptic Gospels are: the call of the disciples (1:35–51), the healing of the official's son (4:46–53), the feeding of the multitude followed by a sea crossing miracle (6:1–21), Peter's confession (6:66–70), the entry into Jerusalem (12:12–15), the cleansing of the temple (2:13–22), the anointing at Bethany (12:1–8), the Last Supper with a prophecy of betrayal (13:1–11), and the basic story of the passion. Events in John that follow Mark's sequence are:

(1) The work of the Baptist
(2) Jesus' departure to Galilee
(3) The feeding of a multitude
(4) Walking on the water
(5) Peter's confession
(6) The departure to Jerusalem
(7) The entry into Jerusalem and the anointing (order rearranged in John)
(8) The Supper with predictions of betrayal and denial
(9) The arrest and the passion narrative

The feeding and sea miracles followed by a discourse on bread in John also has parallels with a double cycle tradition in Mark:

	Mark	Mark	John
(a) Feeding	6:30–44 (4000)	8:1–10 (5000)	6:1–14 (5000)
(b) Sea crossing	6:45–56	8:10	6:16–21
(c) Controversy	7:1–13	8:11–13	6:15
(d) Teaching on Bread	7:14–23	8:14–21	6:22–51

Even though there are verbal differences in the above three accounts, the similar order and themes seem to indicate a common cycle of tradition.

There are also similarities between the Markan and Johannine passion narratives.

	Mark	John
(a) The anointing for burial with similar vocabulary	14:3–9	12:2–8
(b) Prediction of betrayal and denial[35]	14:18–21, 27–31	13:21–30, 36–38
(c) Trial before high priest in the context of Peter's denial	14:54 [55–65] 66–72	18:15–18 [19–24] 25–27
(d) Pilate and the "king of the Jews"	15:2–15	18:33–39
(e) Aspects of the crucifixion	15:20–37	19:16–30

Verbal Parallels

	Mark	John
(a) "Rise take up your pallet and go home" (different paralytics addressed)	2:11	5:8
(b) bread worth two hundred denarii	6:37	6:7
(c) "a pound (jar) of costly ointment of pure nard"	14:3	12:3

35. The bracketing of John's account of the trial by the narrative of Peter's denial, precisely as it appears in Mark, argues favorably for John's dependency on Mark or a pre-Markan tradition.

THEATRON OR KOILON

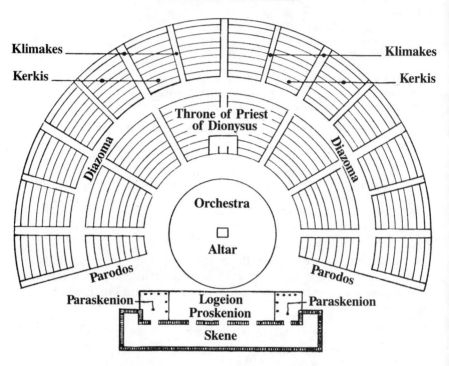

Diagram of Greek theater at Epidaurus. Taken from *W. J. Oates and E. O'Neil, Jr.*, The Complete Greek Drama, vol. 1. © 1938 by Random House. Used with permission.

The use of identical words and phrases lends further support to the view that John was familiar with either Mark's Gospel or traditions used by Mark.

Another literary source relationship seems apparent when John and Luke are compared in the story of the anointing (Jn 12:3–8; Lk 7:36–50). In Jn 12, the two unusual actions of Mary are explainable if John knew Luke's simpler version. In John she *first* anoints the feet of Jesus then dries them with her hair (!), whereas in Luke the woman wipes Jesus' feet with her hair before anointing them. John's version seems more complicated and unusual. Luke's account is simpler and less problematic. Luke is also the earliest Gospel to include the two ritualistic acts. In Mk 14:3–9, for example, the woman only anoints Jesus' head with *no mention* of wiping his feet with her hair. Therefore, it seems plausible, that the author of John derived *both acts* of footwashing and anointing from Luke and added his own curious changes which we read in Jn 12:3-8. Even if John was familiar with the Synoptic Gospels, he did not follow them closely.[36]

The Dramatic Genre: A Comparison with John's Gospel

In our comparison of the Gospel of Mark with Greek tragedy, we stressed the similarities between ancient drama and gospel. Like the Gospel of Mark, John's Gospel may also be viewed as a tragedy.[37] An application of Aristotle's theory of tragedy to the Fourth Gospel is likewise appropriate.

An Application of Aristotle's Theory

John's Prologue. John's prologue (Jn 1:1-18), like most Greek tragedies, provides an introduction and background for the contemporary audience. John's stylistic use of third person singular and plural is reminiscent of the prolegomenon recited by the chorus in Aeschylus' *Supplicants.* The content of the prologue also recalls the opening speech in Euripides' *Hippolytus,* where the goddess Aphrodite describes her power and reign before sketching some of the events up to the drama. In John's prologue, the divine identity and preexistence of the Logos (Word) sets the tone and informs the audience. Then John the Baptist announces the entrance of Jesus the central character.

John's Plot Complication. The Gospel of John conveniently breaks down into the plot structure of: complication (Jn 1:19-12:19), crisis (12:20-26), and denouement (12:27-20:31). In the complication (1:19-2:19), the audience is immediately drawn into the drama of the divine mission of Jesus the Son of God. The different characters (e.g., Nathanael, Nicodemus, the Samaritan woman, the Jews) typify the responses of belief or unbelief to Jesus' identity and mission. The "hours" (2:4; 8:20; "time" 7:6,8,30) unfold the story's plot by raising the questions: when will the hour of Jesus arrive? Why could he not attend a certain feast or be arrested— before his time had come? The statements which envelope the complication section (1:14 and 11:40) raise the question: how will God's glory be revealed? The "signs" that Jesus performed manifest God's glory (2:11), but reach a climax in "the hour" when "the Son of Man should be glorified" (12:23).

---

36. See recent discussion on John and the Synoptics by R. Kysar in *The Fourth Evangelist and His Gospel* (Minneapolis: Augsburg, 1975) 54-66; idem, "The Gospel of John in Current Research," *RelStRev* 9 (4, 1983) 315-16.

37. See the following works on the dramatic character of John: C. Connick, "The Dramatic Character of John," *JBL* 67 (2, 1948) 159-69; E. Lee "The Drama of the Fourth Gospel," *ExpT* 65 (1953-54) 173-76; W. Domeris, "The Johannine Drama," *JTSA* 42 (March 1983) 29-35; N. Flanagan, "The Gospel of John as Drama," *BibToday* 14 (4, 1981) 264-70.

Suspense in the drama is caused by the unbelief and hate of both the Jews and the world (5:16–18,42–47; 8:37–59; 10:19–20,31–33). The schemes and attempts to kill Jesus appear to both jeopardize (8:59; 10:31–33,39; 11:8) and expedite (11:47–53) the accomplishment of Jesus' mission.

Although his disciples are given clues about the "hour" of Jesus' glorification (11:40; 12:7) before ch 12:20–26, the audience has been informed throughout the drama (1:29; 3:14–15; 8:28; 10:11,17; 11:50; 12:16). The disciples and other characters in the story are like those in Sophocles' *Oedipus the King* who follow their roles unaware of the full story which is known to the audience.

John's Plot Crisis. The crisis occurs with the coming of the Greeks (Jn 12:20–26). Their entry was hinted at in Jn 7:35. The many references to the "hour/time" (of glorification 2:4; 5:25,28; 7:6,30; 8:20) make the statements in Jn 12:23 a climactic discovery: "the hour has come for the Son of Man to be glorified!" In accordance with Aristotle's recommendations of achieving ideal tragic effect in the plot (*Poetics* 10–11), the crisis of John (as in Mk 8:27–33) consists of the discovery of the hero's tragic role (Jn 12:23), anticipated reversal of the hero's situation (life to death, 12:24–25), and his subsequent *pathos* or suffering (12:27; 13:21; 19).

John's Plot Denouement. As a result of Jesus' disclosure, the plot moves to its resolution or denouement (12:27–20:31). The denouement has two lines of development: (1) preparing the disciples for Jesus' glorification and departure (Jn 14–17) and (2) the success of the opposition in putting Jesus to death (18–19). The Fourth Evangelist, like Sophocles, uses the well-known farewell discourse form to accomplish the denouement of his plot. Despite its numerous ancient parallels (e.g., Gen 47–49; Dt 31–33; T 12 Patr; Plato, *Phaedo*), the farewell discourse of Jesus (e.g., Jn 14:18–21) seems to recall the farewell address in Sophocles' *Oedipus at Colon*:

> To his wailing daughters he says, "My children, today your father leaves you. This is the end of all that I was, and the end of your task of caring for me. I know how hard it was. Yet it was made lighter by one word—love. I loved you as no one else has done. Now you must live on without me."

Both Jn 14:18–21 and the passage from *Oedipus at Colon* speak of the departure of the father/master, the nearness of the end, and the importance of the ethic of love. Even though the parallels are typical of the genre and the differences are evident (e.g., Oedipus leaves little hope of his return), the concentration of similar themes in two similar passages is noteworthy. Both John and Sophocles appear to use a similar farewell discourse form to accomplish the denouements of their respective plots.

The chief antagonist who brings about Jesus' arrest is Judas, whom Satan has possessed (Jn 6:70–71; 13:2,26–27). It is through Judas (and his Jewish collaborators) that the "ruler of this world," the "evil one" is revealed (14:30; 16:11; 17:12,15). The trial scenes provide the forensic debates with the accusers and judges serving as foils for the hero (18:12–19:16). The forensic setting of John is similar to that of *Prometheus Bound* by Aeschylus. In that play, the attention is on Prometheus and the question of his guilt for breaking a rule of Zeus, i.e., giving humans the knowledge of making fire.

The "hour" of glorification (17:1,4) is accomplished with Christ lifted up on the cross (19:25–27). The somber setting of the burial scene (19:38–20:11) is enlivened by the surprise appearance of the Lord (20:16ff.; *hyporchēmē*). He now affirms the faith of his disciples and bestows on them the Holy Spirit (20:21f.).

John's Epilogue. The epilogue or closing narration (20:30–31)[38] functions like the brief concluding chorus in a Greek tragedy, which often summarizes its contents (e.g., Sophocles *Antigone*; Euripides *Medea*; *Hippolytus*).

Common Motifs

John's Gospel also shares at least six motifs with Greek tragedies, some of which we have already mentioned. First, the content of the prologue (Jn 1:1–18) resembles of the opening speech in Euripides' *Hippolytus*, where the goddess Aphrodite describes her power and reign before sketching some of the events leading up to the drama. Second, the sign performed by Jesus at Cana (Jn 2:1–11) recalls the actions of the god Dionysius who also transformed water into wine (Euripides, *Bacchae* 704–7). Third, the motif of the vicarious suffering of Jesus (Jn 1:29; 10:11, 17–18; 11:50; 12:16, 23–24; 15:13; 19:36–37) is reminiscent of the self-sacrifice of Alcestis who died in place of her husband Admetus (Euripides, *Alcestis*).

Fourth, the farewell discourse of Jesus (e.g., Jn 14:18–21) recalls the farewell address in Sophocles' *Oedipus at Colon*. In this play, a messenger relays to the daughters of Oedipus, the king's farewell words explaining the necessity of his absence from them, the great love he has for them, and the need for them to carry on without him (1585–1658).[39] Even the theme of universal love (e.g., Jn 15) is found in Sophocles' *Antigone* 522–523. The motif of union with God (Jn 14; 17) also has parallels in Sophocles' *Oedipus the King* 314 and *Oedipus at Colon* 247.

Fifth, the trial scenes in John (18:12–19:16) are reminiscent of the forensic debates in Aeschylus, *Prometheus Bound*. The play focuses on the question of the guilt and punishment of Prometheus for his breaking a rule of Zeus by giving humans the knowledge of making fire. Sixth, the motif of the risen Christ who avoids being touched (Jn 20:17) recalls the play

---

38. We regard Jn 21 to be a later addition to the tragic drama of which Jn 1:1–18 was already an intrinsic (although added) part.

39. Oates and O'Neill, *Complete Greek Drama* 1:664–65.

of *Alcestis* by Euripides. Alcestis is brought back from the dead but cannot speak to her husband until she is consecrated after three days (1140–1150).

The above six motifs are only a selection.[40] Some may be coincidental, and others could reflect John's acquaintance with Greek tragedy, since this form of drama was prevalent in the Roman world. It would also be understandable for the Fourth Gospel to share some motifs with other Greek plays, if John is a type of Greek tragedy.

---

40. For other similar motifs of John and Greek tragedies see C. K. Barrett, *The Gospel According to John*, 2nd ed. (Philadelphia: Westminster, 1978) 380, 444, 474, 520.

7

The Ancient Letter Genre

In the previous chapter we looked at NT books that were composed in a basic narrative framework: the Four Gospels and Acts. Although they include large amounts of direct discourse, such as sayings, speeches, and dialogues, the Gospels and Acts mostly contain narrative materials (e.g., miracle stories and historical legends). Also, the direct discourse in these books are joined by narrative comments and summary statements that permeate each work. The epistolary literature is primarily direct discourse. Its small amount of narrative material is mostly autobiographical. Much of its hymns, sayings, and teaching material is part of a dialogue between author and reader. Both the audience and the author are generally specified in this genre. The pronouns that dominate it are characteristic of direct discourse: "I," "we," and "you" (sg. and pl.). Subsumed within the broader category of ancient letter are homilies and expositions. These categories are mostly practical exhortation and doctrinal expositions of Scripture typical of Jewish homilies (e.g., 4 Macc; Tob 4; Wis 1–5) and early Christian sermons (e.g., Acts 13:15–43; Heb; 2 Clem).[1] Also classified under "letter" are the so-called epistles of John. This is merely a convenience, since all do not exhibit the formal characteristics of letters (e.g., 1 Jn has none of the elements of letter form).[2]

THE LETTER GENRE: ITS IMPORTANCE

In the NT twenty-one of the twenty-seven books are labeled "letters" and both Acts and Revelation contain them (Acts 15:23–29; Rev 1:4–3:22).

1. See W. Stenger, "The Ancient Jewish Synagogue Homily," in *Greco-Roman Literature and the NT*, ed. D. Aune (Atlanta: Scholars Press, 1988), 51–70; P. Borgen, *Bread from Heaven* (Leiden: Brill, 1965); D. Schroeder, "Exhortation; Paranesis," *IDBSupp* 303–4, 643; G. Buchanan, *To the Hebrews* (Garden City, N.Y.: Doubleday, 1972).
2. See Brown, *Epistles* 86–100.

Despite its prevalence in the NT, all twenty-one books are not complete letters and the types we find are diverse. The letter to the Hebrews is actually a homily (or sermon), and both 2 Timothy and 2 Peter are farewell discourses with epistolary features. First Peter, Ephesians, and Jude appear to be homilies in letter form; 1 Timothy, Titus, and James are basically exhortations on worship and ethics. First John seems to be a midrash of John's Gospel, and 2 and 3 John are typical letters. Even the undisputed letters of Paul show diversity: Philemon is a typical personal letter and Romans is a long letter essay. The forms of argumentation or rhetoric used by Paul in his letters are also varied.

BASIC CHARACTERISTICS OF ANCIENT LETTERS

The basic characteristics of the letter genre have changed little in history. Letters are a form of written communication between two parties when person-to-person contact is impossible or inappropriate. Letters presuppose a sender and addressee, everyone else is a third party outsider. The sender's side of the dialogue dominates the letter. The addressee's conversation can be inferred, but is not fully articulated until the addressee responds in written form as a sender. Letters are also occasional, written in response to some situation or set of circumstances. Something prompted the sender to write, even if it is merely the fact of physical distance. Letters are often spontaneous, written in reaction to an incident. The above observations apply to all letters, whether they are informal, personal, and private, or formal, official, and public.

Six Basic Types

From the hundreds of letters of antiquity, at least six letter types have been discovered.[3]

1. *personal*–love letters, letters of friendship, private business, commendation or introduction between family or friends, (e.g., Philemon [commendation], papyri letters from Egypt).
2. *business*–dealing with trade taxes, wills, land (e.g., Egyptian papyri).
3. *official*–from political or military leaders to constituents, subservients or superiors (e.g., letters from Augustus, Pliny to Trajan).
4. *public letters*–literary, public pleas, and philosophical treatises (e.g., letters from Isocrates, Plato).
5. *fictitious letters*–purporting to come from heaven, an epistolary novel or pseudonymous (letters of Hippocrates, Letter of Aristeas, 2 Peter, 2 Clement).

3. Material in this section has been derived from: N. A. Dahl, "Letter," *IDBSupp* 538–41 (with helpful bibliography); Doty, *Letters*; Kümmel, *Introduction* 247–52; Roetzel, *Letters*; O. J. F. Seitz, "Letter," *IDB* 4:113–15.

6. *discursive or essay*–exposition of teaching, a monograph (e.g., 2 Maccabees 1; Martyrdom of Polycarp, Paul's letter to the Romans).

Some overlapping of the above categories does occur, since we have personal letters of Roman officials written to friends and family. Fictitious letters include fantastic letters purporting to come from heaven (Hippocrates) and pseudonymous documents written in the name of or attributed to some famous individual (letters of Jeremy, Aristeas, 2 Peter, 2 Clement). The contents of these subcategories vary greatly.

Fixed Patterns

Letters of antiquity followed a basic pattern as they do today. In modern personal letters we see the following fixed forms:

(1) Indication of place and date: St. Louis, Mo.; May 7, 1988
(2) Name of recipient: Dear John
(3) Apology for not writing sooner
(4) Statement of writer's good health and the hope that the recipient is in good health
(5) Body
(6) Salutation: "yours truly" with name of Sender.

In ancient letters we detect the following pattern:

(1) Opening (sender, addressee, greeting)
(2) Thanksgiving, wish for health
(3) Body (formal opening followed by the business which occasioned the letter)
(4) Closing (greetings, wishes for other people, final greeting, wish or prayer, sometimes a date)

Here is an example of an ancient letter using the above fixed form:

Opening: Apion to Epimachus, his father and lord, heartiest greetings.
Thanksgiving: First of all I pray that you are in health and continually prosper and fare well with my sister and her daughter and my brother.
Body: I thank the lord Sarapis that when I was in danger at sea he saved me. Straightway upon entering Misenum I received traveling money from Caesar, three gold pieces. And I am well. I beg you therefore, honored father, write me a few lines, first regarding your health, secondly regarding that of my brother and sister, thirdly that I may welcome respectfully your hand[writing] . . .
Closing: Greetings to Capito, to my brother and sister, to Sernilla and to my friends. I send you by Euctemon a little portrait of myself. My military name is Antonius Maximus. I pray for your good health. Athenonike Company[4]

Most early Christian letters, especially those of Paul, expand various portions and add new features to the above letter pattern. First, the thanksgiving section is usually expanded (e.g., 1 Thes 1:2–2:16; Phil 1:3–11). Second, many early Christian letters add new features such as: (a) an

---

4. Letter derived from: Deissmann, *LAE* 179–83.

eschatological comment which concludes certain sections (1 Thes 3:11–13; 1 Cor 1:8–9; 4:6–13); (b) mention of travel plans (1 Thes 2:17–3:13; Phil 2:19–24), (c) a section of parenesis or ethical exhortations (1 Thes 4:1–5:22; Rom 12:1–15:13; Eph 4:1–6:20), and (d) a doxology or benediction is included (1 Thes 5:28; Rom 15:33; 16:20,25–27). With these features in view, the following outline will be presented on the basic pattern of early Christian letters.

(1) Opening (sender, addressee, greeting)
(2) Thanksgiving (often with a prayer of intercession and an eschatological ending)
(3) Body (formal opening; often having a note on travel plans and an eschatological ending)
(4) Parenesis (ethical exhortation)
(5) Closing (greetings, doxology, benediction)

THE USE OF THE LETTER FORM BY EARLY CHRISTIANS

What type of letters were written by early Christians like the apostle Paul? Using two examples from his undisputed letters we find a diversity of types. Paul's letter to Philemon is a personal letter of recommendation to a friend. It does not appear to be written for the official literary public but to a house-church of several families. There are many parallels from the Egyptian papyri of this letter type. Paul's letter to the Romans, on the other hand, appears to be a letter essay like those of Epicurus and Plutarch.[5] This lengthy exposition of religious teaching and ethics was probably intended to be circulated in Rome and elsewhere.

Four Official Features

Four common features of early Christian letters give them an official quality: (1) the frequent use of an amanuensis or executive secretary (1 Cor 16:21; Rom 16:22; Gal 6:11; 2 Thes 3:17; Col 4:18); (2) the use of co-workers as messengers who deliver the letters (e.g., Rom 16:1–2; Phlm 10–12; 1 Cor 16:10; 2 Cor 8:16–18; Eph 6:21; Col 4:7); (3) the apostolic authority of the sender making the letter an official pronouncement (Rom 1:1,11; 1 Cor 1:1; 2 Cor 1:1; Gal 1:1; Eph 1:1); and (4) the associates of the sender are often included in the opening (1 Cor 1:1; 2 Cor 1:1; Phil 1:1; Phlm 1; Col 1:1). The use of secretaries (Lat. amanuenses) and messengers is typical in ancient letters. An amanuensis' role as the sender's

5. The letters attributed to the 3rd cent. BC Greek philosopher, Epicurus, are found in Diogenes Laertius, *Lives of Eminent Philosophers* 10.35–38; 84–116, 122–35. Those of the 1st cent. AD Greek biographer, Plutarch, are found in his *Moralia* 478A; 502B; 783A.

co-worker combined with the sender's apostolic authority to give most early Christian letters an official quality not unlike that of a ruler's correspondence to his constituents.

Eight Literary Forms

In the letters of Paul and other early Christians we find numerous literary forms, for instance:

1. *Autobiography.* These are statements about the sender's experiences and situation. In the case of Paul they refer to the travels and experiences of his apostolic ministry (2 Cor 1:8–10; 7:5; 12:1–10; Phil 1:12–14; 1 Thes 2:1–12). Some accounts also seek to defend his apostolic authority (Gal 1:11–2:14; 1 Cor 9).

2. *Apocalyptic material.* These unveilings of the end time refer to the Lord's coming, apostolic afflictions and trials, and other more typical features of the apocalyptic (e.g., angels, demons, new Jerusalem, final judgment). They also employ symbolic language and include visions, blessings, and special revelations. Examples are found in 1 Thes 4:13–5:11; 2 Thes 1:5–10; 2:1–17; 1 Cor 15:12–28; Jude; 2 Pet 2–3; Heb 1–2; Revelation.

3. *Catalogues and lists.* These include the Hellenistic lists of vices and virtues (e.g., Gal 5:19–23; Col 3:5–15), household rules (e.g., Col 3:18–4:1; Eph 5:21–6:9; Ti 2:1–10), and rules for the community (e.g., 1 Tim 2; 5; 1 Pet 2:13–3:7). Some lists are merely descriptive and lead to threats of condemnation or a contrast with Christian behavior (Rom 1:18–32; 1 Cor 6:9–11). Other lists are parenetic and are utilized for teaching a moral code of behavior (Col 3:5–11; Gal 5:16–24).

4. *Catechesis.* Specific accounts of teaching on Christian holiness are found in 1 Thes 4:1–9 and 1 Pet 1:13–22. Other passages teach abstinence from evil and the pursuit of righteousness (Col 3:8–4:12; Eph 4:22–25).

5. *Confessional Statements.* These brief honorific titles confessing faith in Jesus as God's agent are found in Rom 10:9; 1 Cor 11:23; and 1 Tim 3:16.

6. *Hymns.* These traditional elements are probably fragments of songs originally used in worship. There are hymns about Christ (Phil 2:2–11; 1 Pet 2:21–24; Col 1:15–20) and baptism (Eph 2:19–22; Ti 3:4–7; Rom 6), to use two examples. Hymnlike passages usually distinguish themselves from their context by a conscious parallelism, unique vocabulary, and special grammatical features.

7. *Kerygma.* This pertains to specific preaching accounts about Christ. They often refer to prophetic fulfillment of Christ, his crucifixion, resurrection, exaltation, and the promise of this coming with a subsequent call to repentance (e.g., Rom 1:1–3; 1 Cor 15:1–7; Gal 1:3–4; see also Acts 2:14–29; 10:36–43).

8. *Prophetic denouncements.* Like the Hebrew prophetic writings, these include: (a) an introduction, (b) a statement of offense, (c) resulting punishment threatened, and (d) a hortatory conclusion (e.g., Gal 1:6–9; Rom 1:18–32; 1 Cor 5:1–13; 2 Thes 1:5–12).

Four Stylistic Features

It is no surprise that the early Christian letters are replete with the stylistic habits and thought patterns of late antiquity. This diversity of literary and stylistic features include: (1) principles of literary balance, (2) figures of speech, (3) rhetorical devices, and (4) grammatical and stylistic peculiarities.

Literary Balance

Two types of literary balance found in Hebrew poetry and Hellenistic literature are evident in early Christian letters: regular and inverted parallelism. Regular parallelism follows the A B: A' B' pattern where the elements of the second group are repeated in the same order as the first. In early Christian letters, as in Hebrew poetry, regular parallelism is usually confined to smaller units and involves contrasting as well as synonymous correspondence. The following pattern from 1 Cor 9:20 is an example of synonymous parallelism:

(A) To the Jews
(B) I become as a Jew
(C) in order to win the Jews

(A') To those under the law
(B') I became as one under the law
(C') that might win those under the law.

Here the thoughts of the first stanza (A B C) are repeated with different words in the second stanza (A' B' C'). Examples of antithetical or contrasting parallelism are found in: 1 Cor 7:29–34; 10:6–10; Rom 4:25; 5:10; 2 Cor 5:13.

Inverted parallelism, or chiasm, is another principle of balance detected in early Christian letters. This introverted A B: B' A' pattern also occurs in Greco-Roman and other early Christian literature (e.g., Herodotus, *History*; Virgil's *Aeneid*; Luke–Acts). In Rom 2:6–11 we find the following chiastic pattern:

(A) God judges all (v 6)
(B) the righteous receive eternal life (v 7)
(C) the wicked receive wrath (v 8)
(C') the wicked experience distress (v 9)
(B') the good experience glory (v 10)
(A') God is impartial (v 11).

Figures of Speech

The language of the early Christian letters, like that of human language in general, abounds with symbolic words and images.[6] Therefore only

---

6. For further study, see Bullinger, *Figures of Speech*; Caird, *Language and Imagery*; Soulen, *Handbook*; N. Turner, *Style*, vol. 4 in Moulton, *Grammar*.

a few examples of this nonliteral use of language will be given. We will look at the figures of comparison and contradiction, as well as rhetorical questions and assertions.

Figures of *comparison* occur when familiar images are employed to clarify, highlight, or dramatize the speaker's ideas by means of analogy or illustration. Comparisons are drawn from family relations, the human body, sickness and death, nature, various trades, war, and athletic contests. Figures of comparison include simile, where the comparison is expressed, and metaphor, where it is implied. Paul's use of simile can be seen in 1 Thes 2:11-12, "*like* a father with his children, we exhorted each one of you." Other examples are found in Phil 2:15,22; Rom 9:27-29; 1 Cor 3:1; 4:13; 2 Cor 6:8-10; Gal 4:14; 1 Peter and James also contain many similes. In metaphors there is greater semantic power. In Gal 5:1, Paul states, "do not submit again to a yoke of slavery," and employs the imagery of slave constraints (cf. Sir 33:25-26) to describe the Galatians' futile lapse into Jewish legalism. Paul also uses slave imagery positively, to depict his obligatory relationship to Christ: Paul, a "slave (Gk. *doulos*) of Christ" (Gal 1:10; Rom 1:1). Other metaphors used by Paul are "sowing and reaping," "*fruit* of the Spirit," "*body* of Christ," and "stumbling block." These familiar images of everyday life were effective vehicles for conveying Paul's teaching.

Figures of *contradiction* are irony and paradox. Irony, a statement which intends to convey its opposite meaning, occurs frequently in 2 Cor 10-13. In these chapters Paul's dialogue with the boastful charlatans of Corinth is full of irony and sarcasm in the Socratic tradition. (See also 1 Cor 4:8; 6:4; 2 Cor 5:3).

Paradox, or an apparent contradiction that may reveal some profound truth, occurs often. For Paul, the crucifixion is a foundational paradox, 1 Cor 1:22-25. Paradoxical statements are also found in 1 Cor 7:22; 2 Cor 4:8-11; 5:17; 6:9-10; 12:10; Phil 3:7; Rom 7:15,19.

Rhetorical questions require no direct answer but are used by the speaker to attract the attention of the hearer. This provocative use of interrogation was widely employed by Hellenistic philosophers like Seneca and Epictetus. Paul in Rom 6:15 asks: "What then? Are we to sin because we are not under law but under grace? By no means!" The answer, generally given, is self-evident but the rhetorical device itself is effective in evoking a response. Rhetorical questions occur frequently in Romans (2:3-4,21-23; 3:1-9; 27-29; 4:1; 6:1; 9:19; 11:1) and James (2:4,6-7,20-21,25; 4:1,4,14).

Rhetorical assertions are numerous, so only a few examples will be given. Hyperbole, or exaggeration for the sake of emphasis, is found in Gal 1:8 "But even if we or *an angel from heaven*, should preach to you a gospel contrary to that which we preached to you, let him be accursed!" See also Gal 4:15; 5:12. Hyperbole is used often in prophetic denouncements or judicial indictments (e.g., Mt 23; Jas 5:1-6). Assertions of understatement, called "meiosis" are also found in Gal 5:23 "against such there is no law" and Rom 1:16 "I am not ashamed of the gospel." Those understatements, the opposite of hyperbole, are used for emphasis or convey a certain effect. Another form of understatement is "litotes," which affirms a fact by denying its opposite: "they make much of you, *for no good purpose*" (Gal 4:17). Litotes is also used in Acts (Acts 12:18; 19:11; 21:39). This cautious use of language was effective in courtroom rhetoric (e.g., Lysias, Cicero).

Rhetorical Devices

Rhetorical devices coincide with the previous category, since ancient techniques of effective speaking and persuasion employed much figurative language. First we will examine those dialogical and rhetorical features that Paul shares with the Hellenistic diatribe, then briefly look at the types of Hellenistic oratory with which the letters of Paul coincide.

Some early Christian letters, e.g., Rom 2-11, Jas 2, seem to employ the dialogical features of the diatribe.[7] This form of discourse and discussion probably originated in philosophical schools, where a teacher would try to expose the errors of his students and lead them into truth. It was previously thought that the diatribe was a form of Cynic propaganda for the masses, but this viewpoint only finds some support in a few sources (e.g., Bion, Dio of Prusa). Most of the primary documents for the diatribe were written by teachers of philosophical schools: e.g., Teles *Bion* (3rd cent. BC); Epictetus *Discourses* (1st cent. AD); Musonius Rufus (1st cent. AD); Plutarch (1st cent. AD); Seneca, *Moral Epistles* (1st cent. AD). Since the diatribe presupposes a student-teacher setting, then it was probably not addressed to outsiders and does not contain polemics against opponents, as some scholars have previously held.

The diatribe envisions two audiences: real and imagined. The real audience is comprised of disciples of the author who are in need of further enlightenment. The imagined audience includes a fictitious dialogue partner or objector who represents a false viewpoint. The dialogue opens with an address of indignation (*apostrophe*) to this imaginary "interlocutor" who is usually a caricature of a proud or pretentious person and represents the false views of the real audience. A dialogical exchange follows where the author resolves objections to his viewpoint or corrects false conclusions drawn from his line of reasoning. These objections and false con-

---

7. See especially: Stowers, *Diatribe*; idem, "Paul's Dialogue with a Fellow Jew in Romans 3:1-9," *CBQ* 46 (4, 1984) 707-22; A. J. Malherbe, "*Mē Genoito* in the Diatribe and Paul," *HTR* 73 (1/2, 1980) 231-40. See also Donfried, *Romans Debate* 132-41.

clusions are usually raised by the imaginary interlocutor. The purpose of the dialogue is to lead the real audience into truth by exposing false thinking or behavior.

The above discussion of diatribe has significance for understanding the argumentation in Romans and James. Both contain many of its dialogical features. In Rom 1-11, for example, the dialogical style is central to the letter's message. Paul and the author of James probably used the diatribe to expose error and lead their readers into a deeper commitment to the Christian life. It is probable that the diatribe was one of the major teaching techniques of early Christianity.

Since the NT letters are primarily written dialogues and discourses, and many are sermons in letter form, they have close affinities with Hellenistic oratory. According to the influential works on persuasion and public speaking by Aristotle, Cicero, and Quintilian there were different types of speeches characterized by a certain arrangement.[8] Political speeches and funeral orations concerned with merits and honor were called epideictic or demonstrative. Their function to display common virtues and values is similar to the purpose of Paul's letter to the Romans (cf. Colossians, Ephesians, Jude, 2 Peter, 2 Timothy). Courtroom or judicial speeches concerned with justice, (accusatory or defensive), coincide well with the apologetic functions of Galatians and 2 Cor 10-13. Speeches that provide advice for future decisions were labeled deliberative or symboleutic. First Corinthians 7-16, where Paul provides specific advice to his readers, seems to fit this category (cf. 2 Cor 8-9, Philemon, Hebrews, James, 1 Timothy, Titus).

The arrangement of these types of speeches falls into the basic pattern of: (a) introduction or exordium (e.g., Gal 1:6-10; Rom 1:1-15; Heb 1:1-4:16); (b) propositio or thesis to be demonstrated (Gal 1:11-12); (c) the facts of the case or narratio (Gal 1:11-2:14; Heb 5:1-6:20); (d) argumentation, called probatio (Gal 3:1-4:31) or confirmatio, Rom 1:18-15:13; Heb 7:1-10:18; and (e) closing summation or peroratio (Gal 6:11-18; Rom 15:14-16:23; Heb 10:19-13:21).

Stylistic Peculiarities

The following examples of stylistic peculiarities will be examined: (a) abrupt changes in syntax and thought, (b) unclear idioms, and (c) borrowings from the Septuagint (LXX).

8. On Hellenistic rhetoric and the NT, see Betz, *Galatians*; G. A. Kennedy, *Interpretation through Rhetorical Criticism* (Chapel Hill: University of North Carolina Press, 1984); W. Wuellner, "Paul's Rhetoric of Argumentation in Romans," *CBQ* 38 (1976) 330-51; idem, "Where Is Rhetorical Criticism Taking Us?" *CBQ* 49 (3, 1987) 448-63.

Abrupt changes in syntax and thought occur frequently in Paul's letters. The technical term for such a sudden break is *anacoluthon* (Gk.), but some of the phenomenon could be interpreted as either a parenthesis (i.e., a clause inserted into a sentence without regard for its syntax) or an interpolation (i.e., a block of inserted material by the author or a later editor).

An example of *anacoluthon* is found in Rom 2:15–16, where Paul is talking about the conscience of the Gentiles serving them as a moral umpire *but* suddenly breaks in with "on that day when, according to my gospel, God judges the secrets of men by Christ Jesus." The change of thought, as well as sentence structure, is sudden and unexpected. It may be either intentional or unintentional, being either a stylistic device to arouse the reader's attention or the result of an author's losing his current train of thought as a new idea is suddenly pursued. Other examples of *anacolutha* are: Gal 2:4–6; 2 Cor 1:22–23; and a large digression in 2 Cor 5:14–6:2.

Parenthetical phrases are often noted in English translations: e.g., Rom 1:13 ("but thus far have been prevented"); 2 Cor 11:21 ("I am speaking as a fool"); 2 Pet 2:8 (entire verse). An interpolation (or gloss) is a larger insertion of material disrupting the original flow of thought. It is either the work of the author or a later editor. In 2 Corinthians it has been argued that 6:14–7:1 is an interpolation by a later editor, because (a) there is no direct connection of 6:14–7:1 to what precedes or follows, (b) 2 Cor 6:13 and 7:2 connect smoothly without the passage, and (c) the vocabulary and conceptions are never or rarely used by Paul elsewhere (leading to the hypothesis that it is non-Pauline). Examples of other possible interpolations are Phil 3:2–4:3 (a later polemical fragment by Paul?) and 1 Thes 2:13–16 (which appears to be a post-70 denouncement of the Jews).

Idiomatic expressions are unclear to modern readers for at least two reasons. First, they are cultural statements foreign to us. Second, the sender often assumes his intended readers are already familiar with their meanings. Remember that we are outsiders reading these ancient letters from a third party perspective. One random example is in Gal 3:20, translated literally: "now the mediator is not of one, but God is one." In v 19 Paul is speaking of the law being ordained by angels through a mediator, but commentators are unclear about what inference Paul is trying to establish in v 20. For other examples of unclear idioms, the meanings of which are important for understanding the overall arguments, see Rom 3:7; 8:22; 1 Cor 2:16c; 15:29 (the last ref. probably reflecting an ancient practice).

Borrowings from the LXX are numerous in early Christian letters. Over seventy direct quotations from the Jewish Scriptures (Gk. or Heb. texts) are made in Paul's letters, as was pointed out in the discussion of source criticism (ch 5). Sometimes explicit mention is made of the source (e.g.,

Rom 1:17; 9:29) and frequently the source is not stated (e.g., Rom 10:13; 1 Cor 2:16; 5:13; 10:26). There are places in the letters of Paul where his entire discussion is permeated with a wide variety of lengthy scriptural quotations: e.g., Rom 9–11 (citing Isaiah, Jeremiah, Hosea, Joel, Deuteronomy, Psalms, Leviticus, Exodus, Proverbs, and 1 Kings). Generally such passages are the most difficult to interpret because the modern reader is unfamiliar with Paul's rabbinic methods of interpreting the Jewish Scriptures.[9] Many of Paul's awkward sentence constructions are also due to his use of septuagintal or Semitic phrasings (Rom 10:5–17). What has been mentioned here of Paul's letters also applies to the non-Pauline correspondence, since all make ample use of the LXX, although the selection of passages and their interpretations are generally different.

9. J. Weingren et al., "Interpretation, History of," *IDBSupp* 436–49; M. Miller, "Midrash," *IDBSupp* 593–97; E. E. Ellis, *Paul's Use of the Old Testament* (Grand Rapids: Baker, reprint 1981, 1957); idem, *Prophecy and Hermeneutic in Early Christianity* (Grand Rapids: Eerdmans, 1978), 147–220; A. Hanson, *Studies in Paul's Technique and Theology* (London, SPCK, 1974), 126–278; Longenecker, *Biblical Exegesis*, 104–32, 205–20.

8

The Genres of the Revelation of John

The ancient book of Revelation with its complex and bizarre imagery continues to be a source of fascination for readers in our modern age of science and technology. Many futuristic organizations share its vision of final disaster for human culture. Survivalist groups take literally its teaching on world tribulation by stockpiling food and arming themselves.

Certain Christians regard the entire book as a blueprint of future events before and after the second coming of Christ. Space exploration, rapid change through computer technology, and the threat of nuclear annihilation might be some external reasons for the recent fascination with Revelation, whereas feelings of alienation, pessimism, and powerlessness might be some internal reasons. Whatever the causes might be, the effects of intense interest in apocalyptic books like Revelation are evident today. What type of literature is the book of Revelation? How do we interpret its bizarre visions and dire warnings?[1]

THE DIVERSE GENRES

Most who read Revelation are impressed by the book's composite nature. It has many diverse forms found in the Gospels, Acts, and early Christian letters. Revelation also shows more dependency on the Jewish Bible for its images and phraseology than any other NT book.

In comparison with the Gospels and Acts, Revelation contains sayings, dialogues, and other forms of direct discourse placed within a narrative

1. For commentaries on Revelation see G. R. Beasley-Murray, *The Book of Revelation*, NCB (London: Oliphants, 1974); G. B. Caird, *A Commentary on the Revelation of St. John the Divine*, HNTC (New York: Harper & Row, 1966); R. H. Charles, *A Critical and Exegetical Commentary on the Revelation of St. John the Divine*, 2 vols., ICC (Edinburgh: T. & T. Clark, 1920); J. M. Ford, *Revelation*, AB 38 (Garden City, N. Y.: Doubleday, 1975); R. H. Mounce, *The Book of Revelation*, NIC (Grand Rapids: Eerdmans, 1977).

framework. The prophetic and apocalyptic materials we find in the Gospels and Acts are especially prevalent in Revelation. Numerous allusions to the Hebrew prophetic writings and the apocalyptic book of Daniel appear in the book. In comparisons with early Christian letters, Revelation is enveloped by a letter form and contains seven letters to churches. Like the early Christian letters, Revelation includes hymns, creeds, catechetical material, ethical exhortation, and both prophetic and apocalyptic material. The composite nature of Revelation has led us to conclude that it is an early Christian prophetic-apocalyptic letter. What components of the book led to such a conclusion?

The Prophetic Genre

The prophetic character of Revelation can be detected from the book's description of itself and from its literary and thematic parallels with the Hebrew prophetic books. First, Revelation describes its own contents as "prophetic" at the beginning and ending of the book (1:3; 22:7,10,18-19). Second, the opening title and motto of Revelation are reminiscent of the prophetic book of Amos (Rev 1:1-3, 7-8; Amos 1:1-2). The messages of both Amos and Revelation are ascribed to obscure individuals (e.g., not to Moses, Adam, or Enoch) and both are described as visions or divine disclosures. Third, Revelation has three visions that commission the prophet or seer to do an appointed task. The first, in Rev 1:9-20, is similar to the inaugural vision of Isa 6. The second, in Rev 4-5, is like the commissioning vision in Ezk 1:5-20. The third, in Rev 10:8-11, has parallels to Ezk 3:1-3 ("eating the scroll") and functions as the center of the book's concentric outline. Fourth, the denouncements upon the churches for misbehavior (Rev 2:1-3:22; excluding the constructive directives) are similar to the prophetic judgment speeches in Amos (1:3-2:6; 4:1-2). Fifth, the following literary forms in Revelation also have parallels in the prophetic books: vision reports (e.g., Rev 4:1-11; 6:1-18; 7:1-8; 14:1-5; cf. Amos 7:1-9; 8:1-3), woe oracles (e.g., Rev 8:13; 12:12; cf. Amos 5:18-20; 6:1-7; Isa 5:8-23; 28:1-38:8; Mic 2:1-4), and a funeral dirge (e.g., Rev 18; cf. Amos 5:1-3; Ezk 26-27). The above are only some of the prophetic features found in Revelation.

The Apocalyptic Genre

The book of Revelation is also apocalyptic in outlook and style.[2] The

---

2. See A. Y. Collins, *The Combat Myth in the Book of Revelation* (Missoula, Mont.: Scholars Press, 1976); Hanson, *Dawn of Apocalyptic*; Koch, *Rediscovery of Apocalyptic*; J. J. Pilch, *What Are They Saying About the Book of Revelation?* (New York: Paulist, 1978); Russell, *The Method and Message of Jewish Apocalyptic*; "Special Issue on

title of the book, "Revelation" (1:1), is from the Greek *apokalypsis* which means "secret unveilings of the end of the age." Revelation has a prophetic character, but its conceptual outlook is closer to apocalyptic. On the one hand, most of the Hebrew prophetic literature awaited a future political ruler in the real politics of plain history. Revelation, on the other hand, does not entertain such nationalistic hopes. Like other apocalyptic writings, Revelation sees the future political scene as hopeless and the human world dominated by angels and demons. According to this perspective, a radical transformation of the world with cosmic catastrophes and a final punishment of the wicked are needed to vindicate the faithful righteous. Examples of apocalyptic literature are: the book of Daniel, 1 Enoch, 2 Esdras, 2 Baruch, Testament/Assumption of Moses, the War Scroll of Qumran (1QM), the Psalms of Thanksgiving (1QH), and the commentary of Habakkuk (1QpHab).[3]

Apocalyptic literature is characterized by the following literary and thematic features. First, there are discourse cycles or visions between a seer and a heavenly being revealing the secrets of human destiny (e.g., Dan 10; 2 Esd 11-12; Rev 4-5; 17). Second, the visions often contain mythical images rich in symbolism: a four-headed leopard with four wings (Dan 7:6), and eagle with twelve wings and three heads (2 Esd 11:1), and a beast with ten horns and seven heads (Rev 13:1). Third, the theme of cosmic catastrophe preceding the end is mentioned: war, fire, earthquake, famine (2 Bar 25-27; 2 Esd 5:1-13; War Scroll, 1QM 1; Rev 6:1-9:21). Fourth, the events of history are regarded as predetermined in fixed periods of time (Dan 9:24; 2 Esd 4:36-37; 2 Bar 25; Rev 6:11; 4:1; 10:7). Fifth, there is to be an end of the present evil order and the beginning of a new age inaugurated by a royal mediator or son of man (Dan 7:1-14; 2 Esd 13; 1 Enoch 69:27-29; Rev 19:11-21). Sixth, there is to be a final judgment of the wicked (T Mos/As Mos 10; War Scroll, 1QM 18-19; Dan 12; Rev 20) and a vindication of the righteous to a state of bliss (1 Enoch 48-50; 1QM 19, Messianic Rule fragment from Qumran; Rev 21-22).

The Epistolary Genre

Both the epistolary framework and the letters section of Revelation comprise our final generic category to examine. After the superscription or title (1:1-3), Revelation reminds us of the opening of an early Christian letter. There is a salutation identifying the recipients as the churches of

Apocalyptic Literature" in *CBQ* 39 (3, 1977); Schmithals, *Apocalyptic*. See also, ch 2, Jewish Background.

3. For primary sources, see Charlesworth, *OTP*, vol. 1; Vermes, *Scrolls*; Dupont-Sommer, *Essene Writings*.

Asia and the sender as John (1:4a). There is also a blessing: "grace and peace" (1:4b–5a) and a doxology: "to him be glory" (1:5b–6). Then, the book ends with a concluding greeting like an early Christian letter: "the grace of the Lord Jesus Christ be with you all. Amen." (22:21). In fact, Rev 22:18–21 has parallels to 1 Cor 16:22–4. Both have a conditional formula "if anyone" (1 Cor 16:22; Rev 22:19) followed by an *anathema* or curse on the disobedient, and the prayer "come Lord Jesus" or *maranatha* (1 Cor 16:22; Rev 22:20) concluding with the wish of grace (1 Cor 16:23; Rev 22:21). The epistolary beginning and ending of Revelation appear to bracket 1:4–22:21 as a complete unit.

In addition to the epistolary framework, there are seven letters to seven churches in the first section of the book (1:4–3:22). The seven letters are similar to 2 and 3 John which contain: an opening address, praise or warning, threats and rewards, promise of a future visit and a final greetings. Upon close examination the seven letters in Revelation have five sections: (1) an address and commission to write (2:1,8,12,18; 3:1,7,14); (2) a messenger formula "these things says the One who . . . " similar to the pronouncement of the Hebrew prophets "thus says the Lord" and followed by a description of the heavenly Christ in the inaugural vision (same verses as above); (3) an exhortation introduced by "I know" which includes some or all of the following:

(a) a description of the situation with "I know that . . . " (2:2–3,13,19; 3:1,8,15)
(b) censure: with the formula, "but I hold it against you . . . " (2:4,14,20) and without this formula (3:2,16–17)
(c) a call to repentance (2:5,16,21; 3:3,19c)
(d) revelatory saying introduced by "see" or "behold" (*idou*, 2:10,22; 3:8,9,20)
(e) announcement of the Lord's coming (2:5,16,25; 3:3,11)
(f) exhortation to hold fast (2:10c,25; 3:2–3,11)

(4) a call to hear the message directed to all: "let him who has ears to hear . . . " (2:7,11,17,29; 3:6,13,22), and (5) an end-time promise: "to the victor I will give . . . " or "he who overcomes will be . . . " (2:7,10c,17b,26; 3:5,12,21).

The seven letters are addressed to seven specific churches that were once located in the ancient province of Asia, which is now the western part of modern Turkey. Although they are an integral part of the book's structure, these letters mirror the problems of early Christians at a particular place and time.

LITERARY TECHNIQUES

An analysis of the structure of Revelation will show that the author did not arrange it in a linear-temporal manner, but in a topical-thematical way.

This observation finds some support in the author's techniques of arrangement and composition.

Intercalation

To clarify the structure and plan of Revelation, let us look at some of the author's techniques of composition. First, the author employs the method of inclusion or intercalation throughout the book. This technique of bracketing material (A B A') was discussed in our analysis of Mark's Gospel. The author frames small segments, large sections and the entire book by this device. In the prophetic introduction, we have the superscription (1:1–3, A) and a motto (1:7–8, A') which brackets the epistolary prescript (1:4–6, B). In Rev 8, the announcement (2, A) and description (6ff., A') of the seven angels with seven trumpets brackets a heavenly liturgy (3–5, B). The reader is therefore required to view these elements as part of an indivisible whole. In larger sections the technique of intercalation is also employed. Between the Babylon visions in 17:1–19:10 (A) and the Jerusalem visions in 21:9–22:5 (A') is inserted the parousia-judgment series in 19:11–21:9 (B). Finally, as mentioned earlier, the entire book (B) is bracketed by an epistolary prescript (1:4–6, A) and conclusion (22:21, A').

Interludes

Closely connected to the technique of intercalation are interludes. These interrupt the progression of the narrative with visions and hymns of end-time salvation (7:1–17; 11:14–19; 12:10; 14:15; 15:24; 19:1–8; 20:4–6). Combined with intercalations, the interludes become part of a double intercalation. For example: Rev 10:1–11:14 is clearly marked as an *interlude* inserted into the cycle of seven trumpets (8:6–9:21, A; 10:1–11:14 B; 11:15–19, A'). At the same time, however, Rev 10:1–11:14 serves as an *introduction* to the following section, Rev 12–14, since it refers to the same period of persecution by the beast (11:7ff.; 13;17).

The vision of the small scroll is also held together by the pattern A (10:1–11:14), B (11:15–19), A' (12–14) and is tied to the trumpet septet of the seven-sealed scroll by the same pattern. By the method of intercalation it is tied at the other end to the bowl septet. The introduction to the bowl septet (15:1–8) is patterned analogously to that of the trumpet septet: appearance of the seven angels 15:1 (A), heavenly liturgy 15:5–8 (B) and the execution of the plagues 16:1ff. (A'). In this sequence 15:2–4 is an *interlude* which at the same time represents an *intercalation* (Rev 14, A; 15:1, B; 15:2–4, A'). The vision of the small prophetic scroll thus reaches a climax in 15:2–4, which at the same time ties it to the bowl septet of the seven sealed scroll. These examples show that the author does not divide the text into separate sections, but interlocks material from one section to the next. Thus the author joins sections together by interweaving and interlacing them through this method of intercalation.

Numerical Arrangements

Another technique used to achieve this interwoven texture of the book is that of numbers and numerical structures. The book has two scroll visions (Rev 5; 10) and four septets or cycles of seven (seven letters 2:1–3:22; seven seals 4:1–8:1; seven trumpets 8:2–9:21; 11:15–19; seven bowls 15:1, 5–16:21). The three plague septets are related to each other as prelude, crescendo, and climax, whereas the letter septet points forward to the visions of end-time salvation.

Chiasm

A further method of composition by which the author seems to have arranged the entire book is inverted parallelism or chiasm, (A B C D C' B' A'). Both the introduction (1:1–8, A) and closing of the work (22:10–22:21, A') contain a letter form, prophetic statements, and a blessing. The inaugural vision and letter septet (1:9–3:22, B) correspond to the visions of final salvation (19:11–22:9, B') in the following manner: (a) there are several points of comparison between the introductory vision of Christ in Rev 19:11–16 and that of the inaugural vision (1:9–20) with its recurrence in 2–3, and (b) the promise to the victorious in Rev 2–3 find its fulfillment in 19:11–22:9. The vision of seven bowls (15:1,5 to 19:10, C') is clearly a continuation of the vision of the seven seals and seven trumpets (4:1–9:21; 11:15–19, C), both of which bracket the central section (10:1–15:4 D) of the small prophetic scroll.

This concentric pattern was widely employed in antiquity. In Greek tragedy, as we have seen, the play unfolds by means of a complication (A), climax (B), and denouement (A'). Revelation shares many other similarities with Greek tragedy.[4] Roman architecture was often characterized by this pattern. Even the seven-branched lampstand in Jewish liturgy, the

---

4. The following studies compare Revelation with Greek tragedy: J. W. Bowman, *The First Christian Drama* (Philadelphia: Westminster, 1955); "The Revelation of John: Its Dramatic Structure and Message," *Int* 9 (1955) 436–53; "Revelation," *IDB* 4:58–70; R. Brewer, "The Influence of Greek Drama on the Apocalypse of John," *ATR* 18 (1936) 74–92; F. Palmer, *The Drama of the Apocalypse* (New York: Macmillan, 1943); J. L. Blevins, "The Genre of Revelation," *RevExp* 77 (3, 1980) 393–408. Blevins points out that six of the seven cities of Asia Minor addressed in Revelation had Greek theaters. Ephesus had the largest with a *seven*-windowed stage. Greek plays also had prologues and epilogues, a number of choruses, interludes, and hymns similar to those in Revelation.

menorah, follows the A B C D C' B' A' pattern.[5]

LITERARY DEVICES

Pre-announcements

Pre-announcements occur when promises to the victor (2–3) are repeated in chs 21–22 and the announcement of final judgment in 14:6–20 is developed in chs 17–20. They have a similar function as foreshadowings in Greek tragedy: i.e., veiled predictions or forewarnings that become increasingly specific as the action of the play unfolds.

Cross-references

Cross references are evident, for example, when the characterizations of Christ in the inaugural vision (1:9–20) recur in Rev 2–3, 14:14ff., and 19:11–16. This device enables the reader to readily identify the character in the narrative.

Contrasts

Contrasts occur in the comparisons between the beast and the Lamb, the great harlot, and the woman in ch 12, as well as the bride of the Lamb, the New Jerusalem. Contrasts effectively distinguish the identity and role of each character, and the nature and function of each object or image.

Symbolism

A common stock of symbols and images are employed throughout the book. For example, the image of the throne has to be seen in connection with other expressions and symbols of kingship in order to grasp its full impact. Symbolic colors (like: purple as royalty or luxury, black as death, and white as joy or victory) as well as symbolic numerals (such as: seven for fullness or completeness, twelve for the twelve tribes or people of God, and three and one-half as incompleteness or imperfection) are basically used the same throughout the book. Finally, the notion of end-time war is intensified and enhanced by a variety of terms and symbols of war.

---

5. For illustrations of this concentric symmetry in other works, see: "Greek Art," in *Encyclopedia Britannica* (Chicago: Encyclopedia Britannica, Inc., 1971) 10:837–40; L. Richmond, "The Temples of Apollo and Divus Augustus on Roman Coins," in *Essays and Studies Presented to William Ridgeway*, ed., E. C. Quiggin (Cambridge: University Press, 1913) 198–212.

THE SYMBOLIC WORLD VIEW

Because Revelation is apocalyptic in outlook and style, it employs much mythical and symbolic language. With other ancient writings, Revelation assumes the mythic world view of a three- storied universe (heaven, earth, hades) inhabited by angels and demons. Like other apocalyptic writings, it visualizes a radical transformation of the world through cosmic catastrophe. Revelation also makes use of well-known mythologies of antiquity. The story of the queen of heaven with the eternal child in ch 12 is one example. The elements of myth are: the woman, the child, his birth and ascension, and the dragon. This myth is international and found in Egypt (Isis, Horus, Seth), Babylon (Demkina, Marduk, Tiamat), Greece (Letho, Apollo, Python) and Palestine (Israel, messiah, Satan or Leviathan). Other examples of popular mythologies are: the heavenly council portrayed as the assembly of the gods (5), the holy wars of the archangel against the serpent (12:7–12), and the god of heaven who defeats the monster of chaos and death to bring forth a new creation (19:11–22:5).

Our usage of myth is not to be understood in a negative, but in a positive and functional sense. Myths are stories about the "world beyond" (religious reality) told in language of "this world" (human reality). Myths are expressed in symbolic language because the realities they convey are too profound or complex to be rationally explained. Myths are important in human culture because they: (a) order human experience with a foundational vision of reality; (b) inform humanity about its identity and destiny; (c) express a saving power in human life; and (d) provide patterns for human actions.

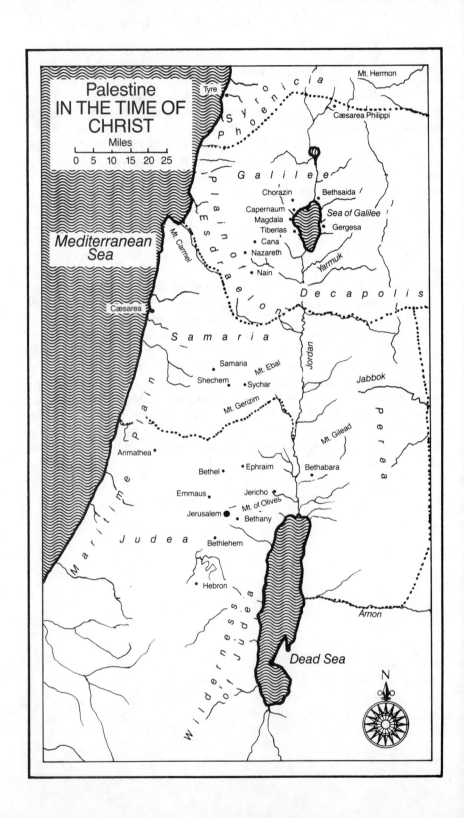

Palestine
IN THE TIME OF CHRIST

Miles
0 5 10 15 20 25

Mediterranean
Sea

Mt. Hermon

Tyre

Cæsarea Philippi

Syro Phoenicia

Plain of Esdraelon

Mt. Carmel

Galilee

Chorazin
Bethsaida
Capernaum
Magdala
Tiberias
Cana
Nazareth
Nain

Sea of Galilee
Gergesa

Yarmuk

Decapolis

Cæsarea

Samaria

Samaria
Shechem
Sychar
Mt. Ebal
Mt. Gerizim

Jordan

Jabbok

Maritime Plain

Arimathea

Bethel
Ephraim
Emmaus
Jericho
Mt. of Olives
Jerusalem
Bethany
Bethlehem

Judea

Mt. Gilead

Bethabara

Perea

Hebron

Wilderness of Judea

Arnon

Dead Sea

N

Part III
The Formation of Early Christianity

9

Reconstructing a Chronology of Jesus' Life

The task of historical reconstruction is a difficult but necessary task. Determining what really happened is not even easy in our own day. Sifting through the accounts of the assassination of John F. Kennedy in 1963 to determine what actually happened on that day in Dallas can be a bewildering enterprise for most people. The many versions of the Watergate affair of 1972 do not answer all the questions about what really happened and why. Historical reconstruction of the NT is necessary, however, because it takes seriously the historicity of this collection. Although the NT accounts are not synonymous with what actually happened, they contain data with which the historian and archaeologist can work.

In developing a chronological scheme, one can establish no certain fixed dates, only probable or plausible ones based on the available evidence. In chronological study, there are differences among scholars. Our views therefore reflect our own conclusions from the available evidence.

Early Christians were not as concerned about exact dating as we are. The synchronism, "in the fifteenth year of the reign of Tiberius" (Lk 3:1), was sufficient to mark the beginning of John the Baptist's ministry. In AD 525 Pope John I asked Dionysius, a Scythian monk to prepare a standard calendar for the Western church using the current dating scheme of AUC, anno urbis conditae (Lat. "from the foundation of Rome"), Dionysius calculated that the Christian era was January 1, 754 AUC and Christ's birth was thought to have been on December 25 immediately preceding it.[1] Therefore, it was 754 AUC = AD 1 in the calendar of Dionysius. The years before this date are denoted "BC" ("before Christ") and after by "AD" (Lat. *anno Domini* = "in the year of the Lord"). However, later research has shown that the *latest* year for Herod's death was 750 AUC, and Christ's

---

1. The traditional day of Christ's birth as December 25th was stated in Hippolytus, *Commentary on Daniel* 4.23.3 (AD 220) and by Chrysostom (AD 386). In the Eastern church, January 6th became the date for both Jesus' birth and the visit of the Magi on his second birthday.

birth according to Matthew, occurred *before* Herod's death (Mt 2:1-8). Therefore the birth of Christ must have been prior to 750 AUC or 4 BC. Josephus also places the death of Herod before a Jewish Passover.[2] This would place the Nativity sometime before March/April of 4 BC.[3]

MINISTRY OF JESUS, AD 29-33

An important chronological notation for the commencement of Jesus' ministry is found in Luke's Gospel:

> In the fifteenth year of the reign of Tiberius Caesar, Pontius Pilate being governor of Judea, and Herod being Tetrarch of Galilee, and his brother Philip tetrarch of the region of Iturea and Trachonitus, and Lysanias tetrarch of Abilene, in the high priesthood of Annas and Caiaphas, the word of God came to John the son of Zechariah in the wilderness, and he went into all the region about Jordan preaching a baptism of repentance for the forgiveness of sins (3:1-3).

The "fifteenth year of the reign of Tiberius" marks the beginning of John's ministry. At the time John was baptizing the people, he also baptized Jesus, which marked the commencement of Jesus' ministry. Therefore the ministry of Jesus began shortly after that of John. The "fifteenth year of Tiberius' reign" was probably reckoned from the death of Caesar Augustus (AD 14).[4] Therefore the date would be AD 28 or 29 for the beginning of John's ministry. This date coheres adequately with the text's other chronological notations and the dates we have established for them. Pilate served as prefect of Judea from AD 26 to 36 or 37,[5] Herod Antipas was tetrarch of Galilee until AD 39; Philip died in AD 34; and Caiaphas was high priest from AD 18 to 37.[6] Therefore, Jesus probably began his ministry around AD 29.

According to Lk 3:23, at the commencement of his ministry Jesus was "about thirty years of age." However, this need not mean that Jesus was exactly thirty but "around (*hosei*) thirty," which could mean any age from

---

2. Josephus, *Ant.* 17.206-233; *War* 2.1-13.

3. See the following work for a good summary of the discussion on the birth of Jesus and the census of Quirinius (Lk 2:1-2): Marshall, *Commentary on Luke* 99-104. We consider the text of Lk 2:1-2 to be too problematic for any attempt to reconstruct a chronology of Jesus' life.

4. The view that the "fifteenth year of Tiberius' reign" included a co-regency with Augustus is not supported by the evidence which reckons Tiberius' reign from the death of Augustus (AD 14), see Josephus, *Ant.* 18.224-237; *War* 2.181-183.

5. Josephus, *Ant.* 18.88-89. Pilate served ten years and was dismissed shortly before Tiberius' death (AD 37). The coinage issued in Judea under Pilate also supports this date.

6. Ibid., 18.29-35; 18.90-95

about 30 to about 33.[7] John 8:57 also states that in the midst of his ministry, Jesus was "not yet fifty years old," which is probably a generalized statement on Jesus' age in contrast to his claim that he existed before Abraham.[8] Therefore, for Jesus to begin his ministry at the age of 33 (4 BC–AD 29) would not conflict with the mention of his age in Lk 3:23.

Even though arguments on the duration of Jesus' ministry range from one to four years,[9] those for a two- or three-year ministry seem more plausible. The two-year position argues that John's Gospel mentions three Passovers (2:13; 6:4; 11:55) implying at least a two-year ministry.[10] This position also transposes John 5 and 6 to make better geographical sense:

John 4 Cana of Galilee
John 6 Sea of Galilee (Passover approaching, v 4)
John 5 Jerusalem (feast of v 1 is Passover)
John 7 Recently left Judea for Galilee

Advocates for the three-year ministry of Jesus make the following case.[11] First, if John's version is correct, certainly more than two years is involved with the mention of *three* Passovers in John (e.g., at least one year has already passed between Jn 2:13 and 6:4!). Second, a plausible case can be made for the death of Jesus at AD 33 instead of AD 30. The last point will be argued in the next section. The following outline supports the three-year ministry of Jesus.[12]

I.   Ministry Before the First Passover
     The beginning of Jesus' ministry was AD 29, after John baptized him, he was tested in the wilderness, called his first disciples and ministered in Capernaum.

II. Ministry from the Passover of 30 to the Passover of 31
     After the AD 30 Passover, Jesus may have ministered in Judea (Jn 3). When John was imprisoned (Mk 1:14), he returned to Galilee.

III. Ministry from Passover of 31 to Passover of 32
     The story about plucking grain on the Sabbath may reflect this period (Mk 2; Lk 6; Mt 12). The Sermon on the Mount and extensive healing activity in Galilee also took place here. John the Baptist is beheaded at this time.

---

7. Hoehner, *Chronological* 37.
8. Ibid., 23.
9. See Hoehner's discussion on the various positions, Ibid., 45–60.
10. Two-year advocates are Epiphanius, *Panarion* 51.30; Schnackenburg, *John* 1:345; G. Caird, "Chronology, New Testament," *IDB* 1:601–2.
11. Three-year advocates are Eusebius, *Eccl Hist* 1.103–4; Hoehner, *Chronological* 55–63; Guthrie, *Introduction* 294–95.
12. Hoehner, *Chronological* 60–62.

IV.   Ministry from Passover of 32 to Passover of 33
      This is probably Jesus' period of retirement from public min-
      istry (Mt 15:21–28; Mk 7:24–30). The confession at Caesarea
      Philippi also takes place here (Mk 8:27–30). Jesus' last journey
      to Jerusalem was to celebrate the Passover of AD 33.

CRUCIFIXION, AD 33

Before we try to determine the year of Jesus' crucifixion, it is important
to clarify on what day he died. First we will discuss the day of the week
and month, then examine the year of his death.

Although both Thursday and Wednesday crucifixions have been argued,[13] the traditional Friday crucifixion of Jesus is perhaps most ten-
able. The three chronological considerations for this position are: (1) The
four Gospels argue that Jesus' body laid in the tomb on the evening of
the day of the preparation (Friday), the day before the Sabbath (Mt 27:62;
28:1; Mk 15:42; Lk 23:54–56; Jn 19:31, 42); (2) Luke tells us that the women
returned home and rested on the Sabbath (Saturday, Lk 23:56). (3) The
four Gospels agree that early on the first day of the week (Sunday) the
women went to the tomb (Mt 28:1; Mk 16:1–2; Lk 24:1; Jn 20:1). The argument from Mt 12:40 that Jesus would be in the heart of the earth for
three days and three nights is parabolic and should not be pressed as
a detailed description. There are OT examples where "three days," and
"three days and nights," are approximations signifying less than the full
72-hour period (e.g., Gen 42:17–18; 2 Chron 10:5,12; Esth 4:16; 5:1; 1 Sam
30:12–13). Therefore, concerning Jesus' death and resurrection there is little
difficulty in viewing "three days and three nights" as fractions of days:
i.e., part of Friday, all of Saturday, and part of Sunday.

Now that we have discussed the day of Jesus' crucifixion, we will examine the day(s) of the month that Jesus ate the last Passover and was
crucified. According to the four Gospels and Paul, Jesus ate the Last Supper the day before his crucifixion (Mt 26:20; Mk 14:17; Lk 22:14; Jn 13:2;
1 Cor 11:23). On what day did Jesus eat the Last Supper? The Synoptics
see Jesus celebrating the Last Supper as a Passover meal on Thursday,
Nisan 14, with the trial and crucifixion on Friday, Nisan 15 (Mk 14:12;
Mt 26:17; Lk 22:7–8), whereas in John the Last Supper was not a Passover meal (Jn 13:1–4). It was celebrated on Thursday, Nisan 13, with the
trial and crucifixion on Friday, Nisan 14 (Jn 18:28; 19:14).

According to John, the time of Jesus' death was when the Paschal lambs
were slain (Jn 1:29; Nisan 14), just before the evening Passover meal (i.e.,
Nisan 15). This explanation assumes that John reckoned "days" from sun-

13. Ibid., 65–71.

set to sunset (e.g., Ex 12:18; Lev 23:32). John's version finds support in a diversity of independent sources: Paul, the Babylonian Talmud, and the Gospel of Peter.[14] Therefore we favor John's version.

Several different explanations have been given to explain the discrepancies in the Synoptics and John concerning the time of the Last Supper, i.e., during or before the Passover. The Synoptics may have been observing the solar calendar like the Qumran sect, which would date the Passover *earlier* than the official day according to the Jewish lunar calendar.[15] Second, perhaps the Synoptics followed the Pharisaic dating of the Passover, whereas John observed the Sadducean scheme (following closely Lev 23:15).[16] Third, the Synoptics adhere to the Galilean method of reckoning a day from sunrise to sunrise (e.g., Dt 16:4; Mt 28:1), but John observes the Judean method of calculating the day from sunset to sunset (e.g., Ex 12:18; Neh 13:19; Mk 4:27; 5:5).[17] According to the Galilean method, the slaying of the Passover lamb would be between 3–5 PM *on Thursday* (Nisan 14), whereas the Judean method would place the ritual between 3–5 PM *on Friday* (Nisan 14). The last explanation, appears to satisfy the data of both the Synoptics and the Gospel of John. The custom is also substantiated by the Mishnah, where Galileans did not work on the day of the Passover, but Judeans worked until midday (*Pesahim* 4.5).

Although the death of Christ was one of the most significant events of history, disagreements still persist about its date. In this century alone dates have been postulated from the broad range of AD 21–36. However, from previous discussion and other significant data, AD 30 or 33 are probable dates for Jesus' crucifixion. First, Pontius Pilate, under whom Jesus was crucified, served as prefect in Judea from AD 26 to 36.[18] Second, both

14. John's account agrees with (a) the Babylonian Talmud, *Sanhedrin* 43a "on the eve of the Passover, Yeshu was hanged"; (b) Paul, 1 Cor 5:7: "Christ, our paschal lamb has been 'sacrificed,' " (presupposing that Christ died just as the paschal lambs were slain for the Passover); and (c) the Gospel of Peter 6: Jesus was delivered to the people "on the day before the unleavened Bread, their feast." These traditions agree with John, although he specifies that Jesus' time of death (Nisan 14) was only *a few hours before* the "day the Passover" (Nisan 15) which began at sunset. Jesus probably hung on the cross for most of the day (Nisan 14) before he actually expired a few hours before sunset (before Nisan 15).

15.1QH 12.4–7; CD 6.18–9; cf. 1 Enoch 72; 74; 2 Enoch 1:1–2; 14–16; 48; A. Jaubert, *The Date of the Last Supper*, trans. I. Rafferty (New York, 1965); Vermes, *Dead Sea Scrolls* 176–77; Cross, *Library of Qumran* 46, n. 71; 103, n. 123; 235, n. 87.

16. H. L. Strack and P. Billerbeck *Kommentar zum Neuen Testament aus Talmud und Midrasch*, 6 vols. (Munich: Beck, 1924) 2.812–53.

17. A sunrise-to-sunrise reckoning for the Passover is presupposed in Josephus, *Ant.* 3.248–251 and a sunset-to-sunset reckoning is presupposed in the Mishnah *Pesahim* 10.9; *Zebahim* 5.8; see Hoehner, *Chronological* 85–90.

18. See n. 5.

The Reckoning of Passover

GALILEAN METHOD Synoptic Reckoning used by Jesus, His disciples, and Pharisees	JUDEAN METHOD John's Reckoning used by Sadducees
THURSDAY Midnight	
Sunrise	
Nisan 14 3-5 p.m. Slaying of Passover lamb	
Sunset	
Last Supper Jesus arrested	Nisan 14
FRIDAY Midnight	
Sunrise	
Nisan 15 6 a.m. Jesus before Pilate 9 a.m. Crucifixion 12-3 p.m. Darkness 3 p.m. Death of Jesus Burial of Jesus	3-5 p.m. Slaying of Passover lamb
Sunset	
	Nisan 15
SATURDAY Midnight	

This presentation is a matter of debate. Anni Jaubert, for example,
has offered a Tuesday Passover for Jesus and his disciples
and a Friday crucifixion on the official Passover, in agreement
with the Book of Jubilees, in which the Passover was always
celebrated on Tuesday.

Adapted from Harold W. Hoehner, "Chronological Aspects of the Life of Christ, Part IV: The Day of Christ's Crucifixion,"
Bibliotheca Sacra, vol. 131, no. 523 (July-September 1954), pp. 241-64. Adapted by permission.
Taken from CHRONOLOGICAL AND BACKGROUND CHARTS OF THE NEW TESTAMENT, by H. Wayne House.
Copyright ©1981 by The Zondervan Corporation. Used by permission.

John and Jesus began their ministries around AD 29 according to our interpretation of Lk 3:1–3.[19] Third, according to astronomical calculations, the
Passover (Nisan 14) took place on Friday in both AD 30 and 33.[20]

We favor AD 33 as the most plausible date, for the following reasons.
First, it allows for at least a three-year ministry from AD 29 to 33. Second,
it places both the deaths of John and Jesus closer to the defeat of Herod
Antipas by Aretas in AD 36. Aretas waged war with Antipas to avenge
both the death of John and the divorce of his daughter by Antipas to marry
Herodias.[21] Third, the accommodating attitude of Pilate towards the Jews
at the trial of Jesus is best understood after AD 31. In the fall of 31, Lucius
Sejanus, a friend of Pilate, was executed under Tiberius for seizing control of the government from AD 26 to 31.[22] As a result, the anti-Jewish

A Chronology of Jesus' Life

Birth of Jesus	5 or 4 BC
Death of Herod the Great	March or April, 4 BC
Prefects begin rule over Judea and Samaria	AD 6
Caiaphas becomes high priest	AD 18
Pilate arrives in Judea	AD 26
Beginning of John and Jesus' ministries	AD 29
Jesus' first Passover after his baptism	AD 30
John the Baptist is imprisoned	AD 30 or 31
Jesus' second Passover	AD 31
Death of John the Baptist	AD 31 or 32
Jesus' third Passover	AD 32
Jesus' final week	March-April AD 33
Entry to Jerusalem	March AD 33
Jesus eats Last Supper, is betrayed, arrested, and tried	Thursday, April 2
Jesus is tried and crucified	Friday, April 3
Jesus is laid in the tomb	Saturday, April 4
Resurrection of Jesus	Sunday, April 5

Adapted from the following work and used with permission from the publisher:
H. W. Hoehner, *Chronological Aspects of the Life of Christ*, 143, Copyright © 1977
by the Zondervan Corporation.

19. We reckon the "fifteenth year of Tiberius' reign" after the death of Augustus (AD 14).
20. See the following work for the contribution of astronomy for dating the
death of Christ: J. Jeremias, *The Eucharistic Words of Jesus*, trans. N. Perrin
(Philadelphia: Fortress, 1966) 36–41.
21. Josephus, *Ant.* 18.109–119. John disapproved of Antipas' divorce from the
daughter of Aretas to marry Herodias and was beheaded as a result (Mk 6:14–29).
22. Tacitus, *Annals* 6.48; Suetonius, *Tiberius* 36; Josephus, *Ant.* 18.179–194.

policies (practiced by Pilate)[23] were lifted and all friends of Sejanus (e.g., Pilate) were in danger of banishment. The situation after AD 31 would make Pilate very accommodating towards the Jews (e.g., Jn 19:12). Fourth, the crucifixion date of AD 33 coheres adequately with the statement in Jn 2:20. It seems to refer to the temple edifice (not the temple precincts completed AD 63) that was completed ca. 18/17 BC or "one year and six months" after Herod began his great temple reconstruction (ca. 20/19 BC; Josephus, *Ant.* 15.380–387, 421–423) and probably asserts that the temple edifice has been standing for "forty-six years," i.e., AD 29/30. This calculation assumes that the statement in Jn 2:20 was made at the outset of Jesus' ministry. Fifth, the reference to Jesus' being *"about* thirty years of age" (Lk 3:23) at the start of his ministry can be adequately explained as an approximate age (i.e., 30–35). As a result of our discussion we favor Friday Nisan 14 (April 3) AD 33 as the date of Jesus' crucifixion.[24]

23. For the cruel anti-Jewish policies of Pilate, see Josephus, *Ant.* 18.55–59; *War* 2.169–177; Philo, *On the Embassy to Gaius* 301–302.

24. The following scholars support AD 33 for the death of Christ: Reicke, *NT Era* 183–4; Hoehner, *Chronological* 103–14; P. L. Maier, "Sejanus, Pilate and the Date of the Crucifixion," *Church History* 37 (March, 1968) 3–13.

10
The Historical Jesus

THE CULTURAL PROBLEM

What was Jesus of Nazareth really like, especially his views and teaching? Was he a superstar? A sentimental teacher of love? A plotting and scheming messiah? A para-zealot revolutionary? An existentialist rabbi? What was Jesus of Nazareth really like and how do we find out about him?

The quest for the historical Jesus is not an easy one, because every person has his or her own conception of Jesus based on a particular cultural and religious context. The history of religious art, for example, provides many different faces of Jesus: a beardless Roman shepherd, a Cynic Greek philosopher, a Byzantine divinity, a grueling and tortured human of medieval Germany, Rembrandt's Renaissance Man, a pious and sentimental-looking white Anglo-Saxon, and an angry black man from an American ghetto. In nineteenth-century Western theology, he was described as a liberal teacher of brotherly love, before Albert Schweitzer argued impressively that Jesus was an urgent preacher of apocalyptic doom.[1]

1. A. Schweitzer, *The Quest of the Historical Jesus*, trans. W. Montgomery from 1906 ed. (New York: Macmillan, 1961; repr. New York: Harper & Row, 1968); survey of 19th cent. scholarship with 1968 intro. by J. M. Robinson. For more current history of Jesus studies, see G. Aulen, *Jesus in Contemporary Historical Research* (Philadelphia: Fortress, 1976); Bornkamm, *Jesus* 1–26; J. W. Bowman, *Which Jesus?* (Philadelphia: Westminster, 1970) helpful survey for beginners; H. Braun, *Jesus of Nazareth. The Man and His Time*, trans. E. Kalin (Philadelphia: Fortress, 1979); H. Conzelmann, *Jesus*, trans. J. Lord (Philadelphia: Fortress, 1973) extensive bibliography; D. Flusser, *Jesus*, trans. R. Walls (New York: Herder and Herder, 1969); J. Jeremias, *The Problem of the Historical Jesus*, trans. N. Perrin (Philadelphia: Fortress, 1964); E. Käsemann, "Blind Alleys in the 'Jesus of History' Controversy," *New Testament Questions of Today* 23–65; J. Klausner, *Jesus of Nazareth* (New York: Macmillan, 1925; Boston: Beacon, 1964); I. H. Marshall, *I Believe in the Historical Jesus* (Grand Rapids: Eerdmans, 1977); H. K. McArthur, ed. *In Search of the Historical Jesus* (New York: Charles Scribner's Sons, 1969) helpful collection of essays; Perrin, *Rediscovering* 15–53; Reumann, *Jesus*; J. M. Robinson, *A New Quest of the*

Not even the NT Gospels are immune from conceptualizing Jesus from their later cultural and religious perspectives. In the Gospels, Jesus is frequently portrayed as: (1) a pious and faithful Jew who is the supreme interpreter of the Torah, a counter to Jewish accusations of "heresy," and (2) the historic founder and present heavenly governor of the Christian church, a response to identity and authority problems in the late first century.

THE SOURCE PROBLEM

Another problem in our quest pertains to the nature of our sources: reliable data outside the NT are scarce, and the NT sources are permeated by the literary techniques and religious perspectives of the authors.

Sources Outside the NT

The sources outside the New Testament provide only bits of information about Jesus.[2]

Jewish and Roman

He is alluded to briefly by Jewish and Roman writers. Although early Christian writers refer to Jesus and his teaching more frequently, few of them are independent of NT influence. The Babylonian Talmud (AD 500) contains an early tradition about "Yeshu of Nazareth" who "practiced sorcery" . . . "led Israel astray" and "was hanged" (crucified?) as a false teacher "on the eve of the Passover" (*Sanhedrin*, 43a). Even though the tradition seems unreliable in other details, it corresponds with John's account of Jesus' execution before the Passover and the derogatory description of Jesus' activities might reflect his great reputation as a miracle worker and teacher among the Jews. In a passage attributed to the Jewish historian Josephus (AD 90), the ministry, death, and resurrection of Jesus are reported (*Ant.* 18.63–64), but it is probably a later Christian interpolation because it reads like a credal statement.

The Roman historian Tacitus (112–113) mentions that in the reign of

---

Historical Jesus (London: SCM, 1959; Philadelphia: Fortress, 1983); E. P. Sanders, *Jesus and Judaism* (Philadelphia: Fortress, 1985); G. Vermes, *Jesus the Jew. A Historian's Reading of the Gospels* (Philadelphia: Fortress, 1973); idem, *Jesus and the World of Judaism* (Philadelphia: Fortress, 1984).

2. For further information, see F. F. Bruce, *Jesus and Christian Origins Outside the New Testament* (Grand Rapids: Eerdmans, 1974); J. D. Crossan, *Sayings Parallels, A Workbook for the Jesus Tradition* (Philadelphia: Fortress, 1986); J. Jeremias, *Unknown Sayings of Jesus*, 3rd ed. (London: SPCK, 1964); Hennecke, *NTA* 1:69–116.

Tiberius Caesar "Chrestus" was given the death penalty by Pontius Pilate, and that the prefect momentarily suppressed the Chrestus sect until it broke out again in Judea and Rome (*Annals* 15.44). This information, however, may have been derived from Christian tradition since Tacitus probably based his account on police interrogations of Christians.

Christian Sources

In Christian sources other than the NT, we have a number of isolated sayings of Jesus, or "agrapha." As examples, we will look at some sayings in Codex Beza, the Gospel of Thomas, the Apocryphon of James, Clement of Alexandria, and Tertullian.[3] In the Codex Beza (D), a sixth-century NT manuscript, an independent Jesus saying occurs after Lk 6:4, stating that:

> When on the same day he saw a man doing work on the Sabbath, he said to him: Man! if you know what you are doing then you are blessed. But if you do not know what you are doing then you are cursed and a transgressor of the law.

This saying, as will be shown, coheres well with what many scholars believe to be an authentic feature of Jesus' teaching: the challenge to make one's own decisions. The apocryphal Gospel of Thomas (AD 200), discovered along with other gnostic writings at Nag Hammadi, Egypt, contains some isolated sayings that could have originated with Jesus. Translations of these sayings are from the *Nag Hammadi Library in English*.[4]

> Jesus said: "He who is near me is near the fire, and he who is far from me is far from the kingdom" (82; Origen).

> Jesus said: "The kingdom of the Father is like a man who wishes to kill a powerful man. He drew the sword in his house, he stuck it into the wall in order to know whether his hand could carry through. Then he slew the powerful man" (98; cf. Lk 14:28–32).

The Apocryphon of James (AD 200?) is another gnostic writing discovered at Nag Hammadi. The translations of these sayings are derived from a recent article.[5]

> Do not cause the kingdom of heaven to become desolate by you (or among you) (13.17–19).

> For the kingdom of heaven is like a spike of wheat, that sprouted in a field. And after it ripened, he (the farmer) sowed its fruit and again filled the field with wheat for another year (12.24–26).

---

3. Hennecke, *NTA* 1:85–116.
4. Robinson, *Nag Hammadi*.
5. C. W. Hedrick, "Kingdom Sayings and Parables of Jesus in the Apocryphon of James: Tradition and Redaction," *NTS* 29 (1982) 1–24.

In the writings of the third-century catholic Christians, Clement of Alexandria and Tertullian of Carthage, we find the following independent Jesus sayings:

> No one can attain the kingdom of heaven who has not gone through temptation (Tertullian, *On Baptism* 20.2).

> Ask for great things, and God will add to you what is small (Clement of Alexandria, *Stromateis* 1,14.158).

The above examples are considered isolated Jesus sayings because they show no clear dependency on the NT Gospels, yet their contents cohere substantially with the teaching of the historical Jesus as most scholars understand it.

NT Sources

The second source problem in our quest for the historical Jesus concerns the religious bias and literary devices of our primary document, the NT. The earliest witness to the historical Jesus is Paul, but his information is scanty in comparison with that of the four Gospels. From the letters of Paul we have allusions to Jesus' ancestry, family, ministry, disciples, betrayal, death, and resurrection, but these are found in kerygmatic and confessional traditions.[6] It is difficult to remove the religious husk in order to get to the historical kernel. Paul's letters contain some sayings attributed to Jesus, like those in 1 Thes 4:15; 1 Cor 7:10–11; 11:23–25, but only the first two appear to be independent of the synoptic tradition. The most authentic agraphon is found, not in Paul's letters but in Acts of the Apostles: "it is necessary to remember the words of the Lord Jesus, that he said, 'it is more blessed to give than to receive' " (20:35).

Even though the four Gospels provide the most information about Jesus, problems arise when (1) the Synoptic Gospels are compared with John and (2) the pervasive religious and literary features are detected in all four.

The Gospel of John

The major differences and minor similarities between John and the Synoptic Gospels raise difficulties for any historical reconstruction.[7] In John, we do not find concise synoptic sayings or parables but long discourses in the form of dramatic monologues or dialogues. The length of Jesus' ministry in John is three or four years, whereas in the synoptic tradition

---

6. The Pauline traditions about Jesus' betrayal, death and resurrection will be consulted in our discussion of these topics in a later chapter. For a more extensive treatment of the Pauline traditions about Jesus, see M. Goguel, *Jesus and the Origins of Christianity, Vol 1: Prolegomena to the Life of Jesus*, trans. O. Wyon (New York: Harper & Row, 1960) 1:105–26.

7. See Goguel, *Jesus*, 1:150–57; Brown, *John* xli–li.

it is one or two. The Synoptic Gospels regard Galilee as the main area of ministry, whereas in John it is Judea. John has Jesus make three visits to Jerusalem during his ministry, whereas the synoptic tradition mentions only one. The Synoptic Gospels have Jesus crucified on the Passover, but John has it before the Passover (cf. *Sanhedrin* 43a). Finally, John includes many unusual stories, themes and symbols not found in the other Gospels. These sharp differences make attempts at harmonization a futile enterprise.

The similarities between John and the Synoptic Gospels concern some general agreements in sequence and a few close parallels. For example, John and Mark follow a similar sequence at certain points: the work of the Baptist, Jesus' departure into Galilee, feeding a multitude, walking on water, Peter's confession, departure to Jerusalem, Jerusalem entry, and anointing (rearranged in John), the supper with predictions of betrayal, the arrest, and the passion. Some close parallels include: the account of Jesus' anointing (Jn 12:3–8; Lk 7:36–50), the cycle of feeding, lake crossing and dialogue (Jn 6:1–51; Mk 6:34–8:21), and the trial scene enveloped by the story of Peter's denial (Jn 18:15–27; Mk 14:53–72). These parallels contribute to source-critical discussions of John and the Synoptics, but are of little relevance for history of Jesus research.

Some contributions that John's Gospel might provide for our historical quest are: additional information about the relationship between Jesus and John the Baptist, the plausibility that Jesus' ministry lasted longer than one year and involved more than one trip to Jerusalem, the focus on the alleged political crimes of Jesus as the main grounds for his execution (19:12,15), his death on the eve of the Passover, and an assortment of Jesus sayings that have some stamp of authenticity (e.g., Jn 3:3,5; 4:32–38,48; 12:24–26; 13:16). The above data, however, are difficult to distinguish from the pervasive literary and religious concerns in the Fourth Gospel. The statement of the author's purpose in writing John also has relevance for our discussion on the literary-religious character of the Synoptic Gospels:

> Now Jesus did many other signs in the presence of his disciples, which are not written in this book; but these are written that you may believe that Jesus is the Christ, the Son of God, and that by believing you may have life in his name (Jn 20:30–31).

Selective use of data to magnify the greatness of Jesus for the life and faith of Christian communities, appears to be the overriding emphasis of both John and the Synoptic Gospels.

The Synoptic Gospels

What we are left with as primary documents for a history of Jesus are the Synoptic Gospels, which are just as religious in emphasis and literary in style as John's Gospel. To explain our point we merely have to review our discussion of the nature of the Gospel material.

First, we must remember that the Gospels in their final form are the end products of a long history of composition involving the use of distinct sources and traditions which originated from various communities of different localities. This original diversity makes a chronology of the life of Jesus a difficult enterprise. Second, there is a gap of three to six decades separating the final composition of the Gospels from the time of Jesus. This gap of time includes many social, cultural, and political changes which would cause the Gospel authors to maintain perceptions and perspectives different from those of Jesus. Historical and cultural distance also explains why many of the early traditions in the Gospels were revised and supplemented by the final authors for their respective audiences that lived decades after Jesus.

Third, the earliest traditions in the Gospels do not necessarily go back to the time of Jesus. Even if it can be shown that a saying originated from Palestine and could be easily translated into an Aramaic idiom, it does not establish with certainty that the saying is directly from Jesus. The reason for this caution is because of the following development immediately after Jesus. Scholars agree that many of the earliest sayings in the Gospel tradition did not originate with Jesus but with early Aramaic-speaking Christians of Palestine, who, like Jesus, were probably itinerant end-time oriented preachers who traveled throughout rural Palestine, often labeled by scholars as the "Jesus movement."[8]

Because of this long history of composition with diverse traditions revised by final authors, the Synoptic Gospels remain ambiguous sources for recovering the authentic sayings of Jesus. In the case of John's Gospel, the history of composition is even longer and more complex, involving at least four phases of tradition from the mid-first to the second centuries. This is why the attempts at constructing a chronology of Jesus' life by harmonizing the accounts of all four Gospels are futile endeavors that disregard the literary and historical character of these writings.

The question that remains is this: how do we attempt to recover the authentic teaching of Jesus? Because the Gospels are collections of independent sayings and stories placed in a certain scheme for religious

---

8. See the classic discussions on the kerygma of the primitive church in Bultmann, *Theology* 1:33–62; and R. Fuller, *The Foundations of New Testament Christology* (London: William Collins Sons, 1965) 23–61. For a current sociological treatment of this period, see Theissen, *Sociology*. Recent dissent on the classic distinctions between Hellenistic and Jewish Christianity is found in Hengel, *Jesus and Paul* 1–47. For a modified position on Palestinian Christianity, utilizing the above research, see Perrin and Duling, *NTIntro* 73–79.

purposes, we can rightfully inquire about the authenticity of these sayings and stories for understanding the message of the historical Jesus.

THE CRITERIA OF AUTHENTICITY

In our quest to discover the historical Jesus , it is necessary to have some standard by which to distinguish the early Jesus material from the later Christian modifications and adaptations. Four useful criteria for making such distinctions have been formulated in the history of Jesus research:[9] (1) Palestinian coloring, (2) dissimilarity or discontinuity, (3) multiple attestation, and (4) coherence or consistency.

Palestinian Coloring

The first criterion of Palestinian coloring actually functions as a negative linguistic and environmental test. No saying can be regarded as authentic if it does not: (a) manifest some Aramaic traits, like translation Greek from an Aramaic original (the native tongue of Jesus) or Hebrew poetic forms, like synonymous or antithetical parallelism, or (b) reflect the life and customs of Palestine, like social and domestic customs, agricultural processes, religious beliefs. Palestinian coloring serves as a negative test because, as we mentioned, many early sayings could have originated from Aramaic-speaking Christians of Palestine who appeared soon after Jesus.

Discontinuity

The second criterion of dissimilarity is the most important and controversial test. A saying or parable is probably authentic if it is dissimilar from characteristic emphases and perspectives of both ancient Judaism and early Christianity. An authentic saying of Jesus would not be a parody of typical Jewish piety or morality (especially of post-70 Judaism); neither would it contain any specific Christian terminology (e.g., gospel, cross, church) or beliefs (e.g., lordship of Christ, imminent return of Christ). For example, the use of "Father" or "Abba" (Aramaic) in addressing God (Lk 11:2; Mk 14:36) is probably authentic because the Jews of Jesus' day preferred an epithet like "Our Heavenly Father," or something similar, and the early church after Jesus reverted to the Jewish mode of address (Mt 6:9).

9. The four criteria of authenticity have been derived from independent research in the following two works: R. Fuller, *A Critical Introduction to the New Testament* (London: Duckworth and Co., 1966, 1971) 94–103, and Perrin, *Rediscovering* 39–47.

The obvious problems with the criterion of dissimilarity are: (a) it ig-
nores material in which Jesus agreed with his Jewish heritage and the
early church agreed with him, and (b) in concentrating on what was distinctive it may present a distorted message of Jesus. In response to the
above problems, the following rationale is presented. Both the fact of cultural assimilation and the nature of the Gospel material require that we
employ the criterion of dissimilarity. The history of Christianity has indicated that every person and group had their own conception of Jesus
based on their particular cultural and religious context (e.g., religious art,
theology). Historical criticism has also shown that the perspectives of the
four evangelists were different from that of Jesus. By the time that the
Gospels were written (80–90) the church had begun to assimilate the institutional structures and organizational outlook of the Judaism of its day
(e.g., elders, church discipline, rules of worship).

Concerning the nature of the gospels, redaction criticism has further
pointed out that the authors constructed their own portraits of Jesus in
response to problems of their particular situation. As a result, scholars
have detected in the Gospels evidence of Jewish caricatures and Christian idealizations of Jesus, as well as the reasons for these formulations.
For instance, in reaction to Jewish accusations of "apostasy," Jesus was
presented by the evangelists as a pious and faithful Jew (Lk) who is the
supreme interpreter of the law (Mt). In response to identity and authority
problems, Jesus was presented as the historic founder and present heavenly governor of the Christian church (Mt, Lk). Secondly, the criterion
of dissimilarity is a relatively certain test. Its judicious use has led to the
distinctive elements in such fundamental concepts as Jesus' proclamation
of the God's rule, his use of parables and wisdom sayings, and the prayer
he taught his disciples (Lk 11:2–4).

Multiple Attestation

The third criterion of multiple attestation is a cross-sectional test to be
used with the others and it focuses on themes or concerns behind a particular saying or parable. If a concern or practice ascribed to Jesus can
be traced back to several independent sources (Mk, Q, M, L, Jn) and different literary forms (parable, wisdom saying, controversy story), it probably is an early "Jesus tradition." As in the criterion of Palestinian coloring,
this test may only bring us back as far as early Palestinian Christianity.
But used in conjunction with the other criteria, it functions as a useful
test of verification. Thus, Jesus' fellowship with tax collectors and outcasts, which has been established as authentic by the criterion of dissimilarity (both the Jews of Jesus' day [Mishnah, *Tohoroth* 7:6] and the early
church [Mt 18:17] scorned them), is also verified by the criterion of mul-

tiple attestation. His association with tax collectors and sinners occurs in prophetic (Mt 11:19/Lk 7:34) and wisdom (Mt 5:46/Lk 6:33) sayings of Q, and in pronouncement (Mk 2:14) and controversy (2:15f.) stories of Mark. The authenticity of this practice of Jesus is attested to in two independent sources (Q, Mk) and four different literary forms.

Coherence

The last criterion of coherence functions as a positive test that builds upon the other criteria. Early material can be accepted as authentic if it coheres or is consistent with material already established as authentic by the other criteria. For example, once the distinctive message of Jesus has been established by the other criteria, Jesus traditions which are consistent with this message can be regarded as authentic. Over one dozen sayings ascribed to Jesus outside the NT (e.g., Gospel of Thomas), bear the stamp of authenticity because they conform closely to the criteria of coherence.

JESUS' LIFE IN OUTLINE

With sensitivity to the difficulties of a quest for the historical Jesus and with attention given to the four criteria for detecting authentic teaching, we will give a brief sketch of the life of Jesus.[10]

Jesus was born about 4 BC to Mary and Joseph the carpenter or stone mason from Nazareth of Galilee. Jesus had brothers, one of whom (James) became prominent in the Palestinian church, and sisters (Mk 6:3). He grew up and was educated in the environment of the rural village life of Galilee, and his native tongue was the language of Palestine, Aramaic. He was baptized by John the Baptist, and the beginning of his ministry was in some way linked with that of the Baptist. In his own ministry Jesus was primarily the one who proclaimed the reign of God and who challenged his hearers to respond to the reality he was proclaiming. The authority and effectiveness of Jesus as proclaimer of God's rule was reinforced by his great reputation as a healer and exorcist. In a world of many gods, demons, and spirits, he was able, by the authority of God and his reign, to help those who were believed to be oppressed by demons. Thus, he moved from village to village, preaching God's reign, healing the sick, ex-

10. Derived from: Perrin and Duling, *NTIntro* 411–12; for a similar but lengthier sketch, see Bornkamm, *Jesus of Nazareth* 53–63.
    On the importance of the empty tomb discovery and the reported appearances of the risen Christ for the birth and growth of earliest Christianity, see: L. T. Johnson, *The Writings of the New Testament, An Interpretation* (Philadelphia: Fortress, 1986) 98–113; H. Jackson, "The Resurrection Belief of the Earliest Church: A Response to the Failure of Prophecy?" *JR* 55 (1975) 415–25; U. Wernick, "Frustrated Beliefs and Early Christianity," *Numen* 22 (1975) 96–130.

orcising demons, and offering hope to the poor. From our evidence it appears that Jesus was a charismatic prophet, preacher, exorcist, and healer, often unconcerned about, or willing to break with, the legal and ritualistic traditions of purity which concerned most of his fellow Jews.

A fundamental concern of Jesus was to bring together into a unified group those who responded to his proclamation of God's reign irrespective of their sex, previous background, or history. A central feature of the life of this group was eating together, sharing a common meal that celebrated their unity in the new relationship with God which they enjoyed on the basis of their response to Jesus' proclamation of God's reign. Because of concern for the unity and stability of his group Jesus challenged the exclusive tendencies and burdensome legalities of the Judaism of his day. This aroused a deep-rooted opposition to him that climaxed shortly before a Passover celebration in Jerusalem when he was arrested, tried by the Jewish authorities on a (trumped up) charge of blasphemy and by the Romans on a charge of sedition, and was executed by crucifixion around AD 33. During his lifetime he had chosen from among his followers a small group of disciples. After Jesus' death, they were convinced by the empty tomb and subsequent visions and prophecies that Jesus was alive and in their midst, enabling them by his Spirit to accomplish great deeds. Thus arose a "Jesus movement," spearheaded by a band of itinerant radicals, who like Jesus, moved about the villages and towns of Palestine, preaching and healing by the authority of Jesus, with the firm conviction that Jesus was alive and would soon return with God's power and authority.

The sketch highlights most of the important events and activities in the life of Jesus. Other information could be added, but what we have mentioned is that which is probable based on the four criteria of authenticity. This cautious procedure has enabled us to present a plausible sketch of the "Jesus of history" with only a minimal amount of the "Christ of faith" portrait found in the Gospels.

11

The Message of Jesus

THE CULTURAL CONTEXT: MESSIANISM

At the time of Jesus, Palestine had many prophets and messiahs.[1] In both Josephus' *Antiquities* and Acts we read about end-time oriented prophets like Judas the Galilean (*Ant.* 18.1–10, 23–25; cf. Acts 5:37), Theudas (*Ant.* 20.97–98; Acts 5:36), the Egyptian prophet (*Ant.* 20.167–172: Acts 21:38), and John the Baptist (18.117; Acts 13:24f.). All of these, except John, advocated armed resistance against Rome. The followers of Judas the Galilean did not seek a coming messiah, since it is stated that "they accepted God alone as their leader and master" (18.169). John the Baptist advocated water baptism as an end-time seal for those who repented and practiced righteousness (*Ant.* 18.116–119). The Egyptian prophet emerged from the wilderness, performed miracles and signs, and gathered a large following of people at the Mount of Olives (*Ant.* 20.167–172). Although there are specific differences, some general similarities between Jesus and these end-time prophets include: an end-time orientation, use of prophetic imagery, the performing of miracles, little or no interest in a coming messiah (unlike the disciples of some), and large followings of people.

Whereas such similarities appear to situate Jesus in the end-time prophetic tradition, the following differences highlight his distinctive emphasis. (1) Unlike most of the end-time prophets, Jesus (like John) did not advocate any program of political resistance, despite his Roman execution for sedition. (2) Although initially affiliated with the ministry of John, it is uncertain if Jesus continued John's practice of water baptism (see, for example, Jn 3:22; 4:2). (3) Jesus did not emphasize the coming

---

1. The following works discuss prophets and messiahs of 1st cent. Palestine: R. Bultmann, *Jesus and the Word*, trans. L. P. Smith et al. (New York: Charles Scribner's Sons, 1958) 20–26; R. Horsley, "Ancient Jewish Banditry and the Revolt Against Rome, AD 66–70," *CBQ* 43 (1981) 409–32; *Jesus and the Politics of His Day*, ed. E. Bammel and C. F. D. Moule (Cambridge: University Press, 1984) 1–68, 109–28; H. Koester, *Introduction* 2:71–72; Schürer and Vermes, *History* 2:488–513.

of God for judgment, but the dawning of God's rule in his own ministry. It was John the Baptist who stressed the coming of God's final judgment and the need for repentance and conversion to escape this "baptism with fire" (Mk 1:2–8; Mt 3; Lk 3). (4) As a result, the conduct of Jesus' disciples was not motivated by the threat of coming judgment, but by the invitation to participate in God's rule (Mk 2:18–20). This last difference underlines the more affirmative and celebrative aspects of Jesus' message when compared with John's, which conforms to the old prophetic tradition (e.g., Amos).

The wisdom, piety, and great deeds attributed to Jesus are also reminiscent of other Jewish holy men of the second temple period. Like Elisha the prophet, Onias the righteous procured rain during a famine by his prayers (Josephus, *Ant.* 14.22). Healings and other miracles were also attributed to the prayers of Hanina ben Dosa, the Jewish sage (Babylonian Talmud *Berakhoth* 33a,34b; *Pesahim* 112b; *Taanith* 24b; *Yoma* 53b).[2] But like some of the Gospel miracles, these embellished accounts tell us more about the convictions of later admirers, rather than the historical situations of these holy men.

THE RHETORICAL TECHNIQUES

Before developing the content of Jesus' message, it is necessary first to understand the imagery and rhetorical techniques central to his teaching. The most important imagery used by Jesus is that connected with God's rule. The phrase "kingdom of God" would call up in the consciousness of any Jew of Jesus' day, the entire experience of Israel under God's sovereignty.[3]

In Israel's history, God was regarded as a great king who created the world, called the patriarchs, delivered Israel from Egypt, guided them through the wilderness, gave them the law, defeated their enemies, and brought them into the promised land. Before the Babylonian exile (586

2. For further discussion of Jesus and "charismatic Judaism," see Vermes, *Jesus the Jew* 58–82; idem, "Hanina ben Dosa," *JJS* 23 (1972) 28–50 and 24 (1973) 51–64; Flusser, *Jesus* 69–70, 93, 95. See also A. Buechler, *Types of Jewish-Palestinian Piety from 70 B.C.E. to 70 C.E.* (London, 1922). On the bold claims and resurrection faith of Jesus' followers, see Johnson, *Writings of the New Testament,* 87–113.

3. See J. Bright, *The Kingdom of God* (Nashville: Abingdon, 1953); O. Evans, "Kingdom of God, of Heaven," *IDB* 3:17–26; *The Kingdom of God,* ed. B. Chilton (London: SPCK; Philadelphia: Fortress, 1984); B. Klappert, "King, Kingdom," *NIDNTT* 2:372–90; H. Kleinknecht, G. von Rad, et al. "*Basileus, Basileia,* etc.," *TDNT* 1:564–93; N. Perrin, *The Kingdom of God in the Teaching of Jesus* (Philadelphia: Westminster, 1963); W. Willis, ed., *The Kingdom of God in 20th-Century Interpretation* (Peabody, Mass.: Hendrickson, 1987).

BC) God's reign over Israel and the nations was envisioned as a future hope in history (ancient prophecy). After the exile and up to the first century AD, especially under the duress of persecution, the Jews believed that God's rule was to be revealed at the end of the age in connection with cosmic catastrophes and spiritual warfare between angels and demons (apocalyptic eschatology). Such vivid and awesome imagery characterized Jesus' announcement that "the rule of God is upon you" (Lk 11:20).

Jesus' rhetorical techniques are evident to anyone who reads his parables and sayings. He often employed hyperbole or overstatement to impart both the dread of first encountering the awesome rule of God and the carefree joy of discovering and participating in it. To concretize his ideas and skillfully transport them to his listeners' situation, Jesus often used figures of analogy, especially parables. He also employed euphemism to instruct his listeners in matters of prayer and forgiveness (e.g., Mk 11:22–25). The teaching of Jesus would have produced in his listeners a wide range of human impressions and moods: intensity, seriousness, conviction, irony, mystery, joyfulness, reverence, and aspiration.

THE CONTENT OF JESUS' MESSAGE

We will summarize the content of Jesus' message by examining the following five themes, which are all related to the proclamation of God's reign: (1) God's rule is present; (2) God alone brings about his rule; (3) God's rule defies human standards; (4) it challenges conventional wisdom; and (5) it reveals God as a merciful father. In order to capture some of the original impressions conveyed by these themes, as well as perceive the vividness and relevance of Jesus' teaching, some application to our own modern situation will be made. Material discussed below is that designated as authentic by our application of the four criteria.

God's Rule Is Present

To anyone reading the sayings of Jesus in Mk 1:15, Mt 11:12, Lk 11:20, and 17:21, the sense of immediacy is striking: God's end-time rule is breaking in! The climax of God's saving activity is at hand! The sense of utter urgency that this message must have imparted to Jesus' listeners might be compared, in our own day, to the horrifying news of nuclear attack or the shocking report that we have terminal cancer. Throughout Israel's history, it must be remembered, the reign of God was viewed as a time of both judgement and salvation. According to Jesus, there is an impending irruption now making itself felt. Speculations about the future coming of God's rule, did not concern him. Jesus proclaimed the reign of God as a reality to be experienced in the lives of his listeners.[4] They were to recognize the reality of God's saving activity in the healings and exorcisms he performed (Lk 11:20), in the fate of John the Baptist (Mt 11:12), and in acts of mercy and love (Mt 5:39–41,44–48).

God Alone Brings about His Rule

Unlike the contemporary end-time prophets who advocated armed resistance to effect God's reign, Jesus saw the new order instituted only by God. Jesus often communicated his views about the development of God's rule by speaking in parables. The parables of Jesus were free from hidden and implicit meanings. Each focused on a main point (x) that was graphically developed by comparing his starting concept (a) to some familiar situation in life (b). The familiar situation is usually developed in the parable (b*) and by analogy the starting concept is developed (a*). This scheme can be outlined in the following manner:

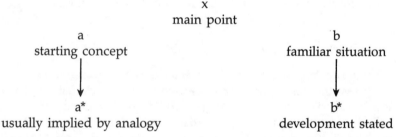

Now we will apply the above scheme to two parables illustrating the divine activity that effects God's rule: the seed growing spontaneously (Mk 4:26–29) and the seed being sown (4:3–8). In the first parable, God's reign (a) is compared to seed growing spontaneously (b), to develop the main point of the miraculous growth of the kingdom (x). Just as the spontaneous growth of the seed into wheat ripe for harvest is not dependent on the farmer (b*), so is the dawning of God's rule not dependent on human activity (a*)—all are the direct result of God's miraculous activity (x). Since the ancient person was prescientific in his understanding of horticulture, this parable of Jesus highlighting the "mysterious" in nature would have made an effective point to his listeners.

The other parable illustrating the dawning of the kingdom as an act

---

4. For further study on the present aspect of the kingdom of God, see Perrin, *Rediscovering* 63–77; idem, *Jesus* 15–34; Perrin and Duling, *NTIntro* 412–15; B. Chilton, *God in Strength: Jesus' Announcement of the Kingdom* (Freistadt: F. Ploechl, 1979); Dodd, *Parables of the Kingdom* 21–84.

of God is that of the seed being sown (Mk 4:3–8). Here the reign of God (a) is compared to seed scattered on a field (b) in order to illustrate again the miraculous growth of the kingdom (x). Just as some of the seed fails to grow but there is still an immense harvest (b*), so it is with God's rule: despite its apparent weaknesses, it will blossom into full glory (a*). In both parables, the human element is passive and dependent on a mysterious, divine force for the results. This miraculous growth, in the understanding of Jesus' listeners, could only be caused by God.

God's Rule Defies Human Standards

Jesus believed that God's emerging reign would bring a crisis to the human situation of his listeners. It would result in a radical self-questioning and complete reversal of human values. In our own day, complete and sudden changes of priorities occur in crisis situations, like war and terminal illness. This new situation announced by Jesus threatened the security and stability provided by the Jewish world view. Jesus' challenge of radical self-questioning can be illustrated by: (1) the parables of the good Samaritan (Lk 10:30–36), the unjust steward (16:1–7), and the Pharisee and tax collector (18:9–14); and (2) those sayings that confront the hearer with a complete reversal of priorities (Lk 9:60; Mt 5:39–41; Mk 8:35; 10:23,25,31; Lk 14:11,26).

In the parable of the good Samaritan (10:30–36), Jesus demands that his listeners "conceive the inconceivable."[5] Only the parable is from Jesus. Therefore, we have separated it from its present context, since the discussion with the lawyer (10:25–29, 37) is probably from the early church. The focal point of the parable is on the goodness of the Samaritan: "which of these three . . . became a neighbor to the man who fell among the robbers?" The parable challenges Jesus' listeners to conceive the inconceivable because (a) both Jesus and his audience were Jewish, and (b) Samaritans were despised by the Jews on both racial and religious grounds. It was not the respectable Jewish priest or Levite that was a neighbor to the injured man, but the hated Samaritan! In order to comprehend better the original impact of Jesus' parable, let us retell the story for modern North American readers:

> One night a man was driving home from church in a suburban neighborhood, his car was stopped by a gang of youths, he was beaten, his car stolen, and he was left on the side of the road unconscious. Now by chance a respected Protestant minister was driving by, but because his schedule was pressing, he drove on (planning to telephone the police later). So also a well-liked deacon at the minister's church passed by the man in his car. But then came a black

5. Perrin and Duling, *NTIntro* 417; see also J. D. Crossan, "Parable and Example in the Teaching of Jesus," *NTS* 18 (1971/72) 285–307.

lesbian who was a professed atheist. As she drove to where the injured man was, she stopped her car, lifted the injured man into it, and drove him to the nearest hospital. Since the man's wallet and identification had been stolen, the black lesbian signed all the admittance papers, contacted the police, and patiently waited at the hospital for the man to regain consciousness. Which of these three became a neighbor to the man who was beaten and robbed?

In the parable of the unjust steward (Lk 16:1–7), Jesus shows how actions contrary to accepted human standards are an acceptable response to the crisis of God's emerging reign. Because vv 8–9 appear to be a later moral application, we regard only vv 1–7 as authentic. The focal point of the parable is the reversal of moral values conveyed by the actions of the steward. In the story, a manager of an estate is about to be relieved of his position by the absentee landlord for negligence. Unable to see any future work opportunities, he pursues a bold course of action. Summoning the landlord's debtors (tenants or merchants with promissory notes), the manager drastically reduces the amount of each debt, with the assurance that they would reciprocate by welcoming him into their homes. As in the parable of the good Samaritan, Jesus "says what cannot be said," and advocates "doing what cannot be done."[6]

In the parable of the unjust steward, Jesus compels his listeners to applaud an act of mercy that is also dishonest. In our own situation it would be like a bank vice president reducing the home loans of his mortgagees by forty per cent! In the context of Jesus' message, this rash decision becomes an acceptable response to the crisis of God's dawning rule; a reign that defies all human conceptions of honesty and justice.

The parable of the Pharisee and the tax collector (Lk 18:9–14) discloses how God's rule reverses all religious values. The Pharisee was a respected member of the Jewish community, whereas the tax collector was viewed by the Jews as a Roman sympathizer and a swindler. In our day, we might compare these two characters to a respectable Protestant minister and a despised panderer (or pimp). The Pharisee's prayer began as an acceptable prayer of thanksgiving (v 11; cf. Ps 17:1–5) but it deteriorates into boasting and self-congratulation at the expense of the other person's defects.[7] The tax collector's prayer is a typical petition of mercy, but because of his humility and sincerity he alone receives God's approval. Although it probably circulated independently of its present context, the following

6. Perrin and Duling, *NTIntro* 418–19.

7. F. Danker, *Jesus and the New Age* (St. Louis: Clayton Publishing House, 1972) 184–86. Some scholars, however, see no deterioration in the Pharisee's prayer (Lk 18:11–12) and tend to heighten the paradox of the parable under a theme like, "I have not come to call the righteous, but sinners to repentance" (Lk 5:32), or "many that are first will be last, and the last, first" (Mk 10:31).

reversal saying of Jesus is an appropriate summary of the parable: "for everyone who exalts himself will be humbled, and he who humbles himself will be exalted" (Lk 18:14).

In addition to parables, Jesus employed short wisdom sayings to challenge his listeners to radical self-questioning and a complete reversal of values. We will list the sayings and only make a brief comment when necessary.

Leave the dead to bury their own dead (Lk 9:60).

If any one strikes you on the right cheek, turn to him the other also; and if any one would sue you and take your tunic, let him have your cloak as well; and if any one forces you to go one mile, go with him two miles (Mt 5:39–41).

In making these impossible demands to shun one's religious and social responsibilities for the dead, become indecently exposed for the legal satisfaction of another, and allow oneself to be forced indefinitely into the service of another (e.g., Roman soldier), Jesus jolts his listeners into making real decisions about their lives and values. The crisis of God's inbreaking rule necessitates radical self-examination.

For whoever would save his life will lose it; and whoever loses his life for [God's reign] will save it (Mk 8:35 [my emendation]).

How hard it will be for those who have riches to come into God's rule. It is easier for a camel to go through the eye of a needle than for a rich man to come into God's rule (Mk 10:23,25 [my translation]).

But many that are first will be last, and the last first (Mk 10:31).

Everyone who exalts himself will be humbled, and he who humbles himself will be exalted (Lk 14:11).

If anyone comes to me and does not hate his own father and mother and wife and children and sisters, yes, and even his own life, he cannot be my disciple (Lk 14:26).

Like the parables examined in this section, these sayings advocate a complete reversal of human values and priorities as a result of the invasion of God's reign in human existence. The contrasts in these sayings are deliberately exaggerated by Jesus to challenge his listeners to reexamine their lives and values in the present.

Even though it is probable that early Palestinian followers of Jesus sought to practice many of these radical sayings (and created some of their own),[8] we are not convinced that Jesus wanted everyone to be poor, homeless, wandering preachers like himself and his followers. This type of lifestyle, however, was typical of many religious and philosophical movements in the Mediterranean world. His obvious appeal to the peasantry and ar-

8. Theissen, *Sociology* 1–24.

tisans of his day and the threat he presented to Jewish exclusivism suggests that Jesus did not envision an ascetic and sectarian community like the Essenes. This observation leads us to believe that Jesus intended a response like radical self-questioning in his use of hyperbole and paradox.

God's Rule Challenges Conventional Wisdom

Closely related to the radical self-questioning of human values was Jesus' challenge to the old ways of comprehending human relations and the world itself. This challenge is best illustrated by the antitheses of the Sermon on the Mount (Mt 5:21–48) and the sayings on religious observance and purity (Mk 2:19,21; 7:15).

Because these sayings of Jesus which are set against the law of Moses ("You heard that it was said . . . but I tell you") are so demanding, some were qualified in later traditions: e.g., "without a cause" (Mt 5:22 KJV); "except for the matter of unchastity" v 32.[9] However, these challenges to the common sense values of Jewish law (e.g., eternal liability for anger not just murder, contra Ex 20:13; adultery of the heart not just the body, contra Ex 20:14) are more than radical demands to be modified and implemented. These antitheses of Jesus were intended to challenge one's secure and complacent view of the world. Like the wisdom sayings mentioned earlier, they were intended to produce a radical questioning of one's present existence because of the inbreaking of God's rule. Since God's future has arrived, humankind's present must be changed.

Jesus' understanding of the present affected by God's future is also evident in his statements on religious observance and purity. The inbreaking of God's rule in Jesus' ministry marks a time of release from normal religious obligations (e.g., fasting) and a time of rejoicing in the experience of God's presence and activity (Mk 2:19). Jesus' ministry also marks a new point of departure, bursting the bonds of old Judaism (2:21). Finally, one of Jesus' most radical challenges to the old way of understanding the world is found in Mk 7:15. The statements in this verse challenge Jesus' listeners to reexamine a basic premise of the Jewish religion: the distinction between sacred and secular.[10] One must now question the presumption that any external circumstances in the world can separate a per-

---

9. In Mt 5:22 the KJV contains the interpolation "without a cause," which is not found in any Greek manuscripts, see Beardslee, *Literary Criticism* 39–40. It has also been convincingly argued that the phrase "except for the matter of unchastity" in Mt 5:32 is a redactional interpolation of Matthew, see for example: Reumann, *Jesus* 339 n. 7.

10. Perrin, *Rediscovering* 149–50. In a similar thematic vein, see D. Bonhoeffer, *The Cost of Discipleship* (New York: Macmillan, 1963), and idem, *Life Together* (New York: Harper & Row, 1954).

son from God. According to Jesus, only the individual person (i.e., his or her own attitude and behavior) is the defiling agent, not foods or other externals. The inbreaking of God's future in the present necessitates such a radical rethinking of the world.

God's Rule Reveals God as a Merciful Father

Jesus' constructive teaching on God as a merciful, understanding, and forgiving Father alleviates some of the urgent, confrontational, and deconstructive aspects of his teaching. Borrowing the modern illustrations used in our discussion of "God's Rule Is Here," the sense of relief and gratitude conveyed by this teaching might be compared to learning that the approaching nuclear attack was a false report or that one's cancer is in complete remission! Even though some of this teaching may have provided positive incentives for those initially confronted with the challenge of God's rule, much of it seems to be addressed to those who have subsequently responded to it. For those early Palestinian Christians who sought to emulate the lifestyle of Jesus, this constructive teaching would help to solidify, inspire, and assure them in their zealous endeavor.

This section will explore Jesus' understanding of God by looking at: (1) the common way he addressed God as "Father" (Mk 14:36); (2) the simplicity of one of his prayers (Lk 11:11–13); (3) his teaching about God as Creator and Provider (Mt 6:25–34; Lk 11:11–13); (4) parables illustrating God's love for sinners (Lk 15:1–10,11–32; Mt 20:1–16); and (5) the divine blessings invoked upon the humble pursuers of justice and mercy (Mt 5:3–8). Some sayings and parables illustrating radical reversal and self-examination also impart the image of God as a merciful Father (e.g., Lk 18:9–14) and the challenge to imitate the Father with human acts of mercy (e.g., Lk 10:30–36; Mt 5:39–41,44–48). Therefore, some previous statements may be alluded to in this section.

In contrast to the elaborate Jewish epithets used of God in Jesus' day, like "O Lord, our God, who art the Creator of heaven and earth, our Shield and the Shield of our fathers," Jesus addressed God by the familial name "Papa" (in Aramaic: "Abba," Mk 14:36). The name "Abba" was probably the original form of address used by Jesus in his prayer and sayings about the "heavenly father" (Mt 6; Lk 11).

The original simplicity of Jesus' prayer is well illustrated in Lk 11:2–4 when compared with a selection of the synagogue prayers dating back to the second temple period:

Blessed art thou, O Lord, God of Abraham, God of Isaac and God of Jacob, the great mighty and revered God, the most high God who bestows loving kindness and possesses all things; who remembers the pious deeds of the Patriarchs and in love will bring a redeemer to their children's children for their name's sake. Forgive us, O our Father for we have sinned; pardon us O our

> King, for we have transgressed; for thou dost pardon and forgive. Look upon our affliction and plead our cause and redeem us speedily for thy name's sake; for thou art a mighty redeemer. Bless this year unto us, O Lord our God, together with every kind of produce thereof, for our welfare; give a blessing upon the face of the earth. O satisfy us with thy goodness, and bless our year like other good years. Blessed art thou, O Lord the redeemer of Israel, who art gracious and dost abundantly forgive, O King, Helper, Savior and Shield.[11]

The prayer, replete with biblical terminology, is not offensive, but the elaborate epithets and laudatory language seem to presuppose a distance between God and humanity that the petitioner is attempting to bridge through appeasement and pacification. The language and assumptions behind such prayers might have been criticized by Jesus (Mt 6:2,5,7). In contrast to the rather sanctimonious petition above, we have the simple prayer of Jesus (emended by us as it might have been uttered by Jesus):

> Papa, may your name be honored; may your rule come. Each day give us the food we need. Forgive us our sins for we forgive everyone who does us wrong. And do not bring us to hard testing.[12]

Both the simple language and conversational style of this prayer presuppose a God who is near and readily responds to the needs of people. This is the image of God that Jesus had.

Jesus' teaching about God as Creator and Provider (Mt 6:25–34; Lk 11:11–13) combines images of God from Jewish wisdom tradition (e.g., Job 12:7–10; 38:41) and his own emphasis on faith in God's future (e.g., Mt 6:33; Lk 11:9). According to the rationale of this teaching, since God has cared for his creation from the past to the present, He can also be trusted to continue it in the future. God is a trustworthy caretaker of his creation (Mt 6:26,28–29) and is more concerned about the welfare of his own people than a human father with his own son (Lk 11:11–13). This message not only alleviates the awesome responsibility conveyed by Jesus' radical challenges, but brings assurance to those who participate in God's rule. The early itinerant Jesus preachers also would have found great consolation in these sayings as they wandered throughout rural Palestine proclaiming the imminent return of their Lord.

In his parables illustrating God's love for sinners (Lk 15:1–10, 11–32; Mt 20:1–16), Jesus again confronts his listeners with a radical reversal of values.

---

11. The lengthy prayer is adapted from Benedictions 1,6,7,9 of the *Shemoneh 'Esreh* or "Eighteen Benedictions," some of which date back to the time of Jesus (in Barrett, *NTB* 162–63). See also the following collection of ancient and modern prayers in W. Simpson, *Jewish Prayer and Worship* (London: SCM, 1965).

12. Our emendation of the Lord's Prayer is based on the TEV and presupposes our application of the four criteria of authenticity. On "Abba," see *BAGD* 1 and *TDNT* 1:5–6.

What kind of respectable father would run down the street joyfully to meet his misfit son and slaughter the fatted calf for him? When would a responsible employer hire idlers on the street to do half a day's wages yet pay them the same amount as the full day workers?[13] It is precisely because of this motif of radical reversal that the theme of God's love for outcasts is so forcefully conveyed. The setting for these parables in the ministry of Jesus appears to be correctly identified in Luke's Gospel. They are Jesus' responses to the Jewish leaders who criticized his ministry to tax collectors and sinners (Lk 15:1-2).

In the parables of the Lost Sheep and Coin (Lk 15:3-10), Jesus reveals God's love for even the most obscure sinner and the great joy experienced by God and his people when even one sinner repents:

> I tell you that thus there will be more joy in heaven over one sinner who repents than over ninety-nine righteous persons who need no repentance (Lk 15:7).

Both the parables of the prodigal son and the laborers in the vineyard can be outlined in a similar manner. Both highlight the same theme of God's love for sinners. In Jesus' parable of the prodigal son (Lk 15:11-32), the vindication of God's love for sinners theme (x) is developed in the following manner: just as the prodigal son (b) was graciously welcomed back by his father despite the protests of the elder brother (b*), so also sinners and outcasts (a) are recipients of God's love despite the protests of the "righteous" Jews (a*). The starting concept (a) and its development (a*) is derived from Lk 15:1-2, i.e., Jesus' associating with tax collectors and sinners. Lk 15:1-2 also provides the appropriate historical context for Jesus' ministry. In the parable of the laborers (Mt 20:1-16), the same theme of God's mercy for sinners (x) unfolds. Just as the owner who hires workmen for his estate (b) picks idlers and gives them the same pay as the regulars, despite their protests (b*), so also is God's love (a) extended freely to sinners and outcasts despite the protests of the "righteous" Jews (a*). The dawning of God's rule in Jesus' ministry results in acts of divine compassion toward Israel's outcasts. These are acts which defy all human standards and expectations.

Our final comments on Jesus' teaching about God concerns the Beatitudes (Mt 5:3-8/Lk 6:20-22). In them Jesus invokes divine favor upon the poor, hungry, and oppressed. The blessings are pronounced as already present. They provide comfort and assurance to those who respond to the challenge of God's rule:

> Blessed are you poor for yours is the kingdom of God.

---

13. Koester, *Introduction* 2:80.

Blessed are you that hunger now, for you shall be satisfied.

Blessed are you that weep now, for you shall laugh.

Blessed are you when men hate you, and when they exclude you and revile you and cast out your name as evil . . .

Rejoice in that day, and leap for joy, for behold, your reward is great in heaven for so their fathers did to the prophets. (Luke 6:20–23)

From our discussion in this section, we observed that the God of Jesus was personal and accessible, good to the poor, glad when the lost are found, overflowing with a father's love for a returning child, and merciful to the despairing and needy. Those who participate in God's reign are not only beneficiaries of the Father's love but also benefactors who extend God's mercy to others in need. Relief and gratitude would be appropriate responses to such good news. So also would be the responses of Jesus' listeners to the experience of divine forgiveness and mercy as participants in God's rule.[14]

14. For further discussion on the teaching of Jesus, see Bornkamm, *Jesus* 64–143; Braun, *Jesus of Nazareth* 36–136; Bultmann, *Jesus and the Word* 27–220; idem, *Theology of the NT* 1:3–32; Conzelmann, *Jesus* 51–81; Flusser, *Jesus*; J. Jeremias, *NT Theology: The Proclamation of Jesus*, trans. J. Bowden (New York: Charles Scribner's Sons, 1971); Klausner, *Jesus of Nazareth*; Manson, *The Sayings of Jesus*; Perrin, *Rediscovering* 54–206; idem, *Jesus* 40–56.

12
A Chronology of Paul's Life

The problems of Pauline chronology are similar to those in the study of Jesus. Evidence is sparse and scattered, and the sources are often dominated by literary and religious purposes. Factors that are distinctive for a chronology of Paul are: (a) we have the apostle's own words about certain events in his life; (b) references to Paul's life in Acts sometimes coincide with statements in Paul's letters; and (c) an ancient inscription confirms the Lukan account of Paul's appearance before Gallio (Acts 18:12–22).

The document of primary importance in determining a chronology of Paul is the Gallio Inscription found at Delphi, Greece (Achaia). Gallio's proconsulship of Achaia, mentioned in Acts 18:12–22, is independently attested by this document and can be dated within narrow limits. The inscription, with conjectural supplements [in square brackets] reads as follows:[1]

> Tiberius [Claudius] Caesar Augustus Germanicus [Pontifex Maximus, in his tribunician] power [year 12, acclaimed Emperor for] the 26th time, father of the country, [consul for the 5th time, censor, sends greetings to the city of Delphi.] I have long been zealous for the city of Delphi [and favorable to it from the] beginning, and I have always observed the cult of the [Pythian] Apollo, [but with regard to] the present stories, and those quarrels of the citizens of which [a report has been made by Lucius] Junios Gallio my friend, and [pro] consul [of Achaea].

A knowledge of stereotyped titles in official inscriptions confirms that the addressor is Claudius who became emperor on January 25, AD 41. The acclamations were irregular but from other inscriptions, we learn that he was acclaimed emperor for the 22nd, 23rd, and 24th times in his 11th year of reign (AD 51) and that the 27th acclamation took place in the second half of his 12th year of reign (AD 52 before August).[2] The 26th ac-

---

1. From: Barrett, *NTB* 48–49, and *BC* 5:461.
2. K. Lake "The Chronology of Acts," in *BC* 5:462–63.

Statue of the Apostle Paul at the Constantinian basilica of St. Paul. Outside-the-Walls, Rome; the fourth-century basilica was destroyed by fire and rebuilt in the nineteenth century. *Photo by Ralph Harris.*

clamation must therefore have taken place at the close of the 11th year (AD 51) or probably the first half of the 12th year: between January 25 and August 1, AD 52. Achaia was a senatorial province, governed by a proconsul, who was customarily appointed by the senate for a one-year term. The one-year appointments were made in early summer (July 1 under Emperor Tiberius). Even though alternative dates have been suggested within the AD 50–53 limit, a convincing case has been made for the Gallio proconsulship of Achaia from July 1, 51 to July 1, 52.[3] Paul's appearance before Gallio (Acts 18:12-22) was probably soon after his accession to office (July AD 51). This would be an opportune occasion for Paul's opponents to gain a fresh hearing and possibly influence the decision of the new incoming proconsul.

3. Jewett, *Chronology* 38–40; G. Lüdemann, *Paul, Apostle to the Gentiles: Studies in Chronology*, trans. F. S. Jones (Philadelphia: Fortress, 1984) 163–64.

Before examining key events in Paul's life, we must state at the outset that priority will be given to the data found in Paul's letters. There are a number of reasons for proceeding in this manner.[4] First, Paul's letters are the earliest data available, predating the Acts of the Apostles by decades. Second, the details in the letters are not motivated by chronological considerations or any assumption regarding the periodization of the church's history. Third, material from the letters is primary historical data and therefore has intrinsic priority over the secondary information we find in the Acts of the Apostles.

These reasons do *not* imply that the data in Paul's letters is free from apologetic and theological influences. The information, however, is closer historically to the events, they are the apostle's own words about his own life, and thus they qualify as eyewitness material. Therefore a general outline of Paul's life must be first worked out from the data of the letters of Paul. Material from Acts is usable in our Pauline chronology only when it does not conflict with the evidence in the letters.[5]

CONVERSION AND CALL, AD 34

The primary data for Paul's conversion and call are found in Gal 1:15–16 and 1 Cor 15:8. Later evidence supporting this event in a more idealized and dramatic manner is Acts 9:1–9; 22:6–21; 26:12–18.[6] In Gal 1:15–16, this is identified as the initial event of Paul's missionary career. It includes a call from God (1:15) and a revealing of God's Son to Paul (1:16). This revelation is identified in 1 Cor 15:8 as a final appearance of the resurrected Christ to his followers. Even though the data from Acts do not include the appearance of Christ as the last of the post-Easter appearances and includes details (e.g., Ananias, blindness, charismata) that are not mentioned in Paul's letters, they agree in the following areas. First, Paul was previously a persecutor of the church (Gal 1:13; 1 Cor 15:9; Acts 26:9–11; 9:1–5). Second, the vision of Christ is connected with Paul's missionary call to the Gentiles (Gal 1:16; Acts 26:16). Third, the whole event is connected with the Syrian city of Damascus (Gal 1:17; Acts 9; 22; 26).

4. Derived from Jewett, *Chronology* 22–24, see also J. Knox, *Chapters in the Life of Paul* (Nashville: Abingdon-Cokesbury, 1950) 13–29; Lüdemann, *Paul* 1–43.

5. See the following article for both possible and probable conflicts between Acts and Paul's letters: P. Vielhauer, "On the 'Paulinism' of Acts," in *SLA* 33–50. See also Lüdemann, *Paul* 23–29.

6. For discussion of the similarities and discrepancies of Acts 9, 22, and 26, along with Paul's letters, see G. Lohfink *The Conversion of St. Paul*, trans. of *Paulus vor Damaskus* (Chicago: Franciscan Herald, 1976) 20–26; C. W. Hedrick, "Paul's Conversion/Call: A Comparative Analysis of the Three Reports in Acts," *JBL* 100 (3, 1981) 415–32.

The Pauline connection of the appearance of Christ as the last post–Easter appearance (not found in Acts) has extrabiblical support. From gnostic and early Christian sources there is a tradition of the post-resurrection appearances of Christ extending eighteen months. The gnostic traditions found in Irenaeus' *Against Heresies* state that post-resurrection appearances lasted eighteen months.[7] The second-century Christian work, the Ascension of Isaiah, mentions post–Easter appearances lasting 545 days (9.16).[8] The second-century Christian gnostic Apocryphon of James refers to 550 days of resurrection appearances (2.20–21).[9] This eighteen-month period may be a historical recollection derived from Pauline tradition.[10]

Basing the dating of Paul's conversion/call on the argument for Jesus' crucifixion at AD 33,[11] we arrive at October of AD 34, eighteen months after the Passover (April). As we proceed in dating the other key events in Paul's life, the AD 34 conversion call will find further support.

FIRST JERUSALEM VISIT, AD 37

Paul states in Gal 1:17–18 that after his conversion/call, he went into Arabia, returned to Damascus, then "after three years" went to Jerusalem for the first time. Second Corinthians 11:32–33 describes this departure from Damascus as an escape from the ethnarch of King Aretas who guarded the city to seize him. Acts 9:22–26 supports the Damascus-Jerusalem sequence of Galatians without referring to the Arabian trip, and also describes the Damascus escape without mentioning the ethnarch of King Aretas.

If Paul's conversion/call was AD 34, and he left Damascus for Jerusalem "after three years," the first Jerusalem visit would take place around AD 37. Is there any datum to substantiate the date for this trip? The historical allusion to the ethnarch of King Aretas guarding Damascus to seize Paul (2 Cor 11:32) may provide this support. The crucial issue will concern the extent of Aretas' rule around AD 37.

Did the Nabatean King Aretas have jurisdiction over Damascus around AD 37? His rule over Nabatea and other regions was from 9 BC to his death

---

7. This tradition is found among the gnostic Ophites (Irenaeus, *Against Heresies* 1.28.7) and the gnostic disciples of Ptolemaeus (1.3.2).
8. Cited in Hennecke, *NTA* 2:657.
9. Robinson, *Nag Hammadi* 30.
10. Jewett, *Chronology* 29.
11. Scholars defending an AD 33 crucifixion are Reicke, *NT Era* 183–84 and Hoehner, *Chronological* 103–14.

in AD 39.[12] Aretas probably did not have control of Damascus until after
the death of Tiberius Caesar (March AD 37). Tiberius discouraged native
client kingdoms and favored Herod Antipas over Aretas in a border conflict between the two in AD 36. However, after the death of Tiberius in
March of 37, there was a change in frontier policy under Emperor Gaius
Caligula. This change of policy would provide a favorable setting for Nabatean control of Damascus. Gaius reestablished a system of client kings
in the east, refrained from any punitive measures against Aretas for the
AD 36 border dispute, and even adopted a friendly attitude towards the
Nabatean king.[13] It was probably during this favorable change of policy
after March AD 37 that Damascus would have been transferred to Nabatean control (2 Cor 11:32). Paul's escape therefore occurred sometime
within the two-year span up to the death of King Aretas in AD 39.

Our discussion provides some support for dating Paul's first Jerusalem
visit at AD 37 (or 38). It also helps to substantiate the AD 34 conversion/call
date three years earlier (Gal 1:15–18). Further confirmation for these dates
will be provided when interlocked with other events in Paul's life.

MISSIONARY ACTIVITY, AD 37–51

The time frame for this period is based on the fourteen-year span between the two Jerusalem trips, mentioned in Gal 1:21; 2:1. After the first
Jerusalem trip, Paul goes into the regions of Syria and Cilicia (1:21) and
"after fourteen years" returns to Jerusalem (2:1).[14] In Acts the references
to Syria and Cilicia in Gal 1:21, find specific support in the allusions to
Paul's trip to Tarsus of Cilicia (Acts 9:30) and his story in Antioch of Syria
(11:25–26; 13:1–2). However, there is no indication that Paul is attempting to be exhaustive in Gal 1:21.[15] Therefore, most of the missionary activities graphically portrayed in Acts 13–14 and 15:36–18:22 probably
occurred at this time.

The date of Paul's second visit to Jerusalem coincides with Paul's appearance before Gallio in Corinth (AD 51). According to Acts 18, after Paul
is acquitted by Gallio, he sailed for Syria (v 18), stopping at Ephesus, Cae-

---

12. Josephus, *Ant.* 10.131–185; 16.293–299; Jewett, *Chronology* 30–33, 121.

13. The above arguments are substantiated in Jewett, *Chronology* 32–33.

14. Discussion of the Jerusalem trips in Acts 11:27–30; 15 and Gal 2:1–10 will
be discussed below.

15. In agreement with H. D. Betz, we regard Gal 1:13–2:14 as the narratio of
Paul's apologetic letter. According to Quintilian's rhetorical handbook, details in
the narratio may be omitted or key events treated later as the cause, the reason
for the conflict. See Betz, "Literary Compositions," *NTS* 21 (1975) 362–67; Lüdemann, *Paul* 54–59.

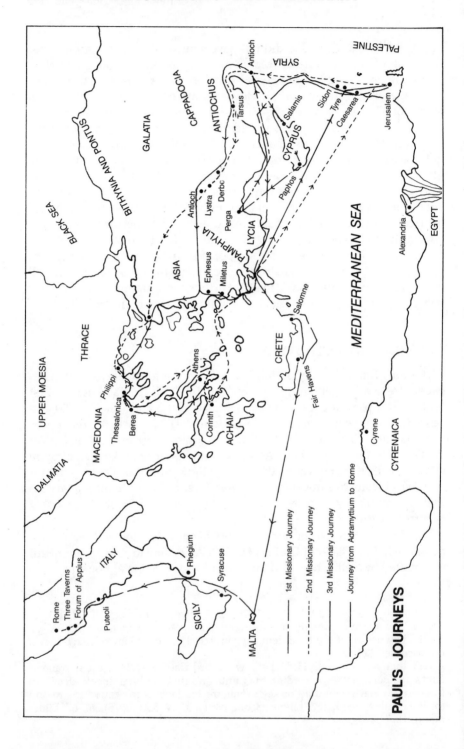

PAUL'S JOURNEYS

————— 1st Missionary Journey

- - - - - 2nd Missionary Journey

————— 3rd Missionary Journey

————— Journey from Adramytium to Rome

sarea, and the church at Jerusalem (v 22). As we have argued at the beginning of this chapter, the summer of AD 51 would have been an opportune time for Paul's opponents to present the apostle before the newly appointed proconsul. The most we can miscalculate on this point is one year (e.g., 50 or 52).

We have placed both missionary journeys of Paul (Acts 13–14, 15:36–18:22) into the fourteen-year framework for the following reasons. First, we have taken seriously the fourteen-year time span (Gal 1:21; 2:1) without resorting to fractions of years (e.g., 12 or 13) where part of a year may be reckoned as a whole year.[16] Second, it takes seriously Paul's busy itinerary in Acts 15:31–18:1. This "second missionary journey" of Paul includes over fifteen stops and covers over 2000 miles. Since Paul traveled on land by foot and by sea in ancient Roman boats, this journey would probably take three or four years.[17] This lengthy time of travel poses problems for anyone attempting to follow the order of Acts and reconcile it with the Gallio inscription.

The order of Acts places the first missionary journey (13–14) before the Jerusalem conference (15). The second journey follows the Jerusalem conference and ends with Paul leaving Corinth (15:36–18:22). The Jerusalem conference and Paul's departure from Corinth limit the time span of the second journey to two or three years.[18] But the distance and time required in the second journey requires three to four years.[19] This is why we have included both the first and second journeys of Paul into the fourteen-year time frame and transposed the conference of Acts 15 to a later period.

SECOND JERUSALEM VISIT, AD 51

It may be necessary at this point to further explain why: (a) the two Jerusalem trips of Acts 11:27–30 and 15 have been transposed to a later date (AD 51) and (b) why both missionary journeys depicted in Acts 13–14 and 15:30–18:22 are included within the fourteen years of Gal 1:21 and 2:1 (AD 37–51). By linking the Gal 2 conference (cf. Acts 15) with Paul's trip "up to" Jerusalem (Acts 18:22), we escape the necessity of positing

16. E.g., counting fractions of years as whole years, one might declare that he or she attended college for *four years* since classes were taken in 1980, 1981, 1982 and 1983. However, this may actually be only *three school years*: (1) fall 1980–spring 1981, (2) fall 1981–spring 1982, (3) fall 1982–spring 1983.

17. Jewett, *Chronology* 59–62.

18. Most scholars date the Jerusalem conference of Acts 15 between 48 and 50, and Paul's departure from Corinth (Gallio inscription) between 51 and 52 (see Caird, "Chronology of New Testament," *IDB* 1:605–7). This time frame usually puts a limit of two to three years on Paul's second missionary journey (15:36–18:22).

19. Jewett, *Chronology* 59–62.

seventeen empty years at the beginning of Paul's ministry and crowding virtually all that is known about his activity into the last few years.[20]

The Jerusalem offering (1 Cor 16:1-8; Rom 15:25-27), designed to bridge the gap between the Palestinian and Hellenistic churches, provided the motivation for the final trip to Jerusalem, although Luke omitted reference to it except for one detail (Acts 25:17). In order to account for the general knowledge in the early church that Paul had indeed brought an offering to Jerusalem, Luke placed the trip back in the early life of Paul in connection with a famine (Acts 11:27-30). Paul is careful to mention only an "acquaintance" trip and a "conference" journey, and this is sufficient to overrule Luke's chronology at this point.[21]

The following is a chart of the Jerusalem trips in both Paul's letters and Acts, reflecting our interpretation:

Jerusalem Visits	Paul	Acts
First trip, AD 37 (acquaintance visit)	Gal 1:18-20	9:26-27
Second trip, AD 51 (apostolic conference)	Gal 2:1-10	Acts 15
Final trip, AD 57 (collection and arrest)	Rom 15:25-27	Acts 21:17-36 [11:27-30]

The dating of the Jerusalem conference will be determined by the relationships of the following texts: Gal 2:1-10; Acts 11:27-30; and Acts 15:1-35. Is Galatians 2 Paul's version of either the Jerusalem conference in Acts 15 or the famine relief visit of Acts 11:27-30? Note the chart of similarities and differences:

	Galatians 2	Acts 11	Acts 15
(1) Paul and associates present	Paul, Barnabas and Titus (v 1)	Barnabas and Paul (v 30)	Barnabas, Paul, and others (v 2)
(2) nature of appointment	by revelation (v 2)	sent by church (v 30)	appointed by church (v 2)
(3) occasion	circumcision of Gentiles by false brethren (vv 3-4)	famine relief (vv 28-29)	circumcision of Gentiles by men from Judea (v 1)
(4) Jerusalem officials present	James, Cephas, John (v 9)	————	Peter, James, apostles, and elders (v 4)

20. Jewett, *Chronology* 79; although he dates the Jerusalem conference earlier (47, possibly 50), Lüdemann finds indications that a Pauline mission (Gal 2:7-8) and even Paul's conflict at Antioch (2:11-14) occurred *before* the conference, Lüdemann, *Paul* 64-75.

21. Ibid.

(5) type of meeting   private (v 2)   ——————   public assembly (4,12–14)

(6) mention of poor   remember the poor (v 10)   relief for famine victims (v 29)   ——————

The similarities between Gal 2 and Acts 15 are the most significant (#1,3,4). The differences (#2,5,6) between Gal 2 and Acts 15 can be explained as two different versions of the same event (#2,6) or as two different meetings on the same occasion (#5). Paul's omission of the apostolic decrees (Acts 15:19–20; 21:25) may have been due to: Paul's own difficulties with such "legalistic" stipulations (Gal 2:6) or the possibility that they were introduced after the conference when Paul made his final trip to Jerusalem (Acts 21:25).

It seems unlikely that Gal 2:10 ("remember the poor") is an allusion to the famine relief visit (Acts 11:27–30). We regard the relief visit as a displaced reference to the collection which Paul brought on his final visit to Jerusalem (Acts 24:17; Rom 15:25–27).[22] In his letters, Paul's only concern for a famine relief is the collection for "the poor among the saints at Jerusalem" (Rom 15:26). The reference to "remember the poor" in Gal 2:10 may even be an indication that the collection for the Jerusalem saints had already begun.[23]

We link the Gal 2 and Acts 15 conference with Paul's trip "up to" Jerusalem after his second missionary journey (Acts 18:22; AD 51) for the following reasons. First, it best conforms to the fourteen-year gap between the two Jerusalem visits (Gal 1:18; 2:1). Second, it allows enough time for Paul to undertake his extensive missionary travels described in Acts 13–14; 15:35–18:22. Third, it takes seriously the priority of Paul's letters over Acts for a Pauline chronology. Because of these reasons, we date the Jerusalem conference at AD 51 (Gal 2 = Acts 15 = Acts 18:22) instead of between 48 and 50 as many scholars have argued.

FURTHER MISSIONARY ACTIVITY, AD 52–57

This period includes Paul's twenty-seven month stay in Ephesus (Acts 19:8–10; Phil 1; 4; Phlm; 2 Cor 1:8) with brief visits to Corinth (2 Cor 2:1; 12:14; 13:1), Troas (2 Cor 2:12), Macedonia (2:13; Acts 20:1), Illyricum (Rom 15:19), and Achaia (Rom 15:25; 16:1; Acts 20:2f.), before Paul's final trip

22. Knox, chs 53–57; Jewett, *Chronology* 79. Lüdemann, however, views Acts 11:27ff. as part of a tripling of Paul's *second* visit to Jerusalem (cf. Acts 15:1ff.; 18:22), Lüdemann, *Paul* 149–57. Nevertheless, in all of the above cases, Acts 11:27–30 is viewed as a Lukan insertion which is chronologically out of place in the narrative.

23. Nickle, *Collection* 59–62; Lüdemann, *Paul* 77–80.

to Jerusalem (Acts 20:16; Rom 15:25). During these years, Paul's "collection for the saints" was begun (spring of 55; 1 Cor 16:1–8), continued among the churches of Macedonia and Achaia (2 Cor 8–9), and was completed for delivery to Jerusalem (AD 57, Rom 15:25–27). All of Paul's undisputed letters were also written at this time, with the exception of 1 Thessalonians (AD 50 from Corinth).

FINAL JERUSALEM VISIT, AD 57

This last journey to Jerusalem is anticipated in Rom 15:25–27 and described in Acts 20:16; 21:1–18. According to Acts, the following events take place in Jerusalem.

(1) Conference with church and participation in a Jewish ritual at the temple (21:17–26)

(2) Seized by a mob in the temple and taken into Roman custody (21:27–36)

(3) Address to multitude and hearing before Sanhedrin (21:39–23:10)

(4) Conspiracy discovered and Paul is transferred to Caesarea (23:11–31)

(5) Paul stays in Caesarea for two years (24:27) where he appears on trial before the procurators Felix and Festus (24–25) and the Herodian King Agrippa II (26).

(6) Paul appeals to Caesar (25:10–12) and is sent to Rome (27:1–28:16)

Some verification for Paul's arrival in Jerusalem at AD 57 can be attained by dating the procuratorships of Felix and Festus (Acts 24–25). If one favors the reports of Josephus over that of Tacitus (as most scholars do), the arrival of Felix as procurator of Judea can be established around AD 52–53.[24] If one follows the progression of Roman procurators in the years prior to the Jewish war (AD 66–70), a date of 59 or 60 can be maintained for the arrival of Festus as the successor of Felix.[25]

Acts 24:27 states that when two years had elapsed (since Paul's transfer to Caesarea as a prisoner), the Roman procurator was succeeded by Porcius Festus. Based on our dating of these procuratorships, Paul's arrival

---

24. Emperor Claudius appointed Felix as Cumanus' successor around the 12th year of his reign (ca. 53), Josephus, *Ant.* 20.134–140.; see also *War* 2.245–249. In Tacitus, *Annals* 12.54 Felix and Cumanus were procurators at the same time over a divided Palestine.

25. Because there are dating problems connected with Josephus' own report on the circumstances immediately following the dismissal of Felix (*Ant.* 20.182–184), we prefer to work back from Josephus' reports on the procurators of Judea from the Jewish War (66–70) back to the years of rule shared by Felix and his successor Festus (ca. 52–62). Festus served for a brief period until his death in AD 61 or 62 (*Ant.* 20.197–203).

in Caesarea would have been around AD 57. According to Acts, Paul's transfer from Jerusalem to Caesarea took place about two weeks after his arrival in Jerusalem around Pentecost, the summer of 57 (Acts 20:16; 21:17,26–27, 22:30; 23:11–12, 31–33).

As a result of our discussion we can outline the chronology of this phase as follows:

(1) Arrival in Jerusalem (Acts 21:17), summer of 57

(2) Hearing before Felix in Caesarea (24:10–22), summer of 57

(3) Hearing before Festus and Agrippa (25–26) after two years (24:27), summer of 59

(4) Departure from Caesarea for Rome (27:1–8), late summer or early fall of 59

JOURNEY TO ROME, AD 59–60

After his appeal to Caesar had been granted (Acts 25:10–12; 26:32), Paul and other prisoners set sail for Italy under Roman custody (27:1). The sea voyage was probably undertaken before the dangerous season for sailing (before mid-September). Paul and the others boarded a sailing vessel to Myra of Lycia (southern Asia Minor) where they transferred to a larger grain ship en route to Italy (27:7–8). As the summer months came to an end, sailing became difficult on the eastern Mediterranean.[26]

Paul and company stayed at Fair Havens after the day of the Atonement "fast" (Acts 27:9). According to the solar calendar, in AD 59, the day of Atonement (Tishri 10) took place on October 5.[27]

Since the dangerous sailing season had begun, the pilot and shipowner attempted to winter at a seaport in Crete (27:9–12). The ship, however, was caught in a gale and driven westward (vv 13–20). Following the chronological notations of Acts (27:20,27,33,39), the boat shipwrecked at Malta in early November of 59 (27:39–28:1). After staying at Malta for three months and three days (28:7,11), they sailed for Rome in early February of 60 and arrived there within two weeks (28:11–16).

According to Acts 28:30, Paul stayed in Rome for "two whole years." He awaited his appeal to Caesar with some degree of freedom. The apostle was also under house arrest and able to receive visitors (28:16–17,23,31).[28]

---

26. J. Smith, *The Voyage and Shipwreck of St. Paul*, reprint of 1880 ed. (Grand Rapids: Baker, 1978) 74–81. For recent discussion see C. J. Hemer, "Euraquilo and Melito," *JTS* (26, 1975) 100–111.

27. Bruce, *Book of Acts* 506.

28. If the variant reading of Acts 28:16 in the Western text (5th cent.) is correct (Paul and the prisoners were handed over to the "stratodeparch") and it refers to the emperor's pretorian guard, the last *single* office holder was Afranius Bur-

EXECUTION, AD 62

The evidence concerning the end of Paul's life is related to the question of the authorship of the Pastoral Letters. References to the "first defense" in 2 Tim 4:16 and his "rescue" in 4:17 have led some scholars to conclude that Paul was released after the two-year imprisonment in Acts 28:30. Since

A Chronology of Paul's Life[29]

Conversion/Call	AD 34 (see Gal 1:15–16; 1 Cor 15:8; Acts 9:1–9)
First Jerusalem visit	AD 37 (Gal 1:18–19; Acts 9:26–28)
Missionary activity	AD 37–51 (Gal 1:21; Acts 13–14; 16:1–18:22)
Second Jerusalem visit:	AD 51 (Gal 2:1–20; Acts 15) apostolic conference
Further missionary work e.g., collection for the saints	(Acts 19–20; 1 Cor 16:1–8; 2 Cor 8–9; Rom 15:25–27)
Final visit to Jerusalem: arrest and imprisonment	AD 57 (Acts 21:17–18, 27–33)
Arrival in Rome	AD 60 (Acts 28:16, 30f.)
Execution of Paul	AD 62 (1 Clem 5; Eusebius, Eccl Hist 2.22)

---

rus who died in AD 62. this variant would establish a latest possible date for Paul's arrival in Rome (Jewett, *Chronology* 44). For a detailed discussion of Acts 28, see C. B. Puskas, "The Conclusion of Luke–Acts: An Investigation of the Literary Function and Theological Significance of Acts 28:16–31," Unpublished Ph.D. dissertation, St. Louis University (Ann Arbor, Mich.: University Microfilms, 1980).

29. Derived from the following work and used with permission by the publisher: Robert Jewett, *A Chronology of Paul's Life*, 98–103, Copyright © 1979 by Fortress Press. For further study on Paul see: K. Stendahl, *Paul among Jews and Gentiles* (Philadelphia: Fortress, 1976); E. Käsemann, *Perspectives on Paul* (Philadelphia: Fortress, 1971); J. P. Sampley, *Pauline Partnership in Christ* (Philadelphia: Fortress, 1980); L. E. Keck, *Paul and His Letters* (Philadelphia: Fortress, 1979); J. Jervell, *The Unknown Paul* (Minneapolis: Augsburg, 1984); H. J. Schoeps, *Paul. The Theology of the Apostle in the Light of Jewish Religious History* (Philadelphia: Westminster, 1961); H. N. Ridderbos, *Paul. An Outline of His Theology* (Grand Rapids: Eerdmans, 1975); W. D. Davies, *Paul and Rabbinic Judaism*, 3rd ed. (Philadelphia: Fortress, 1980); idem, *Jewish and Pauline Studies* (Philadelphia: Fortress, 1984); G. Bornkamm, *Paul* (New York: Harper & Row, 1971); E. P. Sanders, *Paul and Palestinian Judaism* (Philadelphia: Fortress, 1977); W. Meeks, *The First Urban Christians* (Philadelphia: Fortress, 1983); F. F. Bruce, *Paul, Apostle of the Heart Set Free* (Grand Rapids: Eerdmans, 1977); J. Munck, *Paul and the Salvation of Mankind* (Richmond: John Knox, 1959); C. K. Barrett, *The Signs of an Apostle* (Philadelphia: Fortress, 1972).

we contend that the Pastorals were not written by Paul, this evidence should be excluded.[30] The references to Paul's journey to Spain in the Muratorian Fragment and 1 Clem 5 are probably derived from Rom 15:24, although the allusion in 1 Clem 5.7 does not require a mission to Spain interpretation.[31]

The decisive evidence for the death of Paul is in Acts 28:30–31 and 20:24,38. The author of Acts appears to bring his work to a positive conclusion (28:30–31), but seems aware of Paul's death (20:24,38). In all probability the execution of Paul took place immediately after his two-year stay in Rome, under Nero.[32]

The reign of Nero in AD 62 was marked by growing suspicion and the restoration of treason trials. Early in AD 62, the efficient administrator S. A. Burrus had died and the wise advisor Seneca was dismissed. In the summer of AD 62 Octavia, Nero's former wife, was executed. Because Nero's government had changed from one of judicial fairness to treachery and suspicion in early 62, it is unnecessary to link Paul's death with the later persecution of Christians in connection with the great fire of Rome (AD 64).[33]

30. See Kümmel, *Introduction* 370–84, on the authorship and date of the Pastorals.

31. 1 Clem 5.7 states that Paul "reached the limits of the west" before his death. This phrase could refer to Rome, Illyricum or Spain. The death of Peter is also mentioned as contemporary with that of Paul (5.2–5), which cannot be verified.

32. Although influenced by the Pastorals in asserting that Paul was released and retried, Eusebius does state that Paul "suffered martyrdom under Nero" in Rome (Eusebius, *Eccl Hist* 2.22).

33. On Nero, the fire in Rome, and the local persecution of Christians, see Tacitus, *Annals* 15.44 and Sulpicius Severus, *Chronicle* 2.29.

13

The Major Phases of Early Christianity

What can be learned about the origins and development of Christianity from the NT and other relevant documents? The NT not only contains important religious teachings but also includes significant data for reconstructing the beginnings of Christianity. This is why we will attempt to recover the major phases of early Christianity from the NT and other related sources.

Historical reconstruction (to underscore previous discussion) is a difficult but necessary task. It is difficult because the results of this historical inquiry are tentative and (at best) plausible. It is a necessary task because it takes seriously the historicity of the NT.

THE CONTROVERSIAL SUBJECTS

Controversial subjects in our study are: (1) determining the authentic sayings of Jesus; (2) distinguishing the teachings of Jesus from those of his earliest followers (e.g., the "Jesus movement"); (3) identifying the earliest forms of both Jewish and Gentile Christianity; and (4) postulating plausible life-settings from the limited results of form-criticism and sociological analysis.[1] The above subjects are controversial because: our data for early Christianity are minimal, questions still arise about the appropriateness and critical results of our methods, and the pluralistic expressions of Judaism in NT times raise doubts about Jewish and Gentile ethnic distinctions in primitive Christianity. The problems connected with (1), (2), and (4) were discussed in previous chapters,[2] therefore further explanation will be limited to point (3).

---

1. For a concise definition of this diverse field, see "Sociological Interpretation," in Soulen, *Handbook* 179–80.
2. The problems of points (1) and (2) have been discussed in ch 10, The Historical Jesus, and those connected with point (4) in ch 5, under Form Criticism.

The controversy surrounding the early distinctions between Jewish and Gentile Christianity basically involves the detection of pagan religious motifs in the NT. One school of thought finds NT motifs that parallel Gentile/pagan religions (e.g., mystery religions).[3] An opposing school of thought is skeptical of either establishing parallels with "pagan" religions or of restricting these parallels to "Gentile" religions.[4] The controversy continues concerning the nature and extent of the parallels to pagan religions and whether certain motifs or characteristics can be labeled as non-Jewish or pagan.

At least three conclusions can be derived from the controversy of distinguishing between early Jewish and early Gentile Christianity. First, Judaism was a diverse phenomenon in the first century AD. Recent research has shown the prevalence of Hellenistic culture and religion in Palestine since the third century BC.[5] The study of the Nag Hammadi documents has also revealed an independent form of Jewish Gnosticism predating or at least contemporary with Christianity.[6] Second, it must be granted that the earliest Gentile Christians were converts of Jewish Christians, since Jesus' earliest followers were all Jews.[7] Third, all outlines of early Christianity are tentative and subject to revision. Our presentation of the major phases of Christianity will take into account these conclusions.[8]

3. Studies advocating this "history of religions" position are: R. Reitzenstein, *Hellenistic Mystery Religions*, trans. J. Steely of 1927 ed. (Pittsburgh: Pickwick Press, 1978; W. Bousset, *Kyrios Christos*, trans. J. Steely of 1913 ed. (Nashville: Abingdon, 1970); W. Heitmueller, "Hellenistic Christianity before Paul," in Meeks, *Writings* 308–23; Bultmann, *Theology*, 2 vols; A. Nock, *Early Gentile Christianity and Its Hellenistic Background* (New York: Harper & Row, 1964); and Fuller, *Foundations of NT Christology*.

4. Studies which criticize the above "history-of-religions" approach are: (a) those skeptical of the parallels with pagan religions, J. G. Machen, *The Origin of Paul's Religion* (New York: Macmillan, 1925; repr. Eerdmans, 1978); Kim, *Origin of Paul's Gospel*; Hengel, *Jesus and Paul*, (b) those that detect methodological weaknesses in the approach, D. Tiede, *The Charismatic Figure as Miracle Worker* (Missoula, Mont.: Scholars Press, 1972); C. Holladay, *Theios Anēr in Hellenistic Judaism* (Missoula, Mont.: Scholars Press, 1977); (c) Those skeptical of any sharp distinction between Judaism and Hellenism, Hengel *Judaism and Hellenism*; idem, *Jesus and Paul*; I. H. Marshall, "Palestinian and Hellenistic Christianity," *NTS* 19 (1972–73) 271–87; and Brown and Meier, *Antioch* 1–9 (also in *CBQ* 45 [1, 1983] 74–79).

5. Hengel, *Judaism and Hellenism* 58–106, 255–66

6. Rudolph, *Gnosis* 51–52, 277–82.

7. Brown and Meier, *Antioch* 1–9.

8. Our presentation agrees to some extent with the *revised* history-of-religions approach in: Perrin and Duling *NTIntro* 73–91. We have also utilized some of the insights in Brown and Meier, *Antioch*. Note, however, the criticisms of Hengel and others who seek to blur the differences between Judaism and Hellenism: F.

We have divided our presentation into three periods:

(1) Before the destruction of Jerusalem AD 70

(2) From AD 70 to the end of the first century

(3) From the late first to the early second centuries AD

PHASE 1 (AD 30–70)

In this earliest period of Christianity we note two major groups that emerge: rural itinerant charismatics and urban community organizers.[9] Both types persist after AD 70, although the rural itinerant element surfaces only as a minority group afterwards (e.g., Agabus, traveling prophets in the Didache).

The Rural Itinerant Charismatics

This group was comprised of charismatic prophets who traveled through the towns and villages of Palestine, and whose authority derived from a particular message and lifestyle. Like the Cynic itinerant preachers, they left both their families and homes and renounced all wealth and property. Like the Essenes, they were end-time oriented, critical of the Jerusalem authorities, and traveled in the rural areas of Palestine. Their authority was not based on noble origin or past achievements, but was vindicated by their teaching and style of life. Those who would be categorized in this group are: Jesus of Nazareth and his immediate followers, the "Jesus movement."

Jesus of Nazareth

From our discussion of the historical Jesus in chs 9–11, it is easy to conclude that Jesus was a rural itinerant charismatic prophet. This conclusion can be deduced from both his authentic sayings and the basic information we know about him.

First, Jesus grew up in the insignificant town of Nazareth and spent most of his time in the fishing villages of Galilee. The town of Nazareth is almost never mentioned by ancient geographers and historiographers and has no importance in the pre–Christian period (e.g., Jn 1:46). In his Galilean ministry, Jesus frequented the fishing villages of Capernaum,

---

Millar, "The Background of the Maccabean Revolution: Reflections on Martin Hengel's 'Judaism and Hellenism,' " *JJS* 29 (1978) 1–21; Vermes, *Jesus and the World of Judaism* 26, 74.

9. These sociological categories are derived from: Thiessen, *Sociology*; idem, *The Social Setting of Pauline Christianity* (Philadelphia: Fortress, 1982).

Gennesaret, and Bethsaida-Julias. He also spent time in the rural areas of Galilee, Perea, and Judea. Although Jesus probably visited Jerusalem about three times during his ministry, his denouncement of both the temple ritual (e.g., Mk 11:15–19; 14:58) and the Jerusalem authorities (Lk 10:31–32; 18:11; Mt 23:23), reflects the attitudes of a Jew living in a rural area of Palestine.

Second, Jesus was a traveling preacher. This point is evident, not only from his busy itinerary in rural Palestine, but also, by what can be deduced from his teaching. Jesus spoke about leaving family and home (Mk 10:28–30; Lk 9:60; 14:26) as a response to God's dawning rule. He exhorted his disciples, in their preaching itinerary, to rely on the hospitality of friends in the villages and towns they visited (Mt 10:9–11). Many of the radical sayings of Jesus which advocate radical self-questioning and a reversal of values, also presuppose the lifestyle of a poor, homeless, wandering prophet (e.g., Mt 5:29–41; Mk 10:23; Lk 6:20–22).

Third, Jesus was a charismatic prophet. His authority was authenticated by his words and deeds. It was not legitimized by noble lineage (e.g., Mt 13:55) but by his message that God's rule had dawned in his ministry (Mk 1:15; Lk 11:20; 17:21). Even though he had distinctive emphases, Jesus shared similarities with other end-time prophets like John the Baptist (Mk 1; Lk 3). Jesus also refers to himself as a prophet (Mk 6:15; 13:33).

The Jesus Movement

Soon after the death of Jesus, there arose a group of itinerant "Jesus preachers," who, like their master, traveled through villages and towns of Palestine preaching and healing. They were also convinced by his empty tomb and subsequent appearances that God had raised Jesus from the dead and that he would soon return as end-time savior and judge. Despite their efforts to emulate the teaching and lifestyle of Jesus, their eschatology was much more futuristic, since they expected the imminent return of Jesus (Mt 10:23; Mk 9:1; 13:30; Lk 17:23–24). In belief and practice, the Jesus movement may be closer to John the Baptist, whose ascetic practices resembled the Essenes and who also awaited the future coming judgment of God (Mk 1; Lk 3; Mt 3).

It was also at this early stage that Jesus the proclaimer became the one proclaimed. Along with the authentic words and deeds of Jesus a *kerygma* about Jesus' suffering, death, and resurrection developed (Rom 1:2–3; 1 Cor 15:3–4). Both the *kerygma* and the imminent parousia teaching would also function as an interpretive grid through which the Jesus material would be filtered. As a result, authentic Jesus sayings would be more difficult to ascertain.

The contents of the Q document or Synoptic sayings source reflect the beliefs and practices of a rural itinerant charismatic end-time community like the Jesus movement. Such a group would have been responsible for the preservation of the authentic Jesus sayings and the composition of eschatological, prophetic, and wisdom sayings which are found in the collection.

These wandering charismatic missionaries who awaited the near return of Jesus were also counter-culture or skeptical of the Jewish establishment. They were ambivalent towards the Jewish aristocracy of Jerusalem and favored theocracy ("rule by God alone"). Denouncements against the Pharisees in Q which are not from Jesus are derived from this group (Lk 11:42/Mt 23:23; Lk 11:49–52/Mt 23:34–36).

Since this earliest group was probably Aramaic-speaking (Aramaic was the native language of Palestine) they were probably responsible for the preservation and composition of several Aramaic confessions and slogans. From Jesus, they preserved the *Abba* address for God. From Judaism they borrowed the Hebrew *amen* and *hallelujah* vocabulary of worship. To this group can also be ascribed the creation of the confession: *maranatha* "come Lord." Finally, the title "Son of man" (Aram. *bar nasha*) replete with apocalyptic meaning from Daniel and Enoch, was probably employed by this group.

The best representative of this rural itinerant charismatic movement would be the prophet Agabus (cf. Did 12; 13). In Acts 11:28 he "foretold by the Spirit that there would be a great famine over the world; and this took place in the days of Claudius." Foretelling was only one role of the Christian prophet who primarily was a spokesman for Jesus (Acts 2:14–36). In Acts 21:10–11, the prophet predicts Paul's arrest by the Jews and his imprisonment under the Romans in Jerusalem. This passion prediction recalls those about Jesus in Lk 9:22 (rejected by Jewish leaders) and 18:31–32 ("delivered to the Gentiles").[10] Although Agabus is first mentioned as coming down from Jerusalem (11:27), he travels throughout Palestine and Syria to Antioch (v 27). He later journeys to Caesarea "from Judea" (21:10). Agabus seems to fit the category of an itinerant, rural, charismatic prophet.

The Urban Community Organizers

This category involves several different groups in urban centers, like Jerusalem and Syrian Antioch. Each group made converts and organized communities according to its own particular teachings. Most of the groups

---

10. In Acts, both Peter and Paul are also portrayed as itinerant prophets, but both function primarily as "urban community-organizers." For more information on early Christian prophets, see Aune, *Prophecy* 189–232.

were well integrated into the political structure of the Roman world.

According to Acts 6:1, the earliest Christians were first distinguished linguistically: (a) those who conversed in Hebrew and Aramaic, as well as Greek (the "Hebrews") and (b) those who were only Greek-speaking (the "Hellenists").[11] Since they are all Jewish-Christian, each group can be defined in relationship to the Jewish law. Also, within the Hebrew and Aramaic-speaking group, three types can be distinguished by their interpretation and application of the Jewish law.[12]

Hebrew- and Aramaic-Speaking Groups

These groups conversed in Hebrew and/or Aramaic, as well as Greek. They were mostly Christians of Palestinian Jewish descent. Their ties to the Jewish Torah and temple were closer than the Greek-speaking (Hellenistic) Jewish Christians. There are three types within this category distinguished by their relationship to Jewish law.

The first type believed that close observance of the Mosaic law, especially the practice of circumcision, was necessary for salvation. This movement of so-called Judaizers originated in Jerusalem (Acts 15:1,24), and had some success in both Galatia (Gal 1-2) and Philippi (Phil 3). Their law-observant mission to the Gentiles came in conflict with Paul, who did not require that his Gentile converts be circumcised. Even though this sect did not survive after AD 70, its law observant practices and anti-Pauline stance was revived among the Ebionite Christians of the second through fourth centuries.

The second type of Hebrew Christian group had the following features. They did not insist on circumcision as necessary for the salvation of the Gentiles, but did require them to keep some of the Jewish purity laws (Acts 15:19-21; 21:25). This type was a mediating position between that of the Judaizers and Paul, and exerted influence on both. It was headquartered in Jerusalem and its chief spokesmen and leaders were Peter and James (Acts 15; Gal 1:18-19; 2:9). It was probably from this group that the traditions about Jesus' Last Supper and the passion of Jesus with its scriptural fulfillments (Pss 22; 69) were preserved and developed.

This group also sought converts from Gentiles as well as Jews. Even though Paul states that Peter's mission was to the Jews (Gal 2:7), Acts 10:1–

11. Hengel, *Jesus and Paul* 1-29.
12. The above outline is an adaptation of material presented by R. E. Brown in a book that he coauthors with J. P. Meier, *Antioch and Rome* (New York: Paulist Press, 1983) 1-9 and as an article entitled "Not Jewish Christianity and Gentile Christianity but Types of Jewish/Gentile Christianity," *CBQ* (45:1) 74-79. The author has given permission for my use of his work, but obviously my adaptations are my own responsibility.

11:18; 15:7–11 contain the story of Peter's going to the Roman Gentile Cornelius. Also, both the presence of a "Cephas party" at Gentile Corinth (1 Cor 1:12) and the fact that 1 Peter is addressed to Gentile Christians in northern Asia Minor, make little sense unless Peter converted Gentiles. This movement, which originated in Jerusalem, became dominant in Antioch of Syria, Rome, and northern Asia Minor.[13]

The third type of Hebrew Christians included those who neither insisted on circumcision as necessary for the salvation of Gentiles nor required their observance of Jewish food laws. This type of Hebrew Christianity is associated with Syrian Antioch and the Apostle Paul.[14] We regard the apostolic decrees of Acts 15:19–20 to be an interpolation of what later was instituted at Paul's last visit to Jerusalem (Acts 21:25). Paul's conflict with Peter in Antioch (Gal 2:11–14) reflects the viewpoints of type two and type three groups concerning the observance of Jewish food laws. Paul's concern for the collection of the Jerusalem saints (Rom 15:25,31; 1 Cor 16:1–3) shows that he still maintained ties to the type two Hebrew Christians of Jerusalem. Also, Paul even concedes that circumcision has value for the *Jew* if accompanied by faith (Rom 2:25–3:2; 4:2).[15] Finally, according to Acts, Paul and the group associated with him maintained some connection with the Jerusalem temple (Acts 20:16; 21:26; 24:11).

This third group was probably more missionary-minded than group two, since its base of operation was Antioch (Acts 11:19–26; 13:1–3) and its leading spokesman was Paul. As we note from Paul's letters and Acts, they visited the cities of the Jewish diaspora, where they sought to win both Jewish and Gentile converts. Members were conversant in Greek, and some of its leaders spoke Aramaic and Hebrew (e.g., Paul, Silas, Barnabas). They were fully integrated into the political structure of the Roman Empire. This third type of Hebrew Christianity organized Christian communities throughout the Mediterranean world. Paul is the best example of the goal-oriented community-organizer breaking new ground and establishing independent groups apart from Judaism. The influence of this group lasted long after AD 70.

Members of this type of Hebrew Christianity were more theologically venturesome. In their missionary work they probably preferred the titles of "Son of God" and "Lord" over "messiah" and "Son of Man," which would not be understandable to their Gentile audiences. It was probably under their influence that "Jesus Christ" became a name rather than a

13. These localities are deduced from 1 Peter (a document of Petrine Christianity) and Acts 2:4–10.
14. Paul appears to be a Hebrew Christian, since he calls himself a Hebrew (2 Cor 11:22; Phil 3:5) and is portrayed as a Hebrew Christian in Acts (22:2; 26:4–5).
15. In Galatians, Paul sees no value in the circumcision of his *Gentile* converts.

title for Jesus of Nazareth. Great stress was also laid on God's vindicating Jesus by raising him from the dead. The portrait of Jesus as a divine man in whom God worked great miracles (e.g., Apollonius of Tyana, Pythagoras) was also developed by this zealous missionary group. Also, the confession "Jesus is Lord," appropriate in a Greco-Roman context of emperor worship, probably originated here.

Greek-Speaking Jewish Christians

This group came from more Hellenistic families and did not converse in Hebrew or Aramaic (Acts 6:1). Like the two Hebrew Christian groups associated with James and Paul, they did not insist on circumcision as necessary for Gentile salvation. Like Paul, its participants did not require Gentiles to observe Jewish food laws. In addition, the Greek-speaking Jewish Christians saw no abiding significance in the cult of the Jerusalem temple (Acts 7:47–51).[16] Later a more radicalized version of this type of Christianity is encountered in John's Gospel and Hebrews, where the Levitical sacrifices and priesthood are obsolete.

The movement began at Jerusalem and was associated with Stephen (Acts 6:1–5, 8–14). The group was scattered throughout Judea after Stephen's death (8:1). It spread to Samaria with Philip (8:4–6), to Phoenicia, Cyprus and Antioch (11:19–20), and eventually Ephesus (John's Gospel?) and Rome (Hebrews?).

Since this Jewish Christian group was the most Hellenistic, they both conceptualized and communicated their faith in ways different from Hebrew Christians. They probably conceived of Jesus from a Hellenistic viewpoint, such as: a miracle-working hero, or descending and ascending redeemer. Much of this thought is retained in the Synoptic miracle stories (e.g., Mk 4:35–5:43) and early Christian hymns (e.g., Phil 2:6–11; Col 1:15–20; 1 Pet 3:18–19, 22). In competition with the popular cults of the day, this group may have been organized as a superior mystery religion with baptism as an initiation rite and the Lord's Supper as a sacred meal, or as a philosophical school with a succession of teachers and students. This development of Christianity as a Hellenistic religion probably occurred in cities like Antioch, Ephesus, Thessalonica, Corinth, and Rome.

Although Paul was a liberal Hebrew Christian, much of his religious thinking would have paralleled that of the "Hellenistic" Jewish Christians.

16. Contrary to the conservative Hebrew Christian portraits in both Galatians and Acts, some later traditions also have James the brother of Jesus preaching against the temple and its cultic sacrifices (Pseudo-Clementine *Recognitions* 1.64; Epiphanius *Panarion* 30.16.7; 2 Apoc Jas 60.14–23). However, all of the above statements occur in the context of James' martyrdom, a legend which reflects some dependency on the speech and martyrdom of Stephen in Acts 6:1–8:4.

In fact some overlap would be expected between the type three Hebrew Christians and the Greek-speaking Christians (type four). After the destruction of the temple in AD 70 and the break with Judaism, these two groups probably solidified, since disagreements were minor.[17]

It was probably the Gentile converts of both the Greek-speaking Jews and liberal Hebrew Christians that made the biggest contribution to emerging orthodoxy. However, the moderating spirit of consolidation and preservation in early catholicism may also have been influenced by the conservative Hebrew Christianity of James and Peter.

PHASE 2 (AD 70–95)

In this second phase, early Christian groups are responding to: the crisis of the fall of Jerusalem in AD 70, the delay of the Lord's return, the increasing conflicts with Judaism, the emergence of gnostic threats, and sporadic persecution from the Roman government. This period is also characterized by: the writing down of Jesus sayings and stories into gospels, attempts to mediate between various Christian factions, early efforts to combat false teachers, and the endeavor to reassert the influence of the apostles in the late first century. In this section we will examine the following groups: (1) Markan Christianity; (2) the community of Matthew; (3) Lukan Christianity; (4) late Pauline Christianity; and (5) Johannine Christianity.

Markan Christianity

This early movement of Christianity is deduced from what we know about the author of Mark's Gospel and the community he is addressing. In this Gospel, which reads like a Greek tragedy, the author is attempting to address the following issues: the fall of Jerusalem with its accompanying tribulation and persecution, the necessity of Jesus' suffering and death, and the importance of discipleship. The Gospel reflects the viewpoint of Gentile Christians who saw little significance with the Jewish law and tradition.

In Mark 13, the author responds to the fall of Jerusalem and its subsequent tribulation. The reference to the "desolating sacrilege" (v 14), derived from Daniel (11:31; 12:11), probably refers to the destruction of the Jerusalem temple by the Romans in AD 70.[18] Roman persecution of Pal-

---

17. But it must be added, that the Ebionite Christians (3rd cent.) who were more judaistic than Paul (even anti-Paul), also shared with the earlier Rechabites, Essenes, and "Hellenists," a disdain for the temple and sacrificial cult (Pseudo-Clementine, *Recognitions* 1.35–36; 64).

18. Josephus, *War* 6.220–270.

estinian Jews followed this catastrophe and many Jewish Christians fled Judea.[19] Mark incorporates these events within the time frame between the resurrection of Jesus and his return from heaven. During this period many will be led astray by false messiahs (13:5-7; zealot leaders?) and others will undergo persecution for their faith (vv 9-13). Despite these calamities, Mark assures his readers that the end is near and that the Son of Man will soon return in power and glory (v 26). For Mark and his readers, the fall of Jerusalem and its accompanying persecution are part of the tribulation that will precede the end.

Mark's emphasis on Jesus' suffering and death may reveal his attempt to address extreme tendencies in his community. Because the author incorporates material on Jesus' messiahship, his miracles, and Christian discipleship in the context of suffering and death, he may be correcting triumphalist interpretations of these teachings. Perhaps there were factions preoccupied with teachings about Jesus the divine worker of miracles (4:35-5:43) and the healing authority he bestows on his followers (3:14; 6:7,13). Perhaps Mark's community, which was experiencing the hardships of Jerusalem's fall and Jewish persecution (13:9, 14), saw no significance in the prospects of suffering and death (8:31-37; 10:33-45). Maybe the teachings on divine authority and power for believers were not coinciding with the situation of hardship and suffering. These suggestions are especially pertinent if Mark's community was located near Galilee shortly after AD 70 (13:14; 14:28; 16:7).

Mark's community seems to include Gentile converts of Hellenistic Jewish Christians who saw little significance in Pharisaic traditions and temple ritual. Mark's portrait of Jesus' authority to abrogate Jewish law and tradition (2:15-3:6; 7:1-13) demonstrates the radical stance of Mark's community concerning Jewish legalism. Also, Mark's concern for Gentiles (5:1-20; 7:24-30; 15:39), ethnically mixed Galilee (14:28; 16:7), and his attempt to explain Jewish customs for his readers, presuppose a Gentile audience with whom the Jewish customs have little value.

Matthean Christianity

The author of Matthew's Gospel seems to have been a Greek-speaking Jewish Christian, writing to a community in Syrian Antioch at the end of the first century. The author has made use of Mark's Gospel (AD 70) and the statement about a king sending troops and burning a city (22:7) probably refers to Jerusalem's fall. Ignatius of Antioch appears to be the first to cite Matthew's Gospel. Although the author of Matthew is more sensitive to Jewish customs than the author of Mark, Mt 23 reflects a break

19. Mk 13:14; Eusebius, *Eccl Hist* 3.53

between Judaism and Christianity.

Writing from a period later than Mark, Matthew responds to both the delay of the Lord's return as well as Jerusalem's historic fall. For Matthew and his community, the ministry of Jesus is the new sacred time which has fulfilled the hopes of Judaism. Therefore, Jerusalem no longer has significance for the Christian as the sacred place.[20] The Lord's return is still expected, but in the meantime the church must discipline itself (16:18–19; 18:15-20) and make disciples of all nations (24:14; 28:19-20).

Matthew's Gospel seems to represent an attempt to mediate between the conservative Hebrew and radical Gentile elements in his community.[21] The inheritance of the extreme Judaizers is represented by sayings rejecting a Gentile mission (Mt 10:5-6; 15:24) and affirming the law's enduring validity (Mt 5:18/Lk 16:17; Q).

The "James group" that remained in the church would have stressed strict observance of Mosaic law according to Jesus' teaching. This position would have been represented by the Sermon on the Mount sayings which are not contrary to Mosaic law (Mt 5:21-24, 27-29; 6:7), and the exhortation to remain subject to synagogue authorities (23:2-3).

Traditions favoring the Gentile mission (28:16-20) and opposing Pharisaic devotion to the law (6:1-6, 16-18; 15:12-14; 23) might be fostered by the Hellenistic Jewish Christians. Teaching on the radical moral demands that revoked the letter of the Mosaic law (5:33-39) may also have come from this group.

It was the task of Matthew to embrace, reinterpret, and synthesize the competing traditions of Antioch for a new situation. His portrait of Jesus the Messiah and Son of God, who fulfilled Jewish prophecy and properly interprets the law for the church, serves as the standard by which to mediate these divergent traditions. The traditions on Christ's ministry as the new sacred time and the continuity of the church with Christ the Son of God seem to reflect the view of liberal Hebrew Christianity (e.g., Acts 11:19-26). Although Matthew's approach to the law is less abrasive than Paul's, both advocated a mission to the Gentiles without legal restrictions and saw the death-resurrection of Jesus as a pivotal end-time event.[22]

Lukan Christianity

The author of Luke–Acts appears to have been a third-generation Christian (Lk 1:1-4; Acts 2:39) from the Aegean Sea region (Acts 16-21). He

---

20. The Jerusalem temple was never rebuilt after AD 70.
21. See Brown and Meier, *Antioch* 51-57.
22. Brown and Meier, *Antioch* 62-63.

and his readers appear to be a growing Gentile community in need of self-identity and direction as a result of Jewish and pagan antagonism. The author appears to be influenced by Pauline Christianity, although he preserves traditions stemming from both conservative Hebrew Christians (Acts 15:1-35) and radical Hellenists (6:13-14; 7:47-51).

The author of Luke-Acts, like Matthew, responds to both the historic fall of Jerusalem and the delay of the parousia. Luke's description of Jerusalem's capture and destruction is more detailed and coincides with the accounts of Josephus.[23] For Luke, Jerusalem is the city which rejected and persecuted the prophets (Lk 9:51; 13:33-34). It is the place of both Jesus and Paul's passion (Lk 19:31-33; Acts 21:10-14). Therefore the destruction of Jerusalem was a consequence of the city's rejection of the prophets, Jesus, and Paul (Lk 19:41-44).

In Luke's Gospel, the close proximity of Jerusalem's destruction to the parousia (as in Mk) has been severed. The reference to Jerusalem's destruction is more specific (21:20, 24a), but he omits the reference to the false prophets at this point (17:20-23) and adds a reference to an interim period: "until the times of the Gentiles are fulfilled" (21:24b). Luke has thereby lengthened the time between the signs connected with Jerusalem's fall (21:7-24) and those of the parousia (21:25-28).[24]

There are other indications of the delay of the parousia in Luke-Acts. Although certain passages reflect an imminent parousia (Lk 3:9,17; 10:9-11; 18:7-8; 21:32), he identifies "the time is at hand" slogan with false prophets (21:8) and modifies his source in stating that "this [war, tumult] must *first* take place, but the end *will not be at once*" (21:9).[25] For Luke-Acts, there is an extended interim in which the church is to carry on its work and witness in the world (e.g., Acts 1:6-8).

In response to Jewish accusations of heresy and apostasy, the author of Luke-Acts presents Christianity as founded by a faithful Jew (Jesus) carried on by loyal Jews who worshipped in the temple (the Twelve), and extended to the Gentiles by a dedicated Pharisee, Saul of Tarsus (Paul). With this presentation Luke makes his case for Christians as the people of God and recipients of God's promises.

In reaction to Roman suspicions about Christianity as a political threat, Luke appeals for Roman tolerance. According to Luke, Rome must not

23. The mention of Jerusalem being encircled by armies (Lk 21:20) and the building of the palisades or ramps around the city (19:43) coincide with the accounts in Josephus, *War* 5.446-526. The references to Jerusalem leveled to the ground (Lk 19:44) and people slain by swords and led away captive (21:24) coincide with Josephus, *War* 6.220-357.
24. Perrin and Duling, *NTIntro* 298-99.
25. Brackets [ ] and italics are our interpolations.

regard the Christian sect as a rebel group (Acts 5:36–37; 21:38) but a harmless religion (18:14,15) propagating a teaching that even has appeal to Romans (10:1–11:18; 13:7–12).

In order to explain how Christianity became a Gentile religion separate from Judaism, Luke shows how a worldwide mission was God's plan from the beginning. Universal salvation was inaugurated with the coming of Jesus, who fulfilled the Hebrew prophecies (Lk 2:32/Isa 49:6; Lk 3:6/Isa 40:5). These same Hebrew prophecies are also fulfilled in the Gentile mission of Paul (Acts 13:47/Isa 49:6; Acts 28:28/Isa 40:5). A mission to the Gentiles, however, is previewed in Jesus' opening sermon (Lk 4:25–27) and at both the end of the Gospel and the beginning of Acts the resurrected Christ commands his disciples to preach salvation to the nations (Lk 24:47; Acts 1:8). Saul of Tarsus is called to carry the name of Jesus "before Gentiles and kings," and even Peter preaches the gospel to the Roman centurion, Cornelius (Acts 10:1–11:18). Finally, in the missionary travels of Paul, the worldwide mission to the Gentiles becomes a major focus (Acts 13:46–47; 18:6; 19:9–10; 28:28).

Even though Luke–Acts incorporates traditions from both Hebrew and Hellenistic Christianity,[26] the author and his community are most influenced by the theologies of both the James and Paul group, i.e., conservative and liberal Hebrew Christianity. It is clear that the life of Paul was known and revered by the author and his community because of (a) the large amount of space given to him in Acts, (b) the flattering portrait of his activities, and (c) the information about Paul that the author assumes on behalf of his readers (e.g., his letters, his death).

It is also clear that the author and his readers are influenced by the theology of the James group. In Acts 15, all are made to agree with James' view that circumcision is not necessary for the salvation of the Gentiles but that *they should be required to keep some Jewish purity laws* (vv 19–20,28–29; cf. 21:25). The historical Paul would have probably taken issue with these extra conditions (Gal 2:6,12). Also, the portrait of Paul in Acts favors that of the James group. First, Paul seems dependent on the Jerusalem apostles, especially James (9:27; 11:29–30; 15:2,22; 21:17–26). Second, Paul complies with Jewish rituals that were regarded as unimportant in his letters: (a) he circumcised Timothy, whose father was a Gentile, (Acts 16:3; contra Gal 5:2), (b) he participated in a Nazirite vow at the advice of James (Acts 21:23–26; contra Phil 3:2–9).

With the above data, several alternative conclusions can be made. First, Luke and his readers were probably too distant from the times of James

26. Type one, the Judaizers (Acts 15:1, 5), type two, the James and Peter group (15:12–21,28–29; 21:17–26); Type three, the Paul group (15:1–5) and type four, the Hellenists (6:13–14; 7:48–51; 8:4–40).

and Paul to distinguish their theologies. For Luke in his day, the observance of Jewish law as necessary for salvation was no longer an important issue. Second, Luke may have been wanting to reconcile the liberal Pauline theology with the conservative Jacobian theology. In doing this, Luke might have wanted to reconcile Christian factions of his day with a presentation of a harmonistic development of the church. Third, Luke might have been attempting to claim Paul for a more conservative version of Hebrew Christianity, defending the apostle against attacks from Jews and conservative Hebrew Christians (e.g., Acts 21:21).

If Luke–Acts, as we argue, was written in the late first century when early Christianity began to consolidate its traditions and establish normative standards of behavior for congregations, the Gentile church of Luke might be moving in a conservative direction similar to that of the James group or even Judaism around the Jabneh period (90–100).[27] This suggestion might explain the tendency in Luke–Acts to present Paul as a conservative Hebrew Christian in close agreement with James and Peter.

Pauline Christianity

We note from Paul's letters and Acts that he had "fellow workers" and helpers. Many of them survived the apostle and sought to continue and develop his teaching. This practice of teacher-student succession was also found in the philosophical schools of Hellenism and the rabbinic schools of Judaism. The best examples of a Pauline school are the Deutero-Pauline letters: 2 Thessalonians, Colossians, and Ephesians.[28] These books were written in the name of Paul and are close to his thought yet sufficiently different for us to conclude that they were probably not written by the apostle.[29] These writings reflect how they dealt with the delay of the par-

27. For the development of a conservative or legal spirit in early Christian orthodoxy, see our discussion of emerging orthodoxy in chs 14–15.

28. The Pastoral Letters are more distant to Paul's thought and are therefore classed among the late 1st and early 2nd cent. writings of emerging orthodoxy. See Dibelius and Conzelmann, *Pastoral Epistles*; B. Easton, *The Pastoral Epistles* (New York: Harper & Row, 1948); R. Karris, "Background and Significance of the Polemic of the Pastoral Epistles," *JBL* 92 (1973) 549–64.

29. In twentieth-century scholarship, 2 Thess, Col, Eph, and the Pastoral letters have been labeled the *disputed* letters of Paul. They reflect a considerable linguistic, stylistic, historical, and theological *departure* from Paul's undisputed writings (Rom, 1, 2 Cor, Gal, Phil, 1 Thess, Phm). Attempts have been made to explain these problematic features as changes in Paul's thinking over the years, Paul's developing a new theology for a new situation, or his acquisition of a new secretary (amanuensis) (e.g., Guthrie, *NTIntro* 490–508, 551–55, 568–75, 596–622). The vocabulary, style, and theology, however, are *too distinctive* to be explained as simply a change in Paul's thinking or as his addressing a new situation. If a

ousia, false teachings, relations with the Jews, the nature of the church, and Christian ethics.

In 2 Thessalonians, the delay of the parousia is explicitly addressed, whereas in Colossians and Ephesians, it is presupposed. In response to either apocalyptic enthusiasm or gnostic realized eschatology ("the day of the Lord has come" 2:2), the author of 2 Thessalonians speaks of a series of events that must precede the end: (1) the apostasy, (2) the appearance of the rebel, and (3) the disappearance of the "restrainer." This "apocalyptic timetable" in 2 Thes 2 both affirms the distance of the present time from the end and legitimizes the delay of the parousia up to the present.[30] The parousia has not arrived because the three prior conditions have not been met. Nevertheless, hope in the future return of the Lord is maintained (1:7-8).

In both Colossians and Ephesians we mostly find a realized eschatology as a response to the delay of the parousia. In both books, the present benefits of salvation take precedence over the future hope. The future parousia is viewed as either a final day of reward and punishment (Col 3:6, 24; Eph 5:6, 27; 6:13) or the completed phase of one's salvation (Col 1:22; 3:3-4). There is no trace of an imminent parousia.

In these writings, the emphasis is clearly on the future benefits of salvation that can be experienced in the present or have already been experienced in the recent past. God "has delivered us from the dominion of darkness" (Col 1:13), you "were buried with him in baptism, in which you were also raised with him" (2:12; Eph 2:6), "you who were dead in trespasses . . . God made alive" (Col 2:13; Eph 2:5). Those "once estranged" are "now reconciled" (Col 1:22; Eph 2:14-15). In these Deutero-Pauline letters the future dimension almost disappears and hope becomes a symbol of assurance rather than a symbol of anticipation for the end of the age.

The false teachings alluded to in the Deutero-Pauline writings appear to be gnostic, although other possibilities have been given.[31] If 2 Thessa-

---

new secretary was employed, his or her influence was so dominant that it would be more appropriate to identify this secretary as the author. Furthermore, just as each person has distinctive fingerprints and a voiceprint that cannot be imitated completely by anyone else, so each person has a "language print" (Sampley, *Eph,Col* 9-12, 69-71, 73-86, 97-103; J. Bailey, "Who Wrote 2 Thessalonians?" *NTS* 25 (1979) 131-45; F. Beare, "Thessalonians, Second," *IDB* 4;626; Perrin/Duling *NTIntro* 208-22, 384-85. On the issue of pseudonymous writings see K. Koch, "Pseudonymous Writing," *IDBSupp* 712-14; M. Rist, "Pseudepigraphy and the Early Christians," *Studies in NT and Early Christian Literature*, ed. D. Aune (Leiden: Brill, 1972) 3-24; Guthrie, *NTIntro*, 671-84.

30. The emphasis is different from Paul's 1 Thessalonians which affirmed the imminence of Christ's return (4:15, 17; 5:1-5).

31. For a survey of opinion, see Gunther, *Opponents* 3-9.

lonians is opposing gnostic realized eschatology (2:2), this would also explain the admonitions against idleness and disorderly conduct (3:6–13). Since these "troublemakers" have now experienced the final resurrection, they are freed from the bondage of this world and all obligations connected to it. This would be the position of libertine Gnosticism. The statements in Colossians about those whom Christ has now reconciled "in his body of flesh by his death" (1:22) and in Christ "the whole fullness of deity dwells bodily" (2:9) also appear anti-docetic. The denouncement of the "worship of angels" (2:18) may be directed against the aeons of gnostic cosmologies. Even the admonition against those who scrutinize "eating and drinking or in regard to a feast or new moon or sabbaths" (2:16) may be interpreted as Jewish gnostic asceticism. The general harangues against false teachers in Ephesians (4:14–15; 5:6) could apply to any group opposed by the author and his community.

Except for 1 Thes 2:13–16, the mention of the Jews, Israel, or the circumcised mainly concerns Hebrew Christians from the past or present. The Deutero-Pauline interpolation in 1 Thes 2:13–16 denounces the Jews for killing Jesus and probably connects the destruction of Jerusalem with God's wrath.[32] In 2 Thes 1:4–5 there is reference to persecutions and afflictions, but it is unclear if the oppressors are Jews or Roman Gentiles. In Colossians and Ephesians we find Christian reinterpretations of Jewish rites and symbols. Colossians 2:11 refers to a circumcision of Christ made without hands. Ephesians 2:11–16 mention the reconciling of both Jews and Gentiles together in the church through Jesus Christ. In Eph 2:21, the church is also viewed as God's new temple.

The nature of the church is developed in Colossians and Ephesians with some allusions found in 2 Thessalonians. In 2 Thessalonians the Pauline concept of the church as a local assembly is found, but the situation of persecution and false teaching appears post-Pauline. In Colossians and Ephesians, there is added to the Pauline concept of "body of Christ" the motif of Christ as the "head" of the church/body (Col 1:18, 24; 3:15; Eph 1:22–23; 4:15–16; 5:23), who is also the "head" over principalities, powers (Col 2:10), and the entire cosmos (Col 1:18, 20; Eph 1:22). In Ephesians, the church is no longer a house assembly (Phlm 2; Col 4:15) but a universal entity embracing all Christians (Eph 1:22–23; 2:11–22; 3:6, 20; 4:4, 12; 5:24–25, 29–32). The church's mission embraces both heaven and earth (Eph 1:22–23; cf. Col 1:18–20).

In Colossians and Ephesians, the church has assigned offices (Col 1:25; Eph 4:11) and its foundation is built upon the "apostles and prophets" with Christ as the cornerstone (Eph 2:20). In Ephesians, the church is

---

32. B. Pearson, "1 Thes 2:13–16: A Deutero-Pauline Interpolation," *HTR* 64 (1971) 79–94.

not only the body of Christ, but the household of God, the bride of Christ, and the holy temple.

Christian ethics in the Deutero-Pauline writings reflect the situation of a church adjusting to the world. Second Thessalonians adds to its Pauline admonitions the following: "hold to the traditions . . . taught by us" (2:15; cf. 3:6), the avoidance of evil teachers (3:1-3), and a golden rule of labor (3:6-12). Colossians and Ephesians incorporate many ethical exhortations into baptismal instructions for new converts (Col. 3:15-17; Eph 4:17-5:20) and household rules for Christian families (Col 3:18-4:5; Eph 5:21-6:9). The ethical admonitions in the baptismal instructions are conveyed by numerous metaphors (e.g., "put off-put on," "old man-new man," "death-life") illustrating the process of sanctification. The household rules presuppose a hierarchy of authority, typical in ancient Hellenistic society: Christ-husbands-wives-household servants-children.

Although the conservative tone of the Deutero-Pauline writings may parallel a similar mood in contemporary Judaism and echo the spirit of conservative Hebrew Christianity, their radical view of Jewish law and customs places them in the tradition of liberal Hellenistic Christianity. The conservative posture of avoiding false teachings, holding to apostolic traditions, and adjusting to the world as an institution is similar to that of post-Jabneh Judaism (90-100) and may recall the conservative mind set of the James and Peter group. However, the influence of Paul's teaching is obvious (a liberal Hebrew) and a break with Judaism is evident (1 Thes 2:13-16). A Gentile majority emulating the teachings of Paul, yet distant from the concerns of Hebrew Christianity is presupposed in the Deutero-Pauline writings.

These books of the Pauline school contain the following teachings which are characteristic of Hellenistic Christianity separate from Judaism. The legal traditions and feasts are abolished (Col 2:14-17, 20-23; Eph 2:15). All that matters is the circumcision of Christ (baptism?) made without hands (Col 2:11). The Christian church is now the holy temple (Eph 2:21). Although conservative in spirit and Pauline in tradition, the Deutero-Pauline writings share the views of Gentile Hellenistic Christianity separate from Judaism.

Johannine Christianity

In the Gospel and letters of John, as in the Synoptic Gospels, we find a community addressing the issues of Jerusalem's fall, the delay of the parousia, and conflicts with Judaism. Unlike the Synoptic tradition, we encounter a high Christology and realized eschatology arising from a complex Hellenistic Jewish environment (e.g., sectarian, gnostic). The Johannine community is the product of diverse groups of Hebrew and

Hellenistic Christians in conflict with the Jews and each other because of their beliefs about Jesus.

In John's Gospel there is a reference to the destruction of the Jerusalem temple by the Romans ("place" 11:48). In Jn 2 a denouncement of Jesus against the temple (v 19) is spiritualized ("the temple of his body" v 20) and adapted to the post–AD 70 situation when the temple did not exist. Also, Jesus is now the place of divine tabernacling (1:14). Finally, a time is coming when worship in a particular temple will be obsolete (4:21). The last three references reflect the same anti-temple beliefs as the Hellenistic Jews who made converts in Samaria (Acts 6:13–14; 7:47–49; 8:4–5). This Hellenistic group seems to have influenced the Johannine community more than any other type.

John's Gospel responds to the delay of the parousia by reinterpreting many of the future hopes as present realities. Even though the author retains some futuristic beliefs (5:28–29; 6:39–40,44; 12:48b), many of them—resurrection, judgment, eternal life, parousia—are described as realities already present for the believer in the encounter with Jesus (3:17–19,36; 5:24; 6:26–27; 6:40,54; 11:25–26; 12:31).

Conflicts with Judaism are detected at various stages in the development of the Johannine community. There were early conflicts with the Jews over the divine status of Jesus (5:16–18; 8:58–59; 10:33; 19:7), the violation of the Sabbath and the law of Moses (5:16; 7:14,22–24), and the meaning of the Eucharist (6:52). It was probably the confession of Jesus' divine status that caused the Jews to expel the Johannine Christians from the synagogues which they attended (9:22; 12:42–43; 16:2–3). As a result of this expulsion from the synagogues, "the Jews" were regarded as outsiders hardened by God and under Satan's control (8:44; 9:41; 12:37–40; 15:25).[33] The feasts of "the Jews" were now superseded by Jesus' appearing (5:1; 6:4; 7:2). Jesus is the "king of Israel" and believers are "Israelites" (1:47, 49; 12:13). Entry into God's community is not by natural birth but by the will of God (1:12–13; 3:3–7). Jesus is the new temple which has supplanted the old one (2:19–21; 4:21–24). This theological position reflects the beliefs of the Greek-speaking Jewish Christians and their Samaritan converts (Acts 6:13–14; 7:47–49; 8:4–5).

33. Rejection by the Jews and probable difficulty with a Gentile mission (Jn 12:20–23 with 15:18–19) may have convinced the Johannine Christians that the world opposed Jesus (3:19; 7:7; 15:18–19; 16:20), that they should not belong to this world (15:19; 17:16) which is under the power of Satan (12:31,35–36; 14:30). This situation of rejection might explain the world negating-attitude encountered in the Fourth Gospel (typical of Gnosticism and other sectarian movements). The favorable references to the world (1:29; 3:16; 4:42; 6:33,51; 10:35; 12:47; 17:21) presuppose its evil state and magnify the love of God who sent his Son to save it.

In addition to external conflicts with the Jews, there developed internal strife among members of the Johannine community. A high Christology and universalistic emphasis (Jn 3:16–17, 18–21; 4:24; 1 Jn 4:8–9) brought tension with conservative Hebrew Christians.[34] A defensive concentration on Christology against both the "Jews" and Jewish Christians eventually led to a split within the community.

Emphasis on the divinity of Jesus sharpened through polemics against the Jews and Jewish Christians, probably left the question of Jesus' humanity unchallenged and undefined in relation to his divinity. Therefore one group within the Johannine community probably saw the human existence of Jesus as only a stage in the career of the divine Logos and not a significant part of redemption. The only important doctrine for them, was that eternal life had been brought down to people through a divine Son who passed through the world.[35] Knowledge of this doctrine gave one a special communion with God that freed one from worldly duties and responsibilities. These early concepts of the group are on a trajectory towards docetism ("Christ only appeared to be human") and libertine Gnosticism ("freedom from worldly responsibility").

The author of the Johannine letters saw the beliefs and practices of this divine Logos group as a danger to the community. He reaffirms the importance of Jesus' humanity by exaggerating the error of the other group (1 Jn 4:2–3,15; 2 Jn 7,10–11) and by attacking their elitism and perfectionist ideas (1 Jn 1:6, 8; 2:4, 9–11).[36] This reaction caused a schism between the two groups (2:19) and forced the first group (secessionists) toward Gnosticism. The adherents of the author of the letters eventually linked up with the Great Church because of their anti-gnostic stance.

34. There also seems to have been conflicts with adherents from a sect founded by John the Baptizer. Note the number of negative statements disqualifying John as "the light" (1:9), the Messiah, Elijah, the prophet (1:19–24; 3:28), the bridegroom (3:29), or a miracle worker (10:41).

35. We agree with Brown, *Beloved Disciple* 103–44, that the development of the schism was a gradual and subtle process.

36. We follow the view that the same author wrote 1, 2, and 3 John, although he is not the author of the Fourth Gospel. See Brown, *Epistles* 14–35.

14

Emerging Christian Orthodoxy: Part One

"Christianity Adjusting to the World and Becoming an Institution, The Period of Consolidation, Primitive Catholicism, and the Emerging Great Church"—these are some descriptive titles that have been given to this formative stage of early Christianity. This phase was characterized by a general loss of expectation in the immediate return of Christ, a break with Judaism as the "parent religion," doctrinal solidarity, and a fixed organizational structure.[1]

A historian once described this period of early Christianity as a time when: (a) the inner dynamics of the apostolic period were exchanged for laws and rules; (b) the original spontaneity gave way to theological reflection; and (c) the apostolic priority on proclamation became subordinate to the defense of the faith.[2] Although this characterization is in need of some qualification, all religions go through such a process of consolidation. The first generation of founders could be regarded as the pioneers and pilgrims; those original visionaries who were usually counter-culture sectarians led by charismatic leaders. The second generation are the settlers and builders; those community organizers who develop and expand the work of the founders. The third generation are the landed aristocracy who seek to preserve the traditions of their predecessors and have comfortably adjusted to the environment. The values and priorities of this last group have changed the most in comparison with the original and the transitional groups.

It must be noted, however, that these schematizations only account for the major trends and tendencies. The categories must be qualified by such factors as the existence of reactionary groups in the later phases. These "restoration advocates" seek to call the movement back to the original

---

1. For a helpful survey of discussion, see I. H. Marshall, " 'Early Catholicism' in the NT," *New Dimensions* 217–31.
2. A. Harnack, *What Is Christianity?*, trans. B. Saunders, 1900 ed. (New York: Harper & Row, 1957) 190–209.

224 PART III: THE FORMATION OF EARLY CHRISTIANITY

days of spontaneity and charismatic leadership. These reactionaries would either be tolerated or opposed by the movement depending on whether they are perceived as constructive prophets or destructive sectarians. When this and other qualifying factors are incorporated, the above categories remain adequate explanations of a religious movement.

In our broad overview of emerging orthodoxy we will utilize the following early Christian writings: The Pastoral Letters, James, 1 and 2 Peter, Jude, 1, 2, and 3 John, Revelation, 1 Clement, the Didache, the letters of Ignatius, and the works of Justin Martyr. Even though it will be argued that these writings share common characteristics as documents of "emerging orthodoxy," differences in doctrine and organization will also be noted, such as the divergent views of the episcopate in the Pastorals and Ignatius. It is our contention, however, that such differences are best explained when viewed on the same trajectory of thought, with earlier formulations moving toward later refinements. This discussion also assumes that the above writings were composed in the same general period of AD 90–150.[3]

We have also labeled this period as "emerging Christian orthodoxy" because the communities who identified with this movement appear to be on a trajectory of thought moving toward the theology of catholic Christianity in the fourth century, characterized by the Nicene Councils and the writings of Eusebius and Athanasius. The movement of this precursory period is called "*emerging* orthodoxy," because plain distinctions between "right" and "wrong" beliefs were not yet discernible in the late first and early second centuries. The use of "orthodoxy" and "heresy" as technical terms denoting correct and false beliefs rarely occurred until the third and fourth centuries.[4]

In our discussion of emerging orthodoxy we will look at the following characteristics of this phase: conflicts with "false teachings," fixed organizational structure, preservation of the apostolic tradition, credal statements and confessions of faith, developing patterns of worship, normative Christian ethics, and collecting a distinctive literature. Because of its importance for understanding emerging orthodoxy, we will concentrate on conflicts with "false teachings" in this chapter, and the others in the next one.

3. See R. Fuller, G. Sloyan et al., *Hebrews, James, 1 & 2 Peter, Jude, Revelation* (Philadelphia: Fortress, 1977); E. Käsemann, "Paul and Early Catholicism" in *NT Questions Today* trans. W. J. Montague (Philadelphia: Fortress, 1979) 236–51; H. Conzelmann, "Luke's Place in the Development of Early Christianity" in *Studies in Luke–Acts*, eds. L. Keck and J. Martyn (London: SPCK, 1966) 302–9; Perrin and Duling, *NTIntro* 371–95.

4. See our discussion in Appendix A, The Formation of the NT Canon [introductory section], and: R. Kraft, "The Development of the Concept of 'Orthodoxy,'" *Current Issues* 48–56.

CONFLICTS WITH "FALSE TEACHINGS"

One major reason for the emphasis on doctrinal solidarity and structured organization in the late first and mid-second centuries was the presence of sectarian groups in the churches that were viewed as a threat by the majority. As early as the mid-first century we detect the presence of Judaizing Christians in Galatia and Hellenistic Jewish Christians in Achaia (2 Cor), both of which Paul viewed as threats. It is unclear, however, if these groups are sectarians since they might represent the majority opinion of that time. Other "false teachers and teachings" in the churches are alluded to in Mark, Matthew, John, Colossians, and Revelation.[5]

Introductory Concerns

Because most of these "opponents" in the early Christian writings are not specifically named, their exact identities are uncertain.[6] Some tentative conclusions, however, can be drawn from analyzing the invectives and harangues in the NT and other early Christian literature. This analytical procedure, however must be cautiously followed, because a statement about "godless defilers of the flesh," for example, is probably polemical rhetoric with no historical reference intended.[7] Lucian of Samosata, the second century AD satirist, was well known for such rhetorical invectives (e.g., *Alexander the False Prophet*). Lucian and the early Christian writers were merely following a common literary convention. Such exaggerated accusations might be compared to the rhetorical language of political slander in modern times.

Despite these cautionary concerns, the discovery of the Nag Hammadi Codices in southern Egypt in 1945 has provided us with primary texts of a religious and philosophical movement of the third century which was opposed by the Great Church: the Gnostics. Many scholars who have

---

5. See, e.g., T. Weeden, *Mark—Traditions in Conflict* (Philadelphia: Fortress, 1971); Francis and Meeks, *Conflict at Colossae*; D. Georgi, *The Opponents of Paul in 2 Corinthians*; Gunther, *Opponents*.

6. The following work lists the diversity of opinions on the matter: Gunther, *Opponents* 1-9.

7. F. Wisse, "The Epistle of Jude in the History of Heresiology," in M. Krause, ed., *Essays on the Nag Hammadi Texts in Honour of Alexander Böhlig* NHS III (Leiden: Brill, 1972) 133-43; see also G. Vallée, *A Study in Anti-Gnostic Polemics* (Waterloo, Ont.: Wilfred Laurier University Press, 1981).

NB: NT citations in this chapter are from the RSV unless noted otherwise. Citations of gnostic books are from Robinson, *Nag Hammadi* and used with permission. Additions to both NT and gnostic texts by myself or Nag Hammadi translator will be noted by parentheses ( ) or brackets [ ]. All words italicized for emphasis in the citations are mine.

studied these texts are also convinced that they contain traditions much earlier than the third century, since fully developed non-Christian and Jewish-Gnostic systems have been detected. Therefore, when some type of thought correspondence can be established between the invectives of early "orthodox" writings and the contents of the Nag Hammadi documents, one can deduce that the opponents of emerging orthodoxy share similarities with the gnostic communities that produced the Nag Hammadi documents. One can, as a result, label such groups as early gnostic or gnosticizing Christians. The writings of Irenaeus and Epiphanius indicate that Gnosticism was regarded as an opponent by the late second and third centuries. Nonetheless, some caution must be made when we assert that the Gnostics were the opponents of emerging orthodoxy in the late first and early second centuries. The evidence of that period is sparse.

Other candidates for "opponents" of emerging orthodoxy (AD 90–150) are:

Ebionites. An anti-Pauline Jewish Christian group rigidly adhering to the Mosaic Law and espousing a low Christology (i.e., Christ was a great prophet empowered by God to do great works). Sources for this group are found in the second and third-century writings of the Pseudo-Clementine *Homilies* ("Kerygmata of Peter"), the Gospel of the Hebrews (both sources contain some gnostic influences), and the fourth-century work, Eusebius, *Eccl Hist* 3.27.

Marcionites. Led by a radical Paulinist (and gnostic?) of the mid-second century, Marcion of Pontus, who rejected the authority of the Hebrew Bible and drew up his own edited version of the "Christian" Bible; sources for this sect are from: Marcion, *Antitheses*; Justin Martyr *First Apology* 1.26; 58; Tertullian, *Against Marcion*; Hippolytus, *Refutation of All Heresies* 7.38,1–5 (more attention will be given to Marcion in Appendix A).

Montanists. A charismatic, counter-culture, ascetic, and apocalyptic group of the mid-second century; sources for this sect are from Epiphanius *Heresies* and several works by Tertullian.

Cerinthians. A late first-century sect whose founder, Cerinthus, believed that Jesus was a man who received the divine Christ when the supreme power descended upon him at baptism but it subsequently left him when he was crucified (docetism); see Irenaeus, *Against Heresies* 1.26,1; Eusebius, *Eccl Hist* 3.28.

From the mid-second to the fourth centuries it becomes evident that these groups are opposed by orthodox and catholic Christianity, but it is also possible that some incipient forms of these "heresies" surfaced in the late first and early second centuries.

Gnosticism

In this section we will concentrate on the data which correspond closest to what we believe to be some early form of Gnosticism.[8] Reference will also be made to other opponents when the data suggest it.

The data which lend support to early catholic Christianity's opposition to Gnosticism in AD 90–150 are: (1) references to "cleverly devised myths" and "endless genealogies" which are possible allusions to gnostic cosmogonies; (2) opposition to ascetic practices which are characteristic of Gnosticism; (3) denouncements of libertinism which may have been the lifestyle of some Gnostics; (4) countering the belief that the final resurrection is already here; and (5) the refutation of docetic Christology which was (or became) a gnostic doctrine.

Cleverly Devised Myths
References to the "cleverly devised myths" and "endless genealogies" which may be allusions to gnostic cosmogonies ("origins of the world") are numerous:

cleverly devised myths (2 Pet 1:16) myths and endless genealogies (1 Tim 1:4) foolish myths (1 Tim 4:7) strange doctrines or old myths that are useless (Ign Magn 8.1)

Two other supportive references are:

the worship of angels (Col 2:18) idle talk and knowledge (*gnōseōs*) falsely called (1 Tim 6:20)

The above references are taken from different contexts and some of them could be alluding to the practices of (non-gnostic) Jewish groups. Nevertheless, as this section will indicate, there is sufficient evidence to support our original claim that these are anti-gnostic texts.

From such apologists as Irenaeus (ca. 180) and Hippolytus (ca. 220), with confirmation from the Nag Hammadi writings (3rd cent.), we learn about elaborate gnostic conceptualizations of the cosmos. For example, the Valentinian gnostic system (according to Hippolytus) begins with the Unbegotten Father who creates a Dyad, Nous, and Truth, which bring forth Logos and Life, and these produce Man and Church. Ten aeons derive from Nous and Truth, and twelve from Logos and Life. The last aeon of the twelve, Sophia, defects and brings forth an "abortion" without form and incomplete (earth). She also produces the Demiurge from her union with the Fruit of the Pleroma. Thereafter the Father brings forth Horos

---

8. It must be remembered that both Marcion and Cerinthus have ties to Gnosticism. Marcion followed gnostic dualism in making distinctions between an inferior creator God (of the Jews) and a superior Good Father. Cerinthus followed a docetic Christology in arguing that Christ escaped suffering and death on the cross.

so that the aeons may no longer be disturbed by the abortion.⁹ This is
only a brief summary of the elaborate Valentinian gnostic system.
If the authors of the early catholic writings were confronted with such
elaborate gnostic systems, it would be difficult to imagine their response
to be different from the statements we have listed above. The references
in 1 Timothy are striking because the opponents are accused of "idle talk
and knowledge (Gk. *gnōseōs*) falsely called" (6:20). This statement is a
plausible allusion to Gnosticism. The reference in Colossians to the
"worship of angels" (2:18) may also be an allusion to the "syzygies" or
pairs of semi-divine beings (e.g., Nous and Truth) which are a major feature in the gnostic systems.

Both the Valentinian and Basilidian systems would have easily been
identified with "cleverly devised myths" and "endless genealogies" by
early catholic writers.¹⁰ The mention of "genealogies" in 1 Tim 1:4 could
apply to the groups of aeons in the gnostic systems. Even if "genealogy"
in this context has the literal meaning of Jewish lists of family descent
(Gen 5; 10–11), this does not rule out all possible gnostic allusions. We
must remember that both gnostic systems mentioned above contain Jewish as well as Christian elements. Several writings from Nag Hammadi
are also Jewish gnostic (e.g., Apocalypse of Adam, Eugnostos, The
Thunder, The Three Steles of Seth, Paraphrase of Shem).

Asceticism

A second reason for regarding the Gnostics as a group opposed by
emerging orthodoxy is because ascetic practices are denounced which are
similar to those of the Gnostics. Two examples from Colossians and
1 Timothy will be given.

The letter to Colossians urges its readers to let no one pass judgment

9. For a more complete description, see Hippolytus, *Refutation of All Heresies*
29–36; also: Irenaeus, *Against Heresies* 1–8 (Valentinus and his pupil Ptolemaeus).
For a description of the Basilidian system, see Irenaeus, *Against Heresies* 24.3-7;
Hippolytus, *Refutation* 7.20–25,27. For introductory discussion, see Rudolph, *Gnosis* 53–274, 308–26.

10. The reader should be reminded that there are passages in the NT where
it appears that gnostic stories and motifs have been employed in a Christianized
or demythologized form: e.g., the descent and ascent of the heavenly redeemer
in Jn 1; 6; Phil 2:5–11; Col 1:15–20; Eph 2:14–16; 4:8–10,13 has parallels to the
Gnostic Redeemer myth; and the following texts contain various gnostic motifs: 1
Cor 2:6–16 (*aeon, gnōsis, pneumatikos*), Jn 3:18; 9:39; 11:25–26 ("realized escha-
tology"). For further discussion, see R. McL. Wilson, *Gnosis and the NT*
(Philadelphia: Fortress, 1968); Yamauchi, *Pre-Christian Gnosticism; Nag Hammadi,
Gnosticism, and Early Christianity*, ed. C. W. Hedrick and R. Hodgson (Peabody,
Mass.: Hendrickson, 1986).

on them in matters of "eating and drinking or in regard to a feast or new moon or sabbaths" (2:16). The reference to "sabbaths" has led some scholars to conclude that a judaizing heresy is being condemned; however, this assertion would not necessarily rule out a gnostic influence since there were Jewish Gnostics. Also, this denouncement occurs in the same context as both the reference about the "worship of angels (=aeons?)" (v 18) and the anti-docetic statement about Christ: "in him dwells all the fullness (*plērōma*) of deity in *bodily form*" (v 9). The meaning of Col 2:9 will be discussed later in this section.

The passage in 1 Timothy, which also condemns ascetic practices, occurs in a noteworthy context:

> forbidding to marry and to abstain from foods which God *created* to be partaken with thanksgiving by those who believe and *know* (*epiginōskō*) the truth; because everything *created* by God is *good* and nothing is to be rejected if it is received with thanksgiving 4:3-4 (my translation)

The author's disapproval of practices which forbid marriage and abstain from certain foods is substantiated by the appeals to: God's good creation, and believers who know the truth and partake of God's creation with thanksgiving. Both points of the argument appear to be anti-gnostic. First, in gnostic thought the physical world is in complete opposition to the transcendent God; it is therefore inferior, deficient, and doomed to extinction. In both the Valentinian and Basilidian gnostic systems, the creation of the cosmos is attributed to the work of the Demiurge, an inferior and ignoble divine being. Second, believers who gratefully partake of God's good creation are described as those who "know the truth." The assertion can be understood to be a specific reproof against Gnostics who profess to "know" divine secrets. The word *epiginōskō* ("I know"), used in our passage, is a cognate verb form of the noun *gnōsis* ("knowledge") from which the Gnostics get their name.

Most Gnostics followed the ascetic practices condemned by the early Christian writers mentioned above. For example, Irenaeus states the position of Saturnilus, an early Christian gnostic leader:

> Marriage and procreation, he says, are of Satan. Many of his followers abstain also from animal food. (*Against Heresies* 1.31,2)

A similar statement equating marriage and sexual pleasures with the work of Satan can be found in the report of Epiphanius concerning the gnostic leader, Severus (*Panarion* 45.2,1-3). The following Nag Hammadi Codices, advocate an ascetic lifestyle free from fleshly passions, jealousies, and other human vices: Authoritative Teaching (VI,3) 23-24; the Teachings of Silvanus (VII,4) 84,94,105,108; the Sentences of Sextus (XII,1) 172,320, 345,363; the Book of Thomas the Contender (II,7) 139,140-141,145.

For most Gnostics rigorous abstinence was a desired goal. Since both the human body and the physical world were corrupt, it was necessary to gain some mastery over the evil desires of the body and to protect oneself from the allurements of a corrupt world.

Libertinism

A third reason for viewing Gnostics as the opponents of early Catholicism is because libertinism is denounced, which may have been the alternative lifestyle of some Gnostics. The patristic evidence shows that unrestrained license was a second practical response to the gnostic position that "matter" was corrupt (e.g., Clem Alex, *Stromateis* 3.5; Epiphanius, *Panarion* 40.2,4). Since matter was evil and doomed to extinction, Gnostics could also treat their bodies and the physical world as something alien to themselves, towards which they had no obligations and could use or abuse as they please. Irenaeus described their position in the following manner:

> For just as it is impossible that the choic [earthly man] should participate in salvation—since, they say, it is incapable of receiving it—so again it is impossible that the spiritual [person]—and by that they mean themselves—should succumb to decay regardless of what kind of actions it performs. Just as gold, when placed in mud, does not lose its beauty but retains its own nature, since the mud is unable to harm the gold, so they say that they themselves cannot suffer any injury or lose their spiritual substance, whatever material actions they may engage in. For this reason the most perfect among them freely practice everything that is forbidden. . . . For they eat food that was offered to idols with indifference, and they are the first to arrive at any festival party of the gentiles that takes place in honor of the idols, while some of them do not even avoid the murderous spectacle of fights with beasts and single combats which are hateful to God and man. And some, who are immoderately given over to the desires of the flesh, say that they are repaying to the flesh what belongs to the flesh, and to the spirit what belongs to the spirit. And some of them secretly seduce women who are taught this teaching by them . . . And some, openly parading their shameless conduct, seduced any women they fell in love with away from their husbands and treated them as their own wives. (*Against Heresies* 1.6,2–3)

Lengthy descriptions of unusual practices attributed to the libertine Gnostics have been compiled by orthodox writers. Epiphanius, bishop of Salamis (ca. 370), wrote about the *sperma* cult of the Borborites in his book *Panarion* ("Medicine Box" for those afflicted by heresies), chs 25–26. A central ritual of this cult concerned the consumption of semen and menstrual fluids as a sacramental action. The exchanging of sexual partners during a drinking-party is also mentioned (26.4,3–4). Clement of Alexandria (ca. 200) alludes to similar unrestrained practices at an *agape* feast in his *Stromateis* ("Miscellanies" 3.2,4; 7.7,17). It must be noted that evidence is lacking from primary sources, for instance, the Nag Hammadi Codices, to confirm the existence of such libertine practices. Most gnos-

tic groups were strict ascetics, but two factors make the secondary patristic evidence compelling. First, the rationale for libertine Gnosticism,
reported by Irenaeus, substantiates this practice as a viable gnostic op-
tion. Second, the detailed descriptions of the *sperma* cult by Epiphanius,
a zealous defender of orthodoxy and orthopraxy, cannot be easily dismissed as lustful inventions of the author.

We will now examine the denouncements of libertinism by emerging
orthodoxy. Although we must be cautious about deriving historical reconstructions from statements resembling polemical rhetoric, a striking
correlation surfaces when these harangues are compared with the patristic reports on libertine Gnosticism. We will first list the invectives, then
comment on the most important texts.

(that each of you know how to acquire a wife for himself in consecration and
honor,) not in the passion of lust like the heathen who do not know God. (1
Thes 4:4–5)

impious persons who pervert favor into licentiousness (v 4) . . . who indulge
in immorality and go after strange flesh (v 7) . . . these dreamers defile the flesh
[and] despise authority (v 8). But these men revile whatever they do not understand, and by those things that they know by instinct as irrational animals do,
they are destroyed (v 10). These are blemishes on your *agape* feasts, as they
boldly carouse together, looking after themselves (v 12). These are rumblers,
malcontents, following their own passions, loud-mouthed boasters, flattering
people to gain advantage (v 16). In the last days there will be scoffers, following their own ungodly passions. It is these who set up divisions, worldly people,
devoid of the Spirit (vv 18–19). (Jude)

But false prophets also arose among the people, just as there will be false teachers among you, who will secretly bring in destructive heresies. . . . And many
will follow their licentiousness . . . (2:2). [The Lord knows how to punish ungodly men] especially those who indulge in the lust of defiling passion and
despise authority (2:10). They count it pleasure to revel in the daytime. They
are blots and blemishes reveling in their dissipation, carousing with you. They
have eyes full of adultery, insatiable for sin (2:13–14). For, uttering loud boasts
of folly, they entice with licentious passions of the flesh men who have barely
escaped from those who live in error. They promise them freedom, but they
themselves are slaves of corruption (2:18–19). (2 Peter)

But I have a few things against you: you have some there [in Pergamum] who
hold the teachings of Balaam, who taught Balak to put a stumbling block before
the children of Israel, that they might eat food sacrificed to idols and practice
immorality [Num 25:1–2; 31:16]. So you also have some who hold the teachings of the Nicolaitans (Rev 2:14–15). (See 2:6 where the sect is also mentioned
at Ephesus.) But I have this against you, that you tolerate the woman Jezebel,
who calls herself a prophetess and is teaching and beguiling my servants to
practice immorality and to eat food sacrificed to idols. I gave her time to repent, but she refuses to repent of her immorality. Behold, I will throw her on
a sickbed, and those who commit adultery with her I will throw into great tribulation, unless they repent of her doings . . . (2:20–22). But to the rest of you
in Thyatira, who do not hold this teaching, who have not learned [*ginōskō*] what

they call the deep things [*bathos*] of Satan, to you I say, I do not lay upon you any other burden . . . (Rev 2:24). [The beliefs and practices of the cult at Thyatira are similar to those of the Nicolaitans]

Although the invectives of Jude and 2 Peter appear to derive from stock phrases of false prophets in Jewish and early Christian literature,[11] the practices of libertine Gnostics provide the best historical occasion for such polemical rhetoric. One would expect these exaggerated harangues, if the early orthodox writers of Jude and 2 Peter were confronted with unrestrained gnostic behavior.

The references to a specific group called the Nicolaitans in Revelation (2:6,15) provide more certain grounds for identifying a sect with practices similar to the libertine Gnostics. Since the same practice and teaching of immorality and idolatry appear in the church at Thyatira, the Nicolaitans, although not named, were probably present in this church (2:20–25). Although his belief that Nicolaus of Acts 6:5 was its founder is questionable, Irenaeus states that the Nicolaitans forsook true Christian teaching and lived in unrestrained indulgence (*Against Heresies* 1.26.3). Clement of Alexandria (although he also regarded Nicolaus as the founder) mentioned that the Nicolaitans abandoned themselves to pleasures like goats in a life of shameless self-indulgence (*Stromateis* 2.20; 3.24). The earlier beliefs and practices of the Nicolaitans in Asia resemble those of the later Borborites in Egypt (reported by Epiphanius).

Realized Eschatology

A fourth apparently anti-gnostic motif is opposition to the belief that the final resurrection is already here. For most Gnostics, the resurrection of the dead became a personal eschatology and was subject to spiritual interpretation.[12] The resurrection from the dead not only meant the release of the soul through revealed knowledge but also its ascent to the *plērōma* (the "fullness" of the divine realm). Therefore the one who receives "gnosis" has already spiritually attained the resurrection from the dead (or "dead ones" = non-Gnostics). This symbolic and personal interpretation of the resurrection has also been called "realized eschatology."

The gnostic Exegesis on the Soul from Nag Hammadi (II,6) explains this spiritual resurrection in the following manner:

Now it is fitting that the soul regenerate herself and become again as she formerly was. The soul then moves of her own accord. And she received the divine nature from the Father for her rejuvenation, so that she might be restored

11. Wisse, "The Epistle of Jude in the History of Heresiology," *Essays on Nag Hammadi Texts* 133–43.

12. Rudolph, *Gnosis* 189–95.

to the place where originally she had been. This *This is the resurrection that is from the dead*. This is the ransom from captivity. This is the upward journey of ascent to heaven. This is the way of ascent to the Father. (134,7–16,)

It is with this spiritual understanding of the final resurrection that some of the paradoxical statements in the Gospel of Philip (II,3) can be understood, for example:

> Those who say they will die first and then rise are in error. If they do not first receive the resurrection while they live, when they die they will receive nothing, (73,1–5).

Although the Treatise on the Resurrection (I,4) discusses three types of resurrections, the spiritual one is the most important:

> What, then, is the resurrection? It is always the disclosure of those who have [already] risen. (48,4–7)

> Therefore, do not think in part, O Rheginos, nor live in conformity with this flesh for the sake of unanimity, but flee from the divisions and the fetters, and *already you have the resurrection*. (49,10–17)

In the Gospel of Thomas (II,2), we have the following statements:

> His disciples said to Him [Jesus], "When will the repose of the dead come about, and when will the new world come?" He said to them, "What you look forward to has already come but you do not recognize it." (saying 51)

> His disciples said to Him, "When will the Kingdom come?" [Jesus said,] "It will not come by waiting for it. . . . Rather, the Kingdom of the Father is spread out upon the earth, and men do not see it." (saying 113)

Although forms of "realized eschatology" appear in several NT books,[13] emerging orthodoxy saw this symbolic and personal interpretation as a threat to the doctrine of a final resurrection of the dead at the return of Christ (the *parousia*). The realized eschatology of the NT probably did not find too much disagreement with emerging orthodoxy, because this motif was often combined with that of future eschatology, resulting in a modified position, which was in contrast to the radical realized eschatology of the Gnostics.[14] It is this *extreme* symbolic and personal interpretation of eschatology that the writers of emerging orthodoxy attack.

In the Deutero-Pauline writing of 2 Thessalonians (ca. 70–90), for example, the readers are warned not to become excited about a letter purporting to come from the author stating that "the day of the Lord has

13. For examples of realized eschatology, see Jn 3:17–19,36; 6:40, 54; 5:24; 6:26–27; 11:25–26; 12:31. This motif is not unlike that already cited in gnostic literature.

14. For examples of futuristic eschatology in John, see 5:28–29; 6:39–40,44; 12:48b. The reader must also be reminded that John's Gospel was a favorite among Gnostics. The first commentary on the Fourth Gospel was written by the Valentinian teacher Heracleon (ca. 170–180).

come" (2:2). If this teaching of "realized eschatology" is gnostic, it also explains the additional problem in the letter concerning idleness and disorderly conduct (3:6–13). Since these "trouble makers" have now experienced the final resurrection, they are freed from the bondage of this world and all obligations connected with it. This position would therefore reflect that of the libertine Gnostics.

The early catholic writing of 2 Timothy (ca. 100–140) warns its readers of Hymenaeus and Philetus "who have gone far wide of the truth in saying that the resurrection has already taken place" (2:18). Hymenaeus is probably the same person denounced in 1 Tim 1:20. The later Acts of Paul and Thecla (ca. 190) attribute a similar viewpoint to both Demas and Hermogenes the coppersmith:

> And we shall teach thee concerning the resurrection which he [Paul] says is to come, that it has already taken place in the children whom we have, and that we are risen again in that we have come to know the true God (14).[15]

Although the author of 2 Peter (ca. 120) seems to be refuting general doubts about the *parousia* (3:3–4), such scoffing of the second coming could stem from a gnostic interpretation of the final resurrection. Since the resurrection can already be experienced in the present, there is no need for the Gnostic to await it as a future event. These sneering men are also "ruled by their passions" [= libertine Gnostics?] (3:3). It is for such "godless persons" that a final day of judgment is reserved (3:7; see also: 2:17; Jude 7, 15; Ign Smyrn 6.1).

Polycarp, bishop of Smyrna (ca. 150), after alluding to 1 Jn 4:2–3, stated that:

> whosoever perverts the sayings of the Lord to suit his own lusts and says there is neither resurrection nor judgment—such a one is the first-born of Satan. (Pol Phil 7.1)

Because the datum of realized eschatology in Gnosticism corresponds closely to the viewpoint opposed in emerging orthodoxy, the following conclusion can be made. It is probable that the above texts of 2 Thessalonians, 2 Timothy, 2 Peter, and Polycarp's letter are all anti-gnostic.

Docetism
A fifth reason why the writings of emerging orthodoxy appear to be anti-gnostic is because of the refutations we find against a docetic view of Christ. "Docetism" is derived from the Greek verb, *dokeō*, which means "to appear," or "have the appearance of." Applied to the study of Christ

---

15. Hennecke, *NTA* 2:356–57. The above passage appears to be a polemic against the semi-gnostic Paul of the Acts of Paul; Dibelius and Conzelmann, *Pastoral Epistles* 112.

("Christology") it is the doctrine that Christ only had the *appearance* of a human (or "flesh") and consequently neither suffered nor was crucified. Docetism was a necessary part of gnostic anti-cosmic dualism. Since the divine realm is perfect and cannot be tainted by the material world, which is inferior and evil, it was necessary that the divine Christ not appear in real human flesh and not be subject to the human experiences of suffering and death ("God cannot die"). It is in reaction to such a doctrine, that emerging orthodoxy argued that Christ had come "in the flesh."

Docetic Christology plays a significant role in Christian-Gnostic cosmogonies ("origins of the world"). As a Gnostic Redeemer, Christ adapts himself to earthly conditions, but only for a short time, and only in terms of external appearance, since he is the representative of the higher "unworldly" realm.[16] In these cosmogonies, the Redeemer adapts himself to the various spheres (or aeons) inhabited by the angelic beings (archons). Through a change in his outward appearance he outwits the Demiurge (ruler of the world). Then, after completing his task of redemption he is able on his return to overcome them openly and triumphantly.[17]

The Gospel of Philip illustrates this "magic hood" motif found in many gnostic cosmogonies:

> Jesus took them all by stealth, for he did not reveal himself in the manner [in which] he was, but it was in the manner in which [they would] be able to see him that he revealed himself. He revealed himself to [them all. He revealed himself] to the great as great. He [revealed himself] to the small as small. He [revealed himself to the] angels as an angel, and *to men as a man*. Because of this his word hid itself from everyone. Some indeed saw him, thinking they were seeing themselves, but when he appeared to his disciples in glory on the mount he was not small. He became great, but he made the disciples great that they might be able to see him in his greatness. (57,29–58,10)

All of the above adaptations and appearances of Jesus are merely resemblances of various forms that the Gnostic Redeemer assumes. To humanity, Jesus takes on only the "appearance" of a human being, because those "who wear the flesh" are "naked" and cannot "inherit the kingdom," (56,29–34).

The Gospel of Truth speaks of the "spiritualized flesh" of Christ visible only to the initiates:

> For the material ones were strangers and did not see his likeness and had not known him. For *he came by means of fleshly appearance* while nothing blocked his course because it was incorruptibility (and) irresistibility. (31,1–9)

The docetic doctrine which states that Christ was not the one who suf-

16. Rudolph, *Gnosis* (1983) 157.
17. Ibid.

fered and died is illustrated in the First Apocalypse of James:

> The Lord said, "James, do not be concerned for me or for this people [who conspired against me]. I am he who was within me. *Never have I suffered in any way*, nor have I been distressed. And this people has done me no harm. But this (people) existed as a type of the archons, and it [my substitute] deserved to be (destroyed) through them." (31,15–26)

The motif of a substitute for Christ on the cross is found in several gnostic writings. Two examples will be given. In the Second Treatise of the Great Seth, Simon of Cyrene suffers and dies instead of Christ (55,9–56,19). According to the Apocalypse of Peter, it is the "fleshly likeness" of Jesus that is nailed to the cross (81,3–82,14).[18] In both cases, the substitute serves as a deliberate sham to outwit the archons and rulers of the world. This is why, as an onlooker, Christ is often portrayed as the laughing savior.

The early catholic writings react against a docetic interpretation of Christ. The numerous statements in the NT about "Christ coming in the flesh" seem to presuppose such a controversy about Christ's humanity. In the writings of Ignatius and Polycarp, the docetic view is more clearly identified and denounced. We will list the texts and only discuss the most important passages.

> Every spirit which confesses that Jesus Christ has come in the flesh (*sarx*) is of God and every spirit which confesses not Jesus, is not of God; this is the spirit of the antichrist. (1 Jn 4:2–3; also quoted in Pol Phil 7.1 against docetism)

> For many deceivers have gone out into the world, who will not acknowledge the coming of Jesus Christ in the flesh (*sarx*); such a one is the deceiver and the antichrist. (2 Jn 7)

> In the beginning was the Word (*Logos*), and the Word was with God, and the Word was God . . . *all things were made by him*; and without was not anything made that was made. (Jn 1:1–3; see also 1 Jn 1:1–2)

> And the Word became flesh (*sarx*) and dwelt among us (Jn 1:14)

> [The resurrected Christ to his disciples:] See my hands and my feet, that it is I myself; handle me, and see; *for a spirit has not flesh and bones as you see that I have.* (Lk 24:39; also quoted in Ign Smyrn 3.1–2 to counter docetism)

> For Christ also died for sins . . . *being put to death in the flesh* but made alive in the spirit. (1 Pet 3:18)

> Since therefore Christ suffered *in the flesh*, arm yourselves with the same thought, for whoever has suffered *in the flesh* has ceased from sin, so as to live for the rest of the time *in the flesh* no longer by *human passions* but by the will of God. (1 Pet 4:1–2)

---

18. *The Acts of John* 97–102, also has Christ as an onlooker while the Jesus substitute is crucified, in Hennecke, *NTA* 2:232–35. Cerinthus of Asia (ca. 100), considered the first Docetic, also held this view, in Irenaeus, *Against Heresies* 1.26,1.

And you, who once were estranged and hostile in mind . . . he has now reconciled *in his body of flesh by his death*. (Col 1:21–22)

For in him [Christ] the whole fullness of deity dwells bodily [*sōmatikōs*]. (Col 2:9)

[Christ] who was manifested [*phaneroō*] in the flesh (1 Tim 3:16)

In all of the above examples, the words "flesh" (*sarx*) and "body" (*sōma*) denote Christ's actual physical humanity during his earthly existence. We have argued elsewhere that other motifs in Colossians and 1 Timothy are anti-gnostic. We also mentioned that the Gospel of John was acquainted with certain gnostic concepts.

The letters of Ignatius are more explicit in their denouncements of docetic Christology. In Ignatius to the Smyrnaeans, it states that:

He truly suffered even as he also truly raised himself, not as some unbelievers say that his Passion was merely in semblance (*to dokein*), but it is they who are merely in semblance (*to dokein*). (2.1; see also 4.2 and Ign Trall 10.1 for similar anti-docetic statements)

For what does anyone profit me if he praise me but blaspheme my Lord, and do not confess that he was clothed in flesh? But he who says this has denied him absolutely and is clothed with a corpse. (5.2)

The docetic position is here plainly articulated and denounced. The explicit anti-docetic motifs in the letters of Ignatius are significant since they are contemporary with some of the later NT writings (e.g., Pastoral Letters, 2 Pet).

In reaction to docetism, both the appearance of Jesus in the flesh (*sarx*) and his suffering and death are affirmed. Ignatius to the Trallians (9.1–2) states that: "Jesus Christ was truly born, both ate and drank, was truly persecuted . . . was truly crucified and died." Ignatius to the Smyrnaeans (1.2) adds that Christ was: "truly nailed to a tree in the flesh." It is also affirmed that Christ was in the flesh after his resurrection, and that he both ate and drank with the disciples (Lk 24:39) as a being of flesh [*sarkikos*] (Ign Smyrn 3.1–3). Like the NT writings, these affirmations are both reactions to and implicit denouncements of docetism.

15

Emerging Christian Orthodoxy: Part Two

In reaction to the internal threats of Gnosticism and in response to external pressures from both Judaism and the Roman government, early Christianity began to consolidate and define itself as a distinct institution. The passage of time which brought further delay to the hope of Christ's near return, also prompted some rethinking about the church's identity and mission in the world. What resulted from these developments is typical of most religious groups of the third and fourth generations.

In this chapter we shall look at the following characteristics of emerging orthodoxy: a fixed organizational structure, efforts to preserve the apostolic traditions, emphasis on confessions and creeds, the establishment of specific worship patterns, concern for normative Christian ethics, and the emergence of a distinct collection of sacred writings.

A FIXED ORGANIZATIONAL STRUCTURE

In the previous chapter we noticed the great threat that "false teachings" like Gnosticism must have posed for those churches of emerging orthodoxy. One effective measure against false teaching was to establish qualified leadership to preserve the faith. The appointing of bishops and elders who were to continue the teaching of the apostles, became a normative procedure of this period. Criticisms of orthodoxy in the Nag Hammadi Codices reflect this organizational development:

> And there shall be others of those who are outside our number who name themselves bishops and deacons, as if they have received their authority from God. They bend themselves under the judgment of leaders. Those people are dry canals. (Apocalypse of Peter 79.23–31)

> For many have sought after the truth and have not been able to find it; because there has taken hold of them the old leaven of the Pharisees and the scribes of the Law . . . For no one who is under the Law will be able to look up to the truth. (Testimony of Truth 29.13–16, 23–25)

The first quote is probably a gnostic reaction to the early catholic hierarchical organization. Perhaps these Gnostics believed that there was too much "dry" organization among these early catholics and felt that the "dynamic spirit" of the apostolic period was active in their own group. Although the second quote seems to criticize Judaism, it is probably a gnostic criticism of catholic Christianity with its credal statements, traditions, and ethical rules. This analogy to Judaism is significant since developments in early catholicism parallel those in post–Jabneh Judaism (90–100).

A major tendency in the organizational structure of emerging orthodoxy was for leadership to derive its authority from the office rather than personal ability or charisma. In earliest Christian writings, leaders often gained their authority from special abilities and endowments of the Spirit (1 Cor 12:8–10,28–30; Rom 12:3–8); overseers and assistants also surfaced (Phil 1:1), but these roles were yet undefined.

By the late first century, the titles of bishop (*episkopos* "overseer"), elder (*presbyteros*), and deacon (*diakonos* "assistant") denoted specific leadership and service functions in the churches (1 Pet, Jas, 1 Clem, Did). These officials often co-existed with the more ecstatic (and itinerant) teachers and prophets (Did, Hermas). By the early second century, certain organizational developments took place. Even though the Pastorals make no clear distinction between bishop and elder (as in 1 Clem), the ethical qualifications and doctrinal duties of these office-bearers are emphasized. They are to be worthy role-models for the church and to preserve the apostolic teachings against misinterpretation. The letters of Ignatius, however, distinguish the office of bishop from elder and underscore the preeminence of the bishop in a hierarchical scheme (a hierarchy already mentioned in 1 Clem). Therefore, in the writings of Ignatius, the organizational tendency to ascribe authority to the office independent of personal ability and charisma becomes a major emphasis.

The following texts from the Pastoral Letters discuss the ethical qualifications and general responsibilities for the offices of bishop, elder, and deacon. Most contain general virtues required of public officials.[1]

Bishop	Elder	Deacon
1 Tim 3:1–7	1 Tim 4:14	1 Tim 3:8–10, 12f.
Ti 1:7–9	1 Tim 5:17–20	[Phil 1:1; Rom 16:1]
	[1 Pet 5:1–4; Acts	
	20:17, 28–30 Jas 5:14]	

In 1 Tim 5:17–18 elders are described as engaging in the same activities ascribed to the bishop in 3:1–7 and Ti 1:7–9. These activities are: govern-

---

1. See a list describing the good military general in Onosander, *Strategikos*, cited in Dibelius and Conzelmann, *Pastoral Epistles* 159–60.

ing, preaching, and teaching. Also in Ti 1:5-7, "elder" and "bishop" are used interchangeably. The Pastorals also assume a council of elders in the congregation (1 Tim 4:14). However, the nature of their leadership role is unclear.[2] The acquiring of leadership positions seems to have been controlled by the already established leadership. Prospective leaders were tested before being admitted to office (1 Tim 3:10).[3]

In the Pastorals, there also appears to be a synthesis of charisma and office. In 1 Tim 4:14 and 2 Tim 1:6, we note that the office-bearer is recognized as having a prophetic gift. This may have been an attempt to weaken the position of charismatic leaders ("false prophets") who are outside the official structure. Only the qualifications for the office are specified in the Pastorals, but certain conclusions can be drawn about some responsibilities of bishops and elders. They had pastoral responsibility for the membership (1 Tim 5:1-2). They exercised disciplinary authority in the community (1 Tim 5:19-20), and they represented the church to the outside world (1 Tim 3:7).[4]

The office of deacon included deaconesses not wives of deacons (1 Tim 3:8-13). There was no separate title of "deaconess" used, because there is no feminine form for *diakonos*. The basic role of the deacon was that of assistant. Probably assisting in worship and works of charity.[5] Although 1 Peter uses the expression "elders" to denote the older generation (5:1; see also 1 Tim 5:1; Ti 2:2), there already appears to exist a fixed circle of elders (1 Pet 5:1-3). The exhortations on ministry (vv 2-3) presuppose that elders are already engaged in ordered ministry.[6]

In the third letter of John, what appears to be an influential bishop (Diotrephes) is portrayed as an opponent of God (9). He opposes the work of the presbyter (1,9-10) and is possibly trying to gain control over the congregation.[7]

In 1 Clement we see that bishops and deacons were appointed by apostles and are therefore part of a divine hierarchy (42.1-4; 44.2). Obedience to the church officials is therefore enjoined (1.3; 3.3; 21.6). However, no distinctions are made between bishops and presbyters (1.3; 21.6; 44.4-5; 47.6).

The Didache mentions bishops and deacons, but not presbyters (15.1,3). The more ecstatic prophets and teachers also co-exist with the ministry

2. D. C. Verner, *The Household of God: The Social World of the Pastoral Epistles,* SBLDS 71 (Chico, Calif.: Scholars Press, 1983) 149.
3. Ibid., 159.
4. Ibid., 160.
5. Ibid., 150 n. 71.
6. E. Schweizer, *Church Order in the New Testament,* trans. F. Clarke (London: SCM Press, 1961) 111.
7. Ibid., 128 [12C].

of bishops and deacons (11.1f.; 12.3ff.; 13.1f.). This mutual regard for (or toleration of) both the prophet and office bearer is also found in the Shepherd of Hermas.[8]

In the letters of Ignatius, we note the fullest type of divine authority ascribed to the hierarchy of bishop, elders, and deacons (Ign Smyrn 8.1; Phld 7.1; Magn 6.1; Trall 7.2). Even though the relationship of the bishop and elders is close (Ign Eph 4.1; 20.2; Magn 2; 7.1; Trall 2.2; 13.2) their offices are distinct and the prominence of the bishop over the presbytery (council of elders) is evident (Ign Magn 2; 3.1; Phld 7.2; 6.1; Trall 12.2). In this hierarchy of divinely ordained offices, the presbytery is subordinate to the bishop (Ign Trall 12.2) and the deacon is subordinate to both the bishop and presbytery (Ign Magn 2; Eph 2). It seems that over each local church (and region) there was a bishop and council of elders, assisted by deacons. The bishop probably functioned as prophet, chief liturgist, and administrator (Ign Phld 7; Ign Pol 2.2).[9] No worship service or church gathering is valid without the sanction of the bishop and the presbytery (Ign Smyrn 8–9; Magn 4; 7; Phld 12.2; Trall 3.1; 7.2). The church must cling to the bishop as it clings to Christ and as Christ clings to the Father (Ign Eph 5.1; Magn 4; 6.2; Trall 7).

THE PRESERVATION OF APOSTOLIC TRADITIONS

From our previous discussions on opposition to false teachings and fixed organizational structures, it is understandable that emerging orthodoxy would be concerned with "sound doctrine" (1 Tim 1:10, 6:3; 2 Tim 1:13; 4:3; Ti 1:9, 13; 2:1, 8) and "guarding the deposit of the faith" (1 Tim 6:20; 2 Tim 1:14). What were these teachings and why were they regarded as authentic? The question of content will be more fully addressed in the next section on confessions and creeds. The related issues of a standard to measure authentic teachings and the procedures for safeguarding them will concern us here.

The content of the traditions we can easily deduce to be anti-gnostic: the coming of Christ in the flesh, the necessity of his suffering, death, and (bodily) resurrection, hope in the second coming of Christ, and belief in one God. These teachings are expressed in credal statements and confessions of faith (e.g., 1 Cor 15:3–7; 1 Pet 3:18–19,22; 1 Tim 3:10).

It is the succession of tradition or the "apostolic transmission of the faith" that serves as both the standard and safeguard for authentic teachings in emerging orthodoxy. This succession of tradition motif prevails in Chris-

---

8. Schweizer, *Church Order* 157–58.
9. C. Richardson (ed.), *Early Christian Fathers* (New York: Macmillan, 1970) 76.

tian literature after the second century but is also evident in late first century writings. It generally assumes the following pattern: Jesus Christ, who was sent from God, commissioned apostles to spread his teachings, they, in turn, appointed bishops and deacons to preserve this teaching for the church. Similar succession of tradition patterns are found in both the philosophical schools of Hellenism[10] and the rabbinic schools of Judaism.[11]

In the first letter of Clement to Rome (AD 96) we note the typical pattern of the apostolic succession of tradition:

> The apostles received the gospel for us from the Lord Jesus Christ; Jesus, the Christ, was sent from God. Thus Christ is from God and the apostles from Christ. In both instances the orderly procedure depends on God's will. And so the apostles, after receiving their orders and being fully convinced by the resurrection of our Lord Jesus Christ and assured by God's word, went out in the confidence of the Holy Spirit to preach the good news that God's Kingdom was about to come. They preached in country and city, and appointed their first converts, after testing them by the spirit, to be the bishops and deacons of future believers. (42).

Ignatius (ca. 110) often utilized the succession motif, as in the following letter:

> Defer to the bishop and to one another as Jesus Christ did to the Father in the days of his flesh, and as the apostles did to Christ, to the Father and to the Spirit. (Ign Magn 13)

Other examples where the apostolic succession of faith is employed are in the teachings of Papias (ca. 100 in Eusebius, *Eccl Hist* 3.39.3f.), Justin Martyr (*Apology* 1. 66–67), and Irenaeus (*Against Heresies* 1.10; 3.3,4). By the mid and late second century the motif becomes elaborate and detailed (e.g., Irenaeus; Tertullian, *Prescription Against Heresies* 21).

---

10. E.g., the prologue of Laertius, *Lives* (1.12–14) attempts to give almost an exhaustive list of philosophical schools from the time of the Sages (e.g., Thales, Solon, Pherecydes) to the Ionian (Anaximander) and Italian (Pythagoras) schools, to the diverse schools named according to cities (Elians), specific localities (Academics, Stoics), incidental circumstances (Peripatetics), their teachers (Socratics, Epicureans), and those with functional names (Moralists, Dialectician); each school containing lists of teachers and their students in respective lines of succession.

11. For example, the rabbinic tractate *Aboth* ("Fathers"), in the Fourth Division of the Mishnah (AD 200), opens with the following succession of tradition: Moses-Joshua-Elders of Israel-Prophets-Men of the Great Synagogue (the Sopherim), (1.1). The Sopherim ("Wise Men"), represented by Ezra the scribe, were regarded as the founders of the rabbinic tradition (Tannaitic period). This Tannaitic phase, which overlapped with early Christianity, had its own teachers who founded their own schools: e.g., Hillel, Shammai, Gamaliel, Akiba.

In the Pastoral Letters, we note the following pattern:

(1) Paul has been entrusted with the "glorious gospel of the blessed God" (1 Tim 1:11; 2 Tim 1:12)

(2) Paul has publicly entrusted the gospel to Timothy (2 Tim 1:13-14; 1 Tim 6:20)

(3) Now Timothy is exhorted to pass it on to faithful men who will be able to teach others (2 Tim 2:2)

An apostolic succession from Paul to Timothy to elders and bishops is therefore evident. Paul is given special prominence in the Pastoral Letters (1 Tim 6:3; 2 Tim 1:13). First Timothy also has the appearance of being the apostle's last will and testament for the church.

In 2 Peter the letters of Paul are regarded as authoritative (3:15-16) and special prominence is given to Peter, the eyewitness of Christ's transfiguration (1:12-15). Second Peter also reads like a last will and testament of the Apostle Peter.

In Luke-Acts (ca. 90) we have several succession motifs. In Acts 20:17-38, Paul, who was commissioned by Jesus Christ (Acts 9; 22; 26), appoints the Ephesian elders as his successors (Acts 20:28-32). In the preaching summaries of Luke-Acts a *continuity of proclamation* is also detected: Jesus (Lk 4:34; 8:1), disciples (Lk 9:1-2), the Twelve (Acts 4:33; 5:44), others in the early church (Acts 8:4-14), and Paul (Acts 18:11; 19:8; 28:23, 31). Luke 1:1-2, the preface to Luke-Acts, also presupposes *three successive levels of tradition*: (a) the events about Jesus, (b) eyewitnesses and servants of the word, and (c) Luke and his readers.

From these succession of tradition motifs we note two things: only that which is authentic can be passed on from Jesus to the apostles and the church, and the recipients are to participate in the succession of the tradition to preserve and safeguard it. Therefore, the apostolic transmission of the faith serves as both a standard of measurement and the model for preserving it.

This procedure for defining the faith and guarding it is a reaction to the more visionary and individualistic groups, like the Montanists and Gnostics. They superseded the chain of command (apostles and bishops) and claimed to receive their authority and teaching directly from Christ through visions and dreams.[12] Although itinerant charismatic prophetic types were tolerated in early catholic communities, precautions were taken to guard against extremists or "false teachers" (Did 11-12).

---

12. See for example, the Gnostic writings: Apoc Pet 79.23-31 and Test Truth 29.13-25.

FORMULATED CREEDS AND CONFESSIONS

The creeds and confessions of emerging orthodoxy derive from the earliest stratum of Christianity. Kerygmatic and credal statements (Rom 1:1–4; 1 Cor 15:3–7) as well as hymns (e.g., Phil 2:6–11) are found in Paul. Most creeds and confessions originated as hymns in early worship settings (e.g., 1 Tim 3:16) or were summaries of early Christian sermons (Rom 1:1–4; 1 Cor 15:3–7). From these origins, the creeds developed into the standard formulations of the fourth-century Great Church (e.g., Apostles' Creed, Nicene Creed). We will first give examples of creeds and confessions found in the NT, next a "rule of faith" by Tertullian, then an "Old Roman Creed" of the fourth century. Examples of hymns with strong credal content are:

Phil 2:6–11:

> Who, being in the form of God,
>> Did not think it robbery to be equal with God.
>> But emptied himself,
>> Taking the form of a slave.
>
> Becoming in the likeness of men
>> And being found in fashion like a man,
>> He humbled himself,
>> Becoming obedient unto death,
>> Even death on a cross.
>
> Wherefore God highly exalted him
>> and bestowed upon him the name above
>> every name,
>
> That in the name of Jesus every knee may bow
>> in the heavens and on earth,
>> And every tongue confess,
>> "Jesus Christ is Lord."

Col 1:15–20:

> Who is the image of the invisible God,
>> firstborn of all creation
>
> For in him was created everything
>> in heaven and on earth
>
> Everything was created through him
>> and unto him.
>
> And he is before everything
> And everything is united in him
> And he is the head of the body (the church).
>
> Who is the beginning, the firstborn of the dead.
> For in him all the fullness was pleased to dwell,
> And through him to reconcile everything to himself.

1 Pet 3:18-19,22:

> Having been put to death in the flesh,
> Having been made alive in the spirit,
> Having gone to the spirits in prison,
> He preached.
> Who is at the right hand of God,
> Having gone into heaven,
> Angels and authorities and powers having been made
> subject to him.

Eph 2:14-16:

> He is our peace,
> Who has made both one
> And has broken down the dividing wall of the fence.
> In order to make the two into one new man in him
> And to reconcile both in one body to God.

Heb 1:3:

> Who, being the reflection of his glory and the stamp
> of his essence,
> Bearing everything by the word of his power,
> Having made purification for sins,
> Sat down on the right hand of the majesty on high.

1 Tim 3:16:

> Was manifested in the flesh,
> Was vindicated by the Spirit,
> Was seen by angels,
> Was proclaimed among the nations,
> Was believed on in the world,
> Was taken up into glory.

Examples of kerygmatic statements derived from primitive Christian preaching are:

1 Cor 15:3-5:

> Christ died for our sins in accordance with the scriptures, that he was buried that he was raised on the third day in accordance with the scriptures, and that he appeared to Cephas then to the twelve.

Rom 1:1-4:

> The gospel of God which he promised beforehand through his prophets in the holy scriptures, the gospel concerning his Son, who was descended from David according to the flesh and designated Son of David in power according to the Spirit of holiness by his resurrection from the dead, Jesus Christ our Lord.

Rom 10:7-9:

> The word of faith which we preach . . . if you confess with your mouth Jesus

as Lord, and shalt believe in your heart that God raised him from the dead, you shall be saved.

The kerygmatic speeches of Acts also contain some of the basic elements of Christ's death, resurrection, and exaltation, even though it is disputed whether these speeches reflect primitive or late first-century preaching (Acts 2:14–39; 3:13–26; 4:10–12; 5:30–32; 10:36–43; 13:17–41). The following statements are formulated like a pre–Nicene Creed:

2 Tim 2:5–6

> For there is one God and there is one mediator between God and other men, the man Christ Jesus, who gave himself as a ransom for us all, the testimony to which was borne at the proper time.

As a transition from the creeds of emerging orthodoxy to those of the Great Church, we have an example of the "rule of faith" by Tertullian of Carthage:

Tertullian, *Against Praxeas*:

> We, however, as always, the more so now as better equipped through the Paraclete, that leader into all truth, believe (as these do) in one only God, yet subject to this dispensation (which is our word for "economy") that the one only God has also a Son, his Word who has proceeded from himself, by whom all things were made and without whom nothing has been made: that this [Son] was sent by the Father into the virgin and was born of her both man and God. Son of man and Son of God, and was named Jesus Christ: that he suffered, died, and was buried, according to the scriptures and having been raised up by the Father and taken back into heaven, sits at the right hand of the Father and will come to judge the quick and the dead: and that thereafter he, according to his promise, sent from the Father the Holy Spirit, the Paraclete, the sanctifier of the faith of those who believe in the Father and the Son and the Holy Spirit. That this rule has come down from the beginning of the Gospel, even before all former heretics, not to speak of Praxeas of yesterday, will be proved as well by the comparative lateness of all heretics as by the very novelty of Praxeas of yesterday.

The "Old Roman Creed," which later was developed into the traditional "Apostles' Creed" (8th cent. AD) was that of Marcellus, bishop of Galatian Ancyra, delivered to Julius, bishop of Rome (ca. 340).[13]

1. I believe in God almighty
2. And in Christ Jesus, his only son, our Lord
3. Who was born of the Holy Spirit and the Virgin Mary
4. Who was crucified under Pontius Pilate and was buried
5. And the third day rose from the dead
6. Who ascended into heaven

---

13. H. Bettenson, ed., *Documents of the Christian Church*, 2nd ed. (London: Oxford University Press, 1963) 23–24.

7. and sitteth on the right hand of the Father
8. Whence he cometh to judge the living and the dead
9. And in the Holy Spirit
10. The holy church
11. The remission of sins
12. The resurrection of the flesh
13. The life everlasting.

The creeds and confessions of emerging orthodoxy can be viewed as moving on a trajectory toward the creeds of the Great Church. In both Tertullian's "rule of faith" and the Old Roman Creed, elements of earlier credal statements from both 1 Corinthians 15 and 1 Peter 3 can be detected. These particular NT motifs were probably utilized in the creeds of the Great Church because they coincided the best with the beliefs of fourth-century orthodoxy.

ESTABLISHED WORSHIP PATTERNS

By the late first century distinct liturgical patterns are noticeable. Meetings are on the Lord's day, Sunday, the day of Christ's resurrection (1 Cor 16:2; Acts 20:7; Rev 1:10; Did 14.1). Gatherings of families in house churches still continued (1 Cor 16:19; Rom 16:5; Phlm 2; esp. Col 4:15). The ceremony of the breaking of the bread (1 Cor 11:23-25; Did 9) was maintained. The practice of water baptism also continued (Acts 8:36-37; Mt 28:19; Did 7).

Three examples of worship patterns in emerging orthodoxy and the Great Church will be given. The first is from a non-Christian source: Pliny's letter to Trajan (AD 110). The second is from Justin Martyr, *Apology* 1.65-67 and the last is from Hippolytus' *Apostolic Traditions* (220).

Pliny was the Roman governor of Bithynia (AD 110) when he wrote to Emperor Trajan concerning the Christian sect. Although the letter primarily concerns prosecution and punishment of Christians, it includes a glimpse of early catholic worship patterns.

> They were in the habit of meeting on a certain fixed day before it was light, when they sang in alternate verses a hymn to Christ, as to a god, and bound themselves by a solemn oath, not to do any wicked deeds, but never to commit any fraud, theft, or adultery, never to falsify their word, nor deny a trust when they should be called upon to deliver it up; after which it was their custom to separate, and them reassemble to partake of food but food of an ordinary and innocent kind. (Letter 96)

From these verses, we learn that the Christians of Asia Minor met early on Sunday, sang antiphonal hymns to the divine Christ, and bound themselves to a baptismal vow or eucharistic confession (cf. Did 14). The mention of what appears to be a separate *agapē* or fellowship meal later in the day, presupposes an earlier Eucharist celebration: "reassemble to partake of food—but food of an *ordinary* and innocent kind" (cf. 1 Cor 11:17–34; Justin Martyr, *Apology* 1.65–67).

In the writings of Justin Martyr (150) we have a more extensive treatment of the worship service:

> And on the day called Sunday there is a meeting in one place of those who live in cities or the country, and the memoirs of the apostles or the writings of the prophets are read as long as time permits. When the reader has finished, the president in a discourse urges and invites [us] to the imitation of these noble things. Then we all stand up together and offer prayers. And as said before, when we have finished the prayer, bread is brought and wine and water, and the president similarly sends up prayers and thanksgivings to the best of his ability, and the congregation assents, saying the Amen; the distribution and reception of the consecrated [elements] by each, takes place and they are sent to the absent by the deacons. Those who prosper and who so wish contribute each one as much as he chooses to. What is collected is deposited with the president, and he takes care of orphans and widows, and those who are in want on account of sickness or any other cause and those who are in bonds and the strangers who are sojourners among [us] . . . we all hold this common gathering on Sunday (*Apology* 1.67).

By the time of Justin, the *agapē* or fellowship meal had been separated from the Eucharist (*Apology* 1.66–67; Did 9–10). Earlier, they had been combined (1 Cor 11:17–34).

The last example is derived from Hippolytus, bishop of Rome (220). It is a condensed outline of an elaborate Roman baptismal service (*Apostolic Traditions*, 20).

1. Examination of catechumens by presbyter and deacon.[14]
2. Exorcism—by presbyter and deacon with the use of holy water.
3. Fasting and Prayer—catechumens are encouraged to fast on Friday and continue in prayer on Saturday.
4. All night vigil of reading Scripture.
5. Prayer over the waters by presbyter at sunrise on Sunday.
6. Candidates appear in the nude—first children, next men, then women.
7. Candidates are anointed by presbyter with the oil of thanksgiving and oil of exorcism.
8. Candidates descend into the water with presbyter.
9. They confess the common faith of the church: a version of the Old Roman Creed.
10. Triune baptism—they are baptized three times.
11. Candidates are then clothed in white garments.
12. The bishop lays hands on the candidates to receive the Holy Spirit.
13. They are sealed on the forehead to symbolize the seal of the Spirit.
14. They receive the kiss of peace from the bishop

14. Catechumens here were converts to Christianity receiving training in doctrine and discipline before baptism. They are also called candidates for baptism.

15. Then they pray together with the congregation.
16. Finally, they participate with the congregation in the celebration of the Eucharist.

Even though this Roman service is quite elaborate, specifications concerning water baptism are found as early as the Didache (7). It has also been argued that both Ephesians and 1 Peter are baptismal liturgies with epistolary features.[15]

NORMATIVE CHRISTIAN ETHICS

To prevent false teaching and insure sound doctrine ("orthodoxy") emerging orthodoxy focused on the importance of right living ("orthopraxy"). The ethical exhortations (*parenēsēs*) of Paul are emphasized. Paul's list of vices and virtues[16] become commandments to be obeyed. Catalogues of ethical duties are now provided for every member and class in the congregation. These ethical norms exemplify the period of Christianity adjusting to its environment.

In emerging orthodoxy, there were household rules for: husbands (Col 3:19; Eph 5:25–28; 1 Pet 3:7), wives (1 Cor 7:10–11; Col 3:18; Eph 5:22–24; 1 Pet 3:1–6), parents (Col 3:21; Eph 6:4), children (Col 3:20; Eph 6:1–3), household servants (Col 3:22–25; Eph 6:5–8; 1 Pet 2:18–20; Did 4:11), and masters of the household (Col 4:1; Eph 6:9). These rules are based on a hierarchical and patriarchal structure cemented by the principle of obedience. As such they represent an adaptation of early Christianity to the social ethics of the first century.[17]

There were also rules for the congregation. There were specified qualifications and duties for bishops (1 Tim 3:1–7; Ti 1:7–9; Did 15:1–2), elders (= bishops, 1 Tim 5:17–20; 1 Pet 5:1–4; Acts 20:17,28–32) and deacons (1 Tim 3:8–10,11–13; Did 15:1–2). There were also responsibilities delineated for the rich (1 Tim 6:5–10,17–19), young (1 Tim 5:1; 1 Pet 5:5–9), old (1 Tim 5:1–2; Ti 2:2–3), and women in the congregation (1 Tim 2:9–15; 3:1; Ti 2:4–8). Care for widows was also enjoined (1 Tim 5:3–16; Jas 1:27).

---

15. On Ephesians, see Meeks, *Writings* 121–22; on 1 Peter, see F. L. Cross, *1 Peter: A Paschal Liturgy* (London: A. R. Mowbray & Co., 1954).

16. These ethical lists were common in the philosophical preaching of the Hellenistic period (e.g., Stoicism).

17. For Greco-Roman examples, see Philodemus, *Concerning Household Management* 29–30, 38; Arius Didymus, *Epitome* 148–49; Seneca, *Epistles* 89, 94–95; see also Soulen, *Handbook* 91; D. L. Balch, *Let Wives Be Submissive: The Domestic Code in 1 Peter* SBLDS (Chico, Calif.: Scholars Press, 1981); idem, "Household Codes," in *Greco-Roman Literature and the NT*, ed. D. Aune (Atlanta: Scholars Press, 1988) 25–50.

General admonitions were directed to all members (1 Pet 1:22–23; 2:11–12; Col 4:1–8; Did 4:9–10) and instructions on responsibilities to the state were specified (Rom 13:1–7; 1 Pet 3:13–17). Specific rules of church discipline were also provided (Mt 18:15–18).

Finally, church manuals like the Didache (ca. 100) were provided. The Didache contains ethical norms for the congregation (1–6), directions for church ordinances and liturgy (7–10,14), guidelines for discerning false prophets (11–12), and procedures for electing church officers (15).

Lists of vices and virtues compiled for congregations since the time of Paul were also utilized (Gal 5:19–23; Col 3:5,8,12; Eph 4:25–5:20; Did 1–6). These ethical lists are found in the parenetic sections of early Christian letters and resemble the Cynic and Stoic ethics of Hellenism (e.g., Epictetus *Discourses*; Seneca *Moral Epistles*).[18] Parallels to these ethical norms can also be found in rabbinic Judaism (e.g., numerous tractates of the Mishnah).

A DISTINCT COLLECTION OF WRITINGS

By the late first and early second centuries, a collection of Christian writings alongside the authoritative Jewish Scriptures begins to take place. We will examine this development of a distinctive literature in three phases: (1) the original authorities, (2) the earliest collections, and (3) the emergence of NT collections.

The original authorities of Christianity were the Jewish Scriptures. they included the Law, Prophets, and "other books." The last category was undefined in Judaism until the late first century and many early Christians utilized such writings as the Wisdom of Solomon, Enoch, and Judith in their worship, preaching, and teaching.

Along with the Jewish Scriptures was the teaching of Jesus, Paul, and other recognized Christian leaders. The words of Jesus are cited as a new norm on matters of faith and practice by Paul (1 Thes 4:15; 1 Cor 9:14) and other NT writers (Acts 20:35; Rev 2–3). Since Paul and certain recognized teachers were commissioned by Jesus and possessed God's Spirit, they also spoke with God's authority (1 Thes 2:13; 1 Cor 7:25, 40; Rev 1:1–3; 1 Tim 6:13–14; 1 Clem 63.2; Ign Phld 7.1–2).

From the late first century to the time of Marcion (140), the following developments took place. The sayings of Jesus were cited with equal authority as Scripture (2 Pet 3:2; 1 Clem 13:1–2; 46:2–8). Paul's writings were also being circulated (Col 4:16). Clement of Rome makes use of Romans,

18. A. J. Malherbe, *Moral Exhortation, A Greco-Roman Sourcebook* (Philadelphia: Westminster, 1986).

1 Corinthians, and Hebrews. Ignatius of Antioch was familiar with Romans, 1 Corinthians, and Ephesians. The author of 2 Peter also mentions an unspecified collection of Paul's letters (3:15–16).

At this period it is unclear if either written gospels were employed or independent oral sayings of Jesus used. However, the Didache seems to quote directly from Matthew's Gospel (Did 8:2; Mt 6:9–13); Papias of Phrygia (120) is acquainted with Mark's Gospel and a Matthean sayings collection supposedly written in Aramaic (Eusebius, *Eccl Hist* 3.39.15–16).

The first authoritative collection of Christian writings was compiled by Marcion of Pontus. Because he made a sharp distinction between the just, wrathful creator of the Jewish Scriptures (whom he rejected) and the Good Father of Jesus (whom he sought to follow), Marcion rejected the Jewish Scriptures and adhered only to his own edited versions of the Gospel of Luke and ten letters of Paul (Galatians, 1 and 2 Corinthians, Romans, 1 and 2 Thessalonians, Ephesians, Colossians, Philippians, and Philemon).

The period from Marcion to Origen of Alexandria was characterized by several new developments. In reaction to both the selective Scripture of Marcion and the additional gnostic writings and Montanist prophecies, catholic Christians began to specify what writings were authoritative for them.

By the mid to late second centuries, we have Justin Martyr, Irenaeus, Tertullian of Carthage, and Clement of Alexandria supporting the authority of the four Gospels of Matthew, Mark, Luke, and John (although John was avoided in the Syrian churches).

Concerning the use of the letters of Paul and his students in catholic congregations, we note the following developments. Polycarp, the bishop of Asia Minor, was familiar with seven or eight of Paul's letters and alludes to 1 and 2 Timothy. Irenaeus of Lyons made use of Paul's ten letters as well as 1 and 2 Timothy.

The letter to the Hebrews was cited early in 1 Clem 36 and Pol Phil 6.3, but its authority in the West was contested until the fourth century. Certain of the General Epistles circulated during this period. Polycarp was familiar with 1 Peter and 1 John; and Irenaeus cites 1 Peter, 1 and 2 John. The earliest use of Jude is found in 2 Peter.

Justin Martyr was one of the first to cite the book of Revelation as Scripture (*Dialogue* 81). Irenaeus also supported Justin's position. In the East, Clement of Alexandria and Origin regarded Revelation as authoritative, but Dionysius (student of Origen) questioned its authorship and authenticity.

The NT collection of Origen (250) marks the beginning of canonical lists that will culminate in the fourth century. It stated the books of undisputed authority to be those of the four Gospels, the thirteen letters of Paul and his students, 1 Peter, 1 John, Acts, and Revelation. Those books whose authority is disputed (or "spoken against") by various catholic congregations were: 2 Peter, 2 and 3 John, Hebrews, James, and Jude. False writings were those gnostic books like the Gospel of Thomas, the Gospel of the Egyptians, and the Gospel of Basilides. Origen also regarded as authoritative: the Gospel and Preaching of Peter, the Acts of Pilate, the Didache, Barnabas, the Shepherd of Hermas, 1 Clement, and the letters of Ignatius.

By the fourth century, we begin to see a trend towards the acceptance of the twenty-seven books of the NT, although some are still disputed (James, Jude, 2 Peter, 2 and 3 John) and other extra books are recommended (Wisdom of Solomon, Sirach, Didache, Shepherd of Hermas). The Easter Letter of Athanasius (367) becomes the first canonical list to recommend the twenty-seven books of our NT as authoritative. He permits the use of the extra books in the churches.

There are at least four factors that forged the formation of the NT canon. First, it was a reaction to heresy: Marcion's limited Scripture and the extra writings of the Gnostics and Montanists. Second, it was the result of imperial pressure: Emperor Constantine (325) ordered fifty new copies of the Bible for use in catholic churches. Third, the public reception of the twenty-seven books by the congregations of the Great Church were an important deciding factor. Fourth, these books adequately reflected the beliefs and perceptions of catholic Christianity in the fourth century.[19]

---

19. Further explanation of the formation of the NT canon will be provided in Appendix A.

Appendix A:

The Formation of the New Testament Canon

Why twenty-seven books, no more or less? There have been numerous attempts at answering this crucial question of the NT canon. Recent archaeological discoveries, such as the Dead Sea Scrolls and the Nag Hammadi Library, as well as current scholarly research, have challenged many simplistic answers concerning the problem.[1]

Before addressing the question about the twenty-seven books, it is necessary first to clarify three misconceptions concerning the subject and to define important terminology involved in the discussion. The question of "why twenty-seven books?" will then be answered by a historical sketch of the formation of the canon.

SOME MISCONCEPTIONS

Original Unity

The first misconception is the assumption of an early church unified in doctrine and practice. Even though the emphasis on ecclesiastical solidarity in early catholic writings (e.g., Pastoral letters, 1 Clement, Ignatius) seems to convey the idea of an initial unity, it probably presupposes a situation of diversity originating from the apostolic period. The NT supports this view of original diversity in the three examples that follow. First, it is evident that Paul, the apostle to the Gentiles, did not find much agreement with the Jewish Christians in Jerusalem (Gal 2:11–14; cf. Acts 21:17–

---

1. Examples of recent challenges to more simplistic views of the past: H. von Campenhausen, *The Formation of the Christian Bible*, trans. J. A. Baker (Philadelphia: Fortress, 1972); D. Dungan, "The NT Canon in Recent Study," *Int* 29 (4, 1975), 339–51; Farmer and Farkasfalvy, *NT Canon*; E. Kalin, "The Inspired Community: A Glance at Canon History," *CTM* 42 (1971) 541–49; A. Sundberg, "The Bible Canon and the Christian Doctrine of Inspiration," *Int* 29 (4, 1975), 352–71; idem, "Canon of the NT," *IDBSupp*, 136–40.

21). Second, it is clear from the letter of James and Paul's letter to the Romans, that there was a difference of opinion concerning the important teaching of justification by faith (Rom 3:28; Jas 2:24). Third, in the NT we encounter a variety of diverse yet legitimate interpretations of Jesus Christ: Hellenistic and Jewish Christian, as well as apocalyptic and early catholic. Christianity from its inception was characterized by a variety of beliefs and practices.[2]

NT "Orthodoxy" and "Heresy"

The second misconception can be explained in the following three statements. The first builds on the previous discussion of diversity in the NT: Since earliest Christianity was characterized by a variety of different teachings, clear distinctions between "right" and "wrong" beliefs are not always discernible.[3] Second, "orthodoxy" or "heresy" as "correct" or "false religious beliefs" are technical terms characteristic of the period after the NT. The Greek term *orthodoxia* ("correct belief") is not found in the NT, but is frequent in the fourth century.[4] The term *hairesis* generally had a neutral sense in the first century.[5] The technical, negative usage of "heresy" as "false religious belief" rarely occurred until the second and third centuries.[6] Third, rigid orthodox and heretical labels obscure objective historical study by prejudging the positions of both concerned parties before examining them. For example, we want to give the "Judaizers" a chance to be heard as well as the Apostle Paul who opposed them (Gal 1-2).[7] Therefore in our discussion of early Christianity the labels of orthodoxy and heresy will be avoided and more neutral designations preferred, such as: early catholic and gnostic Christianity, Great Church and dissenting Christianity.

2. A comprehensive treatment of original diversity is found in Bauer, *Orthodoxy*, xxi-xxv, 229-40.
3. This point is carefully argued in Kraft, "The Development of the Concept of 'Orthodoxy' in Early Christianity," *Current Issues* 48-56.
4. For example, in the writings of Eusebius, *Eccl Hist* 3.31.6; 6.2.13-14.
5. The neutral sense of *hairesis* as a Jewish sect or party (Acts 5:17; 15:15; Josephus, *Ant.* 13.171) or Christian group (Acts 24:5; 28:22). The usage of *hairesis* with some negative connotation as a "faction" or "schism" in the church: 1 Cor 11:19; Gal 5:20; and possibly Ti 3:10.
6. Ign Trall 6.1 (AD 118); Irenaeus, *Against Heresies* 3, preface and 11.3 (AD 180). The occurrence of "heretical" or "heresies" in Ti 3:10 and 2 Pet 2:2 borders on this negative technical usage, but most scholars date these books in the 2nd cent. On the dating of 1 Peter and the Pastorals, see Koester, *Introduction* 295-305; Kümmel, *Introduction* 366-87, 429-34; Guthrie, *NTIntro* 584-624, 814-51.
7. We are not discounting the importance of discerning "right" from "wrong" teaching for dogmatic and confessional purposes. But since we are not approaching the NT from a confessional perspective, such distinctions could prejudice our attitude towards certain ancient teachings before examining them objectively.

"Canonical" and "Apocryphal" in Early Christianity

The third misconception relates to the use of the labels "canonical" and "apocryphal" when discussing early Christian literature. As we have shown with "orthodoxy" and "heresy," the above labels are also technical terms used after the NT period that tend to prejudice a critical study of the literature. The word "canon" (Gk. *kanōn*, "straight rod, reed") was often used to signify a rule or norm (e.g., Gal 6:16). Applied to the Bible, canon denotes an official list of authoritative writings.

"Apocrypha" (Gk., "kept hidden") was a term often applied to secretive or objectionable literature. In the late second century it was used by Irenaeus in his denouncements of gnostic writings which he considered to be apostolic forgeries. Despite the attempts at censorship by Irenaeus and other Christian polemicists, the circulation of "apocryphal" writings, such as the Gospel of Peter and Acts of Paul, continued for centuries.

Since three misconceptions relating to the NT canon have been addressed, a historical sketch will be provided in response to the question: why twenty-seven books, no more or less? First, the authorities and collections of early Christianity will be examined. Second, the emergence of NT collections will be studied. Third, the canonical lists and their influences will be surveyed. Finally, lingering issues from the Reformation to the present will be addressed.

THE FORMATION OF THE NT CANON

The History of the NT Canon: AD 30–140

What were the written and oral authorities of the earliest Christians before the NT was written? What comprised some of the earliest collections of Christian teachings? These are some of the questions that will be treated in this section.[8]

The Authority of the Jewish Scriptures
Jesus and primitive Christianity were never without a Holy Scripture, since they relied heavily upon the authoritative writings of Judaism. Al-

---

8. The following designations of Christianity will be used in this study: (1) earliest or apostolic Christianity AD 30-70, from the approximate dates of Jesus' ministry to the deaths of most of the apostles; (2) early catholic or post-apostolic Christianity 70–150, after the apostles to the time of Marcion and Justin Martyr, (3) catholic Christianity on its way to becoming the "Great Church," from mid-2nd cent. until the reign of Constantine (324) and the Council of Nicea (325); after 325 catholic Christianity was the Great Church. Some overlap will occur on the above categories.

though all three parts of the later Hebrew Bible were quoted, it is questionable whether there was a closed collection of Jewish Scriptures before the first century. Throughout the Mediterranean world of that time, the Jews used as scripture the two closed collections of the Law and Prophets and also a third undefined group of "other books."[9] This undefined category was later called the "Writings" (Babylonian Talmud, *Sanhedrin* 90b), although this later rabbinic division omitted many widely circulated books, e.g., the Wisdom and Psalms of Solomon, Enoch, and 1 and 2 Maccabees. There is no clear evidence of a closed collection of Jewish Scriptures until after the AD 70 fall of Jerusalem (cf. Josephus, *Against Apion* 1.38–46; 4 Ezra 14). This final stage of consolidation possibly resulted from the late first-century rabbinic discussions at Jabneh. By this time early Christianity had broken away from Judaism and did not adhere completely to a fixed Jewish Bible, since books like the Wisdom of Solomon, Enoch, and Judith were used authoritatively in early Christian writings (e.g., Jas 4:5; Jude 14–15: 1 Clem 27:5; 55:4; Barn 4:3).

The Authority of Jesus

This broad view of Scripture in early Christianity is understandable since the sacred writings were subservient to the authoritative sayings of Jesus (Mt 5:21–45; Jn 5:39–47).[10] As early as the writings of Paul (50–62), words of Jesus are cited as a new norm on matters of faith and practice (e.g., 1 Thes 4:15; 1 Cor 9:14). The citation of Jesus sayings is also evident in the early catholic literature (Acts 20:35; Rev 2–3).

The Authority of Paul and Others

Since Paul and other early Christian leaders were commissioned by Jesus and possessed God's Spirit, they also spoke with God's authority (e.g., 1 Thes 2:13; 1 Cor 7:25,40; Rev 1:1–3; 1 Tim 6:13–14; 1 Clem 63:2; Ign Phld 7:1–2). This was a charismatic living authority which developed in the activities of proclamation and leadership.[11] Even though the author of Revelation claimed inspiration for himself (22:18–19), and some of Paul's letters were intended to be exchanged among the churches (1 Thes 5:27; Col 4:16), this is no indication that early Christian writers were conscious of producing "canonical" Scriptures.[12]

---

9. These undefined "other books" are alluded to in the prologue of the book of Sirach and are exemplified in the broader collections of Scripture in the Dead Sea Scrolls (Qumran) and the Greek Septuagint (LXX). All of the above writings were composed before the NT.

10. Kümmel, *Introduction* 477–78; CHB 1:286–88.

11. Kümmel, *Introduction* 477–78. See especially: E. Kalin, "The Inspired Community: A Glance at Canon History," CTM 42 (1971) 541–49.

12. Kümmel, *Introduction* 477–78.

The Earliest Collections

In the discussion above, we have seen that the authorities of earliest Christianity were the Jewish Scriptures, the sayings of Jesus, the teachings of Paul, and the words of certain early catholic writers. We will now look at some of the earliest collections of sayings and writings that preceded the NT lists of catholic Christianity (140-419).

The authoritative use of Jesus sayings and certain letters of Paul was characteristic of post-apostolic Christianity before Marcion (140). The sayings of Jesus were cited with equal authority as Scripture (1 Clem 13:1-2; 46:2-8; 2 Pet 3:2). Certain writings of Paul including the vaguely Pauline letter to the Hebrews were also circulated. Clement of Rome (96) makes use of Romans, 1 Corinthians, and Hebrews. Ignatius of Antioch (ca. 110) was familiar with Romans, 1 Corinthians, and Ephesians. The author of 2 Peter (120?) also mentioned an unspecified collection of Paul's letters (2 Pet 3:15-16).

Data used to support an early collection of written gospels must be cautiously examined. It is not always clear whether a written gospel or an independent oral saying is cited by early catholic writers, like Clement of Rome and Ignatius. However, the Didache (ca. 90) appears to quote directly from Matthew's Gospel (Did 8.2/Mt 6:9-13) and Papias of Phrygia (120) is acquainted with both the Gospel of Mark and a Matthaean sayings collection in Aramaic (Eusebius, *Eccl Hist* 3.39.15-16). It appears that at least one or two written gospels were being circulated by the early second century.

The appearance of Marcion from Pontus (ca. 130-160) marks a high point in the study of early Christian collections, since he was the first to undertake the task. Influenced by Paulinism (Rom, Gal) and possibly Gnosticism,[13] Marcion made a sharp distinction between a wrathful, inferior creator of the Jewish Scriptures (whom he rejected) and the Good Father of Christ (whom Marcion sought to follow). As a result, he rejected the Hebrew Bible and believed that the true interpretation of Christ and the Father was preserved only in ten letters of Paul (the Pastoral letters ex-

---

13. It was clearly Paul's teaching on law vs. gospel which influenced Marcion's *Antitheses* (143). This work consists of a series of contrasts between the inferior teachings of the Creator/Moses/Law and the superior words and deeds of Christ. See "Marcion" in Meeks, *Writings* 185-92; Farmer and Farkasfalvy, *NT Canon* 58-64,134-41. If Gnosticism also influenced Marcion, it is difficult to understand what type. His distinction between the inferior creator and the Good Father and his claim of a relationship with the Father for those who attain a new recognition of him through Christ have affinities with Gnosticism. But Marcion's teaching lacked the mythological and allegorical characteristics of Gnosticism, which was based on *Jewish* as well as Christian writings. See: E. Pagels, "Gnosticism," *IDBSupp*, 366.

cluded) and the Gospel of Luke, ascribed to Paul's companion. Both the Gospel and apostolic writings were edited and abridged by Marcion (Irenaeus, *Against Heresies* 1.27.2). Despite opposition from Irenaeus and others (e.g., Tertullian, *Against Marcion*), the radical teacher from Pontus was the first to draw up a collection of Christian Scriptures with the two divisions: Gospel and apostolic writings.

The History of the NT Canon: AD 140–250

This period of identifying authoritative Christian writings in catholic Christianity was probably the result of two negative influences: (1) the selective Scripture of Marcion; and (2) the circulation of new gnostic books and Montanist prophecies. Although it is unclear to what extent these two factors influenced the collecting of Christian books by the emerging Great Church, the ambitious efforts of non-catholic Christians provide some explanation for the sudden appearance of Christian collections in the writings of Justin Martyr (150) and Irenaeus (180). Therefore the influences of Marcion, Montanism, and Christian Gnosticism will be discussed as background to our study of emerging NT collections.

Negative Influences

Marcion's rejection of the Jewish Scriptures and his exclusive allegiance to his editions of Luke's Gospel and Paul's ten letters, have already been mentioned. Marcion's ambitious attempt was a deliberate restriction of a much broader use of Christian authorities already evident in the writings of Clement of Rome, Ignatius, and Papias. As a result, Marcion's teachings were denounced by Justin Martyr and Irenaeus, both of whom made use of a broader group of Christian books.

The continuing revelations of Montanism were an opposite extreme from Marcionism, which early catholics also sought to avoid. Montanism was a prophetic movement from Asia Minor that anticipated an imminent end of the world (ca. 170–230). Montanus, the founder, and his two prophetesses Maximilla and Priscilla, claimed to utter new prophecies directly from God. Some of their utterances (influenced by Jn 14–17) are found in the catholic writings of Tertullian (ca. 200) and Epiphanius (ca. 400). Although no Montanist books are extant and the identity of the prophecies as "Scripture" is unclear, the new revelations of Montanism were regarded by the Great Church as an attempt to add to the four Gospels and apostolic writings (Eusebius, *Eccl Hist* 5; Epiphanius, *Panarion* 48).

Another extreme position which appeared to add to the authoritative writings of catholic Christianity was that of Gnosticism. Gnostics advocated spiritual liberation and identity with the divine through revealed knowledge (*gnōsis*). This process of salvation is revealed in elaborate myths of heavenly beings emanating from a transcendent deity that generally involved a story of separation from and restoration to the divine realm. Christian gnostic systems utilized material from, for example, the Synoptic Gospels, John's Gospel, and Paul. Some of the many Christian gnostic writings produced in the second and third centuries were the Gospel of Thomas (1st cent.?), the Gospel and Apocalypse of Peter, and the Gospel of Truth (Nag Hammadi texts). The wide circulation of numerous gnostic Christian writings posed a real threat to the Great Church and the writings to which it adhered. Therefore, Irenaeus and other catholic apologists considered them to be a distortion of their Gospels, apostolic writings, and OT.

The Gospels

With the appearance of Marcion's influential collection and the wide circulation of gnostic gospels, the catholic Christianity began to specify which gospels and apostolic writings were considered authoritative. First, the use of specific gospels and apostolic writings will be noted. Then, the lists of Origen and the Muratorian fragment will be analyzed.

Although the Four Gospels were used by mid-second century, no consensus was reached concerning their exclusive use in catholic Christianity. Justin Martyr of Palestine (150) cites the written Gospels of Matthew, Mark, Luke, and (probably) John as Scripture, calling them the "memoirs of the apostles." Irenaeus of Lyons, Gaul (180), employed fantastic numerology to argue for a closed collection of four Gospels. This closed collection of Matthew, Mark, Luke, and John was supported in the West by Tertullian of Carthage (200) and in the East (possibly) by Clement of Alexandria (200) and Origen (250). However, the exclusive use of four Gospels was contested by the Syrian churches for several centuries.

One reason for the dissension of Syria concerning only four Gospels was due to the work of Tatian from Syria (150). Tatian composed a harmony of four (possibly five) Gospels which was called the *Diatessaron*. Although this first Gospel harmony has been argued as an early witness to a fourfold gospel, the use of four separate Gospels was not a general practice in Syria until the fifth century. It should also be noted that reluctance to use certain individual Gospels, especially John's Gospel, may have been in reaction to its gnostic appeal. For instance, the Valentinian gnostic, Heracleon (170) produced the earliest commentary on the Gospel of John. The Montanists also favored John. Anti-gnostic or anti-Montanist churches (most of which were catholic) would therefore be reluctant to use such a writing. This may explain why the anti-gnostic Syrian churches were reluctant to use separate gospels, but favored the harmonistic arrangement by Tatian.[14]

14. The popularity of the *Diatessaron* continued in Syria until the 5th cent. But the following circumstances contributed to its decline in use. Tatian (who was

The Apostolic Writings

Although a collection of Paul's letters existed before Marcion, the extent of this collection was not defined until the third century. Polycarp, bishop of Smyrna (150), was familiar with seven or eight of Paul's letters (found in Marcion's collection) and alludes to passages from 1 and 2 Timothy (not in Marcion's collection). First and Second Timothy, along with most of Paul's ten letters, were quoted in the writings of Irenaeus (180). After this period the Pastorals (1 and 2 Tim and Ti) are often quoted as the works of Paul.

The letter to the Hebrews was cited early by both Clement of Rome (36) and Polycarp (Pol Phil 6.3); but because of its uncertain authorship, its authenticity was questioned by the West until the fourth century. Tertullian, however, defended the authenticity of Hebrews by arguing that its author was Barnabas, a companion of the Apostle Paul.

This period also marks the circulation of the NT catholic letters. Polycarp appears to quote from 1 Peter and 1 John in his letter to the Philippians. Traces of 1 Peter have also been detected in gnostic writers like Basilides (ca. 125). Irenaeus cites 1 Peter with the words "Peter in his epistle" and also quotes 1 and 2 John, ascribing their authorship to the Apostle John. The earliest use of Jude is found in 2 Peter (ca. 120).[15] Clement of Alexandria and Origen were also familiar with most of the catholic letters.

Justin Martyr was one of the first to cite the book of Revelation as Scripture, ascribing its authorship to the Apostle John (*Dialogues* 81). Irenaeus also supported Justin's position. When the Montanists used this book to support their own ideas, it became controversial among catholic Christians in Asia Minor and Rome. In the East, Clement of Alexandria and Origen considered Revelation to be authoritative, although Dionysius (a disciple of Origen) questioned its authorship and authenticity.

The List of Origen

Origen of Alexandria (250) made use of a large group of early Christian writings. He composed commentaries, homilies, and theological treatises on every OT and NT book that was currently used in the Egyptian

---

a pupil of Justin Martyr) later joined a non-catholic ascetic group (the "Encratites") which was condemned by Irenaeus and Eusebius (Eusebius, *Eccl Hist* 4.19). Hippolytus of Rome (220) accused Tatian of being a pagan Cynic (*Elenchus* 10.18). Bishop Theodoret of Cyrrhus (425) destroyed many copies of the *Diatessaron* because he suspected Tatian of heresy.

15. For further discussion of the view that Jude was a source for 2 Peter, see R. Bauckham, *Jude, 2 Peter* WBC (Waco, Tex.: Word, 1983) 141–43; R. Fuller et al., *Hebrews, James, 1 and 2 Peter* 89–90; Guthrie, *NT Intro* 919–22.

churches. From his numerous works, Eusebius (320) drew up a list of NT books that Origen had used.[16] In this composite list, Eusebius mentions: the Four Gospels, Paul's letters (in his writings, Origen alludes to twelve, excluding Phlm), Hebrews (whose authorship was unknown to him), 1 Peter (Origen doubted the Petrine authorship of 2 Pet), 1 John (he conceded that 2 and 3 Jn may not be genuine), Acts, and Revelation.[17] Elsewhere, Origen rejects the following writings as heretical: the Gospel of the Egyptians, the Gospel of Thomas, the Gospel of Basilides, and the Gospel of Matthias.

The list compiled by Eusebius, however, did not serve as a fixed canon for Origen.[18] Like his predecessor, Clement of Alexandria, Origen used a broader group of Christian writings in an authoritative manner: e.g., the Gospel and Preaching of Peter, the Acts of Pilate, the Didache, Barnabas, the Shepherd of Hermas, 1 Clement, and the letters of Ignatius. Irenaeus also utilized 1 Clement, the Shepherd of Hermas and the writings of Ignatius. Tertullian likewise made use of the Shepherd of Hermas. Such widespread circulation of post-apostolic and pseudonymous writings indicated the fluidity and openendedness of authoritative Christian documents in the second and third centuries.

The Muratorian Fragment

The NT list in the fragment discovered by L. A. Muratori (1740) is significant.[19] Although the beginning and end of the so-called Muratorian Fragment is lost, it appears to affirm a fourfold Gospel. The fragment begins with Luke as the "third gospel book," presupposing Matthew and Mark, and it mentions "the fourth gospel . . . by John." The Acts of the Apostles is mentioned next. In conformity to the seven letters to churches in Asia Minor found in the book of Revelation, Paul is said to have written to seven congregations: Corinth, Ephesus, Philippi, Colossae, Galatia, Thes-

16. Most of Origen's works are found in *ANF* 4. Origen's list is found in Eusebius, *Eccl Hist* 6.25.3ff.; Eusebius also includes an OT list which contains most of the extra books of the Greek OT not found in the Hebrew Bible (e.g., "Maccabees"). For further discussion on Origen and the NT, see Kümmel, *Introduction*, 495f. (contrary to Kümmel, it appears that Eusebius, not Origen, divided the NT into three categories); see Sundberg, "Making the NT Canon," *IOC* 1223.

17. Doubts about James and Jude are also mentioned in Origen's commentaries on *John* (20.10.66) and *Matthew* (17.30).

18. Sundberg, "Making of NT Canon," 1223.

19. The fragment discovered by L. Muratori in the eighteenth century is an early list of authoritative Christian writings found in a mutilated eighth-century Latin manuscript. For further information, see Kümmel, *Introduction*, 491–93; and W. Schneemelcher, "History of NT Canon," in Hennecke *NTA* 1:42–45. For important recent discussion, see Sundberg, "Muratorian Fragment," *IDBSupp*, 609f., and "Canon Muratori: A Fourth Century List," *HTR* 66 (1, 1973), 1–41.

salonica, and Rome. The total number of Paul's letters here is probably nine, since the apostle wrote two letters each to the Corinthians and Thessalonians. Philemon and the Pastoral Epistles are classed together as letters to individuals.

The Muratorian fragment also rejects two forged letters of Paul to the Laodiceans and Alexandrians, which are ascribed to the sect of Marcion. First John is mentioned with the Fourth Gospel. It is unclear precisely what are the two letters "with John's inscription" (e.g., 1 and 2 John or 2 and 3 John?). The letter of Jude is also mentioned later in the manuscript. the Revelation of John is listed again with the Revelation of Peter, although the text states that some do not allow (both of) them to be read in the church. The Wisdom of Solomon is included without a word of caution or endorsement. The book recommended for private and not public reading is the Shepherd of Hermas.

The Muratorian fragment attributes the date and setting of the Shepherd of Hermas "in our time . . . in the city of Rome, when his (Hermas') brother Pius was seated as bishop of the church . . . of Rome." This allusion dates Hermas at about 140–150 and the composition of the Muratorian fragment within a generation of that date ("in our time"). Reference to "catholic church" and "city of Rome" have been interpreted as reflecting Roman origin.

However, the contents of the Muratorian fragment raise problems concerning its early Roman origin, and some have postulated a fourth-century date in the East.[20] First, if the Muratorian list comes from second-century Rome, it had little influence on the early collections of the West.[21] Western sources of the second century reveal no definite acquaintance with the fragment. Second, the contents of the Muratorian fragment are characteristic of fourth-century lists in the East. For examples: the questionable status of Revelation, the disapproval of reading the Shepherd of Hermas in public, and the classification of the Wisdom of Solomon with early Christian writings are all features of fourth-century Eastern lists (cf. Eusebius). If the above criticisms are correct, then the Muratorian fragment preceded and possibly influenced several fourth-century lists, especially the collection of Eusebius (320). The Muratorian fragment, according to this viewpoint, moved West in a codex with other Christian documents (e.g., a book by Chrysostom, 350) to justify the inclusion or exclusion of certain writings in the West (e.g., Hebrews is omitted in the fragment).[22]

20. For the later Eastern dating and problems of early Roman origin, see Sundberg, "Muratorian Fragment," 609f., and "Canon Muratori," 12–25, 34–41.

21. Sundberg, ibid.; cf. J. Daniélou, The Origins of Latin Christianity (Philadelphia: Westminster, 1977) 13–15.

22. Sundberg, "Canon Muratori," 38–41; "Muratorian Fragment," 609–10.

The History of the NT Canon: AD 320–419

The actual formation of a NT canon begins with the compilation of Eusebius (320). It reaches some degree of uniformity with the Easter letter of Athanasius (367) and the councils of North Africa (393–419), although uncertainty concerning the limits of the canon continued in the Syrian churches until the seventh century.

Eusebius

In his *Eccl Hist* 3.25, Eusebius of Caesarea provides a list of Christian Scripture. We will first examine his three categories of writings and then discuss the criteria he used in his categorization. Eusebius divides his canonical list into three categories: acknowledged, disputed, and "heretical." The accepted (Gk. *homolegoumena*) writings are similar to his compilation of Origen's list (6.25.3ff.) except the body of Paul's letters are listed and Hebrews is added to it; he also has reservations about Revelation ("if appropriate"). The "disputed writings" (Gk. *antilegomena*) are subdivided into disputed books "known to many" (Jas, Jude, 2 Pet, and 2 and 3 Jn) and "spurious" or forged apostolic writings: the Acts of Paul, the Shepherd of Hermas, the Apocalypse of Peter, Barnabas, Didache, and Revelation "if appropriate." The third category, the "heretical" documents are those books which are "completely senseless and impious": the Gospels of Peter, Thomas, Matthias (and others), the Acts of Andrew, the Acts of John, and other pseudonymous books which claimed apostolic authorship.

Three observations of the above criteria should be made. First, Eusebius only regarded the *acknowledged* writings as genuine and canonical. Second, although the disputed and spurious writings were rejected by some, they were read publicly in many churches. Therefore most of the disputed writings could be interpreted as quasi-canonical literature. Third, the heretical writings were "totally spurious and foreign to apostolic orthodoxy."[23]

The criteria presupposed in the categorization of Eusebius appear to be three: (1) acceptance by all the churches, (2) apostolic and orthodox contents and (3) apostolic authorship or origins. The heretical writings were probably rejected because they did not adequately meet the above criteria. Eusebius had little difficulty regarding Hebrews as an acknowledged writing since he ascribed its authorship to the Apostle Paul (unlike Origen or Tertullian). But Eusebius had reservations about the apostolic authorship of the Revelation of John. He was probably influenced by the

---

23. *Eccl Hist* 3.31.6. As noted in this discussion, Eusebius identifies his position with "apostolic orthodoxy" and refers to his opponents as "heretics" (3.25.6). By the 4th cent., the lines between true and false religious beliefs were more clearly defined.

skepticism of Dionysius of Alexandria concerning the book's authenticity. Acceptance by the churches was probably the most important criterion that helped gain canonical status for James, Jude, 2 Peter, and 2 and 3 John. Because the above books (including Hebrews) did not adequately meet all three criteria, their status remained disputed in the Western churches until the fourth century.[24]

Athanasius

The first list to have all twenty-seven books of our NT "canonized" (Gk. *kanōnizomena*) was the Easter letter of Athanasius (367), bishop of Alexandria. There was, however, a list of additional books to be read by those being instructed in Christianity: the Wisdom of Solomon with four other Jewish books of the Septuagint (LXX) and the Christian writings of the Didache and Shepherd of Hermas. "Heretical" writings which are falsely assigned an early date and "deceive the innocent" are labeled "the apocrypha" and rejected.

Syria

The twenty-seven book canon of Athanasius greatly influenced the Western synods but had little effect on the Syrian churches. The church councils and synods of North Africa (Hippo 393 and Carthage 397, 419) differed in arrangement but agreed in number with the canon of Athanasius. But the following developments took place in the Syrian churches which challenged the Athanasian canon for centuries. In the fourth century, the *Diatessaron* of Tatian was favored over the Four Gospels. The catholic letters and the book of Revelation were also omitted (e.g., the Doctrine of Addai). In the fifth century the Four Gospels were included, but four catholic letters and Revelation were omitted (the Peshitta or "Syrian Vulgate"). During the sixth and seventh centuries, some degree of conformity to the twenty-seven book canon was eventually attained.[25]

The History of the NT Canon: 1546–Present

During the Reformation period, Erasmus, Cardinal Cajetan, and Martin Luther, despite their theological differences, shared doubts about the apostolic origins of Hebrews, James, 2 Peter, Jude, and 2 and 3 John. Although Luther placed Hebrews, James, Jude, and Revelation at the end

24. These books were disputed in the writings by Cyprian of Carthage (ca. 250) and Hilary of Poitiers, France (ca. 350). There were probably other theological and socio-political factors that induced the skepticism in the West regarding the status of Hebrews and certain catholic letters.
25. See, e.g.: the revision of the Peshitta. For further discussion, see Kümmel, *Introduction* 501–3; *CHB* 1:364–68.

of his NT as the least esteemed, his estimation of 2 Peter, and 2 and 3 John was more favorable than that of Erasmus and Cajetan.[26]

The Council of Trent

In response to lingering doubts about the status of certain NT books and other important factors,[27] the Roman Catholic Church issued a decree on the canon of Scripture at the Council of Trent (1546). Its basic contents and the later responses of Protestantism, will be examined. The decision at Trent maintained that the books of the Latin Vulgate were "sacred and canonical in their entirety, with all their parts."[28] This decree affirmed the equal authority of all twenty-seven books, in contrast to Luther's categories of esteemed and less esteemed books. The council also reaffirmed a broader canon of the OT, which included books labeled by the Reformers as the Apocrypha (e.g., 1 and 2 Maccabees, Wisdom of Solomon, Sirach). Although the Lutheran and Anglican traditions encouraged the reading of these "additional books" for devotional but not doctrinal purposes, the Reformed churches have traditionally rejected them as authoritative writings in any sense (e.g., Westminster Confessions 1647).

The Post-Trent Situation

Despite occasional problems raised by the contents and authorship of such books as James and 2 Peter, all major bodies of Christendom reached general agreement on the canonical status of the twenty-seven books of the NT after Trent. Ecclesiastical agreement, however, did not settle academic debates on the limitations and binding force of the Christian canon.

ACADEMIC DEBATES CONCERNING THE CANON

Since the eighteenth century, questions concerning the dogmatic concept of a canon were raised by scholars like J. S. Semler.[29] Why should historical investigation of early Christianity regard these twenty-seven books as special in comparison with other primary sources? Can the

---

26. D. Guthrie, "Canon of the New Testament," *ZPE* 1:741.

27. The special status ascribed to certain NT books by Luther (Rom, Gal, Eph, Jn, 1 Jn, and 1 Pet) and the secondary status given to the OT books of the Latin Vulgate which were outside the Hebrew Bible by Luther and other Reformers were two key factors.

28. The Latin Vulgate was a 4th-cent. translation of both the OT and NT by Jerome (ca. 345–419) made from earlier Latin, Greek, and Hebrew manuscripts available to him. The OT contains most of the books of the LXX which are not found in the Hebrew Bible. On Vulgate, see *CHB* 1:518–23. Quotation from the decree at Trent is from: Turro and Brown, "Canonicity," *JBC* 67:91.

29. Kümmel, *Introduction* 506.

church regard as binding certain writings whose inclusion into the canon was based essentially on false assumptions? (e.g., that Paul wrote Hebrews or Peter wrote 2 Peter).[30] With the discovery of dissimilar outlooks and differing theologies in the NT (e.g., Jas vs. Rom), the question is raised: which early Christian viewpoint should be valued over the others? Is it possible to have an "actual" canon within a formal canon?[31] Harmonization of diverse NT theologies obscures the real issue or fails to address it. Often, the principle of a canon within a canon is applied, for example, when certain parts of the NT are favored over others: (1) because of their compatibility with church doctrine and practice (e.g., the teachings of Paul and Lutheranism) or (2) because of their chronological closeness to the original apostolic witness (e.g., the letters of Paul and the study of Christian origins). The above questions concerning the limits and normativeness of the NT canon are still being asked today.

THREE EXPLANATIONS OF THE CANON'S FORMATION

Why twenty-seven books, no more or less? The best explanations are found in the history of the Great Church which collected them. First, in reaction to both a selective collection (Marcion) and additional supplements (gnostics), the Great Church adhered to those writings which originated, they believed, from apostolic times and reflected their apostolic "rule of faith."[32] Second, Constantine, the first "Christian" emperor of the Roman Empire, ordered fifty new copies of the Bible for churches of Constantinople (ca. 331). This imperial edict played an important role in deciding which authoritative writings the Great Church would include in its Bible. Third, the public reception of certain books among the com-

---

30. For discussion of the authorship of Hebrews and 2 Peter, see Guthrie, *NT Intro* 685–89, 820–28; Kümmel, *Intro* 401–3, 430–34; Bauckham, *Jude, 2 Peter* 158–62; E. Dinkler, "Hebrews, Letter to," *IDB* 2:572–73; J. Becker, "Peter, Second Letter of," *IDB* 3:767–69.

31. The problem of the degrees of canonicity was raised acutely by Martin Luther (1520) because he gave preeminence to the letters of Paul, John's Gospel, 1 Pet, 1 Jn and secondary rank to Heb, Jas, Jude and Rev. In the 20th cent., E. Käsemann followed a similar position with his "center of the NT" (Paul's letters) and peripheral writings (Pastoral and Catholic letters), *Essays* 94–107.

32. The apostolic rules of faith (or truth) were summaries of the Christian faith, common in the mid-2nd cent. (e.g., Irenaeus, Tertullian), before the formal creeds of Nicea. Although varied in content, they generally contained accounts of the life, death, and resurrection of Jesus Christ derived from oral and written traditions. They served as a basis for instructing converts, a guide for interpreting Scripture, and a defense against heretics.

munities of the Great Church also influenced the limits of the NT canon. For example, the doubts of Eusebius concerning James, Hebrews, and Revelation, were always qualified by statements about their popularity in the churches. In the case of the above books, this acceptance is what ultimately prompted their inclusion in the canon.

SUMMARY

The nature and limits of the twenty-seven books of the NT reflect fundamentally the beliefs and perceptions of the Great Church of the fourth century. This church of the Constantinian era supported its particular convictions about Jesus and the apostles and rejected literature which did not satisfactorily express those beliefs. The modern commitment to a NT canon of twenty-seven books is basically a "vote of confidence" for the decision of the Great Church in the fourth century.[33]

The establishment of the NT canon, then, has favorable and precautionary aspects. The favorable aspect concerns the encapsulized portrait in the canon. A portrait of early Christianity in its diversity and multiplicity.[34] The institution of a canon, appears to legitimize a diversity of fresh and creative responses to Jesus Christ in the modern world. A pluralism of early Christian beliefs and practices (e.g., apocalyptic, early catholic) are canonized as models for modern readers to evaluate, assimilate, or set aside in their attempts to comprehend the NT teachings.

The precautionary point concerns the negative historical consequences of elevating this "classical portrait" of Christian origins at the exclusion of other important primary sources (e.g., Dead Sea Scrolls, Apocrypha, gnostic writings). As the possession of the Great Church, the NT achieved a place of reverence and respect in the church and world. Nevertheless, we must not overlook in our study, the literature of that period which influenced the NT books, attempted to supplement them, or sought to provide alternative viewpoints of Jesus and early Christianity.

---

33. The argument that the NT books attained canonical status, not from church councils, but because of their inherent spiritual and moral contents, does not hold up well for books like Jude, 2 Pet, and 2 and 3 Jn, whose rather meager contents are overshadowed by such "quasi-canonical" books as the informative 1 Clem or the dynamic letters of Ignatius.

34. This concept is developed in Käsemann, "New Testament Canon and the Unity of the Church," *Essays* 103-7.

Appendix B:
English Translations of the New Testament

Why are there so many English translations of the Bible? Which ones are the best? It is important to know what is a reliable English translation and why it is reliable.

Before the King James Version

The translation of the NT from Greek into the vernacular languages of Europe was the aim of Renaissance humanism, and it gained impetus in the Reformation. Luther's translation of the NT into German was published in 1522. It was an example followed in other lands.[1] In England, William Tyndale undertook the task of translation (1494–1536) but faced difficulties because of English hostilities to Luther, led by Henry VIII. He carried out his work in Reformed Europe and finally got his English translation printed in Worms, Germany, in 1526.[2] Although all of the NT and most of the OT were completed, Tyndale died in 1536, leaving unpublished certain manuscripts of the OT. He was proficient in both Greek and Hebrew and his translation influenced subsequent English versions.

The Great Bible (1539)
This translation was a thorough revision of Matthew's Bible (1537; ed. J. Rogers) undertaken by Miles Coverdale (1488–1569), both based on Tyndale's translation. Coverdale's revision was completed in 1539 and was called the Great Bible. It was appointed for use in the churches and was

---

1. See H. Bluhm, "Martin Luther as a Creative Bible Translator," *Andrews University Seminary Bulletin* 22 (1, 1984) 35–44; B. M. Metzger, "Versions, Medieval and Modern," *IDB* 4:773–74; *CHB* 3:94–103, 432–36.
2. See J. F. Mosley, *William Tyndale* (London: SPCK, 1937). For further information on English translations from 1450 to 1650 see F. F. Bruce, "Transmission and Translation of the Bible," *ExBC* 1:48–53; idem, *English Bible*; J. B. Branton, "Versions, English," *IDB* 4:760–68; J. H. Reumann, *Four Centuries of the English Bible* (Philadelphia: Muhlenberg Press, 1961); *CHB* 3:141–68.

the first "authorized version." From 1539 to 1569 it underwent numerous editions.

The Geneva Bible (1560)

The production of the Geneva Bible was begun by English Reformers exiled in Geneva, Switzerland, during the reign of the Catholic Queen Mary (1553–58). The Bible was completed in 1560 and presented to Elizabeth I. Its publication was simultaneous with the establishment of Reformed religion in Scotland. It remained in use long after the KJV and was used by the Pilgrims when they came to America in 1620. To the Pilgrims the KJV was a "fond thing vainly invented." They considered the older version to be the better. The Geneva Bible was favored during the Elizabethan age and was even the Bible of William Shakespeare. The last edition appeared in 1644.

The Bishop's Bible (1568)

Because the radical Reformed and anti-Catholic sentiments of the Geneva Bible were offensive to many, a revision of Coverdale's Great Bible was done in 1568 by Matthew Parker, the archbishop of Canterbury. Called the Bishop's Bible, it omitted many of the controversial notes found in the Geneva Bible. The whole Bible underwent nineteen editions from 1568 to 1606.

The King James Version (1611)

When Elizabeth died in 1603, the crown of England passed to James I, who had ruled Scotland as James VI. To regulate the affairs of the church, he called a conference of clergymen and theologians at Hampton Court (1604). The most important project that resulted from the conference was that a new translation of the Bible should be made and that it should be authorized for use in the churches of England.[3] The new translation was formally a revision of the 1602 edition of the Bishop's Bible. Many other helps and versions were used by the translators, who paid attention throughout to the original text. Forty-seven scholars divided into six panels: three for the OT, two for the NT, and one for the Apocrypha. The draft translation provided by the six panels was finally revised by a committee of twelve. Miles Smith helped to see the work through the press and also wrote the preface. Although it did not receive instant acceptance, this translation became a landmark in the religious history and English-speaking people. Its influence upon English-speaking piety and culture has lasted over three-hundred years.

3. Bruce, *ExBC* 1:49–52; J. P. Lewis, *The English Bible: From KJV to NIV* (Grand Rapids: Baker, 1981) 27–30; Branton, *IDB* 4:766–68; *CHB* 3:164–68.

There are at least two reasons for the enduring use of the KJV. First, absence of controversial notes gave it broader ecclesiastical appeal. Second, it was a literary masterpiece. Its prose rhythms and avoidance of harsh combinations of sound made it useful for public reading. But much of this tribute must be paid to William Tyndale, since he had established the stylistic pattern of the KJV. Nine-tenths of the NT in the KJV are from Tyndale's translation.

Revisions of the King James Version

Although the so-called authorized version[4] established itself at the heart of English-speaking piety and culture, the following three facts remain. First, the translation was based on late and comparatively poor Greek manuscripts, and with the passage of time earlier and better Greek texts were discovered. Second, the translation was based on an inadequate understanding of Hellenistic Greek, something which has greatly improved with the discovery of the Koine Greek papyri from Egypt in the nineteenth century. Third, the English language usage has also changed, so that while some of the phrases of the KJV proved unforgettable, others became unintelligible. The result was that in England in 1870 a revision of the KJV was undertaken.[5]

The English Revised Version (1881)

The English Revised Version of the Bible (ERV) was initiated by the Anglican convocation of Canterbury in 1870. There were two committees of revisers, one for the OT and one for the NT. Although stylistically inferior to the KJV, it was textually superior,[6] since its translation was based on the Alexandrian text advocated by Westcott and Hort. The ERV was also more precise in its rendering of the Greek text. The NT was completed in 1881, the OT in 1885, and the Apocrypha in 1894.

The American Standard Version (1901)

American scholars involved in the ERV project were unhappy with the conservative conditions imposed on the revisers. The ERV appeared to

---

4. We have no evidence *when* it was "authorized" and *by whom* other than the king's own privy council, Bruce, *ExBC* 1:52. See also *CHB* 3:361–63.

5. *CHB* 3:371–73. The *New King James Bible* (1980) is merely an updating of some of the KJV's archaic English expressions with some improvements on translation of the NT Koine Greek. However, the entire translation retains the late and poor Greek text behind the KJV (the "received text"). The NKJV imposes on the form and base of the KJV current English terminology and some recent insights from biblical research. See S. Kubo and W. Specht, *So Many Versions?* rev. ed. (Grand Rapids: Zondervan, 1983) 273–307; Lewis, *English Bible* 331–39; D. Moody, "NKJB," *RevExp* 77 (1978) 110–13.

use no expression that was not current in 1611. The American scholars worked on a new version (based on the best and earliest Gk. mss) without this archaizing policy. They agreed, however, to wait until 1901 to publish it. It was entitled: the American Standard Version (ASV).[7] The translators of the English and American revised versions, like their predecessors with the KJV, sought to keep as close as possible to the exact words and phrasings in the original language. This theory of translation is called formal equivalence.

The Revised Standard Version (1946)

Plans for a new revision of the ASV (1901) were begun in 1937 in America. The result was the Revised Standard Version (RSV) of the Bible. The NT was completed in 1946 and the OT in 1952. The entire Bible was revised in 1962 and 1972. It was produced by American and Canadian scholars and copyrighted by the Division for Christian Education of the National Council of the Churches of Christ in the U.S.A. The Common Bible of the RSV was produced in 1972 with the Roman Catholic and Eastern orthodox portions of the OT (Protestant Apocrypha). As a revision of the KJV, the RSV comes closest to fulfilling the broad purpose once filled by the KJV. Alongside the KJV in the Tyndale tradition stand the ERV, the ASV, and the RSV. The RSV, which was also a committee translation, is stylistically superior to the ERV and ASV and is based on the earliest and best Greek manuscripts reconstructed by modern textual criticism.[8]

Breaks with the King James Version

The New English Bible (1961)

Two examples of translations that break with the KJV tradition are: the New English Bible and the Good News Bible (Today's English Version). The New English Bible (NT 1961, OT 1970) marked a genuine departure in the history of English translations. A team of British Protestant scholars under the general direction of C. H. Dodd set out to produce a "faithful render-

---

6. There are over 5000 differences in the Greek text underlying that of the KJV and that of the RV (ASV), Lewis, English Bible 336.

7. Branton, IDB 4:769-70; Lewis, English Bible ch 4. The NASB (NT 1963; OT 1972) is supposedly a revision of the 1901 American edition. It is very literal in its rendering of the Greek and maintains a conservative Protestant bias. See Kubo and Specht, Versions 222-30; CHB 3:373-74.

8. Like the KJV and revised versions, the RSV attempts to keep as close as possible to the exact words and phrasings in the original language although the RSV has sought to be more intelligible to its modern English readers. It therefore is a less literal translation. See Branton, IDB 4:770-71; B. M. Metzger, "RSV Bible," Duke Divinity Review 44 (1979) 70-87; CHB 377-79.

ing of the best available Greek text into the current speech of our time."[9] The NEB adopts the translation theory of dynamic equivalence: "we have conceived our task to be that of understanding the original as precisely as we could . . . and then saying again in our own native idiom what we believed the author was saying in his."[10] The NEB is not a free paraphrase but has sought to replace Greek constructions and idioms with those of contemporary English. Whereas the RSV follows the formal equivalence practice of reflecting the ambiguity of the original texts, the NEB is concerned to say what the biblical writers meant in the words of contemporary English.[11]

Good News for Modern Man (1966)

The break with the KJV tradition in America came from the American Bible Society. In 1966, a NT translation entitled *Good News for Modern Man* (Today's English Version) appeared. It was the work of Robert G. Bratcher submitted for suggestion and approval to translation consultants of the American Bible and (later) British Foreign Bible Societies. The OT translation appeared in 1971 and the Deutero-canonicals/Apocrypha in 1979 with four subsequent NT editions. The complete work is called the *Good News Bible* (GNB). The GNB (like the NEB) follows the dynamic equivalency theory of translation. This theory applied to the GNB is stated by Eugene Nida: "to try to stimulate in the new reader in the new language the same reaction to the text that the original author wished to stimulate in his first and immediate readers."[12] The GNB seeks to confront the modern reader with the meaning of the original texts in today's standard, everyday English.

Private Translations

The translations reviewed above have all been produced by committees or societies representing major churches, yet anyone at anytime can publish a translation of the NT. Many private translations have appeared in the twentieth century; we shall look at four by Moffatt, Goodspeed, Phillips, and Taylor.

9. C. H. Dodd, "Introduction to the NT," *NEB* (Cambridge; Oxford, 1970) v. See also *CHB* 379-82.

10. Ibid., vii. See also V. Ray, "The Formal vs. the Dynamic Equivalent Principle in NT Translation," *Restoration Quarterly* 25 (1, 1982) 46-56.

11. Harrington, *IntNT* 26-27; J. Roberts, "Dynamic Equivalence in Bible Translation," *Neotestamentica* 8 (1974) 7-20.

12. E. Nida and C. Taber, *The Theory and Practice of Translation* (Leiden: Brill, 1969) 175.

The Moffatt Translation (1913)

James Moffatt, a Scottish NT scholar, published a NT translation in 1913 and the OT in 1924 and entitled it, *The Bible: A New Translation*. Although the NT version was based on the questionable Greek text reconstructed by von Soden, it is a fresh and vigorous translation. Moffatt does not hesitate to trust his scholarly judgment in such matters as rearranging the text of John's Gospel. [13]

The Goodspeed Translation (1927)

The American counterpart of Moffatt is *The Complete Bible: An American Translation* (1927, rev. 1935) by Edgar J. Goodspeed, a scholar from the University of Chicago. His first edition of the NT was begun in 1923. Goodspeed based his NT translation on the more acceptable Greek text of Westcott and Hort with some modification. Utilizing the current studies on the Koine Greek, Goodspeed sought to cast the original thought of the NT writers in the "simplest and clearest of present-day English."

The Phillips Translation (1958)

J. B. Phillips, a vicar of the church of England, published between 1947 and 1957 a NT translation which was later published in one volume: *The New Testament in Modern English* (1958). Making use of the "best available Greek text" (Westcott and Hort), Phillips produced a very lively and readable translation for the ordinary reader. Although he attempted to achieve a dynamic equivalence translation, it frequently approaches paraphrase, translating the ideas from one language to another with less concern for the exact words of the original. Nevertheless, his translation of Paul's letter ("Letters to Young Churches" 1947) was a very popular and successful attempt to clarify the writings of the Apostle Paul.

The Living Bible (1971)

The popular *Living Bible Paraphrased* (1971) by Kenneth Taylor differs from the above translations because it is a paraphrase of the Bible. In his attempt to explain what the NT writers meant, Taylor simplifies, expands and updates the NT idioms and thought-patterns in terms equivalent to our modern English usage. It is a very readable and simple paraphrase, but at numerous points gives the English reader something that the original writer did not intend to say (i.e., *eisegesis*). Although the *Living Bible* (LB) is helpful for young people and casual readers, it was never intended for serious academic study.

---

13. E.g., Jn 3:22–30 is transposed between 2:12 and 2:13; 7:15–24 is placed after 5:47; 12:45–50 is placed in the middle of v 36.

Denominational Translations

The Jerusalem Bible (1966)
The denominational or confessional translations can be divided into two
basic categories: Roman Catholic and Protestant Evangelical. Until recently,
Roman Catholic translations of the Bible were generally from the Latin
Vulgate.[14] Then from 1948 to 1954 a translation of the whole Bible with
introduction and footnotes appeared in French under the editorship of
Jerusalem Dominicans (*La Bible de Jérusalem*). A special English translation and revision of this French Bible was begun by British Catholic scholars under A. Jones and called *The Jerusalem Bible* (1966). The introduction
and footnotes were translated into English and updated. The biblical books
were usually translated from the original languages in comparison with
the French Bible. The *Jerusalem Bible* (JB) has a twofold objective: to trans-
late the Bible into the language we use today and to provide notes that
are neither sectarian nor superficial. Although the JB is more restrained
than the NEB or GNB concerning the theory of dynamic equivalence, it
is written in modern English and avoids the "biblical English" of the KJV
tradition.[15]

In 1985 the *New Jerusalem Bible* was completed under the general editorship of Henry Wansbrough. It is an entire revision and updating of
the *Jerusalem Bible*, based on new insights from the last twenty years of
biblical scholarship.

The New American Bible (1970)
The *New American Bible* is the American counterpart of the British JB.
It was the project of members of the Catholic Biblical Association of
America with some assistance by Protestant scholars. The OT and
Deutero-canonical books were completed in 1969, and the NT in 1970. The
NT is based on the Nestle-Aland Greek text, twenty-fifth edition (1963).
The footnotes of the *New American Bible* (NAB) are even less Roman
Catholic than the JB (although both attempt to be nonsectarian). Even
though it is translated in modern, readable English, it seeks to retain many
of the words and phrasings of the original language. The NAB therefore
tends to follow the formal correspondence theory of translation used in
the RSV and NIV. The Catholic Biblical Association is completing a new
revision of the NAB.

14. In 1935 a NT translation from the Greek text was completed in England
called *the Westminster Version*, the OT was begun in 1934 but never completed, *JBC*
69:172.
15. K. Crim, "Versions, English," *IDBSupp* 935; Harrington, *IntNT*, 27.

The New International Version (1973)

A major translation produced by an international group of Protestant Evangelicals is the *New International Version* of the Bible. The NT was completed in 1973 and the OT in 1978. All translators were committed to the "full authority and complete trustworthiness of the Scriptures." The translators were primarily concerned with the accuracy of the translation and its fidelity to the thought of the NT writers. Therefore the NIV ranks with the RSV and NAB in espousing the formal equivalence theory of translation.[16]

16. For further study on the NIV and other recent translations see L. R. Bailey, ed., *The Word of God* (Atlanta: John Knox, 1982); K. L. Barker, ed., *The NIV: The Making of a Contemporary Translation* (Grand Rapids, Zondervan, 1986); J. R. Kohlenberger, III, *Words about the Word. A Guide to Choosing and Using your Bible* (Grand Rapids: Zondervan, 1987); E. Nida, *Good News for Everyone* (Waco, Tex.: Word, 1977).

Index of Ancient Texts

Author Index